P9-DMK-066

TRUMP AFTERSHOCK

STEPHEN E. STRANG

PRAISE FOR *TRUMP AFTERSHOCK*

Stephen Strang's new book about President Trump is an eye-opener. The part about George Soros and his nefarious operation is riveting. Stephen shows that he is indeed an accomplished reporter who gets to the heart of the issue. I commend Stephen's latest book, *Trump Aftershock,* as a must-read at a time when we are being barraged by false news from the so-called shadow government.

—Dr. M. G. "Pat" Robertson
Founder/Chairman, The Christian Broadcasting Network Inc.
Host, *The 700 Club*

If I wrote a theme song for the Left that captured their frenzied behavior over the last two years, I would definitely title it "Trump Derangement Syndrome." From special counsels with bogus cases built on an unverified "dossier" to social media censorship of conservative voices to liberal bullies who attack administration members—including my own daughter—in public, no one is immune to the tension. Americans feel like watching the news has become a front-row seat to the battle for our nation's very soul. Among the mainstream media very little credit is given to the president for his accomplishments and his unwavering stand for conservative values and freedoms, but this important book you hold in your hands sets the record straight about President Trump and provides insights into the spiritual aspects of Trump's presidency as well. I wrote the foreword for Stephen Strang's last book, *God and Donald Trump,* and now I wholeheartedly endorse his new book, *Trump Aftershock,* and encourage you to read it.

—Mike Huckabee
New York Times Best-Selling Author
Host, *Huckabee* on TBN

On a recent cruise to Alaska, a woman sitting at my table bragged about Stephen Strang's previous book, *God and Donald Trump,* to the lady across the table. Not knowing that I knew Stephen and had also published my latest book with his company, she went on and on. "It's a must-read," she said. "I couldn't put it down!" It made me proud to know Stephen and be interviewed by him for his follow-up book, which you now hold in your hands. *Trump Aftershock* masterfully reveals why Donald Trump's earth-shattering presidency matters—because it is about so much more than Donald Trump; it's a fight to preserve the Judeo-Christian values and freedoms of our great nation for the next generation. If you care about the future of our country, you need to read this book.

—Brigitte Gabriel
New York Times Best-Selling Author
Founder, ACT for America

When my friend Stephen Strang wrote his previous book, *God and Donald Trump,* I couldn't wait to have him on my television show to talk about it because I feared that too many people believed the lies in the mainstream media, and I wanted to help people understand the truth about Donald Trump. That's why I'm so glad Stephen has written this new book, *Trump Aftershock,* because the media's misrepresentation of our president and his agenda has only gotten worse since his election. Stephen's book is one of the only books I know that sets the record straight from a Christian perspective. *Trump Aftershock* is a must-read for politically minded Christians who take religious freedoms and values seriously, who believe we finally have someone in the Oval Office who supports those values, and who are praying that these events will cause our great nation to return to God.

—Jim Bakker
Christian Television Pioneer
Host, *The Jim Bakker Show*

Stephen Strang has had his hand on the pulse beat of America for decades as a distinguished journalist and publisher. In his new book he deftly documents the powerful impact President Trump has had on the nation's culture. The question is, What happens next? And Stephen delivers a hard-hitting look at where the nation is headed.

—Todd Starnes
Fox News Channel
Brooklyn, New York

In the 1960s the United States suffered an aftershock when three Ks were assassinated: John F. Kennedy, Robert Kennedy, and Martin Luther King. Afterward the country experienced rebellion—the "God is dead" movement, the drug and sexual revolution, *Roe v. Wade*, and other signs of moral decay. The country then came face to face with another "aftershock" when, contrary to liberal opinion polls, Donald Trump was elected president. Stephen Strang has written a fantastic book that captures the impact of Trump's extraordinary presidency on our nation and the world, and I encourage you to read it.

—Mike Evans
New York Times Best-Selling Author
Friends of Zion Heritage Center, Jerusalem

Stephen Strang does it again! In *Trump Aftershock*, Strang captures with journalistic brilliance the unprecedented change and impact unleashed by the presidency of Donald J. Trump. Strang not only informs us of what has changed, but he tells us why things have changed. Anyone interested in finding out why 81 percent of Evangelicals voted for and continue to support Donald Trump must read this book!

—Samuel Rodriguez
President, National Hispanic Christian Leadership Conference
Lead Pastor, New Season

I'm glad my friend Stephen Strang has written this book, *Trump Aftershock*, which sets the record straight on the achievements of the Trump administration and the very real opposition he faces. Stephen is not only an author; he's a journalist who heads up a Christian media company we can trust as a source of news that affects our daily lives. We need more voices like Stephen's who are unafraid to speak the truth. Don't believe the lies of the mainstream media. Get the facts from trusted Christian sources such as Stephen Strang, Charisma News, and books such as this. Our president is shaking things up. He needs our support. It's time for all of us to become informed, stand united, and call for an end to the witch hunt investigations, fake news, and hateful rhetoric of those whose agenda is to bring an end to this president and turn our great nation away from God.

—Robert Jeffress
Senior Pastor, First Baptist Dallas
Dallas, Texas

Trump Aftershock is a simple, yet deeply incisive and informative, guide through the political, cultural, and spiritual earthquake generated by President Trump's election and presidency. Anyone truly seeking a deeper understanding of the extraordinary upheaval generated by President Trump's election will find *Trump Aftershock* to be an invaluable resource.

—Dr. Richard Land
President, Southern Evangelical Seminary
Charlotte, North Carolina

An awakening...an uprising...something big is happening...and American culture and the church will never be the same.

I agree with Stephen Strang that "if our nation can begin to truly trust in God and let His light guide our steps, then that's the greatest aftershock of all."

—Tim Clinton
Executive Director, James Dobson Family Institute
President, American Association of Christian Counselors

Trump Aftershock is definitely a "for such a time as this" treatise. President Donald Trump is truly a world shaker, bringing people to their knees in shock or in prayer, depending on the perspective. Kudos to Stephen Strang for articulating the aftershocks to Trump's election in a straightforward and honest way. He has the courage to work the ministry of the scribe for our times.

—Evangelist Alveda C. King
Niece of Dr. Martin Luther King Jr.
Atlanta, Georgia

My friend Stephen Strang has done it again! If you thought his coverage of Trump's election in *God and Donald Trump* was insightful, you'll love reading his new book, *Trump Aftershock*, which provides an eye-opening look at our forty-fifth president and his extraordinary agenda and achievements.

—Jim Garlow
Senior Pastor, Skyline Church
San Diego, California

Stephen Strang has written the definitive narrative of the explosive beginnings of Donald Trump's presidency. Here is the undeniable record of the president who, in spite of his critics, has kept his promises to America. Stephen Strang's journalistic expertise and absolute devotion to accuracy makes this page-turner a must for every citizen. I especially commend it as well to thinking people who may lean left. This book sets the record straight. Finally, Christ followers and the church are challenged not to abandon the public square. Get this book and arm yourself with the weapon of truth.

—Dr. Ron Phillips
Pastor Emeritus, Abba's House
Chattanooga, Tennessee

From the island of Britain I have lived and watched the Trump presidency and feel close to its heartbeat. Stephen Strang's new book, *Trump Aftershock*, is a wonderfully written story, capturing all that I have seen. What caught my eye is that there was a revelation in his writing. It's very detailed commentary, and again he's produced a historical document. Yet it's a fascinating read throughout.

My favorite part was Ronald Reagan's definition of *status quo*: Latin for "the mess we're in."

—Martin Clarke
Chairman, The Martin Clarke Group of Companies
London, England

Stephen Strang is a careful researcher who, in this new book, *Trump Aftershock*, provides documented material for the observer who wants objective truth minus a biased progressive spin. Strang is also a prophetic voice who challenges the reader to work and pray for revival in a day of unprecedented opportunity. As *Trump Aftershock* closes, Strang reminds the reader, "If our nation can begin to truly trust in God and let His light guide our steps, then that's the greatest aftershock of all." God has indeed heard the prayer of His people and has provided proof that there is hope for America. This is not the time for the church to find shelter in a bunker built by fear but to raise up and claim its identity.

—Larry Spargimino, PhD
Pastor, Southwest Radio Church
Oklahoma City, Oklahoma

Most Charisma House Book Group products are available at special quantity discounts for bulk purchase for sales promotions, premiums, fund-raising, and educational needs. For details, write Charisma House Book Group, 600 Rinehart Road, Lake Mary, Florida 32746, or telephone (407) 333-0600.

Trump Aftershock by Stephen E. Strang
Published by FrontLine
Charisma Media/Charisma House Book Group
600 Rinehart Road
Lake Mary, Florida 32746
www.charismahouse.com

Visit the author's website at trumpaftershock.com.

Library of Congress Cataloging-in-Publication Data:
An application to register this book for cataloging has been submitted to the Library of Congress.
International Standard Book Number: 978-1-62999-555-7
E-book ISBN: 978-1-62999-556-4

18 19 20 21 22 — 987654321
Printed in the United States of America

CONTENTS

FOREWORD

For over two years now people have been asking me why I supported Donald Trump as a candidate for president of the United States and why I continue to support him now in his role as the chief executive of our great nation. After all, I was one of the only people from the evangelical camp who endorsed Mr. Trump even before the Iowa caucuses. I determined early on that what ailed the United States would require more than a PR and policy bandage. And if Trump were to get elected, he would need more than bandwagon support.

But to answer the question about my support, much of my motivation came from my background in business. My father came from a family of businesspeople who were not Christians, including my grandfather. But a series of personal tragedies resulted in his early death, at the age of fifty-five. My dad was only fifteen at the time, and he became a Christian because of those sorrowful events. I think he might have gone into the family business if those things hadn't happened. The point is that though the world knows the Falwell name chiefly in the context of my famous clergyman father, most Falwells have been successful entrepreneurs—businessmen and businesswomen.

Even in the context of a nonprofit organization such as Liberty University, I have seen firsthand what applying business principles can do to save an organization. In the late 1980s and 1990s, when donations dried up, we had to create a business model that would keep Liberty alive. In the end not only did we eliminate the debt; we also prospered enough that we've now fulfilled many of the original visions my father had for this university. But Liberty's success didn't come through hazy or lazy leadership.

So that's why I supported Donald Trump early, because the United States is drowning in twenty-one trillion dollars of debt. Trump is a businessman. We haven't had many businessmen who have become president. Instead, we get career politicians who are short on transformative thinking and long on political career preservation. Even though Trump hadn't even decided what all his political views were at that time, I knew that a pragmatic businessman with common sense would come down on the right side of issues. Trump wanted to do what was best for the country. And if you start with that desire—to do what's best for the country and for the common man—then you have no choice but to be a conservative. It's that simple.

I'm proud I supported Donald Trump. And since he's entered the White House, I've stayed in close touch with him, talking to him about once a month. It has become a close friendship. I'm so pleased with how he's kept his promises. He's appointed justices to the lower courts and the Supreme Court who I believe will uphold the Constitution. On matters related to religious liberty, the president has been a godsend. And his deregulation strategies have brought about prosperity for businesses and the American worker. He's done all the things he said he was going to do—even with all the attempts to thwart his administration by fake Republicans in the Senate and all the folks on the left who will stop at nothing to overthrow a duly elected president.

You see, we needed somebody with resolve and backbone. Republicans and Democrats—the parties had become so much alike that you really couldn't tell the difference. Many of them were—and still are—so scared of their shadow and criticism from the press that they waffle on every issue. They put their finger up and see which way the wind is blowing.

But Trump just marches ahead. He doesn't care how much criticism comes his way. And the people don't care either. The people don't care what the press say anymore because they've lost all credibility. That's what Americans have longed to see in their president—somebody who will stand up for the country, stand up for what's right, and not back down in the face of adversity.

Like Stephen Strang does in this book, I compare Trump to Winston Churchill during World War II. Everything looked lost in the face of the onslaught of Hitler's military might. Churchill had to resolve to move ahead anyhow and to never quit. That's what I see in Donald Trump, and I think that's why people support him in spite of all the negatives that get thrown at him.

In this new book by my friend Stephen Strang you will come to a great understanding of all that has been happening since election night. Strang shows how President Trump has exceeded the expectations of his supporters. And Strang reveals how the Left, instead of acknowledging the genuine successes of the Trump administration, are growing in their animus toward the president. Refusing to acknowledge the roaring economy and a renewed sense of optimism and national pride, some on the left (and some on the right) are succumbing to "Trump Derangement Syndrome." And so the rift between the Left and the Right has grown deep, and our national politics are more polarized than ever.

But Strang's book strikes a chord of hopefulness because he believes (as do I) that these days are some of the most extraordinary times in the life of our nation. You'll enjoy *Trump Aftershock*. But even more, it will prompt you to pray and work in your own community to "make America great again."

—Jerry Falwell Jr.
President, Liberty University
Lynchburg, Virginia

INTRODUCTION

SHAKEN TO THE CORE

Donald Trump's election was unexpected. Even for those who worked hardest for his election, the realization that the New York billionaire had actually won struck like an earthquake, shaking everything and everybody. If you read *God and Donald Trump*, you know I believed he *might* win so I flew to New York for his election night party. However, I admit I was nervous. But being there on that historic night, I saw that even his most ardent fans could barely believe it as the returns came in. And that was just the beginning.

The aftershocks have continued ever since the inauguration, affecting politics, business, foreign affairs, and the culture in many new and surprising ways. The panic that ensued on the morning of November 9, 2016, was due mainly to the fact that no one in either party had given much thought to what the world would look like if Hillary Clinton lost the election. The polls and the talking heads had been saying for months that she had it in the bag. She had finally burst through the glass ceiling and was on her way to becoming the first female president of the United States. Then, suddenly, everything changed.

All those big plans would never come to fruition, and the Democrats found themselves staring into the face of a harsh new reality: they were out of power, and the candidate the Left feared more than any other would be taking care of business at the White House. The Obama era was finished, and the world would soon be seeing him and his presidency in a new light. Today we're still dealing with that reality, uncovering secrets and shenanigans long hidden in darkness and doing our best to deal with the aftershocks coming from those stunning revelations.

In Trump's first two years in office the economy has broken out of its decades-long slump and set so many records the *New York Times* had to admit it "ran out of words" to describe the incredible success of the economy under Trump's leadership. Employment numbers have gone through the roof, topping 220,000 new jobs in the month of May 2018, with unemployment falling to 3.8 percent overall, the lowest in eighteen years. At the same time, black unemployment is down to 5.9 percent, an all-time record,[1] and companies announced they were giving thousand-dollar bonuses to more than a million workers.[2] Despite the counterattacks from the Democratic leadership, the American people were ecstatic, and the mainstream media were appalled.

The media were clearly on the other side from day one, but Trump was swept into office by a red wave of Middle Americans who were sick and tired of Washington's way of doing business. They were tired of the liberal talking heads bashing their values and beliefs, and they weren't going to take it anymore. Political observers reported that the people were so frustrated with the government's unwelcome intrusion into their lives that they were on the verge of full-scale revolt. They could feel the country spiraling downward from its previous greatness.

The nation was reaching a point where something had to be done, and that something turned out to be Donald Trump. As Gov. Mike Huckabee told me in an interview for this book, "Quite frankly, the goal of the voters was not to send someone to Washington who would fix anything. They couldn't care less about what our solutions were. They wanted someone to go and burn the place down, and Trump was the guy who seemingly carried a can of gasoline and a lighter every time he went to a rally. He was ready to burn it down, and that excited people."

As it turned out, voters from both sides concluded that there was no hope of finding common ground. Some of them, particularly in blue-collar country, decided to switch rather than fight and moved to the right. But we also witnessed unprecedented confrontations and a level of hostility not seen in this country since the Civil War. Battles over immigration, gun control, taxes, health care, abortion, entitlements, the environment, and everything else were pushing the parties to extremes. Emotions were boiling over in communities all over the country as gangs of leftist thugs and anarchists tried to muscle in on the conversation. But the fact is, President Trump won the 2016 election the old-fashioned way, earning the votes of more than sixty million Americans and winning the electoral votes of thirty states.

It seems the biggest surprise in this developing story was that during the campaign the administration of the outgoing president, aided by the Department of Justice, the FBI, the CIA, and a network of spies and undercover operatives, conducted a search-and-destroy mission against the Trump campaign. Over several months these men and women laid an elaborate trap so that in the unlikely event Trump somehow snatched the victory from the waiting arms of Hillary Clinton, he wouldn't last long enough to do much damage. The fact that this deep-state coup d'état has largely failed and the president has successfully defended his administration is almost as big a miracle as the election itself.

Against All Odds

Donald Trump was an extraordinary candidate who came along at an auspicious time in our history. The challenge for President Trump, as the successor to the first Saul Alinsky–inspired community organizer, would be enormous, but he had the enthusiastic support of millions of voters all across the heartland, and they had his back, just as he had promised he had theirs. The election was evidence of the changing mood of the American voters. Nothing like it had ever happened. Trump's supporters were from every race, creed, and socioeconomic background and from parts of the country that had never been known to back a conservative Republican for the presidency. Nothing better proved that the nation had reached a tipping point.

When Trump first announced his plans to run for the presidency, like many, I wondered if he was actually a conservative. He had been a Democrat and a Republican and an Independent at various times. He was for abortion before he was against it. He was volatile and unpredictable, and many wondered if he might be a bit trigger-happy and lead us into war. As an evangelical Christian, I wondered if he could be trusted to keep his promises to protect religious liberty and help the millions of persecuted Christians around the world.

Since then President Trump has exceeded all expectations. He has proved to have a character trait not shared by many politicians—he actually keeps his promises. He has used the slogan "Promises Made. Promises Kept" and once joked he had kept more promises than he'd made. As Michael Goodwin has pointed out in the *New York Post,* Trump's popularity has made seismic shifts in so many areas that Big Mo (momentum) has switched sides, from left to right. One big reason, he says, is because of the recent Supreme Court rulings favoring Trump's policies. "The first upheld his revised travel ban for a handful of Muslim-majority nations, saying it was within his executive authority. It rebuked lower-court judges who bought the partisan canard that it was a 'Muslim ban.' Their invalid rulings stood in stark contrast to plain readings of the law," Goodwin says, "and show them to be hacks blowing with the political wind."[3]

The second ruling blocked municipal unions from forcing their workers to pay union dues. This would turn out to be a tax cut for workers and deliver a major blow to the Democratic Party in New York, New Jersey, and other blue states. "The nexus between unions and Democrats turned those states into one-party fiefdoms," writes Goodwin, "and resulted in union contracts taxpayers can't afford." Both these rulings were decided on a 5–4 vote, with Justice Anthony Kennedy providing the swing vote. Then with Justice Kennedy's retirement, the president was able to nominate

Brett Kavanaugh as his successor and will likely have a chance to cement his legacy with a second or even a third appointment before his term is over. Decapitating the liberal stranglehold on the court would reduce the strategies of the Left to rubble and provide a wall of defense for conservative principles for generations to come.

Why This Book

This book is my attempt to document what has been happening since Trump's victory in a way that will help readers better understand the political, emotional, and spiritual dimensions of the election that brought us such a complex, unpredictable, and conspicuously gifted leader. Looking back at the headlines, videos, and news clips from the 1980s and 1990s, it's ironic to see how Trump was loved by the media when he was a flamboyant playboy businessman. The *New York Times* said Trump in his heyday got more interview requests than anyone in New York. But when he ran for president as a Republican, the East Coast liberals and their friends in the media made such a hard turn to the left that a new phrase had to be created to describe it: *Trump Derangement Syndrome.*

But once Trump was installed in the White House, he didn't change. Instead, he set out to prove he had real and workable solutions. He got to work fast and accomplished more than anyone could have imagined. He surprised many with his depth of understanding and strength of will. But as I have seen firsthand and will document in these pages, the media have been unwilling to give him credit for his accomplishments. So he uses his rallies and Twitter account to go around the media, and it's working. The media know that his firmest base of support is the evangelical community, and they would love nothing better than to put a wedge between the president and his base—anything to undermine him and his presidency.

During my appearances on the liberal news networks (which Trump calls the fake news networks), I've been asked to explain why evangelical Christians who claim to be so moral could be so hypocritical as to vote for a sinner such as Trump. At times I felt as if I were going into the lion's den to defend the president. Even though I was trained as a secular journalist and worked in the secular media early in my career, I have to agree with Trump's "fake news" moniker. The secular press refuse to give Trump credit for anything. My friend Russell McClanahan once told me, "If Donald Trump came up with a cure for cancer, his critics would say he was putting doctors out of business." Meanwhile, Barack Obama is leading a shadow party funded by leftist radicals such as George Soros, trying to impose his socialist will on the nation, and the mainstream media have little or nothing to say about it.

The rift between Left and Right has grown so deep that it often seems America is at war with itself, and I've written about that in more detail in this book. Trump's unique brand of muscular diplomacy brought the North Koreans to the negotiating table, compelled our trading partners in Europe and China to revise their tariff policies, and helped forge new alliances in the Middle East. Today Israel and Saudi Arabia, which have a common enemy in Iran, are speaking together and sharing resources. Who could have imagined such a thing just a decade ago? And Trump's decision to move the American embassy to Jerusalem was a huge step and a blessing not only for the Jewish community but for Christian Zionists such as me.

In my book *God and Donald Trump* my goal was to take a closer look at God's hand on the man we all perceived as an imperfect leader. Simply surviving the nomination gauntlet, beating out sixteen highly accomplished candidates, was a miracle. As I've already mentioned, I flew to New York for the victory celebration on election night. That gave me a unique perspective, but the story didn't end there, as most of America apparently thought it would. The surprises continue to this day as the aftershocks from Trump's miracle win continue sending tremors and seismic shifts throughout the culture and the world. I believe not only is God shaking the government and culture, but He's also shaking the church, which I explore at the end of this book.

I'm convinced God is using Donald Trump in a remarkable and unprecedented way, not unlike the way he used Winston Churchill and even American general George Patton when it looked as if the Nazis would control all of Europe and the world was hanging in the balance. As I researched and wrote this book, I had the feeling on many occasions that I was recording the history of one of the most extraordinary times in the life of our nation.

Many other books have been written about this man, with many more to come. But my aim has been to offer a perspective the average reader may never see otherwise. Having written from a Christian worldview that sees God's hand at work, I hope I've been able to provide new insights and to give you something to think and pray about as we continue together on this incredible and utterly unexpected adventure.

—Stephen E. Strang
St. Augustine, Florida
June 30, 2018

PART I

AFTERSHOCK AND AWE

CHAPTER 1

CAPITAL PSYCHOSIS

EVER SINCE THE 2016 election and Donald Trump's ascension to the White House, official Washington and the political establishment have been in a state of perpetual pandemonium. There are days when life in the nation's capital looks more like a three-ring circus with animal acts, lion tamers, and troupes of aerialists performing death-defying high-wire acts. There's even a fire-eater or two, not to mention the clowns and occasional dancing bear. But whether this is simply political theater or an outbreak of genuine madness, the melodrama never fails to amuse. It's a spectacle like no other.

Every day the world awakens to new surprises, shocking announcements, and breathtaking revelations. Cable networks and the internet are constantly ablaze with outrageous claims and equally passionate denials. And the president's tweetstorms frequently determine the news cycle for the day. But no matter what any of us may think or say about the pivotal figure of this daily drama, President Donald J. Trump is the undisputed epicenter of attention, and he loves it.

By the time Trump entered the race, in June 2015, coming down the escalator at Trump Tower to the rhythms of Neil Young's hit song "Rockin' in the Free World," he had become a polarizing figure, inspiring equal measures of admiration and anguish. But love him or hate him, this president has initiated shock waves the magnitude of which Washington has never seen before, exposing the ruptures in our political and ideological fault lines and shaking up the status quo.

Intensifying the sense of drama is the fact that the American electorate has been changing in remarkable ways, refusing to accept the empty promises of previous administrations. In the long and confrontational run-up to the 2016 election, millions of voters from the heartland found their voices, forming new coalitions and interest groups and becoming a more volatile force in the political process. Suddenly members of Congress were confronted by a new level of public scrutiny, along with a large dose of righteous anger. Both Democrats and Republicans were forced to adapt, adjust, and amend their tactics for this new and more demanding environment.

Inspired by Trump's campaign promise to "make America great again," millions who had never voted, or who voted routinely and predictably for Democrats, pulled the lever for the Trump team. As a result, Trump and the Republicans were able to celebrate a stunning victory, taking both houses of Congress and the White House for the first time in over a decade. But this was just the beginning. Even though the Democrats suffered a crushing loss, and despite the unexpected defections among the base, the struggle was far from over. In the midst of the post-election festivities new and sinister challenges began appearing almost hourly, and threats to the new administration would grow more frequent and more intense over coming weeks and months.

As the new president would soon discover, the swamp inside the Beltway is full of danger. There are assassins, saboteurs, bounty hunters, and clandestine operatives around every corner on a mission to subvert, entrap, and subdue their prey. Plagued by leaks over the course of his first several months in office, the president and his team began scouring the executive branch to expose faithless or seemingly vulnerable members of the senior staff. The White House exit ramp soon became a thoroughfare for once-trusted allies, including Michael Flynn, Sean Spicer, Anthony Scaramucci, Steve Bannon, Sebastian Gorka, Rob Porter, Gary Cohn, and Hope Hicks, among many others.

Vice President Mike Pence, on the other hand, remained a staunch supporter and confidant. But his loyalty to the president, along with his outspoken Christian faith, exposed the former congressman and Indiana governor to relentless attacks from the Left. In March 2018 left-wing comic John Oliver even took a tasteless swipe at Pence's daughter Charlotte on HBO, mocking the children's book she had written for charity.

Ever since the inauguration the mainstream media have kept up a relentless campaign of contempt for the president, his family, and his key advisors with what can only be described as extreme partisan fervor. In September of the president's first year in office the *Washington Post* reported that 91 percent of Trump's news coverage was negative during the summer of 2017.[1] The article was based on research by the Media Research Center (MRC),[2] which came to much the same conclusion again after a study of early 2018 news coverage. In the first two months of 2018 the television networks seldom reported on Trump's accomplishments. Growth of the economy and jobs netted just twelve minutes, and the positive impact of tax cuts passed in December 2017 received just nine minutes of coverage. Coverage of military success in the war against al Qaeda and ISIS received just eighty-three seconds.[3]

Analysis of evening newscasts on ABC, CBS, and NBC during January and February 2018 reveals that, again, 91 percent of the news concerning the president was negative. Nearly 63 percent was devoted to scandals such as the Russia investigation (204 minutes), allegations of wife beating against White House aide Rob

Porter (54 minutes), and gossip from Michael Wolff's book (most of which has been determined to be wrong and misleading) about the Trump White House (53 minutes).[4] The networks apparently believe their coverage should not be diluted by focusing on any matter where Trump was succeeding. The goal of the mainstream media, as the MRC reports suggest, is no longer objective journalism but support for liberal Trump resistance and the campaign to obstruct, embarrass, and ultimately (with visions of Bob Woodward and Carl Bernstein glory) impeach the president.

On the Record

A rare and surprisingly objective story published by *Newsweek* on the first anniversary of Trump's election victory offered readers a reminder of some of the more notable outbursts from anti-Trump celebrities and commentators. Everyone reacted a little differently, the writer admitted, but the reaction of the liberal contingent was uniformly predictable and unforgiving. "Trump sent the left into a tailspin," the article said, "as he proved the polls and pundits wrong and nabbed more than 300 Electoral College votes. And while some high-profile liberals' concerns may have been warranted...many of their reactions were a little dramatic."[5]

For months before the election MSNBC host Rachel Maddow had assured her audience forcefully and often that Donald Trump could never overcome Hillary Clinton's commanding lead. Pointing to the brightly colored maps showing the changing patterns in battleground states and the results of national polls giving Clinton a clear advantage, Maddow told her fans, "If you do the math associated with all the electoral votes from all the states...and then you say that Donald Trump has the best day in the entire world and completely outperforms expectations and he wins all the toss-up states, he wins all five of those states plus that Electoral College vote in Maine that he's after...even if Donald Trump did win all the toss-up states, he would still lose."[6]

But late on election night it was a different story. Once it was clear Trump had the victory well in hand, an October clip of the MSNBC pundit was widely shared because it seemed to convey her overly dramatic reaction to the election results. "You're awake, by the way," a dispirited Maddow told her viewers. "You're not having a terrible, terrible dream. Also, you're not dead, and you haven't gone to hell. This is your life now." Others had similar reactions. Recognizing that the administration and the agenda were in for a major change, former Obama advisor David Axelrod reacted on CNN to Trump's election, saying, "This was a primal scream on the part of a lot of voters who are disenchanted with the status quo."[7] And he was right about that.

Meanwhile, liberal flamethrower Keith Olbermann declared, "I'd like to begin by congratulating the FBI on its successful coup against the electoral process of the United States of America. You've been working on one of these for a while, boys, and I know everybody at the bureau's just delighted that the 'F' can now also stand for 'Fascist.'"[8] The irony of Olbermann's words would become apparent as we learned more and more about FBI Director James Comey and his chief lieutenants working covertly to undermine the president.

Libertarian author and blogger Andrew Sullivan, in his own fit of disconsolation, wrote that "America has now jumped off a constitutional cliff.... This is now Trump's America. He controls everything from here on forward. He has won this campaign in such a decisive fashion that he owes no one anything. He has destroyed the GOP and remade it in his image. He has humiliated the elites and the elite media. He has embarrassed every pollster and naysayer. He has avenged Obama. And in the coming weeks, Trump will not likely be content to bask in vindication."[9]

Not all the commentators were quite so generous. But journalist and blogger Jeff Jarvis couldn't disguise his elitist bias when he proclaimed, "I'll say it: This is the victory of the uneducated and uninformed. Now more than ever that looks impossible to fix. They now rule."[10] And leftist filmmaker Michael Moore, never one for subtlety, exclaimed, "Take over the Democratic Party and return it to the people. They have failed us miserably....Fire all pundits, predictors, pollsters and anyone else in the media who had a narrative they wouldn't let go of and refused to listen to or acknowledge what was really going on. Those same bloviators will now tell us we must 'heal the divide' and 'come together.'... Turn them off."[11]

Among the more colorful reactions, CNN political commentator Ana Navarro said, "All pollsters should be tarred and feather[ed]. Every single one of them. Next time someone shows me a poll, I'm using it to wrap dead fish."[12] Meanwhile, over at ABC, Joy Behar, cohost of *The View*, expressed shock and dismay that the House, the Senate, and the White House would all be in Republican hands. "And then," she exclaimed, "the FBI has stuck its nasty little nose in the middle of this. Plus the Supreme Court, who knows where that's gonna go? So the only checks and balances we have are us, *The View*. That's it!"[13]

Standing by Their Man

Perhaps most disconcerting for Trump's adversaries is the fact that, regardless of what he says or does, and no matter what scandals or fiascoes the media manage to summon up, the base has remained faithful and continued to support the president and his agenda at all costs. In fact, there seems to be an uncanny pattern to Trump's media disasters. Whether it's his tweets about Deferred Action for Childhood Arrivals, the NFL anthem kneelers, or his criticism of the young Parkland, Florida, anti-gun protesters, every attempt to paint the president as rude, insensitive, or simply wrong falls on deaf ears. And worse, within days or hours a major news event often comes along to confirm that Trump got it right and his accusers missed the boat.

These twists of fate have critics scratching their heads. I experienced their exasperation personally when several national news interviewers started by asking me to explain how Evangelicals can overlook reports of infidelity and still support the president. In essence, these journalists were saying, "What will it take for Trump's evangelical supporters to finally abandon him?" In an editorial for the *Washington Post*, guest columnist and Ohio newspaper publisher Gary Abernathy addressed this question. Over the years, he said, it has been commonly accepted that all presidential candidates will say whatever it takes to win, and once in office those promises are either abandoned or ignored. But not so with this president, who "has remained as constant as the northern star." The writer then asked, "Has Trump really behaved in some new manner that wasn't on full display during the campaign? The outrageous tweets, the bluster, the self-aggrandizement, the insults—Trump the commander in chief is virtually identical to Trump the neophyte candidate."[14]

Even as he exhibits what critics see as negative attributes, Trump has worked diligently to fulfill his campaign promises, including the following:

- Appointing a conservative Supreme Court justice to replace Antonin Scalia
- Making border security a top priority
- Enacting far-reaching and widely popular tax cuts
- Repealing Obamacare
- Empowering American manufacturing and energy production
- Recognizing Jerusalem as Israel's capital and ordering the American embassy to be relocated there

"No one who backed Trump as a candidate, with all his flaws," Abernathy writes, "has been given much reason to abandon him."[15]

Among all his missteps, the one many thought would bring Trump's candidacy to a screeching halt was the *Access Hollywood* tape and the allegations of several women that Trump had sexually assaulted them. But lost on many liberals, Abernathy says, was the fact that the media had already declared during the presidency of Bill Clinton that such stories no longer matter. The Democrats had long-since won the debate. Consequently, Trump was immune on that topic, and, as I referenced in several media interviews, neither *Access Hollywood* nor the more recent Stormy Daniels mess would be enough to slow his momentum. The voters understand that everyone's closet has skeletons, and, the columnist adds, "Trump's closet door has long stood wide open. No new revelations about his personal life were going to shock or shake his supporters."[16]

Surprisingly BBC's US correspondent Katty Kay seems to have come to a similar conclusion. "To understand why somewhere between 35–38% of Americans consistently approve of the job Mr. Trump is doing, you need to reframe the way you look at his voters. It's not what they are for that matters, it's what they are against. So it's not that a third of US voters are fervently on the side of Donald Trump—what's more relevant is that they are adamantly on the opposing side of a culture war that's been brewing here since the 1980s."[17]

Kay continues: "Mr. Trump is against the political establishment (the media, the Republican Party, political grandees like the Bushes and the Clintons) and change (which encompasses everything you had but fear you are losing) and he's against the world (which has taken jobs and sent immigrants to take over America). You can trace the roots of this culture war back to Ronald Reagan's moral majority. Historians may even go back to the civic explosions of the 1960s. If you believe America is engaged in a life-or-death battle over its identity, in which the past looks golden and the future looks, well, brown-ish, then Mr. Trump sounds like he's on your side."[18]

A Matter of Trust

All this, the broadcaster says, explains why Trump's broadsides against the media and the liberal press score major points with the electorate. "Conservatives in the American heartland have long believed, with some justification, that they can't get a fair hearing in America's mainstream press, which they see as overwhelmingly coastal and liberal. They believe the press has made it impossible for them to win elections." The strength of their resentment can be seen in a November 2017 Quinnipiac University poll showing that 80 percent of Republicans trust Trump more than the media. "No wonder his favorite enemy," Kay writes, "is the fake news."[19]

A similar confirmation of this commentator's perspective comes from the London-based periodical *The Economist*, which commissioned a YouGov poll to sample Republican opinions about the media. In the survey of fifteen hundred Americans they found that most Republicans trust the president more than they trust the media. When asked whether they trusted Trump more than the *New York*

Times, the *Washington Post*, or CNN, at least 70 percent sided with the president. Fewer than 15 percent chose the media. (The remaining 15 percent were unsure.)

Republicans also preferred Trump over the establishment Never-Trump journals, the *Weekly Standard* and the *National Review*. Overall the Fox News Channel fared best among all news outlets; nevertheless, 54 percent of Republican poll respondents said they would trust the president over the Fox network if there were ever a conflict of opinion.[20]

One further footnote from radio host Michael Medved may shed a bit of light on the reasons for the gulf between the Left and Right on moral issues (which is something I tried to explain on CNN, MSNBC, and Fox News when the Stormy Daniels story broke). A poll by *The Economist*/YouGov exploring differing views asked respondents if they would be willing to support "a presidential candidate who has done immoral acts in his or her private life."[21] Surprisingly, Democrats were less forgiving than Republicans. Fully 48 percent of Republicans would be willing to back a candidate with moral failings, while only 19 percent of Democrats would. "After three decades of Democratic infatuation with the profoundly imperfect Bill and Hillary," Medved notes, "this counts as a shock."[22]

But going further, the YouGov poll also confirmed that on moral issues such as abortion, gay sex, premarital sex, and doctor-assisted suicide, most Democrats have a very tolerant view. These things are simply matters of personal choice, they said. However, the most surprising finding was that 82 percent of Democrats believe "hunting animals for sport" is morally wrong.[23] If this reflects legitimate concern for all living things, one would think a human infant in its mother's womb would be worthy of protection. "Even if someone doesn't consider the baby to be fully human before delivery," Medved notes, "surely that unborn child deserves as much respect as, say, a deer. Yet Democrats find abortion more acceptable than hunting, by a margin of three to one."[24]

Freedom of Conscience

So much of the bitterness and acrimony in contemporary politics is focused on these issues, which makes the Left's moralizing about the sins of the president all the more surprising. And as I mentioned earlier, the most perplexing issue contributing to existential angst among the members of the liberal establishment is the enigma of Trump's unflagging support among evangelical Christians. I was interviewed by CNN, MSNBC, and Fox News on this very topic, which I'll discuss further in a later chapter. Despite all the sordid revelations about his past misdeeds, the president's favorability ratings among Evangelicals remain as high today as ever. More than 80 percent of white Evangelicals voted for Trump in 2016, and that high level of support has changed very little. Even the most salacious revelations have apparently had no long-term effect on the faithful.

Many books and articles have been written in an attempt to make sense of this conundrum. They've falsely concluded that evangelical Christians are suckers for any outspoken leader with charismatic appeal. They claim Evangelicals are drawn to Donald Trump because he is the charismatic and iconoclastic leader of a large and vocal movement. In other words, they follow him instinctively as a surrogate Christ figure. Nothing better illustrates the folly of secularists claiming to fathom the heart of sincere believers.

Jonathan Wilson-Hartgrove, a religious writer featured in *Time* magazine, declared that Evangelicals are followers of a slaveholder religion, which condemns and subjugates blacks, women, homosexuals, atheists, and believers of all other faiths.[25] Still other commentators, such as former White House speechwriter Michael Gerson, have exploded into print claiming that Christian support for Donald Trump has led to a crisis in evangelicalism.[26] The assumption is apparently that voting for a man with an admittedly imperfect past is an act of hypocrisy, tantamount to outright heresy. But as I've tried to point out, the faithful have not sold their souls; rather, they have taken a calculated position based on the political alternatives and their understanding that all people are sinners.

I've been publishing stories about Evangelicals for the past four decades, so I know the history well. They have watched without recourse as their customs and religious beliefs have come under assault by the education establishment, the media, and, most damaging, the federal courts. Supreme Court rulings in the 1960s stripped prayer and Bible reading from the public schools. There were no riots, no marches. Instead, believers stood by in silence, fearing there was nothing they could do. But that was only the beginning. The Ten Commandments were forbidden in schools and other public spaces, along with inscriptions, symbols, and the accumulated wisdom of the American patriots that had adorned courthouses and monuments for decades. Today Christian bakers, florists, and wedding planners, along with restaurant, hotel, and resort owners, are under the constant threat of losing their livelihood, their homes, and their freedom for simply abiding by the time-honored principles of their faith.

To track these developments, the Washington-based Family Research Council released a report in 2014 titled "Hostility to Religion: The Growing Threat to Religious Liberty in the United States." The study documents numerous examples of overt hostility toward faith in the United States in four areas: (1) attacks on religious expression in the public square; (2) attacks on religious expression in schools and universities; (3) censure of religious viewpoints regarding sexuality; and (4) suppression of religious viewpoints on sexuality using nondiscrimination laws. That catalog of violations, spanning over ten years, contains ninety separate incidents where Christian values and practices have been squelched, prosecuted, and penalized.[27] (In full disclosure, there were also a few instances of hostility toward other religions.)

For those wondering why Christians have consistently favored Donald Trump over his many challengers, writes Hugh Hewitt, this is the overriding reason. Specifically it comes down to clashes exemplified by the case of *Masterpiece Cakeshop, Ltd. v. Colorado Civil Rights Commission*, argued before the US Supreme Court in December 2017. In this case the state of Colorado ruled that Jack Phillips, the owner of Masterpiece Cakeshop, was in violation of state law for his refusal to create custom wedding cakes celebrating same-sex marriage ceremonies. The good news is that on June 4, 2018, the Supreme Court reversed the judgment against the cake shop owner by a surprising seven-to-two vote on the grounds that the Colorado Civil Rights Commission was clearly hostile to Phillips' faith in the initial case. Justice Anthony Kennedy presented the majority opinion, and Justice Neil Gorsuch, joined by Justice Samuel Alito, and Justice Elena Kagan, joined by Justice Stephen Breyer, filed concurring opinions supporting the court's decision.[28] But this is just one example of how the liberal courts have attempted to use politically correct laws to punish people of faith and restrict their freedom of conscience.

Hewitt asks, "Will Americans be allowed to practice their religious beliefs without fear of ruin from secular absolutists? In the view of these voters, elites believe every knee must bend to their secular creed, not just on matters regarding sexual intimacy but also on issues of when life begins and when death ought to be optional. Many people of faith are convinced that their ability to believe, proclaim, and practice their genuine faith convictions is in danger not just of ridicule but also of punishment. They hear themselves routinely—and unfairly—compared to racist bigots."[29]

The discontent is something Donald Trump understands, and this is also why his commitment to appoint strong constitutionalists to the federal courts became such an important incentive for conservative and Christian voters. "For many millions of people of faith," Hewitt explains, "Trump is the last line of defense preventing their having to choose between their religious beliefs and full participation in the community and in business.... This remains a deeply religious country, and many of its most ardent believers distrust the federal courts and elite opinion makers to such a degree that they will make common cause with those who will protect their freedom of conscience. The right to 'free exercise' isn't just one of many important rights to them; it is the central one by far."[30]

Draining the Swamp

During Donald Trump's long and contentious presidential campaign, perhaps no issue was more consistently or more loudly applauded than his promise to "drain the swamp." Thanks to years of disappointments, defeats, and broken promises, the voters understood that their interests had suffered because of interference from powerful forces in Washington working behind the scenes. As a Floridian, I know and understand swamps. There's a five hundred thousand–acre swamp at the end of my street, and bears, coyotes, panthers, and alligators come up from that swamp. Also, I've been both a registered Democrat and Republican at different times. Like Ronald Reagan, I didn't leave the Democratic Party; the Democratic Party left me. Yet I'm often uncomfortable with Republicans who campaign as conservatives and govern as liberals. If anything, many Republicans are as much a part of the swamp as anyone else in Washington.

Candidate Trump said he understood the public's anxiety and pledged to dislodge the stealth players from their comfortable outposts. It was a smart move; however, no issue may have done more to steel the entrenched resistance against him among the legion of K-Street lawyers, lobbyists, and special interest groups accustomed to privileged access to the seat of power.

"Whether or not one supports President Trump," writes James Strock, "the nation has a stake in his success in transforming the way Washington works. This is an area where there is wide agreement outside of the capital." Removing the feeding tube from the swamp dwellers is risky business, but it is one of the most important steps Trump can take to shake up the bureaucratic culture. And it is the most salutary means of deconstructing what Strock calls "the self-sustaining system of politicians, bureaucrats and their supporting cast of lobbyists, journalists, think tank intellectuals, and lawyers."[31]

Even with widespread consensus, draining the swamp could prove to be Trump's greatest challenge, as naysayers and Never Trumpers were quick to point out. But even the liberal *New York Times* agrees it would be a mistake to ignore the importance of this issue. The need to untangle alliances between the unseen political operatives and the legislators and bureaucrats who routinely cater to them is very real, and the public resoundingly agrees. For many crossover voters, the *Times* said, this was the issue that brought them to the polls. The article, written by Brink Lindsey and Steve Teles, went on to say:

> You can't make sense of his shocking victory last year without reference to the downward spiral of public faith in governing elites and established

> institutions. Years of stagnating incomes, combined with dimming prospects for the future, have primed voters for the message that the system is "rigged" and that only an outsider not beholden to the corrupt establishment can clean it up....
>
> The image of the swamp conveys a profound truth about the American economy....One important factor is the capture of the American political system by powerful insiders—big businesses, elite professionals, wealthy homeowners—that use it to entrench their own economic power. In so doing, they protect themselves from competition, fatten their bank accounts with diverted wealth and slow the creative destruction that drives economic growth.[32]

The image these writers evoke is not far from the truth. Even before his January 2018 State of the Union Address, the Trump administration had waded into the swamp and begun the cleanup process, fully embracing 64 percent of the agenda items proposed by the conservative Heritage Foundation for changing the way Washington works.

Pulling America out of the Paris Agreement on climate change turned out to be a major public relations victory for the president, sending a warning salvo across the bow of DC's entrenched climate-change lobby and earning plaudits from his anti-globalist base. Ending Obama-era regulations on net neutrality was another. Then proposing and passing a once-in-a-generation tax reform package—over the objections of legislators from both parties—was an important sequel leading to, contrary to some media warnings, higher take-home pay and bonuses for American workers.

Using the provisions of the Congressional Review Act, the administration worked with Congress to eliminate fourteen regulations adopted in the waning days of the Obama administration. The president made it clear he intended to wage war on overregulation and began by lifting Obama's moratorium on coal leases on federal lands. He then instructed all executive branch agencies to review all new rules, with the goal of eliminating two regulations for every new one. By year's end the administration had withdrawn, delayed, or made inactive fifteen hundred proposed regulations, saving more than $8 billion in lifetime net regulatory costs, with the promise of increasing savings to $9.8 billion with regulatory cost cutting in 2018.[33]

Another priority of President Trump's agenda is the nomination and confirmation of conservative constitutionalist judges, perhaps best illustrated by the appointment of Justice Neil Gorsuch and nomination of Brett Kavanaugh to the United States Supreme Court. Trump also appointed and gained confirmation for twelve circuit court of appeals judges before the end of his first year in office. This was the largest number of appellate judges confirmed during the first year of any American president. However, the challenge would become more complicated the following year, as more than ninety of the president's appointments were blocked in the Senate.

Nominating and confirming strict constitutionalists to the federal bench, as the Trump team has repeatedly pointed out, is an important step in reducing bureaucratic entanglements since most federal cases are settled at the appellate level. As many as eight thousand cases are filed before the Supreme Court each year, which is far more than any court can consider. Plenary review with oral arguments by attorneys for both sides is granted in about eighty cases each term, and as many as a hundred cases may be disposed of without plenary review. Only one of every seven hundred cases heard by the appellate courts will find its way to the Supreme Court, so reducing the number of activist judges, eliminating needless bureaucracy, and resolving disputes at the earliest possible level is a victory for the rule of law.[34]

Resistance and Obstruction

In the aftermath of the 2016 presidential election, the streets of Manhattan, Washington, Chicago, Philadelphia, Portland, and San Francisco often seemed more like war zones, with an orchestrated outburst of vandalism and violence, including verbal and physical assaults against the newly elected president and anyone who voted for him. As reported by the *Los Angeles Times*, many of the protesters were young people who were protesting for the first time in their lives. In some cases, the crowds were organized and manipulated by professional agitators funded by left-wing groups and international anarchist organizations.

Televised images showed thousands of mostly young people marching in front of Trump Tower yelling, "New York hates you!" and "Not my president!" For several days there were anti-Trump demonstrations around the country as left-wing activists and young people on college campuses took up the chant to "resist and obstruct," vowing to make it difficult, if not impossible, for the Trump presidency to succeed. This resistance would take many forms, but none has been more disruptive than the effort to block Trump's nominees to the courts.

When the president began the nomination process for judicial appointments, there were more than one hundred vacancies to be filled, but there was little doubt the minority party would mount an intense counteroffensive to block as many of Trump's appointments as possible. By means of various political and judicial maneuvers, the Republican Senate had successfully prevented the Obama administration from packing the courts with liberal jurists. Trump's supporters celebrated the victory, but the new administration's plans to shift the courts back to the right soon came under equally strong resistance from the Democrats, using political tactics *U.S. News & World Report* described as comparable to "guerrilla warfare."

Although they didn't stop Trump from getting more appellate court judge confirmations during his first year than any other president, by following arcane legislative rules, withholding approval of home-state nominees, and obstructing Trump's nominees in every way possible, Democrats were determined to grind the president's judicial agenda to a halt. The success of these tactics left the justice system with so many vacancies that legal analysts on both sides began calling it a judicial crisis. "We have the Democrats playing politics and putting up huge roadblocks to confirmation," said Carrie Severino, the chief counsel and policy director of the conservative Judicial Crisis Network. "They're attempting to use every procedural tactic that they can to block [Trump's] judges."[35]

In particular, Democrats have taken pains to block nominees who expressed their strongly conservative or Christian views. But Trump has not given up on his plan to install strict constitutionalists on the federal bench and continues to press the Congress for results. By his sixth month in office the president had nominated eighteen people for district court vacancies, fourteen for the circuit courts and the Court of Federal Claims, and twenty-three for US attorneys. As *Business Insider* reported, "During that same time frame in President Barack Obama's first term, Obama had nominated just four district judges, five appeals court judges, and 13 US attorneys. In total, Trump nominated 55 people, and Obama just 22."[36]

The pace of nominations, however, along with Trump's refusal to change directions, only provoked Democrats to intensify their resistance. Liberals fear the confirmation of so many young and conservative judges in the federal courts all across the country will have a long-term impact on the justice system, jeopardizing the progressive agenda for generations to come. The downside of the Democrats' strategy, however, is that the level of obstruction has created a procedural crisis for the courts and the justice system overall. Important cases that ought to be heard and resolved are being delayed for an unreasonable length of time, and some may be held in limbo for years.

Systematic obstruction has made it next to impossible for many well-qualified individuals to survive the confirmation process. As Trump tweeted on March 14, 2018, "Hundreds of good people, including very important Ambassadors and Judges, are being blocked and/or slow walked by the Democrats in the Senate." And he added, "Many important positions in Government are unfilled because of this obstruction. Worst in U.S. history!"[37] As confirmed by the liberal fact-checking agency at the *Tampa Bay Times*, PolitiFact, only 57 percent of Trump's nominees had been confirmed at the time of Trump's tweet, below Obama (67 percent), George W. Bush (78 percent), Bill Clinton (81 percent), and George H. W. Bush (81 percent).[38]

"The last couple of weeks, we have been highlighting Senate Democrats' historic efforts to obstruct the ability of the government to function. A stunning 43 percent of the President's highly qualified nominees are still waiting for confirmation in the Senate," Trump's Press Secretary, Sarah Sanders, said during a March 7, 2018, press briefing. Tactics authorized by Senate minority leader Chuck Schumer, she added, "have led to 102 fewer confirmations than the next closest administration."[39] Subsequently, a spokesman for Senate majority leader Mitch McConnell said, "The Democrats have gone out of their way to block even the most highly qualified nominees that the president has put forward and it has caused necessary delay for our foreign service and national security around the world."[40]

Rules designed to make the Senate more effective have instead made it much less so. During the Obama administration, Democrats complained about Republican obstructionism, but suddenly obstruction and resistance are commended as the only reasonable response to the president's legislative agenda. Under Senate cloture rules any member of the Senate can delay a confirmation vote for up to thirty hours of floor debate. During those thirty hours, no work gets done and none of the president's nominees can move forward.

But Sen. James Lankford (R-Okla.) has drawn attention to the dramatic increase in the number of cloture votes on nominations in the Senate over the past decade. There was a total of nineteen cloture attempts on nominations in the Senate between 1949 and 1992—a sign of the more restrained atmosphere in the Senate at the time. There were eight cloture attempts in 2005, then at least nine every year from 2009 to 2012. In 2017, however, there were sixty-seven cloture attempts. "In 2013, when Obama controlled the White House," writes columnist Debra J. Saunders, "Senate Republicans helped pass a resolution to reduce post-cloture debate time from thirty hours to eight hours for most executive branch nominees. Lankford wants the Senate to pass another such measure to stop the monkey wrenches through 2018, and let nominees rise with fifty-one votes or fall without them."[41]

Thriving on Chaos

From day one the aftershocks of his election have continued, and the Trump presidency has been immersed in controversy. Some Trump observers have wondered why this president finds himself in so many feuds. Whether he is taking on the mainstream media, ousting foreign diplomats, or firing another chief of staff, he is often in the midst of one battle after another. For those who follow his daily Twitter feed, it often appears the president is at war with the world. Donald Trump is confrontational by nature. He is a gifted negotiator and a shrewd business executive who always expects to win. But as Saunders observes, a lot of people believe this atmosphere of conflict and chaos is no accident; it's actually part of a deliberate strategy. Trump is a man who thrives on chaos and loves the excitement of the mano a mano confrontation. As former White House Press Secretary Sean Spicer once remarked, "I think he doesn't back down from a fight."[42]

"Clearly he thrives on chaos," says GOP strategist Alice Stewart. She goes on to say that when Trump shouts, "Fake news," or retweets anti-Muslim videos, "that clearly resonates with his base, and it gets them ginned up and motivated, and it gets them to push their congressmen." Meanwhile, the president is pushing Congress as well to move ahead on his legislative agenda. "But the reality is, his base is not going anywhere. They're going to be with him no matter what."[43]

When Trump fired his first chief of staff, Reince Priebus, and replaced him with John Kelly, many thought the former Marine general would moderate Trump's Twitter storm. But that didn't happen. Instead, Kelly soon discovered Trump's Twitter feed was beyond his control, and there were more than enough day-to-day battles and personnel challenges to worry about. Kelly made it clear his objective was simply to manage the traffic in the Oval Office.[44] The atmosphere of conflict and uncertainty is apparently a symptom of daily life in the White House, but it may also be a reflection of what politics has become in the twenty-first century.

As Kristen Soltis Anderson writes in the *Washington Examiner*, "We are a nation divided, and we are even divided about *why* we are divided. But if one thing unifies us, it is that there is a pervasive sense, across ideological and partisan lines, that something about the way we are living today simply feels unsustainable.... We are experiencing a fraying of our nation that makes it harder to imagine any of the other big issues, like cost of living or national security, seeing improvement.... More than three-in-four Americans think we are greatly divided, a figure that is the highest recorded in decades."[45]

Democratic voters are angry. If they can't get Trump impeached, the goal is to block him every step of the way. Outside of Democrats, most voters don't necessarily want more gridlock or more conflict. According to recent polling data, most voters don't want Congress to open impeachment hearings against the president, but 70 percent of Democrats do.[46] When asked if they would like to have a Democratic Congress as a "check and balance" on President Trump, Democratic voters overwhelmingly say yes, but only three out of ten independents agree, and 21 percent of independents say they would prefer a Republican Congress to support the president.[47]

"What the Democratic base wants out of their party in Congress is simple: to oppose Trump at every turn," Anderson says, "and if possible, to impeach him. . . . If more division and more gridlock are what Democrats are selling, they'll be giving Republicans an enormous gift."[48]

By its very nature, the American two-party system that has been hailed as a model for the world is a battleground where attitudes, ideologies, and worldviews routinely collide. Debate is essential and disagreement is natural in our form of government, but there must also be room for cooperation and reconciliation. To many in both parties Donald Trump's election came as a shock. Some on the right were just as antagonistic as those on the left, and they have been struggling with the aftershock ever since. But whatever happens in coming months and years, and wherever the political class may try to lead us, we must never forget what we have in common. Despite the deeply held convictions that separate us politically, we share a remarkable history, and our legacy of faith, family, and freedom remains a beacon to the world. Republican, Democrat, or Independent, we have a heritage worth defending, whatever the cost.

CHAPTER 2

THE TIPPING POINT

THE HEADLINES CELEBRATING Barack Obama's 2012 election victory were barely off the presses when candidates began lining up for the 2016 presidential campaign. After several months of testing the waters and courting big-money donors, Hillary Clinton announced her candidacy on April 12, 2015. Vermont socialist senator Bernie Sanders emerged soon after, making his first televised statement on April 30, 2015. Sanders was convinced the Democratic faithful were ready for something completely different. They weren't. But there was never much doubt that Hillary would be the Blue-state champion on Election Day even though she carried all the baggage of the Clinton era and a woman had never been nominated or elected president.

The Clintons have a relentless appetite for power, and it was commonly believed that Hillary had struck a deal with Obama in the wake of her 2008 primary loss. She was in her second term as a Democratic senator from New York, and if she would just back off and cooperate, Obama would make sure she received a strategic appointment. Accordingly she was nominated as secretary of state on December 1, 2008, and confirmed just seven weeks later, promising unqualified support for the president until her hour arrived.

Maryland governor Martin O'Malley announced his presidential campaign in May 2015, followed by Rhode Island governor Lincoln Chafee in June, and Virginia senator Jim Webb in July. All were barely known beyond their home states, yet each made a determined run at the Democratic nomination, topping a field of more than a dozen lesser-known hopefuls who never broke the surface. But Clinton's opponents offered little more than party-line arguments on topics ranging from gun control to climate change, leading the *New Republic* to conclude: "Americans Love an Underdog—Just Not Lincoln Chafee, Jim Webb, or Martin O'Malley."[1]

By comparison, the Republican field looked more like the Kentucky Derby: a full-blown horse race, featuring sixteen men and one woman, all of whom were well-known public figures, long accustomed to winning big races. Among this large group were nine current or former governors, five current or former members of Congress, one former corporate CEO, and one distinguished physician.

Of the seventeen candidates, I met or campaigned for five, so I began wondering whom I would support. Would it be Mike Huckabee, for whom I raised money when he came in second for the nomination in 2008? Or maybe Marco Rubio, whom I supported in 2010 when he ran his long-shot race for the US Senate? I met Rick Santorum after supporting him in 2012, and he personally asked me for my support in 2016. Then in 2015 I attended a prayer gathering in Baton Rouge, Louisiana, and was invited to the Governor's Mansion to have dinner and then pray for Bobby Jindal, who was deciding whether he should run for president. Finally, I met and interviewed Sen. Ted Cruz from Texas and decided to endorse him.

I knew each was a devout Christian. Yet as I watched the campaign develop, I realized I could support any of the seventeen in the race over the Democratic candidate—just based on the difference in the political platforms.

All made their pitches with varying degrees of applause and success, but none managed to capture the public's imagination. The candidate who took center stage at every event was the one man every other candidate was determined to defeat. It was Donald Trump against the world, and he was putting on a show.

Despite the high level of discontent with Washington and the public's demand for a two-fisted outsider, most people were surprised when Donald Trump made it official and entered the race. The flamboyant New Yorker had often hinted at a presidential run, but many, including me, saw him as a caricature. He was a reality TV star, showboat, casino owner, and womanizer. Hardly anyone took him seriously until he actually announced. Then, as candidate Trump began to articulate a message that resonated powerfully with discontented voters in the heartland, the crowds at his rallies all across the fruited plain swelled into the tens of thousands, and suddenly the most unlikely candidate was the front-runner.

The Republican National Committee anointed former Florida governor Jeb Bush, but the voters were not impressed. While Bush was not a bad governor, I didn't feel he was ready to lead the nation. It turns out the hardworking people in Middle America were not interested in the Bush family's younger son either. While there were brief flirtations with Cruz, Rubio, John Kasich, and one or two others, the courtship didn't last. Conservative voters were looking for a hard-nosed change agent who would not only upend the balance of power in Washington but also shake up the establishment in both political parties. They wanted a president who could take the heat and drain the swamp of entrenched bureaucrats and policy wonks who were driving the country in the wrong direction and deeper into debt.

Many Americans felt the nation was in a precarious situation, on the verge of disaster or possibly civil war, due to all the radical changes Obama had rammed through over the previous six years. By using executive orders, official memoranda, and "other regulatory dark matter," Obama had circumvented customary legislative procedures in order to implement unpopular directives that would never have passed muster in Congress or the courts.[2]

By the end of his second term, Obama had issued 276 executive orders, yet, as reported by *Forbes* magazine, these weren't even the most disturbing of the administration's major decrees. Confidential memoranda and agency "guidance" publications would be the most problematic for the incoming administration. Lesser known directives may never appear in the *Federal Register,* and it can be tricky to uncover and rescind them. This allows them to direct the policies of unseen and often unaccountable bureaucrats for years to come.[3]

As I have written elsewhere, the elevation of Donald Trump to the presidency of the United States was an act of desperation by the electorate. He was not the sort of person we had come to expect as an American president, but that ultimately proved to be his greatest advantage. He was not a politician. He was not part of the Beltway establishment. He was a barnstormer, a wrecking ball, and, true to his word, he was rattling windows in the White House even before he arrived.

I'll never forget the night Trump was elected, and I can tell you that for the party being evicted from the White House, Trump's election hit like an earthquake, sending shock waves through the political establishment, the media, and Washington watchers around the world. But no one was more devastated than Trump's Democratic rival, who ran for cover on election night, refusing to address the media or admit she had been defeated in royal fashion. Clinton wasn't the only one shaken by Trump's victory, however, and the recriminations and finger-pointing had barely started when the leftist legions took to the streets and the anarchist recoil and resistance movement kicked in with full force.

By November 9, 2016, battalions of left-wing shock troops accompanied by throngs of easily manipulated fellow travelers were being deployed in cities and towns all across the country. The anarchist groups made their intentions known with professionally printed signs, banners, and flags, hoisted by thousands of rent-a-mob zealots bused in to storm the streets of New York, Philadelphia, Los Angeles, Portland, and Washington, DC, on command. No sooner had the demonstrations begun than the liberal news media were celebrating the birth of a movement, portrayed deceptively as a spontaneous outpouring of defiance by ordinary Americans disappointed by the Republican victory.

But these protesters were anything but ordinary. Hiding their faces behind hoodies, balaclava masks, motorcycle helmets, and all-black gear, the anarchists claimed they were there to "resist and obstruct" every move the new president, his cabinet, and the Republican Congress would make. But the mobs, egged on in some cases by European Antifa activists, were hungry for violence as well. Store windows were smashed, cars were overturned and burned, and there were bloody assaults on innocent civilians. For the mainstream media, embarrassed by their own failure to read the mood of the nation or to forecast what had just happened, the violence was apparently a perfectly natural response. Can you imagine if Republicans had reacted this way to Obama's election in 2008? The media would have roundly condemned them or any other protest in any duly qualified election by the losing side.

The Unseen Hand

The street gangs and black bloc anarchists may have been the face of the movement, but the guiding hand behind this carefully scripted insurrection was a man many assumed to be outside the political process. The Hungarian billionaire György Schwartz, better known as George Soros, was no passive observer, as I document in depth later in this book. As perhaps the largest donor to the Democratic Party, he spent $27 million to defeat George W. Bush in 2004 and gave more than $25 million to fund Hillary Clinton's 2016 campaign, along with other Democratic candidates and causes.[4]

He funneled billions to left-wing groups such as MoveOn.org, Media Matters, the Center for American Progress, the Democracy Alliance, the Open Society Foundations, and many others. And according to a 2011 Media Research Center report, Soros has direct ties to thirty mainstream media organizations, undoubtedly to influence and manipulate news coverage in favor of liberal and left-wing politics.[5] Clearly this is not philanthropy.

Soros made much of his fortune by predatory investing, crippling the European economy more than once, and virtually destroying the currency of several nations. In the book *More Money Than God*, financial writer Sebastian Mallaby reveals how Soros used the assets of his Quantum Fund in 1992 to crash the British pound and pocket a billion dollars. He was convicted by a French court in 2002 for raking off more than $2.3 million in 1998 by exploiting insider information and manipulating shares of the French bank Société Générale. His subsequent appeals failed before the European Court, and he was fined 2.2 million euros, equivalent to the amount he profited.[6]

But none of this stopped Soros from creating and funding left-wing groups to undermine democratic institutions, the capitalist system, and the government of the United States. Soros has contributed $32 billion to fund the Open Society Foundations, which work in more than a hundred countries around the world and push an open-borders agenda. In the past no one seemed to understand the danger posed by Soros or the groups he supports. More recently it's become widely known by conservatives that the open-borders policy of such groups is largely responsible for the immigration debacle that has devastated Western Europe and is threatening to do the same in the United States. In the aftermath of Trump's election Soros reportedly gave $18 billion to the foundation for immediate action against the president—meaning more demonstrations and violence if needed.

While claiming to be an independent, objective research organization, Media Matters is better known as a leftist smear machine whose mission is to discredit conservatives by any and all means necessary. The organization is funded by Soros and other left-wing activists through the Democracy Alliance, composed of around one hundred left-leaning millionaires and billionaires, and related 501(c)4 activist organizations. As described by authors David Horowitz and Richard Poe:

> George Soros is the architect of a "Shadow Party" which operates much like a network of holding companies coordinating the disparate branches of this movement, both inside and outside the Democratic Party, and leading them toward the goal of securing state power. Once attained, that power will be used to effect a global transformation—economic, social and political.[7]

Although some in the Democratic Party would be shocked by the degree to which this shadow party has infiltrated and manipulated their community, large numbers of Democrat loyalists have been drawn in as willing participants and defenders of a revolutionary assault on traditional values. Much of the invective directed at Donald Trump and the Republican Party is a direct result of the heated rhetoric emanating from individuals and groups that repudiate the authentic history of this country. Funded by mega-rich ideologues and radicals, these groups and the foot soldiers they've empowered are working methodically to transform the nation into something our ancestors would never recognize and that they would deeply regret.

Like many of the voters who supported Donald Trump in 2016, I had been committed to other candidates early in the race, but we came around because we had seen more than enough of the so-called "progressive agenda." We could see what political correctness and the Left's idea of diversity and tolerance were doing to the country. Trump was a long shot when he entered the fray, but he was saying what conservative and middle-class voters wanted to hear, and a large swath of the electorate realized that Clinton's vision for America would only be more of the same radical "hope and change" they'd suffered through for the past eight years.

Trump was bold, outspoken, abrasive, and unstoppable, but he understood the emotions of the men and women in Middle America. And he understood the importance of the Christian vote, meeting as far back as 2012 with evangelical leaders—most of them Charismatics—to ask that they pray about whether he should run for president. He had grown up in a Presbyterian home and was a friend of Dr. Norman Vincent Peale. But he was known as a playboy billionaire, not a conscientious Christian. Yet, as I described in my first book, he began watching Christian TV in the early 2000s, and he even called my friend Paula White Cain, whose show he watched. I remember Paula telling my wife and me over dinner that her office had gotten a call from a celebrity named Donald Trump, who asked if she would meet with him to discuss spiritual questions he had. A decade later, with Paula's advice, he reached out to Christian leaders, and he promised to take on the issues that concerned people of faith. The Democratic candidate, on the other hand, referred to Trump's evangelical supporters as a "basket of deplorables" and ignored the faith community entirely.

The mainstream media were totally on board with Clinton's campaign, but Donald Trump was swept into office by a wave of support from voters who were sick of the way Washington does business. They weren't listening to the liberal media, and they weren't responding to their polls. They had reached a tipping point, and they weren't going to take it anymore. As Malcolm Gladwell pointed out in his 2000 best seller, *The Tipping Point: How Little Things Can Make a Big Difference*, revolutionary change often comes suddenly and without warning. It happens in nature, and it can happen with people as well. I read this book when it first came out and recommended it to others because it helps explain why unexpected changes happen.

When a large enough group of people reaches a high enough level of frustration, there is often a spontaneous combustion. At first, the overlooked and disenfranchised group members attempt to speak. But if their concerns are ignored or rebuffed, and if there is no sign of improvement, there may be a sudden and irresistible explosion of resentment leading to an unprecedented change of direction. This is obviously what happened in the civil rights movement, and I believe this explains in large part the aftershock we've experienced ever since the 2016 election.[8]

Revolutions don't just happen. They happen because of frustration, disappointments, insults, and provocations of many kinds that compel people to respond in revolutionary ways. Whether they happen in politics or some other area of society, revolutions are always volatile phenomena. They may occur after years of stress and anger, but they are never about just one thing. They result from a long list of offenses, perceived and real, which sets off a natural chain reaction that quickly becomes irreversible. The sudden release of unrelieved pressures is explosive and often leads to unpredictable consequences.

Millions of Americans feel the nation has been going in the wrong direction. The rhetoric we hear in the media, online, or from friends and family reflects the tension that is building in our society. All across the country ordinary Americans are joining forces and donating to candidates who've promised to challenge the direction our leaders have been taking us in for the past forty years. As Richard G. Lee writes in *The Coming Revolution*:

> For the most part these are all ordinary citizens, men and women from all walks of life, and people who have never been politically engaged in this way before. But through their combined efforts, they are speaking out with a new sense of urgency, determined to bring an end to what millions now perceive as arrogant and predatory behavior by Washington bureaucrats and other elected and unelected officials who wield too much power.[9]

There is no mistaking the emotion or the intensity of those who were crying out for change. In the Christian community millions were praying. Large gatherings such as TheCall, led by my friend Lou Engle, were not protesting anything but were publicly interceding for our nation and the need for revival in America. In 2016 Donald Trump was the beneficiary of the public's outrage and an answer to Christians' prayers. The pollsters and pundits had missed it; they reported what they wanted to believe rather than what was actually taking place in the heartland, and this was why the world reacted with shock and awe after the election. They had been manipulated and misled.

Since his inauguration President Trump has been in a pitched battle with the defenders of the previous regime. Turmoil in the Department of Justice, accusations of collusion with Russia, and leaks from his own White House staff and high-level officials in the Department of State and the Pentagon have created a volatile situation. All this illustrates not only the divisions roiling the nation today but the degree to which antagonists within the permanent bureaucracy, along with "deep state" subversives, are working to undermine the legitimacy of the president and leading the nation either wittingly or unwittingly toward the brink of civil war.

TAKING ON THE WORLD

In his address to delegates at the World Economic Forum in Davos, Switzerland, in January 2018, President Trump walked into what many conservatives would have described as "the enemy's camp." Yet when he arrived, he was almost mobbed by well-wishers, one of whom handed him a copy of *God and Donald Trump*. As dozens of onlookers photographed and recorded his every move on their cell phones, he held the book high—something that surprised and pleased me, of course, when I saw the photos on social media. Although he was not initially invited to this confab of globalist power brokers, the president flew to Davos to make a statement, to declare enthusiastically that "America is open for business." He said he was there to offer a hand of friendship and economic opportunity to the world. And in scripted remarks he said, "The world is witnessing the resurgence of a strong and prosperous America....We are competitive once again."[10]

As noted by reporters from the *New York Times* and other media in attendance, his speech to "one of the world's most global meetings" was not what anyone would have expected.[11] A Reuters commentary indicated that many feared Trump's speech would be a "clash of civilizations."[12] After all, this was quintessential George Soros territory, the stomping ground of the Bilderbergs and other secret elite gatherings. But Trump was there to talk about how economic policies implemented since his election were making America a more attractive marketplace for international investors.

"I'm here today," he said, "to represent the interests of the American people, and to affirm America's friendship and partnership in building a better world. Like all nations represented at this great forum, America hopes for a future in which everyone can prosper, and every child can grow up free from violence, poverty, and fear." While avoiding hot-button topics such as climate change, geopolitics, or any of the specific challenges in international diplomacy, Trump told the delegates he would "always put America first, just like the leaders of other countries should put their country first also. But America first does not mean America alone. When the United States grows, so does the world."[13]

As the *New York Times* reported, "Speakers at the World Economic Forum usually celebrate globalization, praise diversity, and decry climate change. So Friday's speech by President Trump, who has at times voiced skepticism on all three stances, was warily awaited by the assembled business and government leaders."[14] But none of those issues was on the president's agenda for this occasion. Instead, he delivered a strong endorsement of recent Republican tax legislation, predicting a surge of optimism when the tax reductions and pay raises kicked in.

The president assured the world's business and government leaders he favors free trade, so long as abusive trade practices toward the United States are reduced and eliminated. Earlier in the week, Commerce Secretary Wilbur Ross had warned that the US was done "being a patsy" on foreign trade and that tariffs on imports were a distinct possibility.[15] But, with only an implicit reference to China, Trump said, "The United States will no longer turn a blind eye to unfair economic practices, including massive intellectual property theft, industrial subsidies, and pervasive state-led economic planning.

"These and other predatory behaviors," he added, "are distorting the global markets and harming businesses and workers, not just in the U.S., but around the globe."[16] The president then emphasized "the importance of raising the prosperity of all Americans, particularly mentioning low unemployment among African-Americans.... He said that the United States was 'lifting up forgotten communities,' and was fulfilling the dreams of Americans for 'a great job, a safe home, and a better life for their children.'"[17]

The impact of the president's words was visible almost immediately in the sudden rise in stock market valuations at home and around the world.[18] The *Irish Examiner* reported that "boosted by a speech by US president Donald Trump that was deemed more measured and presidential, and helped by relief over impressive results by giant chip maker Intel, European stock markets rose and many US stocks hit record highs."[19] Trump pointed out that the US stock market was already "smashing one record after another."[20] During the previous week, the Dow Jones Industrial Average had topped the twenty-six-thousand mark for the first time ever. The record-breaking highs reminded me of an article in the *New York Times* by Andrew Ross Sorkin I had read the week before the election. Sorkin wrote, "Assume, for a moment, that Donald J. Trump wins the presidency... right off the bat, the stock market would fall precipitously."[21]

Then, the day after the election, Princeton University economist Paul Krugman wrote in the *New York Times* that markets were plunging, and, "If the question is when markets will recover, a first-pass answer is never." He also predicted a "global recession" to follow Hillary Clinton's electoral loss—"with no end in sight."[22] Interestingly, not much has been heard from either of them since the stock market has exploded.

The record highs were good news for most investors but not what George Soros was prepared to hear, as he had made clear during his own remarks at Davos one day earlier, claiming that Trump was pushing the world toward nuclear war and trying to establish a right-wing dictatorship in the United States. He said:

> Indeed, the United States is set on a course toward nuclear war by refusing to accept that North Korea has become a nuclear power. This creates a strong incentive for North Korea to develop its nuclear capacity with all possible speed, which in turn may induce the United States to use its nuclear superiority preemptively, in effect to start a nuclear war to prevent a nuclear war—an obviously self-contradictory strategy.[23]

Soros also said that Trump was trying to institute a "mafia state" in the US but had been unable to do so "because the Constitution, other institutions, and a vibrant civil society won't allow it." On the other hand, the eighty-seven-year-old billionaire said he is using his Open Society Foundations—the radical organization to which he had just given another $18 billion—to "[protect] the democratic achievements of the past." And he added, "Not only the survival of open society, but the survival of our entire civilization is at stake."[24]

While many Americans were celebrating the jump in stock prices after Trump's election, Soros reportedly lost as much as a billion dollars. He had invested heavily, expecting a Clinton victory, but he bet on the wrong horse. Taking advantage of his speech at Davos, he went on to make what some journalists perceived as almost "a veiled threat against the president,"[25] saying, "Clearly, I consider the Trump administration a danger to the world. But I regard it as a purely temporary phenomenon that will disappear in 2020, or even sooner."[26] Soros had been in panic mode ever since the election, saying shortly afterward, "We must do something to push back against what's happening here" because of the "dark forces that have been awakened."[27]

A War of Worldviews

What happens when worldviews collide? There may be no better example than the controversy that passes for legislation in the nation's capital today. The two-party system of government is adversarial by nature, providing a vehicle for voters with differing opinions and beliefs to take sides with the political party that best represents their interests. But in recent years the philosophical divide has grown deeper and more entrenched, and despite frequent calls for bipartisanship from beleaguered voters, that's the last thing most voters actually want.

Today's Republican and Democratic parties represent such highly polarized points of view about almost everything that there is little hope of finding common ground, which means that enacting legislation agreeable to both sides is next to impossible. This is obviously the case in the budget battles and threats of government shutdown that occur now with predictable regularity. Disagreements over issues such as immigration, abortion, gun control, taxes, health care, entitlements, the environment, and much more have pushed the parties further and further apart and created deep-seated hostility in Congress and in communities all over America. In my own extended family some relatives refuse to speak to other family members who support Trump. You've likely experienced the same thing in your family.

A researcher at the Brookings Institution, Thomas E. Mann, writes that while the two parties are the "key actors" in government, America's policymakers tend to respond more to their activist base than to the voters who elected them. This partially explains why "public approval of Congress and trust in government have plunged to record depths." But considering the extreme differences in attitudes, beliefs, and worldviews of the two parties, the polarization is inevitable. As Mann writes, the rising level of polarization reflects more than just ideological differences:

> The rough parity between the parties fuels an intense competition for control of the White House and Congress. The stakes are high, because the ideological differences are large, and because both parties have a realistic chance of gaining or maintaining control. This leads to strategic agenda-setting and voting, even on issues with little or no ideological content and a tribalism that is now such a prominent feature of American politics.[28]

Democrats and Republicans often disagree with each other simply because they refuse to agree with the other side on anything. For perspective, it may be helpful to remember that the Left-Right divide didn't start here. The terms Left and Right, and the institutional divide between parties, actually date back to the French Revolution, in 1789, when members of the anti-royalist faction, including the Jacobins, in the French Assemblée Nationale moved to the left side of the chamber to express disdain for the loyalist defenders of the king, who were seated on the right.

The Jacobins were free thinkers and political radicals. Along with other rebel factions, they rejected traditional values, especially the Catholic Church, and led the campaign to eradicate wealthy aristocrats, the clergy, and the French nobility. The violent eruption that took place on July 14, 1789, known as Bastille Day, led in due course to what became known as "The Reign of Terror," in which as many as forty thousand loyalists, business owners, nobles, and clergy were executed in 1793 and 1794. The French Revolution provides a timely warning about the consequences of extreme polarization.

Disputes among government officials have led to bitter feuds in the past—the duel between Aaron Burr and Alexander Hamilton being one notable example—however, most debates today stop well short of physical violence. But nightly news reports make it clear that the standards of civil discourse are breaking down, and debates between the Left and Right are no longer merely academic.

I remember this type of anarchy being espoused during the Vietnam War era, and I saw some of the protests at the University of Florida become violent. I believe the roots of the current problems started back then. But today it is much worse.

Radio talk show host Dennis Prager recently observed that the number one fear in America today is the fear of violence from the Left. Unfortunately, he says, it's already here:

> But as of now, it's only coming from one direction. Left-wing thugs engage in violence and threats of violence with utter impunity. They shut down speakers at colleges; block highways, bridges, and airport terminals; take over college buildings and offices; occupy state capitals; and terrorize individuals at their homes. In order to understand why more violence may be coming, it is essential to understand that left-wing mobs are almost never stopped, arrested or punished. Colleges do nothing to stop them, and civil authorities do nothing to stop them on campuses or anywhere else.[29]

In many cases the police are merely spectators as they watch these "left-wing gangs loot stores, smash business and car windows, and even take over state capitals." The only conclusion one can draw, Prager suggests, is that America's "mayors, police chiefs, and college presidents have no interest in stopping this violence." Left-wing officials tend to sympathize with the lawbreakers. And while local police may have little sympathy for the thugs and generally try to avoid the ideology of both the Left and Right, they've been ordered to stand down in volatile situations. They've been effectively emasculated by corrupt local officials.

I saw firsthand how anarchists tried to stir up racial tensions after the tragic death of seventeen-year-old Trayvon Martin in February 2012 in Sanford, Florida, only a few miles from where I live. When it first happened, it seemed to be just one more tragic death from a handgun. The local black community didn't really know Trayvon because he was visiting from Miami. Initially they were not enraged. Then out-of-town leftist agitators showed up saying Trayvon was killed by a racist white man named George Zimmerman and that the police had let him go. After a difficult trial watched by the nation, it was deemed that Zimmerman (who was actually Hispanic despite his last name) was acting in self-defense and that law enforcement let him go because Florida law allows for use of force in self-defense.

Before the verdict radicals predicted that Sanford would be burned to the ground if Zimmerman were not convicted. The situation was even inflamed by comments made by President Obama. I was personally involved during that period with other local Christian leaders who worked to ease racial tensions. When Zimmerman was acquitted in July 2013, there were demonstrations and small riots in other parts of the country, but thanks to prayer, there was no violence in Sanford.

After the media feeding frenzy over Trayvon Martin's death, the stage was set for higher-than-normal outrage and coverage a year later when a policeman in Ferguson, Missouri, shot a young black man who was attacking him. And of course things escalated with other incidents in Baltimore, Maryland, and other places. By the time Trump was elected, these anarchists and their patrons in the media were poised for more civil unrest when the election didn't go their way.

Liberals in government and the media claim Donald Trump's election created the breakdown in civil discourse. Pointing to the president's "tweetstorms" and verbal attacks on purveyors of so-called fake news, Democrats believe the strong political rhetoric and antagonism ginned up by Republicans has led to a collapse of civil order. A public opinion poll by the Pew Research Center found that Republicans and Democrats are more divided today than at any point in the last two decades,[30] and the partisan divide is deeper and more extensive now than ever. Since the election of President Trump, the polarization has grown deeper and more intense.

As in the French Revolution, more than two centuries ago, the political Left in this country is less inclined to respond to political and philosophical disagreement through discourse and debate. Especially for millennials and younger liberals, mass protests, demonstrations, boycotts, and violent rhetoric from outspoken leaders are the preferred modes of response. The burning of a large Donald Trump figure in Los Angeles on the night after the election, followed months later by comedienne Kathy Griffin holding a replica of Trump's bloody severed head, as well as relentless verbal attacks along the way from Democratic politicians Maxine Waters and Nancy Pelosi, have energized the base and indicated the level of anger boiling over on the Left. Late-night comics from Bill Maher and Jimmy Kimmel to Stephen Colbert and Samantha Bee have focused virtually their entire repertoire on character assassination of the president.

Daniel Lattier, vice president of a Minnesota think tank, believes some of this anger is driven by the constant flow of bad news from the national media. Emotions are already frayed, and many people take their cue from news reports and then react with anger out of self-defense. In this climate, he says, many people have come to see anger as a virtue and a natural defense mechanism. He points to the phrase used by liberal organizers, "If you aren't outraged, then you just aren't paying attention."[31] In this light, anger is seen as a sign of political and cultural awareness. It's how "responsible liberals" do politics. Again, I saw this firsthand with the aftermath of the over-the-top coverage and extreme outrage over Trayvon Martin's death.

But there is a pattern of division on the conservative side as well. Former New York Republican representative Chris Shays says that during his twenty-two years in Congress he often crossed the aisle to work with Democrats. "When I was first elected to Congress, you would have been thrown out…if you couldn't work with the other side," he said. But many members of Congress today have "never known a Congress where Democrats and Republicans worked together for the good of the country." Shays blames the problem on the leaders on both sides attempting to rid the party of moderates. The result is that both parties are being pushed to the extremes.[32] But many conservatives believe compromise with the Left is the cause of many of their social and legislative failures, and the election of Donald Trump was meant to be a significant part of the remedy.

Governing the Ungovernable

The acrimony and anger that are now so pervasive in government have made it more difficult than ever for our representatives to do the nation's business. The atmosphere of infighting and backbiting raises serious questions about the future of the democratic system. How can any elected official expect to govern effectively when the opposition, aided by a compliant media and gangs of radical mercenaries, is able to disrupt every new initiative with impunity? To be specific, how can President Trump fulfill his promises to the American people when he is being blocked, mocked, betrayed, and contradicted at every turn by adversaries in the opposition party and renegades in his own?

Clearly this has been the objective of the Democratic resistance from day one, to resist and obstruct the president's agenda in order to prevent the Republican Congress from achieving success in any area. The tragic irony of this situation, as pointed out by *Washington Times* columnist Charles Hurt, is that the trap to entangle and distract the president was put in place well before Donald Trump was elected. The American standard for electing a president has been heralded as a model for the world, as "the greatest living experiment in self-governance." But what happens when the president is undercut and savaged in the press on a daily basis and prevented from carrying out the mandates of the office? As Hurt says:

> A man can run the gauntlet against more than twenty professional politicians and come out victorious. He can win more than forty Republican primary contests and beat every professional political campaigner out

> there, earning the votes of more than fourteen million Republicans. He can then turn his attention to beating the most powerful, entrenched political machine America has seen in nearly a half-century....But then the powerful established bureaucracy must conduct a massive, sprawling, limitless investigation into any and all aspects of the president we pick.[33]

President Trump won the presidency fair and square, earning the votes of more than sixty million Americans, Hurt points out, winning the electoral votes of the thirty states he needed to take the White House. But at the height of the campaign, it appears the administration of the outgoing president empowered a massive network of spies, subversives, and saboteurs with orders to conduct clandestine operations against candidates of the other party. So they spied, compromised, and exposed whatever they could find and laid an elaborate trap just in case the American people should actually elect Donald Trump as their next president.

In that light Special Counsel Robert Mueller's endless investigation in search of a crime that never happened should come as no surprise, Hurt writes. "It was cooked up long before Mr. Trump even won the election," and it continues like the world's longest case of water torture. But this is apparently "the new standard for 'self-governance' in America." The people can elect anyone they want, but the muckrakers, debunkers, and character assassins will do everything in their power, including inventing bizarre scenarios of international intrigue, to hound the other team from office. So far the effort has been effective, gumming up the works, but these people, says Hurt, have no idea how much the voters and taxpayers actually despise them.[34]

Writing in the Washington journal *The Hill*, James Strock has come to a similar conclusion. Ever since Donald Trump strode into Washington with the confidence of a conqueror, declaring he had come to "drain the swamp," he has been a target of the Left. At times, Strock suggests, the president must "wonder if he's knee deep in the big muddy."[35] His administration has been mired in chaos since the inauguration. Thanks to the obstruction of Senate Democrats, many important cabinet appointments and federal judgeships remain unfilled after months of wrangling. Lawyers and lawsuits are now the news of the day, while the nation's business is being largely ignored.

I started in the newspaper business during the Watergate era. The media back then hated President Richard Nixon and were successful in running him out of office (for much less wrongdoing than the Democrats did in the 2016 election). The media despised Ronald Reagan and George W. Bush almost as much. To a lesser extent they opposed Gerald Ford and George H. W. Bush. A free press is important to hold those in power accountable. I was trained in the highest ethics of journalism at the University of Florida. I'm sad to see how the press are largely not objective and have become the publicity arm of the far Left. I believe the press have become part of the problem—what Donald Trump calls "the swamp," which he pledged to drain.

No president can drain the swamp overnight, and perhaps the president should have known his threat to the vast unseen network of swamp dwellers could become a life-altering experience. Nevertheless, writes Strock, President Trump can "change the weather of Washington politics" by taking the battle to the forces arrayed against him and putting the focus on the members of Congress themselves. An important step would be enforcing regulations that make those who make our laws more accountable to the people they govern. Through statutory and voluntary regulations the president can put the focus back on Congress and introduce measures that will create an environment in which the government can function once again as intended.[36]

Regardless of one's party affiliation, it should be obvious that the nation has a stake in the president's ability to succeed in his job. It should be just as obvious that obstruction hurts not only the president but the entire nation. Draining the swamp means restoring the authority of elected leaders and key officials to do their jobs and eliminating the ability of operatives within the "special interest state" to interfere and obstruct. The system that allows rogue politicians, bureaucrats, lobbyists, journalists, think tank intellectuals, and lawyers to overwhelm the administration with scurrilous charges has helped to create a toxic environment in which almost nothing of importance can be accomplished. Can you imagine trying to do your job with this much opposition coming at you on a daily basis? Yet President Trump is unique in his ability to brush off the harshest criticism and simply ignore it.

Strock points to several areas where regulatory changes could make a big difference—for example, abolishing the pension system for ex-presidents and ex-members of Congress, prohibiting the use of taxpayer funds to subsidize secret settlements of actions against elected officials, removing Obamacare subsidies and special treatment for members of Congress and their staffs, and banning campaign fundraising while Congress is in session. These are a few places where executive action can help to make government more accountable, but taken together, initiatives of this sort would begin the process of reorienting the government and making our leaders more responsive to the citizens they represent.

Putting the burden on Congress to play by the same rules all Americans must abide by sends a message to the voters that the administration is looking after their interests, and it puts Congress on notice with the demand that the members either put up or shut up. That doesn't mean, however, that covert operations will suddenly cease. It will not necessarily restore any semblance of collegiality among members of the opposing parties. And it doesn't mean that sworn enemies such as George Soros, Tim Gill, Tom Steyer, and the league of one hundred leftist billionaires will suddenly walk away from their campaign to impeach or undermine the president. But it's a step in the right direction when some sort of counteroffensive is greatly needed.

According to documents obtained by Judicial Watch through a Freedom of Information Act lawsuit, the Obama administration was actively giving taxpayer dollars to a Far Left group run by George Soros. The documents show that the United States Agency for International Development (USAID) funneled $9 million in taxpayer dollars through its Civil Society Project to support Open Society Foundations operations in Albania. These operations were designed to give the country's socialist government greater control over the judiciary.[37] As disappointing as the news may be, what such discoveries actually show is the lengths to which the previous administration and the deep state would go to perpetuate the leftist agenda.

The report also shows that a group of senators wrote to then secretary of state Rex Tillerson asking for an investigation into allegations that the US government was sending taxpayer dollars to fund Soros' operations in Albania. Judicial Watch President Tom Fitton said, "George Soros is a billionaire and he shouldn't be receiving taxpayer support to advance his radical left agenda to undermine freedom here at home and abroad."[38] But at the same time, billionaire environmentalist Tom Steyer is promoting his "Need to Impeach" campaign in hopes of entangling the commander in chief in legal matters, much as Richard Nixon was handicapped during the Watergate era.

According to one report, Steyer mailed a "guide to impeachment" to 5,171 Democratic candidates across the country to be used as talking points for their political campaigns. "We think avoiding impeachment is a strategic mistake," Steyer strategist Kevin Mack told reporters for the liberal website Axios. "It's what fires up the Democratic base."[39] In the rollout of their plans Steyer and company reached out to millennials in hopes of registering Democratic voters ahead of the 2018 midterm elections. They claim to have more than five million supporters already, but many Democratic candidates have chosen to ignore the impeachment guides for fear of blowback from voters in their home districts.

As reported by Breitbart.com, some observers believe Steyer's efforts are actually an attempt to lay the groundwork for his own presidential campaign in 2020.[40] But the intensity of all these efforts to block and obstruct the president's agenda, by members of Congress and by the unseen forces working to cripple the administration, has escalated the intensity of the struggle in Washington and created an environment in which anything can happen. Who knows when the next disaster will strike, and who knows when the next media bombshell may set off an explosion of partisan fury and retaliation!

I believe Donald Trump was raised up by God at this pivotal time in our history. There were political expressions of the changing mood of the country. But I believe spiritually something was happening. Christians were praying for things to change, and the New York real estate tycoon was actually an answer to prayer. Nothing quite like it had ever happened, and the emergence of a coalition of voters of so many persuasions from so many parts of the country was a phenomenon. And in the early hours of November 9, 2016, it became clear the nation had come to a tipping point.

Neither party fully anticipated what would happen if Clinton lost the election. Democrats were confident, buoyed by dozens of polls, that they had won. They had already completed their lists of cabinet secretaries and department heads for the incoming Clinton administration. But suddenly both parties had to face the fact that the most unlikely candidate had won. Today we are living in the aftermath of that revelation. We hope and pray the tensions will subside and the nation can return to business as usual, but who can predict what may happen if the spectacle that passes for government today continues in the same demented direction in which it has been going.[41]

CHAPTER 3

TRUMP'S FAST-START AGENDA

One fact has become painfully clear to political leaders of both the Left and the Right: Donald Trump did not create the electoral surge that propelled him into office in the 2016 election. Rather, he was the beneficiary of a large and amorphous movement composed of millions of angry and dissatisfied voters from both political parties who were searching for a candidate they could trust.

It was precisely because Trump was so outspoken, so unorthodox, so "not Washington" that the voters responded to him as they did. He was cheered, but he was also scrutinized with considerable skepticism until the voters understood that this was their guy; then he was elevated to his high office on a wave of cautious anticipation.

According to a poll on the general mood of the country, from April 2015 to October 2016, at least 68 percent and as high as 79 percent of Americans were dissatisfied with the way things were going.[1] The anger and resentment of voters for the humiliation they had endured over the previous eight to ten years were smoldering just below the surface. They were on edge, and those with the Clinton campaign were so cocksure of their liberal mandate they completely missed it. Relying on the promises of media sycophants and pollsters, no one, especially Hillary Clinton, ever saw what was about to happen. The hubris of the Left is unfathomable. But if the election of Donald Trump as the forty-fifth president of the United States felt to many like an earthquake, the aftershock was more like a shift of the tectonic plates.

In the first days of his presidency Trump began rescinding Obama's executive orders. In the first six months he secured the confirmation of a conservative Supreme Court justice, ended the Trans-Pacific Partnership, announced his intention to pull America out of the Paris Agreement, and signed forty-two bills into law, including the Veterans Affairs Accountability and Whistleblower Protection Act. By the end of his first year in office he had amassed one of the most impressive lists of accomplishments of any president in history and made it clear he was barely started.

Trump was elected because he was seen as a change agent. He promised to halt the Obama administration's headlong rush toward globalism, to dismantle the deep state and root out the leftist underground covertly transforming the republic into a socialist oligarchy. But in many ways this election was an anomaly. Both candidates ignored the guidance of their respective party leaders, listening more intently to their bases.

For Clinton, this was unfortunate since her base was loud and fiercely combative. As the race heated up, Clinton became "hyper aggressive,"[2] "shrill,"[3] and "annoying."[4] Journalist Bob Woodward surmised on *Morning Joe* that she was "not comfortable with herself."[5] Trump, on the other hand, remained calm, provocative, surprisingly witty, and fully engaged with the crowds at his rallies. His promise to make America great again captured the sentiments of voters who feared something rare and wonderful was being lost.

Trump's campaign slogan, writes Francis Wilkinson in the *Denver Post*, "was expertly crafted to appeal to his core followers. It conveys nationalism, nostalgia and deep pessimism and insecurity about the nation's current status—three pillars of Trump's run—along with the implied agency required to reverse course."[6] The slogan was simple and direct and appealed to our competitive nature. According to a WikiLeaks dump of Clinton's campaign emails, her team waded through eighty-five slogan ideas before eventually settling on "Stronger Together," a phrase Obama had repeatedly used in his speeches.

From the beginning of the campaign Trump courted the religious vote and met privately with pastors, even though several of his primary opponents were strong Evangelicals themselves and initially split the evangelical vote. By contrast, Trump spoke with limited fluency in the language of the faithful, and he had lived most of his adult life as a playboy billionaire. Yet, as I documented in *God and Donald Trump*, in the early 2000s Trump began watching Christian television and reached out to Paula White Cain, saying he had some questions about spiritual things. When he considered running for president in 2012, he asked Paula to gather some of her preacher friends "who knew how to pray" over whether he should run, and he welcomed their prayers with gratitude. These leaders saw he was a changed man and that he had become a champion of their causes in a way that John McCain and Mitt Romney never were. And by the time he ran in the 2016 general election, he was rewarded with the largest Evangelical turnout since exit polls started including white Evangelicals—fully 81 percent of white Evangelicals pulled the lever for Trump in November—which gave him the margin of victory.

He accepted the endorsements of individuals and organizations with whom he had sharp differences of opinion, but believing the adage that "the enemy of my enemy is my friend," he was able to build a formidable coalition to help tackle some of the most intractable problems imaginable.

A New Sheriff in Town

The Trump agenda—elaborated almost daily via Twitter to his over fifty-three million followers and fans—focused on strengthening the economy, restoring the integrity of the federal courts, stopping the overwhelming surge of illegal immigrants, rebuilding the military, and uplifting America's standing in the world. This was a 180-degree shift from the progressive agenda of the Obama administration, which is often referred to as "leading from behind." Fearing it would be losing gains made with activist liberal judges, more and bigger government, and the general leftward drift of the country in the past forty years, the liberal opposition was determined to resist the Trump agenda and destabilize the nation at all costs. The goal was to delegitimize and ultimately impeach Donald Trump, regardless of the cost or the repercussions.

The new president inherited a long and intimidating list of diplomatic problems left unsolved by previous administrations—such as North Korea, the Middle East, NATO, and trade deficits—going back to the Reagan years. Yet from his first day in office he began taking dramatic action to restore the functionality of government. One of the first acts of his administration, within hours of his inauguration, was to issue a memorandum ordering a freeze on new government regulations.

By the end of 2016 the Obama administration had grown the *Federal Register* to 97,069 pages of rules and regulations, more than 10,000 pages longer than any previous administration. This represented 3,853 new or revised regulations, the highest number in eleven years. The order sent by Reince Priebus on behalf of President Trump instructed all departments to "send no regulation to the Office of the Federal Register…until a department or agency head appointed or designated by the President after noon on January 20, 2017, reviews and approves the regulation."[7]

Untangling the administrative web would take time, but Donald Trump wanted to make it clear that there was a new sheriff in town. He was a businessman and entrepreneur, justifiably proud of his prowess as a negotiator, but, as pointed out by Victor Davis Hanson, he did not possess the diplomatic temperament to deal with politicians and dealmakers who had spent their entire careers immersed in the protocols of diplomacy.[8] As Trump makes clear in his book *The Art of the Deal*, his way is more personal, more direct, more intimidating. Many of the issues he would have to confront were long-standing and seemingly insoluble, but for Donald Trump, patience has never been a virtue.

The leader of North Korea bragged he could strike the US mainland with nuclear missiles. China's economy was booming at the expense of the American economy because the Chinese not only violated trade agreements but forced American companies to hand over proprietary technology as the price of doing business in China. When State Department officials' complaints were rejected, rather than threatening sanctions or tariffs, they shut up and went home. Just business as usual.

As far back as 1949 America had been saddled with a significant percentage of the NATO budget, while US military forces were obliged to defend the European continent. At the same time, Mexico was growing rich on remittances from millions of illegal immigrants who had been flooding across our borders for decades. Foreign workers residing in the United States were contributing an estimated $30 billion a year to the Mexican economy. When America complained, Mexican officials fired back, claiming racism, xenophobia, and nativism. Once again, the US government did nothing.

There are common themes in all these international stalemates, and as Hanson points out, "Diplomatic niceties had solved little. American laxity was seen as naiveté to be taken advantage of, not as generous concessions to be returned in kind."[9] These and many other problems had been festering for years, and neither the Clinton, nor the Bush, nor the Obama administration was able to make headway. But that was not Trump's way. He has been described as "a bull in a china shop," but he is a quick study, remarkably perceptive, self-assured, and tenacious.

Donald Trump's way, says Hanson, is to approach such problems much as Alexander the Great had done in the story of the Gordian knot. According to legend, the knot of Gordium was impossible to untie, and anyone who could untie it would become king of Asia. Despite many attempts, no one succeeded; however, when Alexander was given the challenge, he simply pulled out his sword and slashed the knot apart. Subsequently, as king of Macedonia and Persia, he "established the largest empire the ancient world had ever seen."[10]

The analogy is clear enough. Hanson writes, "Before Trump arrived, the niceties of American diplomacy and statecraft had untied none of these knots. But like Alexander, the outsider Trump was not invested in any of the accustomed protocols about untying them. Instead, he pulled out his proverbial sword and began slashing."[11]

In response to Kim Jong-un's threat to push the nuclear button, Trump tweeted back, "I too have a Nuclear Button, but it is a much bigger & more powerful one than his, and my Button works!" and then mocked him as "Little Rocket Man."[12] At the same time, he ordered the US Defense Department to begin expanding our nuclear arsenal and fortifying America's missile defense systems. Trump's way was "winning by intimidation" and threatening Kim in much the same way Kim had threatened others.

Because China's trade policy is so complex and deceptive, it would be difficult to untie that knot by traditional diplomacy, so Trump decided to take the same forceful approach with Chinese president Xi Jinping, announcing in March 2018 that the US would begin levying tariffs on Chinese imports. The 25 percent tariff on $34 billion in Chinese goods went into effect on July 6, 2018, and China responded in kind by implementing a 25 percent tariff on $34 billion in American goods. Some fear an escalating trade war between the two countries, but House Ways and Means Committee chairman Kevin Brady supports President Trump's efforts to challenge China and thinks the two leaders need to meet in person to achieve the best outcome. Brady told Fox Business, "I'm confident this president meeting face-to-face with President Xi can level that playing field, can create a new set of trade rules for both of our countries."[13]

The problems with NATO were equally long-standing, and American defense strategists wanted to know why the US should pay more than a fifth of the entire budget for defending Europe if the other twenty-eight member nations fell short of paying their fair share. In 2017 only four of the other twenty-eight met their commitment of spending at least 2 percent of gross domestic product on defense.

Speaking at NATO headquarters in Brussels in February 2017, Defense Secretary Jim Mattis told the delegates, "America will meet its responsibilities, but if your nations do not want to see America moderate its commitment to the alliance, each of your capitals needs to show its support for our common defense."[14] Shortly thereafter, President Trump confronted NATO delegates, saying, "Over the last eight years, the United States spent more on defense than all other NATO countries combined."[15] No one doubted where the debate was headed, and then on May 27, 2017, Trump tweeted, "Many NATO countries have agreed to step up payments considerably, as they should. Money is beginning to pour in—NATO will be much stronger."[16]

As of this writing, the US has begun erecting a wall on lengthy sections of the southern border, Immigration and Customs Enforcement (ICE) agents have begun conducting raids nationwide, rounding up undocumented immigrants, known criminals, and visa overstayers, and the US has been supporting efforts by Mexico's military to attack the flow of drugs and opioids into this country. From the Oval Office on August 27, 2018, President Trump announced his plan to terminate the North American Free Trade Agreement and enter the new US-Mexico Trade Agreement. He thanked negotiators from both nations for their hard work on the revisions of the twenty-four-year-old agreement he had routinely slammed as "one of the worst deals ever made." In addition to being a "big day for trade," it was one more campaign promise he's kept. He also announced that we would start similar negotiations with Canada immediately.[17]

Beyond Mexico and Canada, the US is in a trade standoff with the European Union and China. But Trump's purpose is to reduce the trade deficit and resolve trade issues in America's favor. Even though other countries are retaliating, the US president refuses to back down, putting America's interest over global ones.

First Things First

For many of Trump's supporters, myself included, nominating a trustworthy conservative to replace the late Antonin Scalia on the Supreme Court was the first order of business. Trump had promised on the campaign trail that he would nominate a staunch constitutionalist. In March 2016 he said he would likely have an opportunity to replace several of the aging liberal justices with conservative picks. Relishing the chance to goad his rivals, he said, "Let me tell you, if they don't win, they're going to have probably four, and could even be five, Supreme Court justices approved that will never allow this country to be the same. It'll take 100 years...."[18]

On January 31, 2017, eleven days after the inauguration, Trump made good on his promise, nominating Neil Gorsuch as associate Supreme Court justice. As the media and the legal establishment began digging into his accomplishments, they found that Gorsuch had eminent academic qualifications and outstanding credentials, having clerked for Justices Anthony Kennedy and Byron White and serving on the Court of Appeals for the Tenth Circuit. Gorsuch would become the first justice ever to be seated on the court with a justice for whom he once clerked.

Then, in July 2018, Trump nominated his second Supreme Court justice, Brett Kavanaugh, who at fifty-three is barely older than Gorsuch. And like Gorsuch, he clerked for Anthony Kennedy, whom he will replace on the high court if confirmed as this book goes to press.

While we don't know when Kavanaugh will be confirmed, Trump's first nominee was confirmed on April 7, in just over two months. And at age forty-nine at the time of his confirmation, Gorsuch would be the youngest member of the court, bringing much-needed support for the three constitutionalists currently serving.

No sooner had he presented the Gorsuch nomination than the president moved on to a long list of nominees to fill more than a hundred vacancies on the federal courts. Again, the goal was to nominate young, highly qualified candidates with strong conservative principles to protect our constitutional rights for decades to come, including especially religious liberty and the right to life. Predictably

Democrats used every trick in the book to block the president's judicial, executive, and diplomatic nominees.

By January 2018 they had kicked back nearly one hundred handpicked and thoroughly vetted nominations to the White House. This was in addition to many ambassador positions being held up in the Senate. By April 2018 only seventy-five of the vacant State Department jobs had been filled.[19] But in response to the Democrats' obstruction of the confirmation process, the president proposed that the Senate be required to remain in session seven days a week until his political and judicial nominees are confirmed.

One of the president's most important executive actions was to expand the religious and conscience exemptions to the contraception mandate of Obamacare to include both nonprofit and for-profit organizations, which was very important to the evangelical community. In the same regard, he ordered the Department of Health and Human Services to create a Conscience and Religious Freedom Division to protect the rights of doctors, nurses, and health care workers who refuse to perform abortions or other procedures that would otherwise violate their religious or conscientious objections. Further, he directed the Department of Justice to publish guidelines for over four hundred departments, agencies, and sub-agencies in the federal government requiring them to safeguard the religious liberty of the parties in all legal actions before the government.

On January 19, 2018, the president took another bold step by addressing the forty-fifth annual March for Life via satellite from the White House Rose Garden, telling them he was especially proud to be the first president to do so. He assured those in attendance, "We are protecting the sanctity of life and the family as the foundation of our society."[20] During his remarks the president announced that he had reinstated the Mexico City Policy that requires all US organizations operating overseas to certify they will not "perform or actively promote abortion as a method of family planning."[21]

He also said he had overturned the Obama-era regulation that prohibited states from defunding abortion service providers, and he emphasized that "Americans are more and more pro-life….In fact, only 12 percent of Americans support abortion on demand at any time." He added that "under my administration, we will always defend the very first right in the Declaration of Independence, and that is the right to life."[22]

The president then went on to mention other accomplishments of his administration. "Tomorrow will mark exactly one year since I took the oath of office. And I will say, our country is doing really well. Our economy is perhaps the best it's ever been. You look at the job numbers; you look at the companies pouring back into our country;

you look at the stock market at an all-time high; unemployment, seventeen-year low. Unemployment for African American workers, at the lowest mark in the history of our country. Unemployment for Hispanics, at a record low in history. Unemployment for women, think of this, at an eighteen-year low."[23]

On October 12, 2017, the White House announced Trump is ending cost-sharing payments to health insurers under Obamacare, and during a White House cabinet meeting on October 16, 2017, Trump added, "Obamacare is finished. It's dead. It's gone. It's no longer—you shouldn't even mention. It's gone. There is no such thing as Obamacare anymore.... It's a concept that couldn't have worked. In its best days it couldn't have worked."[24]

Also on October 12, 2017, the president signed an executive order requiring new regulations to encourage the establishment of cheaper health plans that can be purchased across state lines and allow small-business owners to form coalitions and partnerships with trade groups and others to purchase health insurance. The plans could be designed to suit the needs of the individual employers and the partner organizations and would not be required to offer prescription drug plans or certain other benefits.

One of the most important features of the Senate tax-reform bill passed on December 1, 2017, is the elimination of the individual mandate that penalized taxpayers for choosing not to buy health insurance. After weeks of hotly contested debate, in and out of session, the Senate voted fifty-one to forty-nine to approve the Republican bill. The new law permanently reduces the corporate tax rate from 35 to 21 percent and lowers rates for individuals and families. It places a cap of ten thousand dollars on deductions for state and local taxes, but more importantly the law drives a stake through the heart of Obamacare.

The president said the law will boost the economy, promote new business and industry investment, and encourage companies doing business abroad to bring their workers home and conduct business in the United States. In the wake of these and other changes the White House was buoyed by a University of Michigan survey released in March 2018 showing that consumer confidence had reached a fourteen-year high.[25] Improvements in the economy, rising income levels, and the overall strength of personal finances contributed to the optimism of consumers responding to the poll.

Major Policy Issues

During the campaign Trump had promised to take definitive action against ISIS and the caliphate in Iraq. By October 2017 the Pentagon was able to announce that the "capital of terrorism," in Raqqa, Syria, had fallen to US-led coalition forces. Rex Tillerson, then secretary of state, said the fall of the Islamic State capital was accelerated by decisions made by President Trump. "In January, ISIS was actively plotting terrorist attacks against our allies and our homeland in Raqqa," Tillerson reported. "Nine short months later, it is out of ISIS's control due to critical decisions President Trump made to accelerate the campaign."[26]

In December 2017, military officials reported that ISIS had lost 98 percent of the territory it once held, and intelligence assessments indicated that the number of ISIS fighters, which numbered close to forty-five thousand when the Islamic caliphate rose to power during the Obama administration, was down to fewer than one thousand less than a year after Trump's election. The fall of the caliphate proved to be a crushing blow to the Islamic State.

Few could doubt his determination. When Trump was asked in a 2011 interview how he would deal with the Somali pirates who were attacking ships from the US and other nations in the Indian Ocean, Trump's answer was, "I would wipe them off the face of the earth."[27] Then, five years later, during an Ohio campaign rally in September 2016, he promised that as president he would "utterly destroy ISIS" in Iraq. "We are going to take a swift, strong action to protect the American people from radical Islamic terrorism," he said.[28]

As commander in chief, the president gave the Islamic forces in Syria and Iraq advance warning of his determination to eradicate the threat of ISIS. On April 13, 2017, he authorized the Pentagon to drop the mother of all bombs, the largest nonnuclear weapon in the US arsenal, on ISIS tunnels and underground strongholds in Afghanistan. That event sent a chilling message that this president means business. As long as the Islamic caliphate was growing, gaining new recruits, and expanding its territory, leaders of the militant faction might be able to convince themselves their eighth-century religious jihad was invincible and that Allah was on their side. But with the caliphate gone and the leadership decapitated, the whole world could see the tragedy and the folly of that ill-fated delusion.

According to pollsters tracking the concerns of voters, the central promise of Trump's campaign, and the issue that most often ranks at the tops of all polls, is building a wall on the southern border to stop the flow of immigrants into this country. To start the process, the president began pressing Congress to fund construction of the border wall during his first weeks in office, but it was not until passage of the omnibus spending bill, which contributed a spare $1.6 billion for portions of the wall, that he had sufficient funding to begin construction.

When he signed the bill, on March 23, 2018, the president issued an executive order increasing the number of border patrol agents and customs officials to expedite deportations. Additional funding would be needed to complete the wall, but the president was standing by his promise to "make Mexico pay for it," and who would be bold enough to believe he couldn't do it?

US Customs and Border Protection reported a 23.7 percent reduction in immigrants entering the country illegally during the 2017 fiscal year, and this was without the wall being completed. It was becoming clear to would-be immigrants and the international community at large that this American president was more serious about curtailing illegal immigration than any of his predecessors. As promised throughout the campaign, Trump was actually putting Americans first, and fear of what would happen under the new Trump administration made many prospective border crossers decide it would be much safer to stay home.

Richard Baris also reports that 92 percent of illegal aliens arrested by ICE since Trump's election either had criminal convictions or criminal charges pending or were already ICE fugitives or repeat offenders. Contrary to the sensationalized media reports accusing the administration of criminalizing the dreamers and allowing barbaric treatment of border crossers by customs officers—"ripping babies out of their mother's arms"—the facts make it perfectly clear that these were not innocent victims, and the media's narrative was little more than cheap theatrics.[29]

Continuing his fight against the pro-immigration forces within the United States, the president issued an executive order requesting the Department of Justice and Homeland Security withhold "federal funds, except as mandated by law," from any city or municipality declaring itself to be a "sanctuary city."[30] He had talked a lot about sanctuary cities on the campaign trail, and many Americans were pleased to see him taking action against these lawless cities.

The president had also promised to make energy policy a major issue in his administration, and he began by opening the Arctic National Wildlife Refuge (ANWR) for energy development. For decades Republicans had made promises to allow oil drilling in ANWR, but strong opposition from the Left blocked their efforts. Yet later, when drilling in ANWR was included in the president's signature tax bill, there was only limited resistance. Proponents of the bill argued that drilling in ANWR would benefit domestic oil and gas producers and allow the US to import less from hostile sources, such as Russia, Venezuela, and the Middle East. Meanwhile, the House Committee on Natural Resources reported that developing the natural resources in ANWR would help to generate around 130,000 new jobs and $440 billion in new revenue.

According to political writer Mason Weaver, President Trump pulled off a major coup with the signing of the omnibus spending bill, basically persuading Congress to release billions of dollars in "discretionary funding" that would give the executive branch broad powers to fund and defund a variety of initiatives. To gain the support of Senate Democrats, the president agreed to certain measures he was strongly against, such as allowing Planned Parenthood to be eligible for federal funding for another year. That was something he had forcefully resisted, but stonewalling the issue would have dragged out deliberations and risked a major roadblock to other vital issues.

The heated debate over the omnibus bill was becoming an obstruction and a political football the president wanted to avoid, so he worked to get the best deal he could get. Congress, not the president, is in charge of federal funding, so he eventually agreed to these measures and signed the bill. However, the president has the ability to direct how the money is used, says Weaver, and he has discretionary authority to spend or not spend any monies that are not otherwise required by law to be spent.[31]

The federal government must pay for mandatory social programs such as Social Security and Medicare. But agencies such as the Department of Energy, the Department of Housing and Urban Development, the Department of Education, the Department of Defense, and the State Department are all paid by discretionary funding. The president enjoys broad powers to determine how, or even if, these funds are spent. For the president to get things he wants through Congress, he generally has to accept a number of things he does not want. During the brouhaha over the omnibus bill, both friends and enemies of the president claimed he had switched sides. He was allowing measures to be funded he had once declared unacceptable. But, Weaver says, the president "TRUMPED" them all.[32]

In Trump's tweet posted shortly after signing the spending bill, he said, "Building a great Border Wall, with drugs (poison) and enemy combatants pouring into our Country, is all about National Defense. Build WALL through M!"[33] What he was saying was that he would be using a portion of the money designated in the bill for the military to build the wall, and the Swamp, much to their chagrin, had just funded it.

Even though countries such as North Korea, China, and Russia have shown themselves to be hostile to America's interests in the world, the United States Congress has consistently given aid and comfort to these enemy nations, sometimes through unfair trade policies that penalize American business. When President Trump signed the omnibus spending bill, demanding substantial increases for the military, it was with the understanding that he could apportion that money to do the greatest good, defending the nation not only on foreign battlefields but on our own borders.

"The U.S. Army Corps of Engineers," says Weaver, "is the premier construction organization in the world. It can build, maintain and establish projects anywhere and under any circumstances. It is engaged in more than 130 countries. The military responds to national disasters like hurricane, fires and other national disasters. If it can build roads, buildings and schools in Iraq and a border wall between Afghanistan and Pakistan, the south Texas and San Diego County deserts will be no problem for them."[34]

Making America Great

Because of the importance of a strong and growing economy, the president's first big meeting was with a group of the nation's top corporate executives to discuss priorities of the Trump administration and the importance of doing business in the US. Among those in attendance were the CEOs of Ford Motor Company, Lockheed Martin, Dow Chemical, Dell Technologies, US Steel, Whirlpool, and six others. The president told the group that tax cuts for business and the elimination of unnecessary and punitive regulations would be a top priority of his administration, and he encouraged manufacturers with overseas operations to bring the business back home. "There will be advantages to companies that do indeed make their products here," he said.[35]

After the meeting Dow Chemical CEO Andrew Liveris told CNBC during a live interview that he and others were enthusiastic about Trump's strong support. "My whole sense of this administration in the 30 days of working with them is urgency on the business side. They really want to get the barriers out of the way," he said. "If it goes much beyond the fall, I would be staggered." The repeal of Obamacare may be a higher priority, he said, but tax reform was "right up there." Liveris also said that "all the CEOs that were here today and in the last meeting, are very encouraged by the pro-business policies of President Trump and his Cabinet." He added, "Some of us have said this is the most pro-business administration since the Founding Fathers. There is no question that the language of business is occurring here at the White House."[36]

Since Trump took office the stock market has boomed, which I'll discuss further in chapter 7, "Trump's Booming Economy." Even though the market took a sudden plunge in February 2018, some analysts believe the event was orchestrated by billionaire adversaries of the president who manipulated large transactions to distract from recent market gains. Obama administration officials had projected a long-term downturn and said 2 percent growth would be "the new normal." But, in fact, the Dow Jones Industrial Average hit record highs seventy times in 2017. Individual 401(k) average values in June 2017 were 9.6 percent higher than they were a year earlier, and a Bank of America analyst forecasted the S&P 500 and NASDAQ Composite would rise another 12 and 16 percent, respectively, in 2018.

By the fourth quarter of 2017 the economy was projected to top 3 percent growth. The National Association of Manufacturers noted that in the second quarter of 2018 "according to the...*Manufacturers' Outlook Survey*, an astounding 95.1 percent of manufacturers registered a positive outlook for their company, the highest level recorded in the survey's 20-year history."[37] Richard Baris says, "Trump's policies have fueled historic levels of optimism among consumers and businesses."[38]

As he had promised, Donald Trump's first year in office was one of the fastest starts for any administration in American history, not only creating and empowering new measures but ending others that were costing taxpayers millions of dollars. For example, he ordered all federal agencies to cut two regulations for every new one. The point was to reduce the number of regulations, which would in turn reduce the net cost of doing the people's business. One of the best ways to help the economy is by taking the shackles off American companies by reducing red tape and simplifying and streamlining the government.

Within days of taking office the president ordered a freeze on all federal hiring, other than the military, national security, and public safety personnel. He then ordered the Department of Justice to withdraw an Obama administration policy to allow transgender students in public schools "to use the restroom with which they identify." The purpose was for all such issues to be left to the states.

Among other important initiatives, the Environmental Protection Agency, under the leadership of Scott Pruitt, dismantled the Waters of the United States and the Clean Power Plan, which had been put in place by Obama regulations. The Federal Communications Commission, under the direction of Ajit Pai, ended the dangerous and disingenuous net neutrality scheme. And the Department of Education, under the leadership of Betsy DeVos, rescinded the guidance from the Obama administration on how schools should handle sexual assaults under Title IX federal law, which had created "kangaroo courts" that denied defense rights of the accused and often destroyed the lives of individuals without the benefit of due process.

On March 21, 2017, still within his first hundred days in office, President Trump signed the National Aeronautics and Space Administration Transition Authorization Act of 2017. The space shuttle program ended in 2011, essentially turning NASA into an outreach program. The Obama administration even told the head of NASA to make "reaching out to the Muslim world" one of the space agency's top priorities.[39] In restoring the agency to its legitimate function, Trump's law calls for a $19.5 billion NASA budget and asks the space agency to reach Mars by 2033. In response, NASA's acting administrator, Robert Lightfoot, said the bill "ensures our nation's space program will remain the world's leader in pioneering new frontiers in exploration, innovation, and scientific achievement."[40]

In the same vein, President Trump also signed the White House Space Policy Directive 1 on December 11, 2017, supporting research and development for the transportation of humans to the moon, Mars, and other celestial destinations. The program, which is a public/private partnership developed by independent research scientists, is an example of the administration's support of technology and innovation and forward-thinking scientific research, aimed at renewing America's leadership in space exploration. This program was created by the unanimous support of the new National Space Council, chaired by Vice President Mike Pence.

If Donald Trump had done nothing more than stop Hillary Clinton, who is, in my opinion, the most corrupt candidate to ever run for president, he would have been successful to me. But when he said he wanted to make America great again, it was not just a slogan but a vision that propelled this president to accomplish more than any of us could have imagined. Looking at the success of the president's policies during the first two years of his administration, it's hard not to be impressed. Just the items enumerated in this chapter make an impressive list of accomplishments. In every list compiled by the media tracking the success or failure of Trump's campaign promises, he's batting way over .500. Whether we're looking at his first day, first month, first hundred days, or even his first year in office, President Trump has been able to marshal the support needed to accomplish almost all his goals. This is remarkable when you consider that he has been fighting an ongoing battle with the media and holding firm against a recalcitrant Congress.

Much of the time his own party has been as much trouble as the Democratic resistance, and good news that celebrates his successes has only been reported by a few sources: the White House Press Office, the Fox network, a handful of friendly publications, and the president's own tweets. But the American people have been watching. As in the campaign, they're intrigued by this man. They're hopeful, and ultimately they will be the judges who determine the legacy of the Donald Trump administration.

CHAPTER 4

IN THE LION'S DEN

THE LIBERAL MEDIA in this country were focused on bringing down Donald Trump from the day he first announced he was running for the presidency. It began during the primaries, when political analysts and network anchors treated the possibility of Trump's winning the nomination as a joke, never thinking he might actually win. The outlandish things he said and tweeted were not politically correct. Surely, they thought, the next outrage coming from Trump's mouth would be the straw that breaks the camel's back.

As a journalist, I'm part of the media, so I'll be sharing some personal experiences in this chapter. But first let me give you an overview. In the world of the elite media, liberal pundits and talking heads are the gatekeepers. They control access to the public, and they determine winners and losers based on the kind of coverage they decide to give them. They knew that any misstep, emphasized and repeated endlessly, would be enough to end the career of an aspiring candidate. After all, it happened in 1987 when a full-on media barrage ended the presidential campaign of Sen. Gary Hart only a week after reporters found he had spent the weekend with Donna Rice. And before that, in 1972, Sen. Edmund Muskie lost his bid for the presidency when reporters spotted tears on his face (that he claimed was melted snow) after he and his wife were criticized. He had been the front-runner, but the report of the senator openly crying ruined him politically. And Muskie's candidacy was before the days of 24/7 cable news and websites posting breaking news in real time.

And what about John Edwards, the fair-haired senator from North Carolina who was on the ticket with John Kerry in 2004? After the loss to George W. Bush, Edwards decided to run on his own in 2008, but the tabloids and later the mainstream media revealed he had been involved in a long-term affair with a campaign worker while his wife was dying of breast cancer. He later admitted fathering a child with the woman. Not only was his political career destroyed, but he was indicted on charges that he used campaign money to hush everything up. One charge was dropped, and the others ended in a mistrial, after which the government dropped the case.

Every politician is concerned about a slip of the tongue in a debate or a misstep on the campaign trail. The slightest bobble could be just enough to do the candidate in. And in the world of political correctness a poor choice of words can be fatal. So when Donald Trump came down the escalator in Trump Tower to announce his candidacy on June 16, 2015, and promptly talked about the problems with illegal immigrants and plans for building a wall, the pundits predicted his campaign would be aborted before it could get off the pad. After all, they said, it's not politically correct to criticize "undocumented immigrants."

However, Trump survived that onslaught, just as he did when he made comments about Sen. John McCain, saying he was only considered to be a hero because he'd been a prisoner of war in Vietnam. When Trump said, "I like people who weren't captured,"[1] the pundits were sure they finally had him. But once again, it didn't happen. Nevertheless, the back-and-forth has continued into his presidency where every perceived misstep the president makes is reported by the media as the last straw.

Prior to the election Trump's media critics were certain his ignorance of foreign policy would prove to be his weak spot. He was not a politician, and his knowledge of international relations was minuscule. So when he challenged Russia and Iran, and threatened to unleash holy hell on ISIS and the jihadists in Iraq, it was clear to the talking heads on CNN, MSNBC, and every liberal news outlet that Trump was done for. But within forty-eight hours Russia and Iran were making conciliatory noises, and not long afterward US forces in Iraq were crushing the jihadists in Mosul and Kirkuk.[2]

Fast-forward to late 2017. After surviving one controversy after another, and while managing to avoid the daily onslaught of the Mueller investigation into alleged collusion with the Russians, the media were grasping at every little thread. Democratic attorney and former Harvard law professor Alan Dershowitz pointed out that even if there were evidence of collusion, there is no federal statute prohibiting it. But the cable networks couldn't stop chattering about the Russia probe, the "Steele Dossier" (which has been totally discredited), and the possibility of a full-blown star chamber investigation leading to impeachment.

But hope springs eternal, and just as Russiagate seemed to be fading, Stormy Daniels appeared out of nowhere, and the late-nights were all a-twitter! Daniels' claims of a one-night stand with Trump in 2006 suddenly became the headline of the day. It didn't matter that Trump's playboy past had not sidelined his campaign or his election. If the *Access Hollywood* tapes that recorded Trump making vulgar comments about women didn't slow him down, it's hard to imagine anything of a sexual nature was going to stop him. A number of women came forward—none seemed to have a very credible story—and one by one they slid back into the shadows within days.

Stormy Daniels was all over the news for weeks, but her accusations didn't seem to hurt the president. When it was revealed that Trump's former attorney Michael Cohen (who later pleaded guilty to several tax fraud and campaign violation charges) had paid Daniels to be quiet, the porn star was briefly back in the headlines, but it was looking more and more as if Trump were bulletproof. The more the media pounded on him, dredging the gutters for any scandal they could find, the harder Trump's supporters fought back. It's hard to imagine that any new revelation could have made them change their minds.

The media story line was this: How could a man this immoral deserve to serve as president? Any Christians supporting Donald Trump, the media argued, were hypocrites. But actually, the hypocrisy went the other way. After a steady drumbeat of "It's only sex!" and "Sex between consenting adults is not a crime!" during the Clinton years, where did this sudden burst of outrage that Trump was not adhering to the media's newfound moral standard come from?

The press never seemed to be concerned when John Kennedy and Bill Clinton had multiple affairs while serving in the White House. Why not? Of course everyone knows the answer: Kennedy and Clinton were Democrats, and Trump is a conservative Republican. Those kinds of behaviors by Trump or anyone else cannot be approved of by Bible-believing Christians, least of all me. I didn't support Trump initially because of concerns over his lifestyle. I supported Ted Cruz until he dropped out of the race. But while I don't agree with the Never Trumpers who don't think Trump exemplifies biblical standards of behavior, either in the bedroom or in his Twitter feed, I do agree that Christians must hold up biblical standards in our culture, even as the culture at large has mostly rejected them.

Defending the Indefensible

A Never Trumper attacked me on Facebook during the election because I endorsed Donald Trump. She enumerated his many transgressions. I usually don't respond to such posts, but that time I did. I agreed that what she said about Trump was true, but it was like a speck in his eye compared with the log in the eye of Hillary Clinton. Not only did Clinton endorse left-wing positions on partial-birth abortion and same-sex marriage; she was probably the most corrupt person ever to run for president. After the email scandal; after her campaign paid over $1 million to Fusion GPS for opposition research on Trump, which resulted in a thirty-five-page dossier; and after what many believe was her involvement in a bribery scheme with Russia, namely the

Uranium One deal, why weren't these self-righteous, Bible-believing Christians saying, "Never Hillary"?

At some point during the campaign I began to see that Trump had changed, and those behaviors seemed to be in his past. At that point I backed him wholeheartedly, not because I approved of his playboy reputation, his multiple marriages, or his involvement with gambling (among other things) but partly because of whom he was running against. When the Stormy Daniels scandal erupted, the pundits were saying Trump would finally lose the strong support he received from Charismatics and Evangelicals. Driving a wedge between Trump and his base was important to the Left, especially if his evangelical supporters could be shown to be hypocrites. They had a story line. Now all they needed was a contingent of evangelical leaders who could give them the sound bites they needed.

At that time the PR firm that represents my company had been pitching me to appear on some of the network talk shows to discuss my book *God and Donald Trump* to little avail. But the day Stormy Daniels told her lackluster story to Anderson Cooper, I got a call that CNN wanted to interview me about it less than three hours before Cooper's highly promoted interview with the porn star.

What was I to do? It was a Sunday afternoon, and I'd just gotten back from being out of the country and hadn't been following the news. Plus, I wondered, What happens when a conservative author goes into the studio with the liberal media minutes before a blockbuster interview designed to discredit and perhaps destroy a sitting president? How would they treat someone like me on and off camera? To make matters worse, my wife, who is no fan of CNN, warned me not to do it, comparing the network to a pit of vipers. However, I wanted to be able to talk about my book to a new audience and hopefully speak frankly about the faith issues, trying to explain why most Evangelicals still support Trump in spite of his lifestyle issues.

I was running some errands when my cell phone rang with the interview request from our PR firm. I said it would take twenty minutes to get home and at least half an hour to get ready, and it was a forty-five-minute drive to the studio, on the other side of Orlando. There was no way I could handle the logistics with such a short window of time. I asked the PR person to tell them I'd love to be a guest another time, fully expecting that nothing would materialize. But much to my surprise, the next day word came that CNN wanted to interview me, but we didn't know what day. That gave me lots of time and plenty to worry about! Would I look stupid defending behavior that is indefensible? Was CNN really as bad as most conservatives, including President Trump, thought? Would I say something that could be used out of context to make Evangelicals look bad?

I decided many years ago that, no matter what the consequences may be, I would be willing to walk through the doors the Lord opens for me. So after consulting with a couple of friends and praying about it, I decided to walk through this door, even if it was a door to a pit of vipers. I decided the worst thing that could happen is that people might laugh at me, or that the experience would be so negative I would never do another interview on CNN. I knew I would be going in to alien territory, but at least I would have tried.

As we were waiting to find out what day they wanted to do the interview, I tuned in to CNN's early morning program, *New Day*, to get a feel for what to expect. The coanchors, Chris Cuomo and Alisyn Camerota, were interviewing some conservative guy, and they seemed respectful. They weren't as aggressive as I expected. When the invitation finally came, the producers asked me to go to the studio on a Wednesday during Holy Week. I would have to be up at 4:00 a.m. to make it there by 6:00 a.m., and I would be on the air at about 6:50 a.m.

I've done many television interviews but almost always on Christian programs. So while the interviews were friendly, the experience helped me to relax, to be myself, to pay attention to the interviewer, and to forget everything else. And above all, my wife told me after seeing one of the shows, "Smile, Steve! Tell them you're glad to be there." But I also sensed there was a higher purpose to my being on the air, and it wasn't about me or my book. So I decided just to be myself, be friendly, and try to give positive answers no matter how I might be treated.

I had been told we would talk about Stormy Daniels and Trump and why Evangelicals still support him. Before going to the studio, I did my own poll, asking friends and colleagues if they felt this scandal would seriously damage Trump. I didn't think so, and neither did they. While my poll was hardly scientific, it gave me confidence I would be speaking for the majority of Evangelicals.

I was interviewed by Camerota, who began the segment by stating: "Explain to us again how it is that Evangelicals are willing to overlook these reports of infidelity and other things to support President Trump."[3]

"That's easy for me," I told her. "Donald Trump has had a reputation as a playboy going back to the '80s." I said, "I didn't support Donald Trump for a long time because…I didn't approve of, you know, what I knew as his lifestyle."

Camerota asked, "So what changed?" which gave me the opening I was hoping for.

I said, "I think he changed. I really do. And I talk about this in my book *God and Donald Trump*. I interviewed him in 2016 and expected sort of the brash personality that you see in the media." I added, "I found him to be respectful, to be—actually be a little bit humble."

"And people knew that he was not perfect. I bring that up again and again in my book because we Christians know that you have to have forgiveness and that God can change lives and that the leaders in the Bible that we read about from King David on were not perfect in any way, shape, or form."

She retorted, "But in order to receive forgiveness, don't you have to confess your sins?...Isn't that a tenet of the Bible? I mean, don't you have to own up to these things? You know, Donald Trump famously said he's never asked God for forgiveness."

Obviously she was asking me "gotcha" questions, hoping for a sound bite CNN could play again and again, proving their predetermined premise that Evangelicals were beginning to turn their backs on Donald Trump.

At the time, I didn't feel Camerota was being confrontational—I was focused on giving cogent answers and making it look like a conversation even though she was in New York City and I was in a dark studio in Orlando, Florida, trying to relate to a camera lens as if it were the interviewer I could not see. But when I saw the video later, her demeanor seemed confrontational. And I could see how she was trying to bait me again and again. But I didn't take the bait. Instead, I tried to bring the discussion back to what Christians believe or what the Bible says.

When she asked what the Bible says about forgiveness, I remarked that I was glad she was quoting the Bible! I shifted the discussion to Donald Trump's policies that Evangelicals like. Later, friends who saw the interview complimented me on my "zinger." Actually at the time, I didn't see it as a zinger, nor a particularly important point. I went into the interview just wanting to answer their questions, not to debate or make them look bad. I had prayed that the Lord would give me the words to say.

Later, Camerota asked me if Evangelicals were intentionally looking the other way when it came to Trump's sexual past. I believe the Lord prompted me to say that if so, it was no worse than when the mainstream media looked the other way when President John Kennedy and, later, President Bill Clinton had multiple affairs while occupying the White House. I had not even thought of that ahead of time as a likely line of questioning or a talking point I should repeat.

Interestingly Camerota did not argue my point other than to allude to the fact that I was doing what the press did—looking the other way. I reminded her that I am a journalist too. She's probably used to dealing with evangelical pastors, not someone who has a journalism degree and has interviewed four presidents. I felt good about how the interview went. I was doing it more to speak up about the Lord and to interject, in my small way, the spiritual significance of what's happening in our country and the conversion of events that brought us to elect Donald Trump—and not just to sell more books. By that point my book had already been on the Christian best-sellers list since the month it came out.

Usually whenever I've done a media interview, we see a spike in sales on Amazon from people who first hear about the book in the interview. They go to their computers and order it online. After this appearance, however, we saw a very little spike in sales. At first it surprised me, but then I realized that the viewers of CNN are not as likely to read a book on God and Donald Trump as viewers of Christian media, where I generally appear. Later, a friend reminded me that CNN's ratings are so low that maybe not many people were watching at 6:50 a.m., when I was on the air.

When I was interviewed on *Fox & Friends* two months earlier, I was getting texts and emails before I left the studio. Friends who just happened to have had the TV on weren't expecting to see me there, and they dashed off a congratulatory note. I received very little feedback like that after my two appearances on CNN and MSNBC. Maybe it's because my friends normally watch Fox and not those other networks.

Prophetic Voices

Previously I had done many radio and television interviews to promote my book *God and Donald Trump*. I noticed as I did them that, without necessarily planning to, I repeated certain themes. One of them was the fact that several modern-day prophets had predicted that, against all odds, Donald Trump would be the next president of the United States. This had happened as far back as 2007, and it's something I documented in the book. Months before the election I had written about the prophetic voices in *Charisma* magazine, in print and online.

Those prophecies may have sounded ridiculous or impossible to some people, but Trump was elected, just as the prophets had said. The prophecies were one reason I had enough confidence to fly to New York for the election night party. I know it seems crazy, but somehow, some way, God intervened in that election and saved us from "corrupt Hillary" becoming president.

When the interviewers asked me how Evangelicals could bring themselves to vote for a man so flawed, I found myself saying that millions of Christians were praying that somehow God would shift the direction in which this nation is headed. I said God answered our prayers in a way we didn't expect, with a person we didn't necessarily like. But once Trump began to implement his policies, we were sure we had made the right choice.

Like I've already mentioned, I didn't support Trump initially for the same reason some Evangelicals still don't support him: his lifestyle and brash behavior were not what Christians expect from their national leaders. As I've said on many occasions,

I publicly endorsed Ted Cruz and supported him until the day he dropped out. By then I had become aware of the comparisons between Donald Trump and the Persian king Cyrus the Great, a pagan who was used by God to let the Israelites return from captivity to Jerusalem.

The Scripture in Isaiah says, "Thus says the LORD to Cyrus, His anointed...I have even called you by your name; I have named you, though you have not known Me" (45:1–4). I first heard this from my friend Lance Wallnau, but I document in *God and Donald Trump* that others had made the same comparison.

In my case, I reasoned that if God could use King Cyrus to accomplish His purposes, He could certainly use Donald Trump. Of course, I also supported him because of his stated support for Christian issues, which was the opposite of what his opponent said and believed. But it wasn't just Charismatic prophets who made the Cyrus–Trump comparison. Temple organizations issued a "temple coin" in early 2018 with Trump's profile, and right behind him there's a rendering of King Cyrus. Most of the writing is in Hebrew, but it also says in English: "Cyrus-Balfour-Trump Declaration 2018."[4]

Of course, the secular press couldn't care less about comparisons to kings in the Old Testament. But they are obsessed with the "hypocrisy" of churchgoing, Bible-believing Christians supporting a playboy from New York.

Praying Up a Storm

Since I had never been on CNN before, I was surprised when I got a second invitation to be interviewed, this time on an afternoon CNN broadcast hosted by Ryan Nobles on Easter Sunday. Nobles was less confrontational than Camerota, but he asked some good questions. For example, when he asked about Trump's behavior and quoted Franklin Graham saying Trump is a changed man from the time of these alleged affairs, he gave me the best opening of any of my interviews to speak up for the Lord.

"You know, the whole essence of Christianity," I said, "is that God is able to change people through the power of the gospel."[5] I told Nobles that in my book I documented that in the early 2000s Trump began tuning in to Christian TV shows, watching ministers such as Paula White. And I mentioned how he allowed pastors and others to gather around him and lay hands on him and pray in the Pentecostal style.

I told him that Trump seems to enjoy the prayers. I was even bold enough to add a comment that probably made no sense to Nobles: "I've been told that he enjoys what we Christians call the anointing." Of course, that comment was a sound bite, and I didn't have time to elaborate or explain how, during the election, Trump would speak at rallies in Ohio often held in Charismatic churches, and how he was present as these people worshipped and prayed in their usual Charismatic style, often led by Pastor Frank Amedia of Canfield, Ohio, who is my personal friend. When Christians pray and there is a sense that the Lord is present in that place, Pentecostals call that the anointing. It's something you feel when you worship deeply. Amedia, who had considerable access to candidate and later President Trump, told me that Trump would ask him to "pray up a storm" because Trump seemed to enjoy that presence.

As I walked through the doors of secular media interviews that God had opened, I was beginning to see that I could speak up for the gospel and they wouldn't contradict me—even if only because it was Holy Week. In an interview on Good Friday with Craig Melvin on MSNBC, he asked me, Besides Neil Gorsuch's appointment to the Supreme Court, "what else do Evangelicals point to as a win from this president from a legislative or policy standpoint?" So I turned the discussion back to the fact that there were millions of "evangelical Christians who believed the country was going in the wrong way, and we prayed. We prayed that God would somehow do something to shift the direction of our country, and here He raised up a man who we didn't necessarily even like, in the form of Donald Trump. He has done more for religious liberty and helping persecuted Christians and the kinds of causes that Christians feel are important than any president, I think, in my lifetime."[6]

I cited protecting religious liberty, helping persecuted Christians, and the fact that he believes the Johnson Amendment to the IRS Code—which limits churches and nonprofits from endorsing candidates, a clear breach of their First Amendment rights—should be repealed by Congress. Meanwhile the president issued an executive order that the Johnson Amendment should not be enforced until the law can be changed.

Predictably Melvin said something about the separation of church and state. When I saw the show later, I realized I could have said something about that fallacy. The words *separation of church and state* don't appear in the Constitution. It's a convenient phrase plucked from thin air by Thomas Jefferson to assure a Baptist group in Connecticut that the government would make no law restricting their religious freedoms. Here's what the amendment actually says: "Congress shall make no law respecting an establishment of religion or prohibiting the free exercise thereof," and then the document adds that Congress cannot abridge "the freedom of speech, or of the press; or the right of the people peaceably to assemble, and to petition the Government for a redress of grievances."[7]

When the media cite the First Amendment, they are usually referring to the freedom of the press, which I also strongly support. But notice that freedom of religion, which government cannot prohibit "the free exercise thereof," comes before the other freedoms.

Melvin then cited a poll that seemed to prove his point that Trump was losing evangelical support. I doubt the poll because it was probably done by the same people who predicted Hillary Clinton would win by a landslide. But I hadn't heard of it, so I cited my own "poll" based on statements from all the people I'd talked to, indicating that none of them have changed their minds about Trump. "There have been many, many opportunities to change our mind about Trump," I told him, "but he has come through again and again. He is standing strong. He is trying to make America great again, and most evangelical Christians, like me, are praying that somehow America will become morally and spiritually great again."

The mainstream media don't seem to get it. Conservative Christians want a spiritually great nation, and while we're interested in tax cuts and foreign policy, the real issue for us is whether his policies will help or hurt the Christian community and whether they're moving our nation in the right direction. Since the election of Donald Trump, I believe things are going in the right direction. I believe Donald Trump has our interests at heart, or I wouldn't defend him as I do.

I made the same point with Camerota. I said, "The issue for me and for millions of Evangelicals is his policies. He supports the kind of policies that we think are important."[8] Political pundit Marc A. Thiessen, whom I admire for his clearheaded commentary on the Fox News Channel, agreed with me when he wrote an op-ed in the *Washington Post,* published on March 23, 2018, titled "Why Conservative Christians Stick With Trump."

Thiessen wrote: "He is a deeply flawed man. But Trump has shown one moral quality as president that deserves admiration: He keeps his promises. During the 2016 campaign, Trump pledged to defend religious liberty, stand up for unborn life and appoint conservative jurists to the Supreme Court and federal appeals courts. And he has done exactly what he promised."[9]

Further proof that he's backing Christian issues, such as cutting back on abortion, can be found in the literature and advertising put out by pro-abortion lobby NARAL, Thiessen adds, that "complains that Trump has been 'relentless' on these fronts, declaring his administration 'the worst...that we've ever seen.'"

Thiessen gives a long list of accomplishments documented elsewhere in this book and concludes his op-ed saying: "No one upholds Trump as moral exemplar. He is not the most religious president we have ever had, but he may be the most pro-religion president. Christian conservatives are judging Trump not by his faith, but by his works. And when it comes to life and liberty, his works are good."

Donald Trump's election was "shock and awe" to the status quo and to the direction of the nation, as I've described in part 1. But that was only the beginning. To make America great again, Donald Trump was now "going on the offensive."

PART II

GOING ON OFFENSE

CHAPTER 5

TRUMP'S BULLY PULPIT

THROUGHOUT THE 1980s and 1990s Donald Trump was a media sensation. Flamboyant, witty, and fabulously wealthy, he was one of the most successful real estate moguls in New York and the nation, and the media couldn't get enough. Magazines, newspapers, radio, and TV—he was everywhere. He was a multimillionaire, married with one child, and a highly sought-after public figure in 1980 when he was invited to NBC's Manhattan studios for a sit-down interview with the network's celebrity anchor Tom Brokaw on *The Today Show*.

"Mr. Trump, what's left in your life?" Brokaw asked. "You're 33 years old, you're worth all this money. You say you didn't say that you want to be worth a billion dollars."[1] Trump had been described as brash and egotistical. He had grown up in the borough of Queens, then earned an Ivy League degree from the Wharton School and followed his millionaire father into business. He had reason to be vain, and he clearly relished his success. He wasn't shy about his wealth and surely believed he would soon be a billionaire. But he was always polite in interviews and, as pointed out by *The Atlantic*, even somewhat humble.

"No, I really don't," he answered Brokaw. "I just want to keep busy and keep active and be interested in what I do. And that's all there is to life as far as I'm concerned." Little by little, and one sound bite after another, the handsome young real estate developer from New York City was becoming a national celebrity and household name.[2] Completing the repairs on Central Park's Wollman ice-skating rink in record time and $750,000 under budget, after the original contractor had run over budget and out of time, dramatically elevated his celebrity status with New Yorkers.

I remember reading how he humiliated the city of New York by completing the Wollman ice-skating rink when they couldn't. But overall I wasn't impressed by him because of his playboy reputation, and I had no interest in following his career. I never would have dreamed that thirty years later he'd be elected the forty-fifth president of the United States.

Trump's fortunes rose and fell repeatedly throughout the 1990s, but by 2004 he was on the move, with three nationally televised beauty pageants, a best-selling book, a string of casinos, and his own reality TV show, *The Apprentice*, which was just beginning its stunning fifteen-season run. His signature property, Trump Tower, completed in 1983 on Fifth Avenue in the heart of midtown Manhattan, was the world headquarters of the growing Trump empire. A feature by James Traub in the *New York Times Magazine* said, "Trump probably receives more requests for interviews than any other private citizen in New York."[3]

"The rules that govern others just don't apply to Trump," Traub asserted. "With him, it's celebrity that breeds success rather than the other way around. And Trump has never been a bigger celebrity than he is now, thanks to the astounding success of 'The Apprentice,' which has been nominated for four Emmys and began its second season last week." And to top it off, he said, "*The Art of the Deal*, which was published in 1987, sold 835,000 copies in hardcover alone."[4] The Trump Organization weathered its share of problems, including bankruptcies and lawsuits of various kinds, but the success of his book and the weekly television exposure were giving "The Donald" a much bigger audience. As Traub writes:

> More than forty million people watched the first season's last episode…when Trump anointed the winner. The show was the top-rated new series and tied with "The West Wing" for attracting TV's most affluent prime-time demographic. "The Apprentice" almost single-handedly rescued the lagging fortunes of NBC, the network that broadcast it.[5]

With all his success, Trump had ascended to the Olympus of the celebrity culture, where the likes of Oprah, Martha Stewart, Ralph Lauren, and hip-hop artist P. Diddy reigned. "Now comes the Donald, with his own hit TV show, his own golf courses, his own magazine—*Trump World*, whose first issue just arrived on the newsstands—and his name-bearing collection of shirts, ties, suits and a fragrance. The suits and the fragrance are a done deal, and on the others he's just got to say the word."[6]

But as they say, *tempus fugit* ("time flies"), and for many younger voters, all this describes a Donald Trump they've never known. For the mainstream media, in particular, the luster of the rising star has evaporated, and the man who would become America's forty-fifth president has become an object of scorn. But the existential question is, How is it possible that someone with so much success, charm, and public acclaim could suddenly become the most controversial and divisive person on the planet? What changed?

I believe that Donald Trump changed. As I describe elsewhere, he began watching Christian television and asking questions to Christian leaders such as Paula White Cain. In the process his politics changed. He became opposed to abortion and embraced other conservative causes. Is it little wonder the liberal media elite didn't like the new conservative Trump any more than they liked those in America who, as Barack Obama famously said, cling to their "guns or religion."[7]

As the crowds at his presidential campaign rallies in cities and towns all over America have demonstrated, Donald Trump is still celebrated and admired by millions of regular Americans. At the same time, however, he is cursed and reviled with equal measures of fear and loathing by Hollywood, academia, and the New York elites. His favorability rating, topping 50 percent in early 2018, was slightly better than his unfavorables.[8] But among liberals, progressives, and the mainstream media, there are no words to describe the seething hatred that rises within them whenever his name is mentioned.

Branding America

On the day he announced his candidacy, Trump told the crowd assembled in the lobby of Trump Tower, "We need somebody that can take the brand of the United States and make it great again.... We need somebody that literally will take this country and make it great again. We can do that.... So ladies and gentlemen, I am officially running for president of the United States."[9] At that point the *Washington Post* reported, "Trump enters the race with nearly unmatched name recognition and a powerful real estate brand—but a reputation for a quick temper and attention-grabbing celebrity feuds."[10]

It's true Trump had traded barbs with the likes of Arianna Huffington, Rosie O'Donnell, Cher, Mitt Romney, and others. He was never shy about saying what was on his mind. But his most far-reaching and provocative feud occurred in 2011 when Barack Obama decided to mock Trump at the annual White House Correspondents' Dinner. In the midst of the birther controversy, dating back to his 2008 campaign, document analysts found inconsistencies in Obama's birth certificate, and Trump said more than once that he suspected the document was a forgery. The media and politicians on both sides disputed the claims, but Obama was not satisfied with that.[11]

During the dinner, with Donald Trump seated only a few feet away, Obama quipped, "No one is prouder to put this birth certificate matter to rest than the Donald. And that's because he can finally get back to focusing on the issues that matter—like, did we fake the moon landing? What really happened in Roswell?

And where are Biggie and Tupac?" Clearly enjoying the laughter at Trump's expense, the president added, "Say what you will about Mr. Trump, he certainly would bring some change to the White House."[12] At that point a large, garish image of the White House remodeled to resemble an over-the-top Las Vegas casino was projected on the ballroom's video screen.

Obama's jab hit the target, and video of the event shows an unsmiling, steel-jawed Donald doing his best to restrain his natural instincts. But many political observers believe that was the precise moment when Trump decided he would enter the race for the White House. Nevertheless, the jousting match between Trump and Obama didn't end there. In August 2012, in the midst of Obama's second campaign, Trump tweeted, "An 'extremely credible source' has called my office and told me that @BarackObama's birth certificate is a fraud."[13] Then, just weeks before the 2014 midterm election, Trump tweeted, "I am starting to think that there is something seriously wrong with President Obama's mental health.... Psycho!"[14]

The 2011 episode still resonates strongly with the individuals at the center of the feud, particularly in light of the shocking lapse of judgment by the organizers of the 2018 White House Correspondents' Dinner. The vulgar and tasteless assault on Press Secretary Sarah Sanders and the president by comedienne Michelle Wolf merely emphasized the level of hatred at the heart of the Left-Right divide. Obama acolytes and liberals in the media celebrated Wolf's attack, but Donald Trump is not without resources of his own.

Since becoming president and taking occupancy of the White House, he has made history with his Twitter account. As columnist James Lewis points out, Donald Trump is the only president since Ronald Reagan to be able to bypass the mainstream media to reach directly into the hearts of the American people.[15] He uses Twitter, often to the chagrin of his team of advisors, not only to congratulate private citizens for their heroism and public service but as his primary defensive weapon against an antagonistic press. Explaining his motivation, Trump said: "I use Social Media not because I like to, but because it is the only way to fight a VERY dishonest and unfair 'press,' now often referred to as Fake News Media. Phony and non-existent 'sources' are being used more often than ever. Many stories & reports a pure fiction!"[16]

As soon as he was identified as a possible Republican candidate, Trump became a target of the Left. Every word, every act, and every step were scrutinized and dissected by reporters eager for a scoop. But despite the almost compulsive animosity he generates in the Left, Trump is prime time. He is the headline of every newscast, and like it or not, he is the media's cash cow.

Writing in *Fortune* magazine, Mathew Ingram cites a study by TV analyst Andrew Tyndall during the 2016 campaign that found that Trump was receiving the lion's share of network news coverage—a combined total of 327 minutes on ABC, CBS, and NBC in 2015. Compare this with Jeb Bush and Ben Carson, who got only 57 minutes each; Marco Rubio, who got approximately 22 minutes; and Ted Cruz, who received just 21 minutes of coverage. And that does not include the virtually around-the-clock coverage Trump was getting on the cable networks.

One reason Trump is easy to cover: "He is effectively a one-man media machine, especially through his Twitter account," Ingram says, "where he picks fights and lobs grenades at everyone from the other candidates to Taylor Swift." As Tim Dickinson, a writer for *Rolling Stone*, pointed out in a February 2016 tweetstorm, "Trump's 6.5 million followers make him about the same size as the CBS evening news....He is his own media entity."[17]

Of course, the number of Trump's followers has skyrocketed since the campaign, and his influence has only grown. But as much as the media may dislike him, they can't live without him. "Need to boost traffic?" Ingram says. "Run a couple more Trump stories with a few tweets embedded in them, and you're good....Although he is a media entity in his own right, the candidate relies on TV networks and newspapers and websites not just to give him coverage but to provide a nice punching bag for him to use when he is criticizing the liberal orthodoxy and how it doesn't understand him."[18]

The Media's Blind Spot

According to the poll of polls compiled by RealClearPolitics, which includes a statistical average of multiple popularity surveys, the president's average job approval in May 2018 was around 43 percent,[19] which is apparently a complete puzzle to Trump's media critics. Despite their best efforts, the combined forces of the mainstream media, the DNC, Hollywood liberals, and the entire progressive establishment, Trump remains relevant and immensely popular with voters in Middle America. Nothing could be more perplexing. But this is the media's blind spot. Not only are they angry about the outcome of the election, but they're also embarrassed that they've failed to draw the nation over to their enlightened point of view.

The networks' expert analysts repeatedly misread the pulse of the nation throughout the 2016 election cycle, and they apparently had little or no impact on Trump's popularity ratings. They still can't comprehend how the man they vilified for months was able to win the votes of sixty-three million Americans. This may explain why CNN's James Acosta, a longtime and frequently disruptive critic of the president, concluded that the American people lack the intelligence to see through Donald Trump's act. As Acosta stated during an interview with *Variety*, "They don't have all their facilities in some cases—their elevator might not hit all floors."[20]

I saw this hostility toward Trump on CNN firsthand when I was interviewed twice about Stormy Daniels around Easter in 2018. As I tell elsewhere in this book, they were only interested in grilling me on how devout Evangelicals could possibly back someone as immoral as Donald Trump, even comparing him to Harvey Weinstein. I said we don't approve of those lifestyle issues from the past; we place more importance on Trump's policies.

For more than two years the media have conducted around-the-clock aerial bombing of the president's character, motives, and intelligence while ignoring and generally misrepresenting his accomplishments with the economy, jobs, taxes, foreign policy, the military, and border security. The impression among a majority of the general public is that the media's focus is predicated almost entirely on talking points and broadsides supplied by the DNC. "What we have here," writes John Nolte, "is more proof that the media are no longer able to sway public opinion or move the needle. While Trump's job approval sits at 43 percent, trust in the media sits at just 41 percent. But even that 41 percent is skewed. It is only Democrats who support the media at a respectable level of 62 percent."[21]

The animus behind the media's ongoing assault has not been lost on the public. As Gallup reported in January 2018, 43 percent of Americans believe the media support our democracy "poorly" or "very poorly," while just 28 percent say they support democracy "well" or "very well." And less than half of Americans in the survey (44 percent) were able to name even one objective news source. In addition, Americans of all political persuasions, Gallup found, believe the spread of inaccurate information on the internet is also a major problem, with 76 percent of Republicans, 71 percent of Democrats, and 75 percent of independents holding this view.[22]

Meanwhile, only 14 percent of Republicans believe the media get their facts straight. And only 37 percent of independents—a critical target group for both parties—say the media get their facts straight.[23] In other words, outside the solidly blue precincts of East and West Coast liberals, most of America no longer trusts the media. And as John Nolte says, "Why would they? The media are a fake news factory that for nearly two years have told us lie after lie about Trump's colluding with Russia—and now, we have learned that was a big, fat hoax fabricated by the Deep State, CNN, and BuzzFeed."[24]

For more than half a century, since at least the end of the Second World War, surveys have shown that what most Americans really want is peace and prosperity. By the end of his second year in the White House, most Americans believe Donald

Trump has delivered on his promises. Income levels have risen steadily, taxes are lower, the nation is in no immediate danger of war, and living standards in the US are some of the best in the world. In early 2018 Nolte speculated that, more than likely, the voters will judge Trump on that basis in future midterm and general elections. But for the most part, Nolte writes, "They can see through the smoke of the media lies and the pundit hysteria, and they are starting to understand that 'sources tell us' is Greek for 'this is fake news.'"[25]

Examples of media mistakes and miscues are not hard to find. During a rally in Florida on February 19, 2017, Trump referred to news of recent attacks in Sweden and said, "Look at what's happening... in Sweden. Sweden, who would believe this? Sweden. They took in large numbers [of immigrants]. They're having problems like they never thought possible." The following day the liberal UK news outlet *The Guardian* claimed he made it up and said, "Trump cites non-existent terror attack."[26]

In fact, Trump was referring to comments by filmmaker Ami Horowitz, who had been interviewed by Tucker Carlson the previous evening on Fox News. He said there was "an absolute surge in both gun violence and rape in Sweden once they began this open-door policy." He went on to speak about Sweden's "no-go zones," saying, "These are areas that cops won't even enter, because it's too dangerous for them."[27] Subsequently, *The Guardian*, CNN, and other outlets had to report that the president had not invented the story but was referring to the filmmaker's remarks.

On January 20, 2017, while the Trump administration was still moving into the White House, *Time* magazine reporter Zeke Miller tweeted that the bust of Martin Luther King Jr. had been removed from the Oval Office—surely a sign of Trump's racist views. Of course, Miller had to apologize the following day after Sean Spicer tweeted a photo of Dr. King's bust still sitting on its pedestal in the Oval Office. It turns out someone was standing in front of the bust when Miller was in the Oval Office, and Miller didn't bother to double-check.[28]

In the chaos surrounding the firing of White House National Security Advisor Michael Flynn, ABC TV correspondent Brian Ross reported during a live broadcast that Flynn was prepared to testify that Trump had ordered him to contact Russian operatives about policy issues while Trump was still a candidate. Because of the suggestion that Trump could be impeached if evidence of collusion was confirmed, Ross' report sent shock waves through the financial community, and the Dow Jones plunged 350 points. Later it was shown that Trump was already in office at the time of the incident in question and not a candidate. The network later corrected the report, and Ross was publicly disgraced and handed a four-week suspension.[29] He later resigned in disgrace.

Trump's Twitter Wars

Amidst all the accusations, threats, and insinuations from the mainstream media, the president was waging a war of his own, taking the attack directly to the major networks and cable news organizations for promulgating "fake news." During a report by Jeff Zeleny on CNN's *The Lead With Jake Tapper*, aired on May 29, 2017, a tweet by Trump was shown saying, "It is my opinion that many of the leaks coming out of the White House are fabricated lies made up by the #FakeNews media." He added that, "The Fake News Media works hard at disparaging & demeaning my use of social media because they don't want America to hear the real story!"[30]

In June 2017 Trump tweeted, "Sorry folks, but if I would have relied on the Fake News of CNN, NBC, ABC, CBS, washpost or nytimes, I would have had ZERO chance winning WH."[31] That tweet received almost 25,000 retweets and 102,000 likes.

Earlier the same day, after he was criticized for chastising London's mayor, Sadiq Khan, in the wake of a series of terrorist attacks in that city, Trump tweeted, "The FAKE MSM is working so hard trying to get me not to use Social Media. They hate that I can get the honest and unfiltered message out."[32] Then, ten days later, he tweeted, "The Fake News Media hates when I use what has turned out to be my very powerful Social Media—over 100 million people! I can go around them."[33]

When you compare Trump's followers (105 million[34] as of July 2018) with those of major news outlets, it's clear that he doesn't need the media to get his message out. The most-watched cable television news network for sixteen years straight is Fox News, with an average primetime audience of 2.4 million viewers (Sean Hannity leads the way with an average of 3.368 million viewers for his 9:00 p.m. show); *CNN Breaking News* is "the most-followed news account on Twitter," with 54.5 million followers; and the *New York Times* tops the newspaper category with 41.6 Twitter followers.[35] Trump eclipses them all.

As the media piled on, many of his critics apparently resented Trump not so much for his political agenda as for defending himself with Twitter and his outspoken public comments. But Trump refused to stop his verbal assaults. Responding to an NBC News report on April 30, 2018, citing several anonymous sources claiming White House Chief of Staff Gen. John Kelly had called the president "an idiot," Trump fired back, "The Fake News is going crazy making up false stories and using only unnamed sources (who don't exist). They are totally unhinged, and the great success of this Administration is making them do and say things that even they can't believe they are saying. Truly bad people!"[36]

A short time later the president took a shot at the Mueller investigation looking into possible collusion with the Russians, saying, "The White House is running very smoothly despite phony Witch Hunts etc. There is great Energy and unending Stamina, both necessary to get things done. We are accomplishing the unthinkable and setting positive records while doing so! Fake News is going 'bonkers!'"[37] No doubt part of the anger that provoked the president's tweets on this occasion was generated by the scandal that had erupted two nights earlier. On April 28 comedienne Michelle Wolf had taken the stage at the White House Correspondents' Dinner and unleashed a vulgar tirade against not only the president but also White House Press Secretary Sarah Sanders, who was sitting on the dais just a few feet away. Sanders kept her cool and acted with decorum, just as she does in heated daily press briefings or when asked a few months later to leave a restaurant in Virginia because the owner and some employees don't like President Trump's policies.

Wolf showed no mercy or tolerance for her targets, and very little humor, attacking Sanders' personality, appearance, and professionalism. In her monologue Wolf called Sanders an "Uncle Tom but for white women" and said she thought of the press secretary as Aunt Lydia, one of the darkest characters in the television series *The Handmaid's Tale*. Among her caustic jibes, she said, "Every time Sarah steps up to the podium I get excited, because I'm not really sure what we're going to get—you know, a press briefing, a bunch of lies or divided into softball teams.... I actually really like Sarah, I think she's very resourceful. She burns facts, and then she uses that ash to create a perfect smoky eye. Like maybe she's born with it, maybe it's lies."[38]

To their credit, some who attended the dinner, and a handful of others who witnessed the event or heard about it, chastised the comedienne and called for an apology from the White House Correspondents' Association for Wolf's offensive harangue. NBC News commentator Andrea Mitchell, no friend of the White House, tweeted, "Apology is owed to @PressSec and others grossly insulted [by] Michelle Wolf at White House Correspondents Assoc dinner which started with uplifting heartfelt speech by @margarettalev—comedian was worst since Imus insulted Clinton's."[39] Former White House Chief of Staff Reince Priebus called it "an R/X rated spectacle that started poorly and ended up in the bottom of the canyon. Another victory for @realDonaldTrump for not attending and proving his point once again. The room was uncomfortable. Trump lovers and even a large number of Trump haters were pretty miserable."[40]

The same evening, Gov. Mike Huckabee responded to Wolf and the organizers for their humiliation of his daughter, pointing out the hypocrisy of liberals who claim "hate speech" is not free speech. "Those who think that the tasteless classless bullying at the WHCD was an example of the 1st Amendment should never condemn bullying, bigoted comments, racist bile or hate speech." And the former Republican presidential candidate added, "People should be free to speak but held accountable for it."[41]

I was particularly horrified about this treatment because I've known Sarah ever since I was involved in her father's unsuccessful presidential primary bid in 2008. She was an impressive young woman then and has grown by leaps and bounds since then. She has one of the highest-pressure jobs in Washington, and she does it while juggling the responsibilities of raising three young children.

President Trump was obviously shocked that his press secretary, who attended the dinner as his proxy, became a sacrificial lamb to Michelle Wolf's vicious attacks. When he tweeted his response the following day, he said, "The White House Correspondents' Dinner was a failure last year, but this year was an embarrassment to everyone associated with it. The filthy 'comedian' totally bombed (couldn't even deliver her lines—much like the Seth Meyers weak performance). Put Dinner to rest, or start over!"[42]

Later he emphasized what he had been saying all along, that the media are hopelessly biased against him and his administration. "The White House Correspondents' Dinner is DEAD as we know it," he said. "This was a total disaster and an embarrassment to our great Country and all that it stands for. FAKE NEWS is alive and well and beautifully represented on Saturday night!"[43] In response to the angry reactions she and the event organizers were receiving, Margaret Talev, president of the White House Correspondents' Association, admitted that Wolf's performance was not in "the spirit" of the annual media event.

"Last night's program was meant to offer a unifying message about our common commitment to a vigorous and free press while honoring civility, great reporting and scholarship winners, not to divide people," she said in a prepared statement forwarded to the press. "Unfortunately, the entertainer's monologue was not in the spirit of that mission." When asked how she responded to Wolf's "jokes," Talev said, "Some of them made me uncomfortable and did not embody the spirit of the night."[44]

No doubt Talev was anxious to mend fences, but Fox News journalist Liz Peek took issue with her remarks. "Ms. Talev is wrong," she said and emphasized that "the assault was very much in keeping with how the liberal media views the White House. They detest President Trump, and the feeling is mutual. CNN, the *New York Times*, MSNBC and the rest cannot forgive President Trump for having denied Hillary Clinton her 'inevitable' presidency." Then the writer added:

Hillary wasn't the only one measuring the drapes in the Oval Office; the media world looked forward to four—maybe eight!—more years of an administration with whom they saw eye-to-eye, with whom they could craft stories polishing up outcomes and burying unpleasant realities. With whom they could indulge in token spats knowing that they undeniably controlled the message, and the country's future direction.[45]

Irreconcilable Differences

A study conducted by two researchers from the Reuters Institute at the University of Oxford examined the public's growing distrust of the media. Their findings indicated that those who do not trust the news media—which came to 25 percent of the respondents in their sample—accuse the media of bias, spin, and hidden agendas. The research reported that "a significant proportion of the public feels that powerful people are using the media to push their own political or economic interests, rather than represent ordinary readers or viewers.... In many countries, particularly the US and UK," they say, "some media outlets are seen as taking sides, encouraging an increasingly polarised set of opinions." Based on their findings, the Reuters report suggests that "journalists and news publications should be far more open about their biases and clearer about distinguishing news from opinion and news."[46]

Based on more immediate factors, however, such as the Correspondents' Dinner and the ongoing war of words between the president and his adversaries in the media, a reconciliation of any kind seems highly improbable. Americans are consuming more news today than at any time in history, and according to a research paper by Dr. Neil Johnson, a physicist with the University of Miami's Complexity interdisciplinary group, the constant flow of negative news has pushed the nation toward "a state of pure polarization." And the researcher added that "the size of the extremes of the left and right are now so large that they outnumber those in the middle ground."[47]

As a scientist, Johnson told the *Miami Herald* he generally expects surveys to produce results in the shape of a bell curve; that is, responses tend to cluster in the middle range, with outlying responses trending to one side or the other. But when exploring the degree of political and social polarization in the general population today, he found that responses were greatest at polar opposite ends—meaning, he said, "The mere act of absorbing news that everyone else is seeing causes a polarizing effect." When asked if there was hope for turning things around and encouraging greater consensus and moderation, Johnson replied, "Not really."[48]

The reality of the irreconcilable differences between the Left and Right can be seen almost anytime in the daily confrontations on cable TV, in Trump's tweetstorms, and in the verbal battles taking place in the halls of Congress. I saw this animosity the morning after the election in New York. I didn't get to bed after Trump's victory party until about 4:00 a.m., so I ate a late breakfast right before they began serving lunch. A young woman sitting a few feet away was watching an anti-Trump video with foul language on her smartphone. I didn't want to listen to it throughout breakfast, so I asked her to turn it down. Nothing was said about Trump. She must have thought I looked like a Republican because she began a tirade against me that caused everyone in the restaurant to turn and stare. She also insisted on moving to another part of the restaurant. It was my encounter with the vitriol to the inauguration we'd see around the country the rest of the day until now.

While the animosity is genuine, the combatants are not fighting on a level playing field. The mainstream media have the advantage of technology and 24/7 news and commentary by a bevy of immaculately tailored commentators broadcasting over airwaves and the internet into millions of homes. But the president has his bully pulpit.

President Theodore Roosevelt used the term *bully pulpit* in a 1909 speech, saying, "I suppose my critics will call that preaching, but I have got such a bully pulpit!" He was referring to the extraordinary influence he enjoyed as president of the United States.[49] (For what it's worth, Theodore Roosevelt is one of the presidents I admire most, and I believe he is a distant cousin of mine.) For Donald Trump, his bully pulpit consists mainly of the unprecedented power of his Twitter feed and his unique ability to grab headlines regardless of what he says or does.

As Victor Davis Hanson explains, Donald Trump is dangerous to the progressive agenda. "In military terms, he is a strategic B-52 on a deep mission. Trump targets the enemy's homeland, even as his opponents' far-flung and attenuated expeditionary armies bog down abroad." The power the president wields is not necessarily found in the success of his political maneuvers but in his remarkable powers of persuasion. The 63 million Americans who voted for Donald Trump sent him to Washington with a mandate, and poll after poll reveals they're mostly convinced he is keeping his part of the bargain. I agree with Hanson, who writes:

> More than half the nation has lost confidence in progressivism, the administrative state, and the Republican hierarchy and establishment.... They feel that most of his targets have it coming and that the resulting chaos, within limits, is much-needed purging. Out of the daily conundrum, Trump nevertheless has managed so far to achieve greater prosperity at home and stability abroad than did Obama, while the

> reputation of a habitually prejudiced media is plummeting fast. Where critics see chaos, some voters are likely to see clarity and comeuppance.[50]

Furthermore, Hanson says the media's unrelenting barrage of bad news and personal attacks have energized Trump to become even more combative and outlandish. "In the past, when a progressive tagged a Republican politician as some sort of irredeemable or deplorable bigot, he often inched left in search of penance or to preempt further attacks."[51] But that has never been Trump's way. He punches back even harder, with more than half the nation cheering him on. According to the conservative Heritage Foundation, by January 2018 the president had already completed 64 percent of his agenda and nearly two-thirds of the 334 policy objectives recommended in the *Mandate for Leadership*, which has been published as a guide for incoming presidential administrations since 1981.[52] And he has done it while constantly fighting a defensive rearguard action against the Left's outcry over his policies.

The Heritage Foundation feels the standouts in Trump's list of achievements include the following:

- Leaving the Paris Climate Accord
- Repealing net neutrality
- Negotiating a $54 billion increase in military spending
- Reinstating the Mexico City Policy on abortion
- Removing restrictions on the development of America's natural resources
- Withdrawing from the costly and ineffective UNESCO organization
- Ordering dramatic reforms in a wide range of costly and ineffective government agencies

These are all policies the vast majority of Americans support, and whether or not the public may like the language and behavior of the president, writes Hanson, "Trump voters now still believe that the mostly positive message matters more than the flawed messenger."[53]

Overplaying Their Hand

In spite of the fact that Trump is himself a New Yorker, it's not easy for the New York liberals to understand let alone appreciate that most of the rest of America doesn't agree with them. It reminds me of the iconic cover of the March 29, 1976, issue of the *New Yorker*. It showed a close-up of Manhattan from the perspective of

Ninth Avenue, looking westward to Tenth Avenue and beyond to a wide Hudson and a tiny US continent with only a few mountains, and beyond that the Pacific Ocean, with only Japan, China, and Russia in the distance.[54] It shows how provincial New Yorker thinking (both the magazine and the people) was even back then.

When Salena Zito, a writer for the *New York Post*, took a trip out of Manhattan to look into the attitudes of men and women in the Midwest, she was surprised to find widespread support for the president, even in the formerly Democrat-controlled counties of northeastern Ohio. One of the voters she interviewed in her two-part series did not vote for Trump but has nevertheless become a fan and supporter. "If he continues to stick to his guns and do what he is doing," he said, "I'd vote for him if he ran again." He didn't like Trump as a candidate, but he was "enjoying the heck out of his presidency."[55]

But that's not all the reporter discovered. The man told her he is frustrated by the way the media treat President Trump, especially in comparison with the way they fawned over President Obama: "They really do not give him a fair shake," he said. The perceived bias against Trump has changed the way he sees him, and "instead of [it] pushing him away from the president, he is more intrigued by him."[56]

Zito says the opinions she found in this and other parts of the heartland defy the conventional wisdom of national news outlets. The mainstream media seem unable to grasp the fact that Trump's base isn't going anywhere or that they believe his leadership has been successful overall. But even more problematic for Democratic loyalists are the results of a *Washington Post*–ABC News poll released in April 2018 showing many Clinton voters are feeling remorse for their support of the Democratic candidate. Further, the poll suggests that if the election were repeated today, Trump would win not only the electoral college but the popular vote as well. Researchers found that 15 percent of Clinton's voters would vote for a different candidate if the election were to take place again. On the other hand, just 4 percent of Trump voters said they would change their vote.[57]

The poll also showed that while 58 percent of Americans think Trump is out of touch, most respondents felt the Democratic Party is even more out of touch than Trump or the Republican Party. Fully 67 percent expressed the opinion that Democrats are out of touch, including nearly half of the respondents who identified as Democrats.[58] When Zito asked her interviewee why he thought the media missed it so badly, he said, "The national media just doesn't get the people it covers. It didn't last year. It still doesn't." In interview after interview, she said, voters told her they don't find their views expressed anywhere in the national media. They understand they're not the center of the universe, but they would like to be included in the coverage.[59] One of the reasons I wrote *God and Donald Trump* and this book is to tell the untold stories of the election and Trump that few in the elite media ever cover.

For people in small-town America, Zito wrote in her companion article for the *Post*, today's political climate is difficult to comprehend. They see the way the media talk about Trump and his supporters. They may not like all of it, but they like the slogan, "Make America Great Again." It's inspirational and forward-looking, something bigger than themselves. Zito then cites a Quinnipiac poll from April 2018 that indicates that 58 percent of white voters without a college degree approve of Trump's job performance, with 44 percent approving strongly. Summing up what she learned in her exploratory journey, Zito says:

> The honest truth is it is still Nov. 8, 2016, in this country. If you voted for Trump you are, for the most part, optimistic about what he can do in the future. And if you didn't vote for him, you still believe he is not worthy of the presidency. No fancy corporate billboards are going to change anyone's mind. Where his supporters go next is anyone's guess, but because they are a force to be reckoned with in modern politics, shouldn't we stop treating them like anthropological studies and start listening to what they have to say?[60]

As many observers on both sides of the fence have asserted, a backlash against the media is building in many parts of the country. "Mainstream media have overplayed their hand with their unceasing and venomous attacks on Donald Trump," writes Darrell Delamaide for *MarketWatch*. "He, of course, has fueled the flames with his petulant taunts, but at the end of the day, it is the media that have squandered their credibility. Their obsession with possible Russian collusion with the Trump campaign, even in the absence of hard evidence, has not only blocked Trump's agenda but has kept Democrats and other opponents from offering anything like a constructive alternative."[61]

It has gotten to the point, many would say, that the media's "breaking news" consists mainly of vague reports of administration officials meeting with shadowy figures, deemed shadowy mostly because there are no credible sources. As Donald Trump has argued all along, the fake news stories are "too numerous to count," says Glenn Greenwald in The Intercept, as he cites numerous examples from mainstream publications such as the *Washington Post*, MSNBC, Slate, *The Guardian*, and the *New York Times*.[62]

Since the press are generally sanctimonious, they rarely admit they are wrong unless backed into a corner. Early in my career I remember a *Washington Post* reporter named Janet Cooke won a Pulitzer for a heart-rending article about an eight-year-old boy named Jimmy in Washington, DC, who was addicted to heroin and later died. It was a total fabrication, and she returned her Pulitzer, the only person to ever do that.

Closer to home was the sad story of Jack Kelley from *USA Today*, whom I knew in the 1980s as a committed Christian—one of the few in secular media. He was nominated for a Pulitzer in 2002. But in 2004 he resigned in disgrace when it was revealed he'd been fabricating stories for years, including a page-one story in 1999 in which he reported on a typed Yugoslav Army order to "cleanse" a village in Kosovo.

Fast-forward to 2016 and Donald Trump's presidency, and there is a new generation of journalists who, for all intents and purposes, are fabricating stories in an attempt to take him down. "The reporters behind these stories apparently think of themselves as the new generation of journalism heroes, mirroring the exploits of Bob Woodward and Carl Bernstein in exposing the Watergate scandal and bringing down President Richard Nixon," says Delamaide. But even Woodward believes the media's pursuit of Trump is over the top and recently called for more "fair-mindedness" in their reporting.[63]

Speaking with Fox talk host Sean Hannity about "violent rhetoric" in the media, liberal feminist Camille Paglia said, "There's no journalism left. What's happened to the *New York Times*? What's happened to the major networks? It's an outrage." Former CBS reporter Sharyl Attkisson, who authored the sensational new book *The Smear: How Shady Political Operatives and Fake News Control What You See, What You Think, and How You Vote*, says the media's constant pounding on the president and his administration has caused them to lose credibility with a majority of the public. "We want to critically and carefully cover our institutions and powerful politicians," she said. "But when you do it in such a way that the public no longer believes what they're getting is the whole truth or sometimes the truth at all, you've undercut yourself because we'll get into an area where people hardly believe anything they hear at first blush."[64]

This has been Donald Trump's message since he entered the campaign, and if, as Shakespeare wrote, the past is prologue of things to come, the provocations will continue, the battles will rage, and the president's bully pulpit will be as busy as ever.

CHAPTER 6

MUSCULAR DIPLOMACY

SPEAKING TO REPORTERS outside the White House on June 8, 2018, shortly before leaving for the G7 summit in the Canadian province of Quebec, President Trump said he was looking forward to his meeting with North Korean leader Kim Jong-un, scheduled for June 12. The president assured reporters he was well prepared for the meeting. "I always believe in preparation," he said, "but I've been preparing all my life."[1] Trump had engaged in a number of well-publicized verbal spats with the G7 leaders during his brief stay in Canada and left a day early, skipping discussion of the environment and climate change in order to fly to Singapore's Sentosa Island, where he and Kim were to discuss ending the rogue regime's nuclear weapons program.

Sometime later White House correspondents and political opponents scoffed at Trump's comments, saying it was a stretch to claim he'd been preparing for negotiation with the Korean dictator all his life. But then a video from October 1999 surfaced on YouTube in which the late Tim Russert interviewed the future president on NBC's *Meet the Press*. During the conversation Russert said, "You say that you, as president, would be willing to launch a preemptive strike against North Korea's nuclear capability." To that Trump responded, "First I'd negotiate....And I'd make sure that we tried to get the best deal possible." In three or four years, he said, North Korea would have nuclear weapons pointed all over the world and specifically at the United States. Then he added:

> The biggest problem this world has is nuclear proliferation, and we have a country out there, North Korea, which is sort of wacko, which is not...a bunch of dummies, and they are going out and they are developing nuclear weapons. And they're not doing it because they're having fun doing it. They're doing it for a reason. And wouldn't it be good to sit down and really negotiate something? And I do mean negotiate. Now, if that negotiation doesn't work, you'd better solve that problem now than solve it later, Tim. And you know it, and every politician knows it, and nobody wants to talk about it.[2]

Suddenly it was clear that, for at least two decades, Donald Trump had been thinking about how to deal with a tyrant such as Kim Jong-un. And fortunately his face-to-face meeting with Kim proved to be everything he was hoping for. Speaking to reporters afterward, he said he was hopeful for the prospects of peace but warned that the summit was just "the beginning of an arduous process." He said the sanctions on North Korea would remain in place until the goals of the negotiation were met. "The past does not have to define the future," he said. "Yesterday's conflict does not have to be tomorrow's war.... There is no limit to what North Korea can achieve when it gives up its nuclear weapons and embraces commerce and engagement with the rest of the world."[3]

When asked about North Korea's shameful record of human rights abuses, Trump said the North Koreans would be "doing something" to improve the situation. Then, asked how he could praise Kim Jong-un when the North Korean was such a brutal dictator, he spoke about Otto Warmbier, the twenty-two-year-old American university student who was detained by the North Koreans and imprisoned for taking a propaganda banner. Warmbier suffered a devastating brain injury while in custody but was released on June 12, 2017, under intense pressure from the United States.

He was medically evacuated to the United States on June 13, 2017, and died six days later, having never regained consciousness. But the president said it was Warmbier's captivity, injury, and death that ultimately led to the summit in Singapore. "Otto did not die in vain," he said. The young man's tragic death inspired both sides to strive for peace. "Otto Warmbier is a very special person and he will be for a long time, in my life. His parents are good friends of mine.... Special young man. And I have to say, special parents, special people." And he also said, "I think without Otto, this would not have happened."[4]

The president said later the State Department would not remove sanctions on North Korea without "significant improvement" on human rights. He indicated he had discussed the issue of kidnapped Japanese citizens with Kim, but specific language was not included in the document they signed due to time constraints. They did reach an agreement, however, on repatriation of the remains of American soldiers missing in action during the Korean War, saying the process would begin immediately. He also indicated the US would cease joint military exercises with South Korea if the North Koreans followed through on Kim's promises.[5]

At the conclusion of the summit the two leaders addressed a crowd of at least twenty-five hundred journalists from around the world. "We're very proud of what took place today," Trump said. "I think our whole relationship with North Korea and the Korean Peninsula is going to be a very much different situation than it has in the past." During the televised ceremony in which the president and the Korean dictator signed a joint statement of accord, Kim Jong-un thanked Trump for making the face-to-face talks possible. "We had a historic meeting and decided to leave the past behind," he said, adding that "the world will see a major change."[6]

A Time of Awakening

On the morning after the summit there was a sense the world had shifted on its axis and everything was upside down, in a very good way. President Trump had done it. He met with Kim Jong-un in a neutral location, shook hands, and signed an accord committing to the elimination of nuclear weapons on the Korean peninsula. No other sitting American president had ever spoken to North Korea's leader since the beginning of the Korean War, almost seventy years ago, not even by telephone. But Donald Trump took a chance, and the world was suddenly a better and safer place, and the American president was its most powerful leader.

At the conclusion of negotiations, even the mainstream media had to admit that Donald Trump, his presidency, and the entire international community had achieved an important milestone. Around the world there was relief and thanksgiving. The provocative former NBA star Dennis Rodman played a part as well. Proudly sporting his MAGA hat and multiple piercings, he assured the president that Kim Jong-un was ready to talk. Rodman had developed an unusual friendship with the Korean dictator and pleaded with tears in his eyes for Trump to give the summit a chance. In a matter of hours the sword that had threatened the world—and especially Asian nations—ever since the hostilities began in 1950 was being lifted.

The media overlooked several fascinating spiritual parallels between Trump and Kim as journalists focused on the political aspects of the summit. In 1907 a Christian revival in Pyongyang, Korea, had such an impact that missionaries called the city the "Jerusalem of Asia."[7] In fact, Kim Jong-un's great-great-grandfather became a pastor, and Kim's great-grandfather, an elder who raised his son, the future dictator, as a Presbyterian. For nearly four decades Christianity was much stronger in northern Korea than in South Korea. But Kim Il-sung, the dictator who brought communism to North Korea, not only rejected Christianity but made North Korea one of the most oppressive regimes on earth, crushing free speech and religious rights.

When the Korean War began, there were thirty-five hundred churches in North Korea. Today there are two official churches, for propaganda purposes, and as many as 120,000 confessing Christians being held in labor camps.[8] More than 100,000 North Korean refugees are currently residing in China awaiting a chance to be repatriated to South Korea, but fewer than 100 are able to be evacuated each month. Groups supporting the effort have said that if one out of every 140 of the fourteen million South Korean Christians teamed up to evacuate just one refugee each, the backlog could be cleared.[9] Millions are praying for reconciliation, but progress has been painfully slow.

Interestingly, President Donald Trump was raised a Presbyterian by his mother, a native of the Outer Hebrides Islands in Scotland, where there was a tremendous spiritual revival from 1948 to 1952—ironically almost the exact years of the Korean War. The awakening was so widespread and inspiring that the Hebrides were known for a time as the "Jerusalem of the British Isles."[10] According to Scottish sources familiar with the events and the individuals involved, two sisters, Peggy and Christine Smith, ages eighty-two and eighty-four, prayed for years to see God move in their small fishing village on the island of Lewis, and their faithful prayers helped spark a revival. The movement that followed spread throughout Scotland and the British Commonwealth.[11] Several sources have reported that the two elderly sisters were Donald Trump's great aunts. In researching for this book, I couldn't verify that they were his great aunts, but regardless, his family would have been impacted by the revival in some way.

The 2018 summit in Singapore was an answer to prayer for the thousands of South Koreans who had been praying fervently for the reunification of Korea and for revival in the North. President Moon Jae-in of South Korea said in the days before the summit that the people of his country were praying for Trump to "create a miraculous result."[12] I have visited South Korea several times, and each time, I attended huge prayer services, where I was aware they were praying for their northern neighbor—even as the repression seemed to grow and as famine decimated the population.

South Korean leader Jeffrey Yoon, director of Church Growth International in Seoul, told me that Korean Christians have been praying not only for the North Korean Christians but also for the reunification of the two nations ever since the Korean War ended, and praying for God to open doors to North Korea. In May 2018, when the Singapore summit was on again, off again, my friend and mentor Alex Clattenburg was in Seoul to attend a board meeting of Church Growth International, and he witnessed this again. Alex, who is lead pastor of Church in the Son in Orlando, Florida, has served on the board, founded by famous Korean pastor David Yonggi Cho.

Alex attended a rally on May 18, 2018, at the Seoul World Cup Stadium, seating 66,700. The enthusiastic six-hour prayer meeting ("the closest thing to heaven I've ever experienced," he told me) was focused on the reunification of Korea and revival in North Korea. "We trust God has been doing something and [are] sure that it will happen and will be successful," Jeffrey Yoon said.

In spite of its Christian heritage, North Korea has become one of the most repressive governments on earth, implementing the infamous "songbun system," in which the entire population has been sorted into social classes according to their perceived loyalty to socialism and the regime. As reported by the organization Liberty in North Korea:

> The regime silenced anyone who opposed the system with extreme prejudice. Free speech became an offense punishable by imprisonment or even death. Worse, when one was arrested, up to three generations of their family would be sent to political prison camps. The regime instructed children to inform on their parents, and neighbors to inform on each other. Under these conditions, the North Korean people became fearful and distrusting of each other.[13]

In 2016 *Christianity Today* magazine reported that Christians in North Korea face rape, torture, enslavement, and being killed for their faith in the most dehumanizing ways. According to a report from Christian Solidarity Worldwide, freedom of religion has been "largely non-existent" for three generations of the Kim family's dictatorship. "Religious beliefs are seen as a threat to the loyalty demanded by the Supreme Leader, so anyone holding these beliefs is severely persecuted," the report says. "Christians suffer significantly because of the anti-revolutionary and imperialist labels attached to them by the country's leadership."[14]

Most Westerners know there isn't much freedom in North Korea, but most of the attention in recent years has been focused on North Korea's nuclear capability, especially with Kim's propensity to fire missiles he said could carry a nuclear warhead. He even boasted he could send missiles as far as the West Coast of the United States. But as Russell Goldman wrote in the *New York Times*, US efforts to counter Kim's nuclear ambitions did not begin when President Trump threatened the Korean regime with "fire and fury." Goldman writes, "For decades, Mr. Trump's predecessors have waded into the diplomatic mire, trying to threaten or cajole North Korea's ruling family into abandoning the country's weapons programs. Each failed."[15]

Goldman reports that during the 1990s Bill Clinton lifted sanctions that had been there for decades, supplied five hundred thousand tons of oil a year, and provided $4 billion in aid. None of this deterred North Korea from developing its nuclear capability.

President George W. Bush took a different tactic by confronting the North Koreans. I remember Bush's 2002 State of the Union Address, in which he referred to North Korea, Iraq, and Iran as an "axis of evil." Bush's goal was to punish North Korea with sanctions until it toppled. But that didn't work either.

Next, President Obama decided a policy of "strategic patience," choosing to wait out the hermit nation until it realized it would be to its advantage to make a good-faith effort at renewed peace talks. Instead, Goldman says, "The North pursued its weapons program and launched a series of cyberattacks on American businesses."[16] While Obama was president, Kim Jong-un, a grandson of the country's founder, was declared leader after the death of his father, Kim Jong-il, reportedly ten days before his twenty-eighth birthday.

American diplomats initially hoped Kim Jong-un would break from his predecessors' policies, but instead he took a more aggressive position. In September 2016 he tested a nuclear warhead he claimed could be attached to a long-range missile and later threatened he could hit not only Japan and Guam but also the continent of North America. Many feared Kim was crazy enough to do it. But President Trump was having none of it, and instead of "strategic patience," he countered with threats of "fire and fury" in August 2017. "North Korea best not make any more threats to the United States," Trump told journalists at his club in Bedminster, New Jersey. "They will be met with fire and fury like the world has never seen."[17]

Shortly after this he began calling the young North Korean dictator "Little Rocket Man," making his critics scream that Trump was risking nuclear war and should be more diplomatic. Instead of nuclear war, Kim agreed to come to the negotiating table. But when Kim began to bluster about the terms he was being offered, Trump canceled the meeting. Within hours a conciliatory statement was issued by the North Korean Vice Minister of Foreign Affairs, and Kim sent an emissary to Washington, DC, a few days later with a letter to Trump officially asking for the summit to be reinstated. This was yet another example of Trump's strong leadership and negotiating ability, even if he was overly aggressive in his approach.

Trump told Sean Hannity of Fox News in Singapore after the summit ended that he felt foolish and hated having to use harsh rhetoric to condemn North Korea and Kim Jong-un, but he felt he had to do it to bring the countries together. This implies that the overly aggressive approach in his tweets was strategic. It also shows that the president is willing to sacrifice his reputation for what he believes is best for the country.[18]

A Glimmer of Hope

At the conclusion of the meetings in Singapore, the president was asked by reporters if he had spoken to Kim about the plight of persecuted Christians during their closed-door sessions. "We…brought it up very strongly," he said, adding that "Franklin Graham…spent and spends a tremendous amount of time in North Korea. He's got it very close to his heart. It did come up, and things will be happening."[19] Later, back in Washington, he was asked by a CNN reporter why he had not confronted Kim more directly for the regime's human rights abuses, and the president said, "I don't want to see a nuclear weapon destroy you and your family."[20] The implication was that changes would come, but the negotiation was still delicate at this early stage to push Kim further.

Franklin Graham is best known for his important work with the Christian relief group Samaritan's Purse, but his family has been involved in missionary activities in China and Korea for more than a hundred years. His maternal grandparents, Dr. L. Nelson Bell and Virginia Leftwich Bell, served as medical missionaries in China for twenty-five years, from 1916 to 1941, and Franklin's aunt and uncle Virginia Bell Somerville and Dr. John Somerville followed in their footsteps, serving as Presbyterian medical missionaries in South Korea for many more years. In addition to the influence of his father, evangelist Billy Graham, and his hands-on ministry in many parts of the world, Franklin's concern for the people of Korea is deep and multigenerational.

Under Graham's leadership, Samaritan's Purse has supplied aid and ministry in North Korea by "distributing food, furnishing agricultural aid, supplying flood relief, improving medical facilities, equipping TB treatment centers, and providing mobile clinics."[21] In response to severe flooding in North Korea in 2007, Graham and his ministry team flew a Boeing 747 loaded with seventy-five tons of food and emergency medical supplies, valued at more than $8 million, to the capital city of Pyongyang. The nation had been hit by the heaviest flooding in decades, which led to a humanitarian disaster all across the country. An estimated six hundred North Koreans were dead or missing, and more than one hundred thousand were left homeless. "In spite of the political differences that divide our two countries," Graham said at the time, "we need to do all we can to care for the people of North Korea."[22]

At the conclusion of the Singapore summit, Graham expressed his gratitude to the president and posted his reaction on Facebook, saying, "Thank you, Mr. President, Mike Pompeo, and all of the administration's advisors for being willing to work for peace. We owe you our support and gratitude in this effort. The Bible tells us to 'seek peace, and pursue it' (Psalm 34:14). Millions of people bathed the

Singapore meetings in prayer—Americans, North Koreans, South Koreans, people around the world were praying. Let's ask God to continue to work in the hearts and minds of these leaders."[23]

Open Doors USA, the Christian watchdog group founded by the Dutch Christian leader known as Brother Andrew, who famously smuggled Bibles into the former Soviet Union and Eastern Europe for many years, has ranked North Korea as the number one persecutor of Christians for the past seventeen years. According to David Curry, president of Open Doors, "President Trump's decision to address North Korea's human rights atrocities was diplomatically bold, and we are particularly glad to hear the president say he brought up the plight of the more than 300,000 Christians who face persecution and even death under the regime of Kim Jong Un."[24]

In North Korea, he said, as many as "120,000 Christians have already been confined in prison camps, where conditions remain deplorable....I hold out hope that human rights and denuclearization in North Korea need not be mutually exclusive endeavors." He added, "For this reason, we are prayerfully and cautiously optimistic for our fellow Christians in North Korea, for whom there is now at least a glimmer of hope that did not exist prior to President Trump's meeting with the dictator."[25]

In an article for our online news service, CharismaNews.com, news director Jessilyn Justice reported that Christians in the north are severely persecuted and can only practice their faith in secret. To avoid suspicion, prayer meetings must be discreet and in secret locations, often with no more than two or three worshippers at a time. If discovered, Christians are subject to detention and imprisonment in political prison camps, where they are charged with crimes against the state. Punishment in these camps may include extrajudicial killing, enslavement, forced labor, torture, rape and sexual violence, and other inhumane acts.

Eyewitness reports documented by escapees tell of Christians being hung on crosses and suspended over a fire, being crushed under a steamroller, being herded off bridges into rocky chasms and deep waters, and even being trampled underfoot by military guards and others. And sadly many North Korean Christians who manage to escape into China are forcibly repatriated to North Korea, where they are subsequently imprisoned and subjected to the most brutal forms of reprisal and torture.[26]

The intervention and relief organization Christian Solidarity Worldwide has said that America and its allies cannot afford to shy away from the moral mandate to hold the Korean dictator, Kim Jong-un, responsible for the human rights abuses of his regime. For the Korean Christians who have been imprisoned, tortured, and subjected to hideous forms of execution, their only crime was expressing their faith in God and holding religious beliefs other than those approved by the communist regime. As the Open Doors report explains:

> For three generations, everything in the country focused on idolizing the leading Kim family. Christians are seen as hostile elements in society that have to be eradicated. Due to the constant indoctrination permeating the whole country, neighbors and even family members are highly watchful and report any suspicious religious activity to the authorities.[27]

While the friendly images of President Trump and Kim Jong-un may be comforting, and while we're hopeful these negotiations may offer a pathway to denuclearization, says Vernon Brewer, CEO and founder of World Help, the North Korean Christians are no safer today than they were before the Singapore Summit.[28] The president must not fail to continue putting pressure on Kim for changes in the regime's totalitarian practices.

Brewer also says, "Believing in Jesus is still a crime that can land a Christ-follower in a labor camp or prison—which, in many cases, amounts to a death sentence. Yet, here's the most amazing thing: the underground church of North Korea continues to grow! Believers continue to risk their lives to get their hands on a Bible. As we celebrate the US and North Korean leaders meeting together, we cannot forget our North Korean brothers and sisters. We must continue speaking up and praying for them. They are still waiting for their own victory."[29]

World Help has been using a variety of clandestine means to provide Bibles for North Korean Christians. Although Trump said denuclearization was the top priority of his summit meetings with Kim, he said that the North Korean leader reacted very well when asked about taking steps to eliminate human rights abuses in his country. "I believe it's a rough situation over there," Trump said. "There's no question about it. And we did discuss it today pretty strongly. I mean, knowing what the main purpose of what we were doing is: denuking. But discussed it at pretty good length. We'll be doing something on it….It's rough in a lot of places, by the way. Not just there. But it's rough, and we will continue that. And I think, ultimately, we'll agree to something. But it was discussed at length outside of the nuclear situation, one of the primary topics."[30]

Trump also said he would halt the military exercises held regularly by US and South Korean forces as long as negotiations remain on track, and he said Kim Jong-un also agreed to allow international workers to retrieve the remains of US soldiers killed during the Korean War. Referring to what comes next in the negotiation during a post-summit interview on Fox News, Trump said, "I just think that we are now going to start the process of denuclearization of North Korea, and I believe that he's going back and will start it virtually immediately—and he's already indicated that."[31]

Praying for Miracles

In another report for *Charisma* magazine, author and evangelist Lee Grady predicted that, with all the incredible changes taking place today all over the world, Kim Jong-un would soon "fling open [North Korea's] doors to Christianity and join the 21st century." Many readers were critical of the idea, Grady told me, either because they didn't trust the motivations or the honesty of Kim, or possibly because they feared the author of *The Art of the Deal* might not be up to the challenge. "But I'm sticking to my prediction," Grady said. "I personally believe North Korea's future is not in the hands of Kim, Trump, or any other human. I believe the sovereign Lord of the nations is engineering this miracle."[32]

If we step back and think for a moment about how strange it is for North Korea to be considering any sort of change to its barbaric practices after seventy years of brutal repression, we would have to see that something miraculous is happening. Grady says the world is on the verge of a truly historic breakthrough, that the prospects for an earth-shaking reversal of fortunes could be much closer than we know, and changes of that magnitude are desperately needed.

"As many as three million North Koreans starved in the 1990s," says Grady. "The economy is so poor that more than 6 million people are malnourished today, and one-third of all North Korean children are stunted because of starvation. The average person earns…$1,800 per year, making North Korea one of the poorest countries on earth. Yet it has an army of 1.2 million soldiers—twice the size of South Korea's military." Even though the founder of the totalitarian regime, Kim Il-sung, died in 1994, the government gave him "the office of the eternal presidency," and he is worshipped as a god by followers of the Juche religion.

Today there are more than thirty-four thousand statues of Kim Il-sung in the country—one statue for every seven hundred fifty North Koreans. The dead leader's embalmed body is on display in the Kumsusan Palace of the Sun, the most popular tourist site in the country. All citizens of North Korea are required to wear a badge that features Kim Il-sung's face. Furthermore, Grady writes, in North Korea it is not 2018. It's the year 107, which, according to North Korea's Juche calendar, commemorates the birth of Kim Il-sung in 1912. North Koreans born on July 8 or December 17 are not allowed to celebrate their birthday, because Kim Il-sung and his son, Kim Jong-il, died on those days.

The loyal subjects of the current dictator, Kim Jong-un, believe he can control the weather. His official biography published by the government says Kim learned to walk and talk before the age of six months and that he can control the weather with his moods. The regime's propaganda ministry also convinced the people of North Korea that a new star appeared in the sky on the day Kim Il-sung was born. Schools in the north are indoctrination centers where children are brainwashed from the earliest grades. They are taught the song "We Have Nothing to Envy in the World" and are expected to bring their own desks and chairs to school. In addition, children are required to do government work during school hours, but parents who can afford it are allowed to bribe the teachers to keep their children from doing hard labor.

Unlike conditions in South Korea, which is an advanced and technologically sophisticated society, the electrical grid in North Korea is so inadequate that most people have no lighting in their homes. Nighttime images taken by satellites from space show a country immersed in darkness; however, visitors to the North have reported that the people have come to love the darkness because it gives them the only privacy they ever experience. But travel is incredibly difficult, Lee Grady writes, because only 3 percent of the roads in North Korea are paved. Even so, the roads are rarely used by civilians since very few own private vehicles. A small, elite group of North Koreans have access to the internet, but all online content is filtered by the government.

Farmers have little or no access to chemical fertilizers, so the government requires that the people of North Korea produce a certain quantity of human waste. In fact, many families put locks on their outdoor toilets to keep neighbors from stealing waste to meet the government quota. Christians are often ridiculed, says Grady, because we believe demons are real and that demonic forces are working behind the scenes to affect world events.

"Why is that so hard to believe?" he says. "I can't understand how anyone can look at the bleak situation in North Korea and not believe the devil exists. Thankfully, the Bible also says Christ overcame Satan's power through His death and resurrection—and that God's kingdom will expand wherever the gospel is preached." That, says Grady, is why he is expecting to see miracles in North Korea.[33]

Peace Through Strength

As a Christian author and publisher, I place high priority on religious freedom for all people. But it is only one of the many ways President Trump is making a difference beyond the borders of the United States. As I've discussed earlier, Trump is pushing our NATO allies to pay their share of the cost of defending Europe after dragging their feet for decades. He also met in Helsinki with Russian president Vladimir Putin in July 2018. Even though his press conference with Putin at the summit set off shock waves of political and media speculation, one thing is certain: Donald Trump does not take the conventional approach to anything, including diplomacy. Rather than rushing to judgment like many in the media and political arenas, I believe that in the long run there will be meaningful progress for America as a result of Trump's atypical foreign policy meetings and tactics—whether with Russia, Syria, Iran, North Korea, China, Ukraine, or elsewhere.

At times it appeared President Trump had world leaders such as Chinese President Xi Jinping and French President Emmanuel Macron eating out of his hand, and he has gone head to head with the elites in Davos, Switzerland, at the World Economic Forum. All of that, as he has said, is part of "making America great again," restoring the spirit of American exceptionalism and putting America first on the global stage. This is his passion, and it seems to be guiding everything about his policy, both domestic and international.

Trump's single-mindedness reminds me of a story James Watt told me when he was the US Secretary of the Interior under President Ronald Reagan. I had the privilege of interviewing Secretary Watt at his office in Washington, DC, and wrote a cover story about him in *Charisma* magazine in 1983. He told me that Reagan's number one priority was to defeat Soviet communism. Now, these were the days when most Americans, including me, assumed we would have to coexist with communism all our lives.

I'm old enough to remember the Cuban Missile Crisis of 1962 and how some Floridians actually built bomb shelters because there was such a fear of war with the Soviets. I also remember that Reagan inherited a horrible economy from Jimmy Carter. Inflation was 14 percent in 1980, and I can remember paying interest rates as high as 20 percent when I started my media company in the early 1980s. The recession of 1981–82 was the worst since the Great Depression.

So what was the president to do if he wanted to defeat the Soviets when it looked nearly impossible? First, he needed a strong military. For a strong military, he needed a healthy economy. For a healthy economy, he needed to manage the resources of our great country better. That's where James Watt came in. The Department of the Interior is more than the department that oversees the national parks and the buildings in Washington. It can give leases for drilling for oil and gas. It decides how much timber can be harvested at any given time. Watt knew he had to do his job well so the economy would grow, which allowed the United States to have a strong military that could help bring the Soviets to their knees. When the Soviet Union broke apart a decade later, I remembered what Watt told me.

President Trump believes that to make America great again, we must rebuild our military. And to get a clear-eyed perspective on what's happening in the military, I contacted my friend retired general Jerry Boykin. During his thirty-six-year career, he spent thirteen years in Delta Force and was involved in several high-profile missions, including the Black Hawk Down incident in Mogadishu, Somalia. He also served as deputy undersecretary of defense for intelligence under President George W. Bush. He is known as an outspoken Christian leader who now serves as executive vice president of the Family Research Council in Washington, DC.

When I asked the general about changes in the military since President Trump's election, he quoted Gen. Douglas MacArthur, who told cadets at West Point in 1962 that "your mission remains fixed, determined, inviolable. It is to win our wars," adding that the mission has not changed. The general believes President Obama failed to understand that simple concept and, therefore, was willing to allow military readiness to languish, eventually reaching a state where the military could no longer expect to win the nation's wars.

Such a lapse of judgment created a critical national security risk. Donald Trump's objective has been to restore military readiness, and he's doing that. He unleashed the military to do its job. In a little more than a year, Iraqi and Syrian forces supported by a US-led coalition regained most of the territory in Syria and Iraq that ISIS had captured, significantly reducing its ability to mount war and commit acts of terrorism in other parts of the world.

While al Qaeda existed in Iraq before Obama, the emergence of ISIS resulted from a fallout between Osama bin Laden and a renegade Iraqi leader named Abu Bakr al-Baghdadi, who became the head of ISIS as it expanded into Syria. ISIS, after all, stands for Islamic State of Iraq and Syria, denoting their desire for an empire without borders, a caliphate that fanatical Muslims believe will one day cover all the world. Because of that, some radicals call it "the Islamic State," suggesting the caliphate is much bigger than just Syria and Iraq. At one time ISIS seemed unstoppable as it expanded its territory exponentially.

Even though the US had been bogged down in the war in Iraq for more than a decade and had been fighting in Afghanistan since 2001, we couldn't seem to win. "But then Trump comes in, and in one year, Trump—as the commander in chief, through his military—has taken back over 90 percent of the territory that ISIS controlled in Iraq and Syria," Boykin told me. "So, what happened? He gave our military rules of engagement that allowed them to win. The Obama administration never talked about winning. Again, go back to MacArthur... your mission is to win the nation's wars."

One of the greatest hindrances to winning wars was sequestration, a provision in the Budget Control Act of 2011 that imposed across-the-board spending cuts if Congress and the White House could not agree on targeted reductions aimed at reducing the budget deficit. Trump campaigned on getting rid of sequestration and increasing the military budget, and he has done exactly that, which has made a huge difference in being able to equip our military. "Now you have a president who understands the concept of winning, to include in wartime, in combat. Obama never understood that.... He had people in the battlefield just to play, not to win," Boykin said. "Just think of how long we fought against ISIS and how little success we had against ISIS during the Obama administration," he told me.

FOR SUCH A TIME

The general believes the new commander in chief changed the rules of engagement and is in the process of giving the military the resources they need, which Boykin feels has been Trump's most significant accomplishment. This has put America's armed forces on the right course to be able to win the nation's wars. Boykin predicted to me that Trump will go down in history as the president who gave our military everything they needed to be successful against our adversaries on the battlefield, and the proof is the fact that ISIS has now lost over 90 percent of its territory.[34]

The lack of willingness to fight was only one of the ways Obama hurt the military, he said. While the wars in the Middle East dragged on, Obama decided it was time to end the "don't ask, don't tell" policy and told gay people they could serve openly in the military. Then he said the military would pay for hormone treatment and gender reassignment surgery for those in the military who felt they were transgender.

"Obama used our military as a social experiment testing; they were almost like lab rats," Boykin said. "And along comes Mr. Trump who says, 'This makes no sense to me whatsoever, and we're not going to do this,' and he bans transgenders from the military. Now, what he does have to contend with, which is a serious issue, is what do you do about those people that came out under the Obama administration, in good faith, believing that their government was going to stand behind their pledge to allow them to come out?"

Boykin pointed out that conventional wisdom says "you have to let them continue to serve or give them huge incentives to go ahead and get out on their own. But if they want to stay, you've got to let them serve because it's a good faith issue." This was the official position, Boykin said, but there's more to consider. "Hold on!" he told me. "How does that contribute to readiness in the military? You're bringing in people that you know are going to be non-deployable at a time when we need every man and woman fully capable of deploying and fighting and winning the nation's wars. It always comes back to the issue of can we win the nation's wars in our military?"

So now, he said, "You've got a situation where you're bringing in people you know will not be able to deploy for some period of time, plus you're going to use taxpayers' dollars that could be used for beans and bullets for our military being spent to get a person hormone therapy and gender reassignment surgery, and what is the logic of that? How does that contribute to making our military capable of winning the nation's wars? And the answer is, it doesn't," he said. And that's why the president made a sound, ethical decision to restrict military enlistments.

Meanwhile, three unelected judges in the federal judicial system decided that Trump's actions were unconstitutional, and by mid-2018 that case was still winding its way through the courts. But General Boykin asks, "As the commander in chief under article 2 of the Constitution, if Mr. Obama had the authority to say you can come out and serve openly, why does Mr. Trump not have the same authority to be able to say, 'I'm changing that policy'? Because the president of the United States is responsible for the military as the commander in chief, and he is responsible for the composition, the deployment, the training, the state of readiness of our military."

But this was not the only social experiment, Boykin told me. In 2010 the Obama administration repealed "don't ask, don't tell." There have always been homosexuals serving in the military; the question was whether they would be able to serve openly. Obama made a pledge to usher in the repeal of the "don't ask, don't tell" policy, and he did it. He also decided to put women in the infantry and special operations. Boykin said Obama considered it an issue of fairness to put women in ground combat roles where they've never been allowed before. But once again, he said, "How does it contribute to readiness? And the answer is, it really doesn't. But that's another one of the social experiments."

General Boykin said he is absolutely convinced Donald Trump has been "raised up for such a time as this." And he added, "I think it's no different than Winston Churchill, who saved the world from annihilation or subjugation to the Nazi regime." Churchill would never meet the standards of an evangelical Christian, he said, and Donald Trump may not either. Nevertheless, he believes Donald Trump was chosen for this job at this time. "He does not speak the language of Evangelicals, but he is indebted to the Evangelicals because he knows that, whatever they have, it is real. And I think God is using him in a very powerful way to give America an opportunity to get our act together and turn this nation around through Donald Trump's leadership."

I felt those were encouraging words from a soldier and a patriot who knows what it means to be ready in every situation, regardless of the risks or the potential consequences. It seems clear now that President Trump's patience with Kim Jong-un is based on his strategic assessment of those very things—the risk of taking no action and the potential consequence of pushing too hard during the critical early stages of the negotiations. It's a delicate balance and not a sign of weakness or indecision.

According to a report on the Fox News Channel, two Norwegian lawmakers have officially nominated President Trump for the 2019 Nobel Peace Prize as a result of his historic summit meeting with Kim Jong-un. The story, which aired on the Sean Hannity television broadcast on June 13, 2018, indicates that the politicians from Norway's populist Progress Party announced their decision within hours of Trump's meeting with the communist dictator and praised the president for his ability to bring the North Korean leader to the negotiating table. President Obama received the award in 2009 before he had taken any significant diplomatic actions, based on the Nobel committee's hopes he would be a defender of world peace, but his administration was plagued by wars throughout his presidency.

There is no question that the people of North Korea need and deserve an advocate who is dedicated to the peace process. They need material goods, food, hope, and the freedom to express their beliefs openly. But the challenge is immense, and peace will likely only come if President Trump, Secretary of State Mike Pompeo, and their teams of negotiators and operatives can somehow convince the North Korean dictator that it's in his own best interest to dispose of his weapons and throw open the doors of the hermit kingdom. If President Trump can accomplish that feat, he will undoubtedly deserve his place in history. But if changes of that magnitude are to happen, it will be through the power of muscular diplomacy supported by the power of faithful and unrelenting prayer.

CHAPTER 7

TRUMP'S BOOMING ECONOMY

No matter how hard the liberal media may try to refocus the world's attention on other issues, the good news coming from President Trump's booming economy is impossible to ignore. Take, for example, this review of the blazing hot economy from *U.S. News & World Report*: "Wall Street opened 2018 on a winning note Tuesday, bidding Nasdaq to its first-ever close above 7,000 points following a rally in technology shares. At the closing bell, the tech-rich Nasdaq Composite Index had jumped 1.5 percent to end the first session of the year at 7,006.90. The S&P 500 also notched a fresh record, gaining 0.8 percent to close at 2,695.79, while the Dow Jones Industrial Average rose 0.4 percent to 24,824.01, about 13 points below its all-time record."[1] All this is actually happening, and all at the same time.

As economics analyst Peter Roff explains in his special report, this means "America is up to its eyeballs in good economic news." The Dow broke 26,000 on the first trading day of the new year. Unemployment was down to 3.75 percent as of June 2018, the lowest since 1969, and black unemployment was the lowest it had been since the Bureau of Labor Statistics started keeping track in 1972.

Under Barack Obama, black unemployment peaked at 16.5 percent. By June 2018, inspired by the pro-business climate created by the Trump administration, it was down to 5.9 percent. Boosted by all the good news, the labor market added 223,000 jobs the same month, of which 218,000 were in the private sector, and average hourly pay increased from $26.84 to $26.92.[2] But the good news just keeps on coming.

The monthly Economic Optimism Index, a collaboration of *Investor's Business Daily* and TechnoMetrica, measures the confidence of consumers, workers, and investors in the overall strength of the economy. A score above fifty indicates optimism, while a score below fifty indicates pessimism. As reported by *Investor's Business Daily*, the optimism scale jumped more than 6 percent in January 2018 (to 55.1). The following month the index hit 56.7. By June 1, 2018, even the *New York Times* felt compelled to say, "We ran out of words to describe how good the jobs numbers are," adding that "the economy is in a sweet spot, with steady growth and broad improvement in the labor market."[3]

This was the kind of growth Donald Trump had promised throughout the campaign and the confirmation his administration had been waiting for. Celebrating the moment, the president tweeted on June 4:

> In many ways this is the greatest economy in the HISTORY of America and the best time EVER to look for a job![4]

Of course, it didn't take long for the naysayers to jump in, and Bloomberg quibbled that "labeling a single economic era as the greatest in history is subjective because there's no agreed-upon metric." But then it added, "Judging solely by gross domestic product, perhaps the simplest way to gauge a nation's progress, the decades that followed World War II were the hottest in American history. Pent-up consumer demand, a housing boom and a vibrant manufacturing sector all melded into the economy's Golden Age."[5]

No one would deny that the post-war era was a unique growth period for the nation, but that was sixty years ago, and Trump's enthusiasm today is being stoked by the fact that more Americans than ever are finding good, productive employment and making their lives better. Jobs in most sectors are at an all-time high, and layoffs nationwide are down to where they stood in December 1990. In addition, corporate spending on capital goods is way up, and growth in gross domestic product (GDP) has now reached 4.1 percent. With such strong economic reports, businesses began raising wages, paying bonuses, and announcing expansion plans.

GDP is the best way to measure whether an economy is growing, and the Federal Reserve projected that GDP for the second quarter of 2018 would top 4.8 percent. "That's a number not seen since the days of Reagan," says columnist Wayne Allyn Root. "The USA has moved back to #1 in the world in the global economic competitiveness index. Thanks to President Trump's massive tax cuts and killing of regulations, we're now ahead of booming economies like Singapore, Hong Kong and Switzerland."[6]

But if you haven't heard any of these numbers, says Peter Roff, you shouldn't be too surprised. The mainstream media steadfastly refuse to give the president the credit he and his administration deserve for this record-breaking economy. What's going on, he says, is "akin to a conspiracy of silence intended to ensure no one gives President Donald Trump credit for the economic turnaround."[7]

I've heard talking head liberals on cable TV say the economy is only good because of how President Obama teed it up for Trump with what Obama called his "shovel-ready" stimulus plan in 2009. But I agree with what Roff, an expert whose analysis I respect, wrote: "If Obama had anything to do with the good numbers" that started before the election, it was only because the markets were responding to the fact that, no matter who won in November 2016, Obama and "his regulatory happy band of progressive central planners would soon be gone."[8]

In his outstanding article on the *U.S. News & World Report* website, Roff says it may be difficult to accept that numbers this good are due solely to Trump's policies, but they are what they are. As proof, he quotes Patrice Lee Onwuka of the Independent Women's Forum, saying unemployment for blacks in the US had declined from 7.9 percent in December 2016 to 6.8 percent at the end of 2017, which "is a significant achievement."

The economy, as Onwuka sees it, "is improving for black America and should continue to get better as pro-growth and pro-family policies expand our resources and deliver better opportunities."[9] But the real question may be, How is it possible that this is not front-page news?

> How is it the 24-hour cable networks that are willing to devote hours of programming to the impact of what President Trump said or might have said in a private meeting with senators discussing immigration policy aren't holding televised townhalls and bringing in the best economic minds in the country to explain why the issue of black unemployment—which many had relegated to the burial ground of insoluble problems—has suddenly taken a turn for the better?[10]

What's going on, Roff writes, is more than just media bias. The media seemed to think Presidents Reagan and Bush were too dumb to do the job. With Trump, he says, it's more than that:

> It's open hostility to the man reflected in a general unwillingness to cover anything good that he does and anything good that might be happening because of the policies he's put in place. The same people who could never accept that he won the nomination when they all said it was improbable and that he won the presidency despite their projections and polls that showed it would be impossible for him to do so are so vested in proving they were ultimately right that they are not only rooting for him to fail, they are trying to cause it to happen.[11]

Even if Trump invites a certain amount of abuse from the liberal media for his adversarial tone and the strong language he uses in his tweets, it's not a fair fight. For one reason, Donald Trump is not the kind of person who runs from a fight; in fact, he seems to enjoy it. And thanks to his tweets, public comments, and even the occasional leaks of his private remarks, the public understands the nature of the battle, and they're not blind to the success his administration is having with the economy. They can see the impact all this good news is having in the marketplace, and despite the criticism and incessant denials from the media and liberal politicians in both parties, his favorability ratings are very high.

Unfortunately politics is not really about what's good for the country. Too often it's about what's good for the party. So when companies such as AT&T, Wells Fargo, and Visa announced they would be giving one-time bonuses, pay increases, or benefits increases for employees and credited the GOP's December 2017 tax legislation for the economic boost, Democratic House minority leader Nancy Pelosi went on the attack, calling the projected one thousand–dollar bonuses "crumbs." She said, "In terms of the bonus that corporate America received versus the crumbs that they are giving workers to kind of put the schmooze on, is so pathetic." Then, when Walmart, which had been a target of years of bad press and picket lines because of low wages, announced the company would increase the minimum hourly wage to eleven dollars and offered longtime employees a one thousand–dollar bonus, Trump's Democratic and media critics called it a publicity stunt.[12]

But the blowback from Pelosi's remarks and the criticism leveled at employers who were offering cash bonuses was fast and furious. Working men and women all over the country criticized Pelosi for the arrogance and insensitivity of her comments. In candid televised interviews several indicated that an extra thousand dollars is not crumbs to most working families and for a multimillionaire such as Pelosi to say something so rude and thoughtless only shows how out of touch she really is. In a speech during a congressional retreat in West Virginia on February 1, 2018, the president fired back. To West Virginia's miners and factory workers, a thousand dollars means a great deal, and Pelosi's comment, he said, was about as sensitive as Hillary Clinton's claim that half of Trump's supporters are a "basket of deplorables."[13]

Making the Economy Great Again

Throughout his campaign Donald Trump promised to free up the economy to do what it does best, increase prosperity for all Americans. Sure enough, writes economist Andy Puzder, "that's exactly what happened." As taxes were cut and antibusiness regulations eliminated, businesses invested, GDP growth climbed during Trump's first full three quarters to a 3.1 percent average, and the unemployment rate fell to a low not seen since 2000. Obama confidently predicted in 2010 that GDP would "exceed 4 percent per year in 2012–2014."[14]

However, Obama never had even one year of 3 percent GDP growth. In 2016, says Puzder, GDP growth averaged a dismal 1.5 percent, adding that Obama's appointees implemented progressive policies and anti-business regulations that caused the economy to fail "to produce enough good paying jobs, [while] people dropped out of the labor force, wages stagnated, paths to the middle class closed, and income inequality increased." Puzder says it was predictable that "progressive economic policies produced the very problems" the administration claimed it wanted to alleviate.[15]

In early 2017 the Trump administration was forecasting 3 percent GDP growth, but Obama economist Lee Branstetter claimed it was "essentially mathematically impossible to get the growth they're talking about." Obama administration economist Jason Furman forecast ten years of GDP growth of "around 2 percent a year." Obama economist Larry Summers said that believing in Trump's forecast of 3 or 4 percent GDP growth was like believing "in tooth fairies and ludicrous supply-side economics." But the progressives guessed wrong. With GDP growth averaging 3.1 percent for over three straight quarters, the Congressional Budget Office forecast an even higher rate of 3.3 percent growth in 2018. To that Puzder said:

> With economy freed from the heavy hand of government, the economic optimism is palpable. The National Association of Manufacturers recently reported that 93 percent of American manufacturers are optimistic about their future. That's the highest number in the survey's 20-year history up from 56.6 percent just last year. The National Federation of Independent Businesses' Small Business Optimism Index for March, reached its 16th consecutive month in the top five percent of 45 years of survey readings.[16]

By January 2018 more Americans were employed in the labor force than at any time in the nation's history. According to the National Federation of Independent Business, the major problem facing businesses today isn't taxes or regulations any longer; it's finding qualified employees. Says Puzder, "Some might call that a capitalist comeback. But it's no surprise to those of us who, to paraphrase President Kennedy, appreciate how quickly the rising tide of capitalism can lift all boats."[17]

The American people are aware of the changes taking place. In March a Gallup poll reported that barely a third of Americans were greatly worried about the economy, and less than a quarter were greatly worried about unemployment—the lowest numbers since Gallup began reporting the data in 2001. The most significant decline in both measures occurred after President Trump took office. In that light, says Puzder, "it would be nice if, for once, those on the Progressive left could set aside their disdain for the president long enough to see American capitalism for what it is: an unmatched engine for creating prosperity and opportunity, empowering consumers instead of elites, and offering people of all backgrounds a good job and a better life."[18]

Americans know that the economy is doing much better under President Trump than the eight years of stagnation we experienced under Obama. Economic policy during the previous administration was based on increasing taxes on those who create wealth in order to create government programs that would allow the Democrats to redistribute money and benefits to potential Democratic voters. Building support through "disingenuous sound bites about fairness and decency," says Puzder, there was little time or interest for creating policies that might actually encourage economic growth.

President Clinton has admitted that he raised taxes too much during his presidency. With input and advice from the Republican House of Representatives and Speaker Newt Gingrich, Clinton agreed to cut capital gains taxes, reform welfare, deregulate the banks, balance the budget, and shrink the size of government. He said famously during his 1996 State of the Union address that "the era of big government is over." Unfortunately that's not the message coming from Democrats today. For progressive Democrats, economic growth comes second to expanding the size and power of government.

As CEO of CKE Restaurants during the Obama years, Puzder says he was often confronted by journalists asking "how restaurants could employ people in part-time and entry-level jobs with salaries too low to support a family. The discussion would invariably turn to a $15 minimum wage, automation, or 'corporate greed.'" But the dynamics have changed since then, he says, and thanks to Trump's booming economy the unemployment rate is now at the lowest level in almost two decades. Despite a record 155 million people in the labor force in March 2018, there were a record high 6.6 million jobs available. According to Puzder:

> The number of people working in construction is at its highest level since June 2008, and there were an additional 248,000 job openings that month. The number of people working in manufacturing is at the highest level since December 2008, with 391,000 additional job openings.
>
> According to a recent survey by the National Association of Manufacturers, 72 percent of manufacturers are increasing workers' wages and benefits, while 77 percent are hiring more workers.[19]

Since Barack Obama left office, the economy has done a 180-degree turnaround, going from a situation "where the problem was workers being unable to find good-paying jobs to an economy where the problem is businesses being unable to find workers to fill good-paying jobs."

This has come about, Puzder says, because of President Trump's commitment to "lowering taxes and shrinking the size of government through deregulation. It was not the result of higher taxes or expanded government programs. In fact, the number of Americans dependent on government benefits is declining. The monthly average of initial unemployment benefit claims is at a low last seen forty-five years ago. The number of people receiving SNAP benefits (food stamps) has also dropped—by over 2.5 million people since President Trump took office."[20]

The president's approach to the economy, according to his son Donald Trump Jr., is designed to help the working class "forgotten man" in the heartland, rather than the coastal elites and "the rich," as the president's opponents have claimed. Trump Jr., who has taken over day-to-day operations of the Trump Organization along with his younger brother, Eric, said the latest jobs numbers that show 3.8 percent unemployment and record low unemployment for blacks, Hispanics, and women are an indication of the success of Trump's policies—a level of success that has left the antagonistic media almost speechless. "And again," Trump Jr. said, "if the *New York Times* is saying they don't have words to describe how good these numbers are, they're not doing that with joy." [21]

As his father said throughout the 2016 presidential campaign, the goal is to make it possible for average blue-collar workers to succeed—and that's what's happening. "The forgotten men that we campaigned on—they're getting the real benefit of that," he said. "That's not helping billionaires and the narrative they're trying to sell. That's helping real, blue-collar, hardworking, patriotic Americans. They're getting better wages. There's more demand for their work. They're able to do that. They're able to support their families better. That helps their family structure. Everything—I mean, this is what we campaigned on. This is what my father ran on. This is helping the people in what was the forgotten land everywhere between New York City and Malibu that the Democratic Party establishment has forgotten about for decades."[22]

Trump Jr. added that following through on campaign promises is unusual for a president, but his dad is not like most politicians. He is committed to seeing Americans succeed. "That was the thesis of his whole campaign, and guess what? He's actually doing it....Promises made, promises kept. Time and time again. That's not coming from guys who are fans of DJT. That's coming from guys like the *Washington Post* who are saying, 'Hey, Trump is keeping his campaign promises.'"[23]

"I see the new Democratic spin," he said. "'We're going to be about jobs.' Really? Where have you been for thirty years?" This president has created more jobs than anyone before him in the same amount of time. Now Democrats are saying they're going to run against him in the midterms and in 2020 on the same concepts: oppressive taxes, ridiculous overregulation, and all the progressive policies that are now the basic foundations of their party! "It makes no sense whatsoever," Trump Jr. said, "but we have to remember that," and he added that if Trump wins a second term in 2020, the administration can really get the country back on track. "It's really incredible, and it's an incredible opportunity that we can't squander."[24]

The Economic Outlook

Based on a wide range of key indicators, the US economic outlook is very strong. The GDP growth rate is expected to remain between 2 and 3 percent, which is "the ideal range" according to analysts at TheBalance.com. Unemployment is forecast to continue at a natural pace, and the risks of both inflation and deflation are moderate and well within a normal range. That's what most market and finance experts would call "a Goldilocks economy," they say. Not too strong, not too weak, but just right. President Trump had predicted economic growth of 4 percent during the campaign (a number tempered later by Treasury Chief Steven Mnuchin because many analysts believe growth at such a high rate can lead to overconfident investing when prudence is the best policy in a changing economy). But Trump is not easily dissuaded from his goals for unprecedented growth, and on July 27, 2018, when the GDP report for the second quarter of 2018 came out, growth had climbed to 4.1 percent—signaling a historic economic turnaround and another campaign promise kept. Trump touted the numbers as "amazing" and "terrific" and rightly so.[25]

Short-term interest rates—the prime rate for bank loans, London InterBank Offered Rate (LIBOR), most adjustable-rate and interest-only loans, and credit card rates—are controlled by the federal funds rate. The Federal Open Market Committee raised the federal funds rate to 1.5 percent in December 2017, with expectations of increasing to 2.1 percent in 2018, 2.7 percent in 2019, and 2.9 percent in 2020. The last time the Fed raised rates was in 2005, and the sudden increase on that occasion contributed to the sub-prime mortgage crisis. Some observers in the housing industry have suggested real estate markets could crash in the next couple of years. However, the differences between the housing market today and the situation in 2007 makes such a somber scenario highly unlikely.[26]

My good friend Joe Bert, a certified financial professional in Longwood, Florida, who I trust with my own investments, reviewed this chapter at my request and pointed out that while the stock market is the gauge the average person uses to judge the health of the economy, it is not nearly as valid as many other elements discussed on these pages. He told me, "No one can predict the short-term movement in the stock market, but the milestones and accomplishments you mention in your book bode well for a positive long-term upward trend." I take that as strong encouragement.

While the economy looks really strong as I write this book in mid-2018, that could change, and there could be a dip in the stock market. If that happens, remain calm. That's the best advice for anyone invested in the stock market because markets go down and later go back up. Of course, corrections are inevitable, but when commodity prices such as gold, oil, and coffee plummet, experts will tell you they always return to the mean. As the nation moves beyond the effects of the lackluster Obama years, the booming Trump economy has made this a great time to reduce debt, build savings, and improve personal financial positions in practical, not speculative, ways.

But as good as all this good news has been for the Trump administration, there is still a dark cloud that has hovered over the nation's financial well-being for more than a century, since the presidency of Woodrow Wilson and longer: the national debt. There may be no greater threat to America's financial future and national security than the uninterrupted growth of the national debt over the past fifty years.

According to the Department of the Treasury, "the term *national debt* refers to the direct financial liabilities of the United States government."[27] Its website explains the different concepts that can refer to the national debt:

- **Public debt** comes from public debt securities issued by the US Treasury. These consist mainly of marketable securities such as Treasury bills, notes, and bonds; United States savings bonds held by individual investors; and a long list of special securities issued to state and local governments.
- **Debt held by the public** excludes the portion of public debt held by government accounts.
- **Gross federal debt** is made up of public debt securities and a small amount of securities issued by government agencies.[28]

"Debt held by the public," the Treasury Department says, "is the most meaningful of these concepts and measures the cumulative amount outstanding that the government has borrowed to finance deficits."[29] Congress and the White House have been obligated to settle this liability for generations, yet the national debt continues to skyrocket, and little is being done to resolve the debt crisis hanging over our heads.

In testimony before the Senate Select Committee on Intelligence on February 13, 2018, the US director of National Intelligence, Dan Coats, told lawmakers he believes our growing national debt is the single biggest threat to America's national security. Coats, who served as a Republican senator from Indiana for sixteen years, outlined a series of rising global and cyber threats the United States faces from adversaries such as North Korea, Russia, Iran, and China. But he also warned against the greatest internal threat, which he said could undermine the American economic and national security. He said, "I'm concerned that our increasing fractious political process, particularly with respect to federal spending, is threatening our ability to properly defend our nation both in the short term and especially in the long term. The failure to address our long-term fiscal situation," he said, "has increased the national debt to over $20 trillion and growing."[30]

The intelligence director's comments echo the warning of Admiral Michael Mullen, former chairman of the Joint Chiefs of Staff, seven years earlier when he said, on September 22, 2011, "I believe the single, biggest threat to our national security is debt."[31] According to Arizona congressman Andy Biggs, both of these highly placed defense experts got it right. The United States faces many existential threats, he said, from ISIS, rogue nations such as Iran and North Korea, illegal immigration, and much more. But the single greatest danger for America's peace and security is our inability to bring our national debt under control.

As of May 4, 2018, the public debt stood at $21,037,962,909,322.34. In less than a year the US saw the debt surpass $20 trillion in September 2017 and $21 trillion in March 2018. During the 2018 fiscal year Congress passed seven short-term spending bills, including the $1.3 trillion omnibus package signed by the president in March. None of these spending bills balanced the federal budget or reduced spending. Worse still, by passing these short-term continuing resolutions, Congress dismissed "regular order," which would have allowed members of Congress to consider amendments to the bills.

Instead of cutting spending, Congress extended the debt ceiling to accommodate projected capital spending requirements. Consequently, the congressman said, we're at risk of defaulting on current debt obligations and jeopardizing our economic stability. Analysts for Moody's Financial Metrics said in August 2017 that "rising entitlement costs and rising interest rates will cause the US's fiscal position to further erode over the next decade, absent measures to reduce those costs or to raise additional revenues."[32] Our nation must face this challenge.

During an address to military and government officials, Secretary of Defense James Mattis warned in January 2018 that "no nation in history has maintained its military power that was not economically viable and did not keep its fiscal house in order." And

Director of National Intelligence Dan Coats stated, "Our continued plunge into debt is unsustainable and represents a dire future threat to our economy and to our national security." Representative Biggs also warned that "the United States is racing toward a fiscal cliff," and Congress is doing very little to save the nation from a ruinous fate. But thankfully, he added, President Donald Trump and his administration realize the urgency of this crisis and are committed to finding a responsible solution.[33]

"In his National Security Strategy," Biggs said, "Mr. Trump highlighted the need to reduce the debt through fiscal responsibility." No one denies the severe consequences that would befall the nation if for some reason we were to default on this debt. But Biggs believes the Trump administration sees the ongoing threat for what it is, even if too few in Congress recognize the danger. "It is past time for my colleagues to become serious about balancing our budget and making significant cuts to federal spending," he says. "If we do not change our course, we will be part of one of the worst catastrophes this nation has ever experienced: the crash of the American economy and the demise of a superpower."[34]

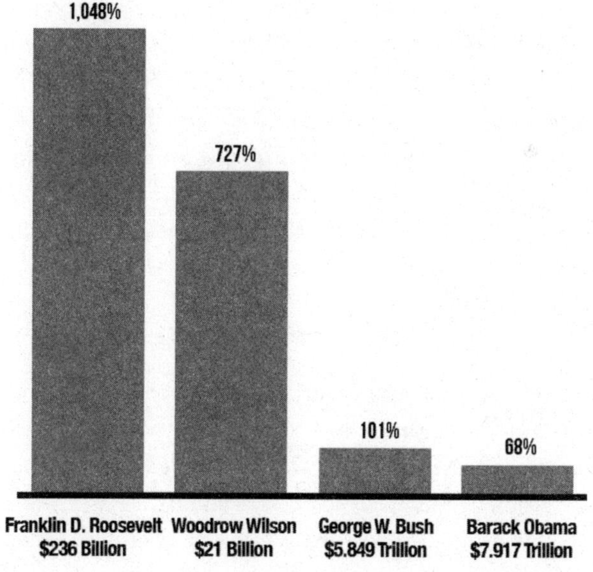

For a better idea of how the government got to this point and how various presidents have dealt with the debt problem, it's informative to know which administrations added the most to the national debt. Predictably, President Franklin D. Roosevelt increased the debt the most percentagewise. As reported by Kimberly Amadeo at The Balance, FDR only added $236 billion to the debt, which seems low by today's standards, but this was a 1,048 percent increase from the $23 billion debt left by his predecessor. The causes were both the Great Depression, which decreased revenues and created countless agencies and programs to help those unemployed, and World War II. War spending was Roosevelt's most substantial contribution to the debt, adding $209 billion, according to Amadeo.[35]

Woodrow Wilson, president during World War I, came in second percentagewise, adding $21 billion—a 727 percent increase in debt over the $2.9 billion left by President Taft.

Barack Obama made the fifth-largest increase percentagewise (a 68 percent increase over seven years), but he ranks number one at increasing the national debt dollarwise, adding $7.917 trillion, according to Amadeo's research.[36]

The second-highest dollar amount added to the national debt came during the presidency of George W. Bush, who, according to Amadeo, added $5.849 trillion to the debt (the fourth-largest increase percentagewise). Like Wilson and Roosevelt, financing war was a huge factor in the increase during Bush's tenure. In Bush's case, the terrorist attacks on 9/11 launched the War on Terror in both Afghanistan and Iraq. President Bush also dealt with a recession in 2001 by passing enormous tax cuts that reduced revenue even further and increased the nation's debt.

Based on current plans, President Trump's projected fiscal year 2019 budget calls for a 41 percent increase from the $20.245 trillion in debt left by Obama, adding $8.282 trillion to the national debt. If this happens, Amadeo concludes, Trump will replace Bush as adding the second-highest dollar amount in history, and he will add almost as much in one term as Obama added in two terms.[37] But the president has an alternative strategy for dealing with the unfolding crisis of debt.

Trump's Audacious Gamble

America is perched atop a financial time bomb. Everyone knows this, yet the members of Congress can't bring themselves to reduce spending. "Why?" asks Garland Tucker. "Because the American public refuses to demand congressional action." Tucker, a senior fellow with the John Locke Foundation, says there are "two primary aspects to the spending crisis: the staggering explosion of federal debt" and the increased dependency on government by millions of Americans. The debate over such things is always focused on the financial issues, he says, but the heart of this matter is really a moral issue, and it's high time the nation came to grip with the problems before our financial sins catch up with us.[38]

According to Tucker, "Since the onset of the Great Society's War on Poverty in the mid-1960s, the US has spent...more than $15 trillion in means-tested entitlement programs. Between 1960 and 2010, federal entitlement spending increased from 19 percent to 43 percent of annual federal spending....These programs were designed not only to eliminate poverty but to eradicate the root causes of poverty. The results? The overall poverty rate in 1966 stood at 14.7 percent, while in 2013 it stood at 14.5 percent." In other words, nothing changed. "By any standard of measurement," says Tucker, "these programs were a disastrous investment."[39]

The US government redistributed income on a massive scale, and since the spending was financed with larger and larger deficits, the debt burden was shifted to yet unborn generations of Americans. This is now a huge moral issue for the American people. As former US budget director and Indiana governor Mitch Daniels said at the time, echoing the warning attributed to the eighteenth-century Scottish historian Alexander Tytler, "As a people, we have discovered the ability to vote ourselves largesse from the federal treasury in such vast quantities that we are destroying our own chances at prosperity." Or in the words of American Enterprise Institute President Arthur Brooks, we have become a nation of takers, not makers.[40]

We know that President Trump signed a $1.3 trillion omnibus bill in March 2018. As Tucker points out, "With this most recent installment in America's sad descent into this fiscal and moral crisis, our deficit is projected to reach $850 billion for 2018." House Speaker Paul Ryan said he was determined to tackle entitlement spending, but the Senate and the president would have to join in if anything productive were to happen.[41] Or, as Jesse Hathaway, a research fellow with the Heartland Institute, puts it, "There's an ominous ticking sound at the bottom of this fiscal hole. If our representatives in Washington, DC, don't listen and keep digging the nation deeper toward disaster, the American people, especially children, are the ones who'll end up suffering the most from the impending debt explosion."[42]

Donald Trump's audacious gamble is his unshakable faith that current levels of economic growth will continue and that increased revenue from taxes and the lowered cost of government due to substantial reductions in the bureaucracy and costly regulations, along with increased revenue from tariffs on international goods, will begin the process of lowering the debt to a sustainable level. As pointed out by Bloomberg columnist Conor Sen, the president is conducting a risky experiment, allowing the government to run one of the largest budget deficits of any nation, outside wartime or a recession, in hopes that this will somehow propel economic growth to a much higher level. "Irresponsible as that might sound," writes Sen, "it actually makes some sense."[43]

"In the long run," he says, "economic growth is a function of two variables: population and productivity. For decades America has had plenty of both. Birth rates were ample, and any additional labor could be attracted from [other places if needed]. From 1947 to 2007, workers' output per hour grew at an average annual rate of 2.3 percent. So for the most part, American presidents could focus on improving rather than reviving growth." But after the recession of 2008, the variables changed. Labor-force growth began slowing as baby boomers reached retirement age. At the same time, productivity began to decline as well.

"The Obama administration," writes Sen, "accepted the new reality." The administration's annual budget report in 2016 projected inflation-adjusted growth of GDP at just 2.2 percent for the next decade. Rather than addressing the impending debt crisis, however, Obama's economists offered "traditional ideas such as immigration reform, more cross-border trade, infrastructure spending, and education investments."[44]

Donald Trump, on the other hand, has taken a much more aggressive approach, projecting an annual growth rate of 3 percent over the next decade, which is high but healthy. This kind of growth won't come from the population, says Sen, particularly with the administration's plans to restrict immigration, which means that productivity will have to increase tremendously. Tariffs on imports such as steel and aluminum and foreign-made automobiles will bring in new revenue but, at the same time, could make domestic output more expensive. By mid-2018 the plans to implement tariffs on major imports were still subject to change, but the administration made it clear the long-term balance of trade favoring China and other nations would have to change, and while the tariff rates could change, Trump's policy would favor American business.

While the Bloomberg organization has expressed doubt about aspects of Trump's plan, the omnibus bill in March 2018 and tax cuts signed into law in December 2017 prompted companies of all sizes in all segments of the market to commit to greater capital investments, increasing the size of the workforce, and higher salaries, thereby attracting more and better workers. As the writer says, there's no certainty about how Trump's tax cuts will help in the long run or how long the current momentum in the economy will last. But so far, the prospects are very good, and the president is using his bully pulpit to help encourage business owners and their employees to take advantage of the prosperous economic climate.

Donald Trump's gamble is that economic growth and productivity will get a boost from the government's tax cuts and spending plans. Treasury Secretary Steven Mnuchin said during a Bloomberg interview on February 22, 2018, "There are a lot of ways to have the economy grow....You can have wage inflation and not necessarily have inflation concerns in general."[45] Data from earlier that month showed an unexpectedly large jump in salaries, which spooked global markets for a time. The new data fueled concerns that rapidly rising wages would push inflation upward faster than expected and force the Federal Reserve to hike interest rates quicker than anticipated, but that did not happen, and the markets began a slow but steady climb upward.

The idea that Trump's policies "could lead to wage growth without inflation" is surprisingly similar, Sen pointed out, to policies presented by Bernie Sanders during the 2016 campaign. "By running the economy hot and making labor more expensive," Sen writes, "the government can induce businesses to do more investment than they would in a normal economy. Ever since the financial crisis, a weak economy has discouraged many businesses from investing, leading to weaker productivity growth. So why not try the opposite?" Trump's gamble is "a theory that has not been tested in decades," writes Sen, but it is an intriguing idea, and he asks:

> What are the potential risks and rewards? Sticking with the status quo promises more of the same underperformance—annual real GDP growth of about 2 percent. The deficit experiment has two possible outcomes. In the best case, the US gets some form of productivity miracle. In the other, rising inflation forces the Fed to raise interest rates to cool off the economy, triggering a recession.[46]

Double-digit inflation like we experienced during the 1970s is not what today's investors, economists, and policymakers are worried about. In advanced economies, says the writer, central banks now have better tools for dealing with inflation of that kind. But weak productivity remains a major concern for economies with aging populations and a need to provide higher levels of support for seniors and other segments of society. While Republicans and Democrats will certainly disagree on the best way to deal with deficits and spending, the options Trump offers are intriguing and possibly even inspired.[47]

The Obama model was based on tax increases, investments in infrastructure and education, and reduced military spending (although military spending increased every year through 2011 before it decreased). It was a policy of low expectations and low return on investment. Trump's model, on the other hand, calls for full-throttle acceleration of the economy, lowering taxes, boosting jobs and productivity, and cheering the market from his bully pulpit.

The balance of risks, as the Bloomberg columnist concludes, points toward taking Trump's gamble. Whether it turns out to be Trump or the next chief executive who comes up with a brilliant plan, someone is going to take that gamble, and the long-range benefit will be not only a bigger and more impressive list of winners but a chance to roll back the national debt to a more manageable level. And knowing what we do about this president, who would doubt such a thing can actually happen?

CHAPTER 8

BILLIONAIRE RADICALS

Hundreds of chauffeur-driven limousines, at least two hundred helicopters, more than one thousand private jets, and six feet of new snow descended on the resort town of Davos-Klosters, known as the highest town in the Swiss Alps, for the annual meeting of the World Economic Forum. The guest list included more than three thousand of the world's top bankers, business leaders, and entrepreneurs, along with senior diplomats and heads of state from nearly seventy countries. Outside the inner circle of billionaire elites roamed a gaggle of pop stars and celebrities anxious to boost their activist credentials and mingle with the richest and most powerful men and women in the world.

The agenda for the weeklong event, from January 23 to 26, 2018, included more than four hundred sessions and panel discussions focusing on climate change, ecology of the oceans, technology, the internet, economic growth, energy, sustainability, education, geopolitics, poverty, open borders, and global migration. The stated theme of the event was "creating a shared future in a fractured world," but the overriding objective of this forum, as it has been every year since the event began in 1971, was building a consensus on how global elites can overcome the populist impulse and "improve the state of the world."[1]

Although his attendance was widely publicized by forum organizers and vigorously debated by the media, Donald Trump was not an official guest at first. He went anyway, he said, because the United States is the most powerful nation on the planet, with an economic engine like no other, and it was important for him to be there. The president told the *Wall Street Journal* he was going to Davos as a cheerleader for the American economy, to draw attention to his administration's economic successes.[2] CNN Money described it as "Trump vs. the global elite, on their home turf."[3]

The president's speech was greeted with mixed reviews. Many attendees were predisposed to denounce his remarks, regardless of what he said. But others were pleasantly surprised by the measured and diplomatic tone of his presentation. He began by saying, "It's a privilege to be here at this forum where leaders in business, science, art, diplomacy, and world affairs have gathered for many, many years to discuss how we can advance prosperity, security, and peace. I'm here today to represent the interests of the American people and to affirm America's friendship and partnership in building a better world."[4]

He went on to say that the US economy has created more than $7 trillion in new wealth since his election, along with 2.4 million jobs. "The stock market is smashing one record after another," he said. At the same time, consumer, business, and manufacturing confidence are at the highest levels in decades, and unemployment for African American and Hispanic workers is the lowest on record. His message to the world was that "America is open for business, and we are competitive once again."[5]

Even the reflexively critical *New York Times* noted that "a rough consensus emerged over Mr. Trump's two-day visit that his administration had shown itself to be more pragmatic than advertised. Many were inclined to view the president's most extreme positions as just aggressive bargaining postures."[6] After the speech the US president was swarmed by curious and enthusiastic delegates seeking selfies, autographs, or a few words with him. At one point, as he was greeting arriving members, someone handed him a copy of my book *God and Donald Trump*. With only a brief glance at the cover featuring his image, he lifted the book high over his head for everyone to see. Needless to say, that was a highlight and a complete surprise for me as well.

During the question-and-answer session following his speech, moderated by German engineer Klaus Schwab, the founder and executive chairman of the forum, the president was relaxed and affable. But when asked about his relationship with the media, he said, "As a businessman I was always treated really well by the press. The numbers speak and things happen, but I've always really had a very good press. And it wasn't until I became a politician that I realized how nasty, how mean, how vicious, and how fake the press can be."[7]

Predictably, those remarks sparked a chorus of boos from members of the international press standing in the back of the room. But no matter what anyone may think of Donald Trump, there can be little doubt the media have been aggressively antagonistic toward him since day one. The major media have engaged in what columnist Victor Davis Hanson describes as "a veritable slow-motion effort to remove an elected presidency." While Trump's tweets may be rude or insensitive, Hanson says, "no man is an island," and in many cases the president is simply defending himself against an avalanche of scurrilous charges. "Trump may be ego-driven and have a proverbially thin skin," he says, "but even a rhino would finally chafe under the 24/7 media detestation of his person, his family, and his presidency."[8]

A Thousand Tentacles

Since I was trained as a secular journalist, I have watched with interest the press's animosity during the campaign and first term. When I began my career during the Watergate era, I saw the press hound Richard Nixon out of office for doing far less than Hillary Clinton, who has been given VIP treatment by the media. I began to understand several decades ago that despite what is seen, there are forces at work that are often malevolent. As a Christian, I believe in a spiritual world that often manifests itself in the political world. So when Donald Trump began talking about draining the swamp and people began talking about the deep state, it wasn't hard for me to believe.

I knew this had to be grappled with in any book about the aftershocks of Donald Trump's election. Yet my expertise is centered more on the inner workings of the evangelical community and church history than on the globalists who are moving to one world government—something not hard for me to believe in the light of my eschatological view of history. When it came time to write this chapter, I wondered if I should include it. Yet I've received feedback from readers of *God and Donald Trump* thanking me for daring to emphasize how Trump is shaking up the globalist agenda, which is why he is opposed by so many. Since I'm no expert, I'm glad I had researchers and editors to help pull together this difficult, but important, chapter. In addition, the internet gives access to many things written about globalism and Trump and what I see as sinister forces behind the scenes.

To understand why the media have become so aggressively anti-Trump, it may help to know that Far Left billionaires, including George Soros, former New York mayor Michael Bloomberg, hedge-fund guru Tom Steyer, eBay founder Pierre Omidyar, and super-investor Warren Buffett, have been on a spending binge over the past fifteen years, buying newspapers, funding websites, and creating a phalanx of nonprofit advocacy groups to promote ultraliberal policies and to undermine conservatives and their organizations.

According to a multiyear research project by the Media Research Center (MRC), these billionaires, along with Soros' son Jonathan Soros, have contributed more than $2.7 billion since 2000 to groups pushing abortion, climate change alarmism, and gun control, and supporting a long list of handpicked liberal politicians. On his own, Soros has spent at least $52 million building a network of newspapers, news organizations, and journalistic institutions.[9]

But the tentacles of this octopus are not limited to the billionaire's connections to news organizations such as ABC, NBC, the *New York Times* and the *Washington Post*. As the MRC reports, the *Columbia Journalism Review* (*CJR*) provides a long list of investigative reporting projects funded by Soros foundations. Among them are activist groups such as ProPublica, the Center for Public Integrity, the Center for Investigative Reporting, and New Orleans' The Lens, all funded, in turn, by the Soros-funded Open Society Foundations. The Columbia School of Journalism, which produces *CJR*—considered the journalistic gold standard when I was majoring in journalism four decades ago—has received at least $600,000 from Soros, the MRC report reveals.

The most renowned journalism school in the nation isn't the only thing Soros funds. He uses his fortune to influence journalism industry associations such as the National Federation of Community Broadcasters, the National Association of Hispanic Journalists, and the Committee to Protect Journalists. He also supports the Organization of News Ombudsmen, which lists fifty-seven associate and retired members from periodicals and news organizations around the world:

"A news ombudsman," their website states, "receives and investigates complaints from newspaper readers or listeners or viewers of radio and television stations about accuracy, fairness, balance and good taste in news coverage."[10] But anyone with the least knowledge of Soros and his leftist agenda can only wonder about the group's objectivity and balance.

Soros' money also goes to the Investigative News Network and the James L. Knight Foundation, which has offices in eight large and midsized cities and eighteen smaller ones and is associated with the former Knight chain of newspapers.[11]

Warren Buffett, whom many see only as your friendly neighborhood billionaire, has one of the most aggressively liberal portfolios in the nation. "Buffett began buying up small and midsized newspapers in 2012, spending millions on an industry most people believed to be dying. Forty-six of the seventy-five papers he owned as of July 2014," the MRC reports, "were strategically located in the crucial swing states of Iowa, Virginia, North Carolina, and Florida."[12] Meanwhile, the Susan Thompson Buffett Foundation, named for his late wife, donated at least $1.2 billion to support abortion and contraception worldwide.

Radical environmentalist activist Tom Steyer and the younger Soros have funded liberal news or news-related websites such as the Center for Public Integrity, Media Matters, the Center for Ecoliteracy, and the Center for American Progress. Steyer, whose super PAC spent nearly $100 million to support Democrats during the 2016 campaign, has also spent $20 million for a national "Need to Impeach" advertising campaign, which many observers see as the first stage of Steyer's bid for the presidency in 2020. And these are just a few of the billionaire radicals working to undermine the president and the will of the American people.

Explaining the impact of such generosity, a 2017 report from the Capital Research Center says:

> When media are covering news stories at election time and seek to explain some complex policy point, Soros's generous funding means there's always an Open Society Foundations–linked group ready to answer reporters' calls and emails on just about any conceivable issue. In the US alone, Open Society Foundations are providing grants in many key areas, among them justice, drug policy, equality, democracy, economic advancement, national security, and human rights.[13]

There should be no question as to what sort of answers reporters are getting from the Soros-funded foundation. Sharing a seeming like-mindedness with Soros are Steyer, Michael Bloomberg, and Amazon.com founder Jeff Bezos, all of whom are rumored to be partners of the group known as the Democracy Alliance, founded by Rob Stein following the reelection victory of President George W. Bush. George Soros and Peter B. Lewis, the late CEO of Progressive Insurance, have been among the more well-known partners. The alliance is made up of approximately 110 wealthy donors and liberal activists who fund so-called "progressive" groups and policies. To be part of the group, partners must sign a confidentiality agreement and consent to contribute at least $200,000 a year to causes and groups the Democracy Alliance recommends. However, most partners contribute a great deal more than that. The alliance has helped distribute more than $500 million to liberal organizations since its founding, in 2005.

According to staff writers at the *Washington Post*, "This exclusive donor club includes millionaires such as Susie Tompkins Buell and her husband, Mark Buell, major backers of Sen. Hillary Rodham Clinton" when she campaigned for the senate in 2008. Bernard L. Schwartz, retired chief executive of Loral Space & Communications Inc., is another alliance donor who said he joined the group because it "is most helpful for big donors who lack the time to closely examine their political investment options." Fred Baron, a trial lawyer, longtime Democratic donor, and member of the alliance, agreed: "The piece that has always been lacking in our giving is long-term infrastructure investments."[14]

Writers at the *Post* said, "There also are a few 'institutional investors,' such as the Service Employees International Union (SEIU), that pay a $50,000 annual fee and agree to spend $1 million on alliance-backed efforts."[15] Soros also funds foundations that fund other foundations, including the Tides Foundation, and as many as two hundred hard-left groups such as the Alliance for Global Justice and organizations associated with Antifa, which make donations, in turn, to a long list of anarchist and ultraliberal causes. MoveOn.org, Black Lives Matter, and Planned Parenthood are Soros' favorites. In 2015 alone Soros' Foundation to Promote Open Society made a total of $431 million in contributions and grants to far-left groups, so-called "anti-fascist" causes, and other causes around the world.[16]

The amounts being paid out by these groups that can be obtained from tax forms and news reports are likely an understatement of the amounts actually given. A full accounting would be difficult to compile because so many of the Soros-funded operations include their own media and direct-action subgroups.[17]

Asra Q. Nomani, who has written for the *New York Times*, reported that many of the "spontaneous" disturbances taking place following the November elections were actually bought and paid for by the Soros direct-action network of black bloc radical groups. Virtually all the organizations involved in the anti-Trump demonstrations that rocked New York and other cities in January 2017 had ties to Soros. And Nomani pointed out that Soros also had ties to more than fifty protest groups involved with the Women's March on Washington, DC, which took place with massive publicity on the day after Trump's election. All these groups were funded by Soros-related organizations.[18]

The Power of Persuasion

It should be apparent that the impact of these groups is not limited to their influence at ABC, CBS, NBC, or the *New York Times* and the *Washington Post*. *CJR*, which bills itself as "a media watchdog," lists several investigative reporting projects funded by one or more of the Soros foundations. The News Frontier Database, organized by the Columbia School of Journalism, includes seven different investigative projects funded by Soros' Open Society Institute.

Along with the liberal watchdog group ProPublica, Soros funds the Center for Public Integrity, the Center for Investigative Reporting, and New Orleans' The Lens. But by any measure the Democracy Alliance has proved to be Soros' most powerful and most dangerously effective creation. According to the *Washington Post*:

> The Democracy Alliance works essentially as a cooperative for donors, allowing them to coordinate their giving so that it has more influence. To become a "partner," as members are referred to internally, requires a $25,000 entry fee and annual dues of $30,000 to cover alliance operations as well as some of its contributions to start-up liberal groups. Beyond this, partners also agree to spend at least $200,000 annually on organizations that have been endorsed by the alliance. Essentially, the alliance serves as the accreditation agency for political advocacy groups.

> This accreditation process is the root of Democracy Alliance's influence. If a group does not receive the alliance's blessing, dozens of the nation's wealthiest political contributors as a practical matter become off-limits for fundraising purposes. Many of these contributors give away far more than the $200,000 requirement...45 percent of 95 partners gave $300,000 or better in the initial round of grants [in October 2005], according to a source familiar with the organization.[19]

As of July 2018, Amazon.com founder Jeff Bezos, who bought the *Washington Post* in 2013, is now the richest man in America, with an estimated wealth of $147 billion. Microsoft founder Bill Gates, who ranked first for most of the last twenty years, comes in second, with $96 billion in 2018, and Warren Buffett was third, with an $83.2 billion fortune.

Facebook founder Mark Zuckerberg is the fourth-richest American, with $68.4 billion, and Oracle cofounder, executive chairman, and chief technology officer Larry Ellison is the seventh-richest American, with assets of $54.2 billion. Meanwhile, the infamous Koch brothers, Charles and David, who have often been attacked in the press for their support of conservative causes, rank twelfth and thirteenth on Bloomberg's list of billionaires, with assets of $47 billion each.[20]

The Bill & Melinda Gates Foundation has invested billions of dollars in programs dedicated to ending poverty and increasing access to health care in developing countries. As of a speech he gave in October 2017, Gates is committed to the Common Core education initiative and is involved in developing curricula and professional development aligned with Common Core. Taco Bell heir Rob McKay, who formerly served as chairman of the Democracy Alliance, was one of the earliest supporters of Barack Obama's community organizing project, Organizing for America, now known as Organizing for Action.

Billionaire oilman George Kaiser, who gambled and lost a fortune on the Solyndra energy debacle, has invested heavily in Oklahoma politics and was a fund-raiser for Barack Obama's 2008 presidential campaign. Along with Drummond Pike, the creator of the Tides Foundation, and Tim Gill, the megadonor bankrolling the LGBT movement and supporters in the Democratic Party, almost all these billionaires have been engaged in the effort to resist and obstruct the president's conservative agenda and squash the religious Right. Gill was quoted in an interview for *Rolling Stone* in June 2017 saying, "We're going to punish the wicked."[21]

A software programmer who struck it rich during the dot-com boom, Gill said his efforts to block religious freedom bills in Southern states have really paid off. Using threats and strong-arm tactics, the Gill Foundation convinced more than one hundred corporations, including Coca-Cola, Google, and Marriott Hotels, to pull their business out of the state of Georgia to protest the Religious Freedom Restoration Act—which had passed—causing Republican governor Nathan Deal to veto it. Gill has donated more than $400 million to help fund the LGBT movement.

Today Gill's foundation is carrying out similar operations all across the South, with operations such as the attack on North Carolina governor Pat McCrory, who signed a state law regulating public restrooms, locker rooms, and other facilities on the basis of biological sex. In this case Gill's operatives put pressure on organizations such as PayPal and the National Basketball Association to pull out of the state. Consequently Governor McCrory lost his reelection bid in 2016 in spite of strong support from Christians in North Carolina to the state's Democratic attorney general, Roy Cooper, who had attended meetings in New York with a group of left-wing donors. At the time, Gill said the North Carolina governor's race was a "must-win" for the LGBT movement.[22] Sadly in this instance they won.

The Christian Response

Few conservative Americans, much less Bible-believing Christians, are aware of the magnitude of the forces who oppose not only Trump but the basic Judeo-Christian values our country was built on. They may have heard a few things and are hopefully beginning to wake up to the threats, and I'm hoping that even this book may help spur responsible action to stop what are essentially terrorist tactics against our way of life.

Consider Gill wanting to "punish the wicked"—that's you and me. Because we believe the Bible says any sex outside marriage, including homosexuality, is wrong, we are now being labeled wicked. There's even a law awaiting concurrence in amendments in the California legislature that would criminalize helping people who want to change their sexual orientation. While the law has been amended to specifically ban "advertising, offering for sale, or selling services constituting sexual orientation change efforts," it still explicitly states, "This bill intends to make clear that sexual orientation change efforts are an unlawful practice,"[23] leaving the door open for books that say homosexuality is a sin or for speaking out against homosexuality in the pulpit to be considered criminal. Backers of this horrible law say the ban doesn't include selling the Bible, which clearly says homosexuality is sin. But I believe that unless there is a backlash and the law fails either in the California legislature or in the courts (because it is such a blatant violation of constitutional religious freedoms), it's only a matter of time until the Bible is banned as "hate speech."

I believe that these people who hate Trump hate him only because he is standing up for the kind of values Christians believe are right. And he's a disrupter of the leftist agenda, which is not only political but opposes God. To me, this is no different from Sanballat and Tobiah, who opposed Nehemiah as he rebuilt Jerusalem, or Haman, who wanted to kill all the Jews. There have always been those who oppose God. And often they seem to win, at least for the short term. I believe God is raising up a standard against this, but in the natural it doesn't look good.

For example, it seems most of the billionaires are leftists, and they are investing their billions to promote ungodly agendas from abortion to LGBT issues to political policies such as open borders and socialism. Thank God there are some billionaires such as the Cathy family, owners of Chick-fil-A, and the Green family, owners of Hobby Lobby, who are examples of godly values. But they make up only a small fraction of US billionaires.

Consider, too, the difference between the influence of the church and the money and influence of these billionaire radicals on the culture. While there are many good ministries, and some of them are large, even the largest are tiny compared with the kinds of numbers we are describing here. And thanks to Lyndon Johnson, who pushed through an amendment to the tax code in 1954 saying any nonprofits that backed candidates could lose their tax-exempt status, churches have had a muzzle for more than six decades. And it has had a chilling effect beyond the actual regulation in that pastors and other religious leaders are meek and don't attempt to speak out on moral issues lest it be deemed political. Thankfully President Donald Trump sees this as a violation of the freedom of speech of pastors and other Christians and has issued an executive order to not enforce the Johnson Amendment while he's working with Congress to permanently change the law.

As I've said so many times, we are not wrestling with flesh and blood but against principalities and powers and evil in high places. This is spiritual warfare, and I hope this book is a call for believers to battle these forces in the spiritual realm. The reason I'm going into this detail is to document what is occurring so our eyes are open. Those who attack our political institutions and even President Trump have an even more insidious agenda that is demonic to its core. And the poster boy for this deceptive, vile agenda is George Soros, who has been the undisputed ring leader of this globalist cabal.

Born György Schwartz on August 12, 1930, in Budapest, Hungary, Soros came from a family of nonpracticing Jews who changed the family name during the rise of Adolf Hitler in order to assimilate into the city's Christian population. By the mid-1940s, when the Nazis invaded the country and began the systematic extermination of Hungarian Jews, Soros worked with a man, later identified as his godfather, whose job was confiscating property from Jews who were being rounded up and shipped off to the concentration camps.

At age fourteen, Soros was his godfather's helper, confiscating the property of Holocaust victims. Close to a half million Hungarian Jews were sent to their deaths at that time. During a now infamous interview with Steve Kroft on CBS TV's *60 Minutes* in 1998, Soros said that his experience "created no problem at all." Surprised by his coldness, Kroft asked, "No feeling of guilt?" to which Soros responded, "No."[24] In another interview Soros referred to his time as a Nazi collaborator as "the happiest year of my life."[25]

For a short time after the war Soros scrambled to make a living and sold seaside souvenirs. He was eventually admitted to the London School of Economics, then landed a job with the investment house Singer & Friedlander in London in 1954 as a clerk. Soros has said he was hired because the managing director was Hungarian.[26] In 1956, he moved to New York where he worked as a stock analyst and trader while applying to become a naturalized American citizen. He founded Soros Fund Management in 1970, where he solidified his fortune.

Soros is best known in Europe as "the man who broke the Bank of England." Betting heavily on the devaluation of the British pound, he made a billion dollars in one transaction and virtually crashed the English economy. According to his Open Society website, "George Soros launched his philanthropic work in South Africa in 1979. Since then he has given over $32 billion to fund the Open Society Foundations, which work in over 100 countries around the world."[27] But make no mistake; the aim of the "open borders" advocates is to eliminate nation states as we know them, along with their individual laws, customs, currencies, and traditions, in order to empower a global cadre of educated and progressive elites to rule all the people.

In their 2006 book, *The Shadow Party*, David Horowitz and Richard Poe reveal that Soros' private philanthropy provides funding for organizations that support not only open borders but "abortion rights, atheism, drug legalization, sex education, euthanasia, feminism, gun control, globalization, mass immigration, gay marriage and other radical experiments in social engineering."[28] A list of the many nongovernment organizations receiving Soros funds can be found at DiscoverTheNetworks.org.[29]

The Religious Left

Soros spends untold millions of dollars pushing his open borders and illegal immigration agenda in order to achieve what the Left foresees as a "permanent progressive majority." The push for amnesty and voting rights for illegals is a fundamental part of his open-society plans for breaking down borders and creating what amounts to a one world government run by a global elite. Soros knows, however, that conservative and Christian voters will never willingly support those goals, so he uses his wealth to mobilize hundreds of militant leftist organizations to protest, create disturbances, and arouse so much pandemonium and fear that those who disagree with his objectives will be too intimidated to resist.

But, as Rebecca Hagelin writes for Townhall.com, it goes even further because Soros also believes that if enough money is thrown their way, even the most ardent traditionalists can be bought off. And this is particularly true for liberal and left-leaning ministers such as the Rev. Jim Wallis, who founded the Christian social justice organization Sojourners in 1971 and serves as founder and president of the liberal *Sojourners* magazine.[30] Between 2004 and 2007 the Sojourners organization received grants from Soros-funded groups totaling $325,000, according to a *National Review* report by Jay Richards, which are part of at least forty-nine separate foundation grants between 2003 and 2009 totaling $2,159,346. "Not one of these," Richards discovered, "is from a discernibly conservative foundation. Very few are from discernibly Christian foundations."[31]

Father Robert Sirico, president of the Acton Institute, reported in the *Washington Times* that the Soros-funded Open Society Policy Center had made donations totaling $650,000 to two faith-based organizations. If anyone were to conclude that Soros has found religion, Sirico says, they would soon discover that "the motivation for the philanthropy… is far more banal." Whether they are "faith-based" is a matter of debate, but the organizations Faith in Public Life (FPL) and PICO National Network (renamed Faith in Action in 2018) are actually grassroots political action networks. In his initial funding of these groups, Sirico discovered through a review of leaked documents, Soros was attempting to mobilize ten thousand volunteers to influence the Catholic Church during the visit of Pope Francis to the United States in 2015. On the surface, he says, the donations seem benign. However:

> What's disconcerting is the crass political intention to manipulate church leaders that is evident from the leaked documents. One gets the impression that Mr. Soros and his fellow travelers view the leadership of the religious community generally and the Catholic Church in particular as mere useful idiots to be manipulated to further their own political and, frankly, secularist agenda.[32]

In an article for the Capital Research Center, Neil Maghami reports that FPL bills itself as a network of faith leaders and is identified on the organization's website as "a national network of nearly 50,000 clergy and faith leaders united in the prophetic pursuit of justice and the common good. With staff in four states and growing, we work closely with our members to take strategic moral action that shapes policy both locally and nationally. We believe that faith leaders have unique moral power to influence public debates and build more just and equitable communities."[33] Founded in 2005 and based in Washington, DC, FPL received approximately $1.7 million in grants from the Foundation to Promote Open Society between 2012 and 2015 and reported revenue of $2.252 million in 2015.[34]

Leading the charge against the religious Right is the Rev. Jennifer Butler, who serves as executive director of FPL and is the former chairperson of the White House Council on Faith and Neighborhood Partnerships for the Obama administration. FPL has engaged in a vigorous and ongoing assault on President Trump and his pro-America, pro-business, pro-faith agenda. On November 23, 2016, FPL circulated a letter signed by fifteen hundred clergy condemning President Trump's "cabinet of bigotry," calling them the "ambassadors of hatred, bigotry and intimidation."[35]

On January 9, 2017, Reverend Butler and associates organized a protest march of two hundred "moral leaders" on Capitol Hill to oppose the president's nomination of Sen. Jeff Sessions as attorney general. A short time later FPL circulated an op-ed by the director of the group's Catholic outreach, John Gehring, which said, "People of faith who want to give moral cover to Trump's actions turn their backs on Jesus."[36] Then, on February 23, the organization issued a press release about a letter signed by four thousand clergy condemning "any policy change that would bar refugees based on their religion or nationality," referring to Trump's ban on Muslim refugees.[37]

On March 6, 2017, FPL issued a press release about a press conference to "condemn President Trump's executive order banning the entry of immigrants and visitors from Muslim-majority countries."[38] Then, in April, they issued a press release about a prayer vigil in the nation's capital "to urge Congress to reject President Trump's sinful and immoral federal budget proposal, which makes deeply destructive cuts to programs that address human needs in order to increase Pentagon spending."[39] To further their left-wing agenda, FPL has also published a voter guide, *Faith, Values and the 2016 Election: Toward a Politics of the Golden Rule*, endorsed by some two hundred religious leaders representing various Christian, Jewish, and Muslim organizations. Predictably, the guide focused on global warming, immigration, gun control, racial justice, national security, and the economy, with little mention of actual faith.

In June 2013, Maghami reports, another intervention by FPL into Catholic matters took the form of a pamphlet titled "Be Not Afraid?" The pamphlet criticizes the Catholic Campaign for Human Development, a once-reliable source of funding for "grassroots community organizing," for giving in to pressure from "conservative Catholic activists and their ideological allies on the political right" and defunding various organizations for political reasons.[40] A June 2017 *Foundation Watch* article offers a helpful analysis of this situation.[41]

The authors of the pamphlet asserted that the newly appointed bishop of the diocese of Santa Rosa, California, Fr. Robert Vasa, had a role in denying funding to the radical North Bay Organizing Project in that city. Vasa expressed distaste for the group's "Alinsky-style organizing."[42] The reference to the Hillary Clinton mentor Saul Alinsky, the author of *Rules for Radicals* and a notorious Marxist organizer, ought to set off alarms for anyone who understands what the acolytes of Alinsky are really all about.

The other organization, Faith in Action, is active in more than twenty states. The organization's website and literature identified Faith in Action as "a national network of faith-based community organizations working to create innovative solutions to problems facing urban, suburban, and rural communities."[43] It was founded in 1972 by Fr. John Baumann, SJ, between his first and second year of seminary. While doing fieldwork in Chicago, Baumann had contact with Alinsky. Baumann says he was deeply impressed by the radical organizer's arguments and manner. In a 2014 interview published by Holy Names University, Baumann describes how the meeting with Alinsky changed his life, promoting his dedication to community activism.[44]

From 2012 to 2015 FPL received just under $1.9 million from the Foundation to Promote Open Society. But these are not the only religiously oriented, pro-Alinsky organizations on the Open Society grantee list. There's also the Gamaliel Foundation, which has received $550,000 from the Foundation to Promote Open Society since 2012. For a look at the foundation's ties to community organizer Barack Obama, the article "The Gamaliel Foundation: Alinsky-Inspired Group Uses Stealth Tactics to Manipulate Church Congregations," in the July 2010 issue of *Foundation Watch* magazine, provides a closer look at the way Soros money is used.[45]

But the war against Christian values isn't limited to those on the Far Left, such as FPL and Faith in Action. On the CBS Sunday morning program *Face the Nation*, *Washington Post* columnist Michael Gerson, a liberal Evangelical, was asked to comment on the evangelical leaders who supported the president during the Stormy Daniels scandal. The former speechwriter for President George W. Bush replied, "Well, they are acting like, you know, slimy political operatives, not moral leaders. They are essentially saying, in order to get benefits for themselves, in a certain way—they talk about religious liberty and other issues—but to get benefits for themselves, they are willing to wink at Stormy Daniels and wink at misogyny and wink at nativism."[46]

My friend Tony Perkins, the president of the Family Research Council, who was accused of moral duplicity by Gerson in an article for *The Atlantic*, responded by saying his decision to support Donald Trump was due to the dramatic contrast between the two candidates and the good that Trump's conservative agenda would do. "Religious freedom is being restored," he said, "pro-life policies being advanced—the infrastructure of leftist government being dismantled. That's why Gerson and the Left are so enraged." Dr. Robert Jeffress, pastor of Dallas' First Baptist Church and an advisor to the president, agreed: "We are supporting this president because of his policies."[47]

Meanwhile, Dr. Richard Land, president of Southern Evangelical Seminary, said evangelicals "feel culturally and politically besieged" and "feel like their government has been weaponized against them." During a radio interview, Land said, "In a fallen sinful world, sometimes we are forced to make a choice between the lesser evil and the greater evil. And if we do not choose to help the lesser evil triumph over the greater evil, we become morally responsible for the greater evil prevailing." He added, "However immoral you may think Donald Trump is, Mrs. Clinton is more immoral." He added that liberal Evangelicals such as Mike Gerson have missed the point.[48] I could not agree more, and I've described elsewhere that I've made that point not only in *God and Donald Trump* but in various media interviews as well.

Assessing the Impact

David Horowitz and Richard Poe conclude their powerful exposé of George Soros and the Shadow Party, saying:

> Using the power of his great purse and his brilliantly manipulative institutional vision, Soros has constructed a party, a Shadow Party, unlike any in American history. It is not an American-style party that is accountable to the people and subject to their will, but is more like a Leninist vanguard party, fully as conspiratorial and just as unaccountable. Moreover, it is a party improbably constructed by a financial tycoon, skilled at the manipulation of money and markets.[49]

Soros designed and built the open-borders conspiracy out of "institutional elements plucked from every level of the existing social hierarchy." In the process he has helped to mobilize "the party of rebels," they say, "but also the party of rulers—a corporate unity of capital and labor," using the resources of some of the wealthiest and most powerful men and women in the world. And day by day this oligarchy of billionaire radicals is being "insinuated into the heart of the American system."[50]

In another assessment of the impact of the billionaire radicals and their brand of left-wing activism, *Investor's Business Daily* observes:

> This is the real world of progressive politics: Billionaires, big shots, insiders, Washington elites, big unions, all colluding to fracture our democracy into pieces and set one group of Americans against another, for maximum political benefit and power. To this end, they give hundreds of millions of dollars to the Democratic Party, ignore or insult the Constitution, and treat the U.S. political system as a personal toy with which to radically change the very fabric of our nation.[51]

Clearly the damage that can be inflicted on a constitutional republic by actors at this level is immense. That's why it is so important for conservative and Christian Americans to resist the agenda of the radical Left and, at the same time, support the political alternative.

In his concluding remarks to the members of the World Economic Forum in Davos, President Trump pointed out that success is more than money and more than political strategy. "To be successful," he said, "it is not enough to invest in our economy. We must invest in our people. When people are forgotten, the world becomes fractured. Only by hearing and responding to the voices of the forgotten can we create a bright future that is truly shared by all." And in dramatic contrast to the "one world" philosophy of the open-border activists, he said, "The nation's greatness is more than the sum of its production. A nation's greatness is the sum of its citizens: the values, pride, love, devotion, and character of the people who call that nation home."[52]

Looking around the room at the rich and powerful who had come to see what Donald Trump was all about, he said:

> Represented in this room are some of the remarkable citizens from all over the world. You are national leaders, business titans, industry giants, and many of the brightest minds in many fields. Each of you has the power to change hearts, transform lives, and shape your countries' destinies. With this power comes an obligation, however—a duty of loyalty to the people, workers, and customers who have made you who you are.[53]

In closing, he said, "Let us resolve to use our power, our resources, and our voices, not just for ourselves, but for our people—to lift their burdens, to raise their hopes, and to empower their dreams; to protect their families, their communities, their histories, and their futures." That's why he made the decision to run for office, and that's what is happening today in America. By listening to the people and working for their interests, he said, the results have been amazing. "It's why new businesses and investment are flooding in. It's why our unemployment rate is the lowest it's been in so many decades. It's why America's future has never been brighter." And he asked the billionaires of Davos to be part of "this incredible future we are building together."[54]

In 2016, as the November presidential election was rapidly approaching, the Politico website reported that George Soros was more politically active than he had been in years, motivated, they said, by his fear of the recent successes of the conservative political agenda and particularly by Donald Trump, whom Soros accused of "'doing the work of ISIS' by stoking fears." More than any other liberal donor, the writers said, Soros has the greatest "potential to catalyze giving by other rich activists."[55] Considering what we know about the power and influence of the billionaire radicals, the website's almost casual observation ought to be a wake-up call. If there is anything to be learned by taking a closer look at the men and women who are funding the Left today, it is the importance of understanding who these people are, what they have said, and where they are investing their treasure.

While there's cause for alarm in what the billionaire radicals are saying and doing, there is also cause for Christians to rejoice. While the radicals accuse Donald Trump of stirring up "fears," it is they who are fearful that the leftist victories they have scored for half a century may be in jeopardy and it's not a forgone conclusion their side wins. That should be an encouragement but remind us that the fight is not over and we must continue to pray, especially because the man who embodies the recent radical shift to the left much more than any of these largely unknown billionaires is Barack Obama. And he continues to have an agenda even after his term has ended.

CHAPTER 9

OBAMA'S THIRD TERM

When Barack Obama won his Senate seat in 2004, he was a forty-three-year-old former law professor making $85,000 a year. By the time he left the White House in 2017, he was worth an estimated $20 million. Three-fourths of that, according to a review of sixteen years of Obama's tax returns and financial records by *Forbes* magazine, came from book deals. Just $3.7 million came from the former president's government salaries. As Dan Alexander writes:

> The former president didn't waste much time capitalizing on his story once he got to the nation's capital. In January 2005, the same month he joined the Senate, he got approval from its ethics committee for a $1.9 million advance against royalties with Random House for two nonfiction books and one children's book. The Obamas, who had earned less than $300,000 every year from 2000 to 2004, made an average of $2.4 million annually over the next four years, even before Barack got elected president.[1]

At the time, Michelle Obama was vice president of community and external affairs at the University of Chicago Hospitals, where she earned $317,000 in 2005 and $274,000 in 2006. Her personal income tapered off during Obama's presidential campaign, *Forbes* relates. "Then came the big money." When the Clintons left the White House in 2005, Hillary claimed they were "dead broke," but since that time they've taken in more than $240 million, mainly from high-paid speeches and book deals.[2] Following their example, and with the aid of their billionaire supporters, the Obamas would no doubt have an opportunity to take in much more.

As best-selling author Peter Schweizer has explained, money is a big part of the game in Washington politics. "For many, serving in Congress is the best job they will ever get. Besides the income, they are rewarded with power and responsibility. But increasingly, members are leveraging that power and responsibility to create wealth, too....Under crony capitalism," he says, "access to government officials who can dole out grants, special tax breaks, and subsidies is an alternate path to wealth."[3] And it's not just Congress. However much wealth our legislators can accumulate while in office, those at the top of the food chain are doing infinitely better.

Ever since the renegade days of Tammany Hall more than a century ago, the manipulation of government monies by corrupt politicians has been a fact of life. But funneling taxpayer money to friends and supporters, the researchers tell us, has exploded in recent years. With federal expenditures now topping $3 trillion, government officials have "extraordinary opportunities to get a piece of the action."[4] Most Americans would be shocked at the number of government checks being paid out to some of the richest Americans. Shelling out millions can be tricky, Schweizer writes. But if expenditures are presented to the public as an "economic stimulus plan" that creates jobs, then programs such as Obama's "alternative energy" schemes enable government officials to distribute billions to a handpicked set of deserving entrepreneurs.

In fact, Washington has doled out billions in cash and federal loan guarantees to favored individuals in the alternative energy business. When Obama moved into the White House, in January 2009, he immediately began speaking about the need for billions of dollars for an "economic stimulus" to jump-start the struggling economy. Then, of course, more billions were needed for expanding internet access and creating a "smart grid" to guarantee adequate and secure energy resources. Schweizer says:

> Almost entirely unreported by the media is the fact that an overwhelming amount of this money has been directed to wealthy financial backers of President Obama and the Democratic Party.... Many recipients served on the President's campaign finance committee, or functioned as campaign donation "bundlers" (coordinators of individual contributions that can be combined into large gifts), or were major contributors themselves. In short, they raised and donated *millions* for Obama's 2008 campaign, and in return, the companies they own or lead have received *billions* in government-backed loans and outright grants.[5]

Obama assured taxpayers that distribution of the money would be based on merit, rather than political friendships. But, as Schweizer relates, that's not what happened.

A large proportion of the winners of Department of Energy (DOE) stimulus program grants and loans were companies with Obama-campaign connections. Several members of Obama's finance committee and campaign bundlers were selected to receive guaranteed loans, and politicians who supported Obama launched alternative-energy companies and obtained large government grants.

In one program alone, the 1705 government-backed loan program, Obama-connected companies received more than $16.4 billion of the total government allocation. All these firms were owned or operated primarily by Obama's financial backers. As Schweizer says, "Their political largesse is probably the best investment they ever made in alternative energy. It brought them returns many times over."[6] These were DOE initiatives, but internal memos show that the DOE did not handle the grant review process alone. All loans and grants were required to be reviewed by the White House before they could be approved.[7]

The return from the administration's alternative energy investments, however, was not what the public had been led to believe. By 2015, ten years in, the Government Accountability Office reported in its audit that over $800 million in loans had already defaulted under the Energy Department program.[8] All told, in fiscal years 2010 and 2011 there were 345 different federal initiatives supporting solar energy, and just 65 of those initiatives accounted for more than 1,500 solar energy projects managed by six federal agencies.[9] Spending from 2009 to 2014 was estimated in excess of $150 billion on solar energy and other renewable energy projects. The IRS reported that tax breaks for solar and alternative electricity initiatives cost the country nearly $9 billion annually in lost revenue.

Only a tiny share—about 2.2 percent—of America's electricity was generated by wind and solar, and even then it was unreliable, impractical, and expensive, according to a *Forbes* analysis. "All we've really gained for the effort and expense…is the creation of a solar energy establishment, made up of bureaucrats, academics and rent-seeking corporations, whose primary interest isn't generating power, but pocketing public resources.…With so little to show for so many costly initiatives, it should be clear to the objective observer that federal solar power efforts haven't been a productive or prudent use of precious tax dollars."[10]

Post-Presidential Contingencies

In the weeks after Donald Trump's stunning victory, as members of Obama's inner circle came face to face with the reality of their electoral defeat, those who were closest to the president over the past eight years couldn't escape the feeling that "this wasn't how the script was meant to play out. This wasn't how the Obama years were supposed to end." But as political correspondent Jason Zengerle pointed out in a January 17, 2017, article for GQ magazine, this wasn't going to be the end. Instead, it was the beginning of Obama's third term.[11]

I can remember back to how Harry Truman became a beloved elder statesman but stayed out of politics after he left office. It was like that with Presidents Eisenhower,

Johnson, Nixon, and Ford. Only Jimmy Carter has stayed in the limelight, but that is mainly doing do-gooder projects such as Habitat for Humanity. Ronald Reagan, both Bushes, and even Bill Clinton have stayed out of the political limelight. Like all the other chief executives who have wrapped up their season on the nation's biggest stage, the Obamas would find ways to unwind, enjoying another Hawaiian vacation no doubt and setting up their new home in Washington, DC's upscale Kalorama neighborhood. But this was going to be a much bigger change than they or any of their friends, advisors, and confidants had anticipated. With a Clinton victory, Obama would have continued to influence national policy for a decade or more. He would have had a leading role. But if anything of that nature were to happen now, in the shadows of the Trump administration and the Republican-controlled Congress, it would require a different set of rules. It would have to be carried out behind the scenes.

As former Obama advisor Dan Pfeiffer explained to Zengerle, "For the first time in eight years, as Obama seeks to comfort Americans going through a traumatic event, he knows in the back of his mind that his life has also irrevocably changed. This time, it's not a town in Oklahoma flattened by a tornado; it's him." Pfeiffer said the Obama legacy could have continued for generations if the Democrats had won three in a row. Everyone in Obama's circle believed a Clinton win would guarantee Obama's legacy. Then he added, "Some of the battles that would have been settled with a Clinton win will now continue for the next four to twenty years."[12]

Another Obama advisor told the writer there was a contingency for what Obama's post-presidency would look like, depending on a Clinton victory. "Then Trump happened and that threw it all in the trash bin. Now it's Plan B." The new contingency called for a strategic realignment. Everyone who knows him, Zengerle writes, knows that Obama would never be content sitting on the sidelines, as Bush and Clinton had done. Rather, he would be looking for the right moment to get back in the action, "so as to achieve maximum impact."[13]

The most likely outcome, according to those who know him best, would be to engage in a feud with Trump over a major policy issue, such as the effort to kill Obamacare, the Iran deal, or any of the various EPA initiatives his administration had promoted. The attempt to eradicate every last vestige of Obama's legacy could easily set off a major political battle. The biggest question confronting Obama, the GQ article contends, would be when and how to attack. Pfeiffer told the writer that former Obama staffers had no illusions about what lay ahead. "No one will view it as sufficient to sit on the sidelines." Like their boss, the former White House crew was already preparing for the battle that was just getting started.[14]

Community Organizer in Chief

The community-organizing former president has set up shop in the shadow of the White House. According to author and researcher Paul Sperry, a former Hoover Institution media fellow, Barack Obama is waging a political insurgency behind the scenes, funding and training radical protest groups to resist Trump's policies and scheming to flip the GOP majority by turning red states blue. Sperry writes:

> From his sprawling DC office not far from the White House, where he oversees a full-time staff of 20, Obama has held regular meetings with Democratic lawmakers, as well as DNC chief Tom Perez, whom he personally helped install to run the Democratic Party. Obama has also met with his attorney general, Eric Holder, to craft a strategy to redraw congressional district maps in Democrats' favor, according to Politico. Holder now runs the National Democratic Redistricting Committee, which Obama helped his old friend launch.[15]

The organization he created while still in office, Organizing for Action (OFA), has now become the organizing and training hub of the anti-Trump resistance, says Sperry. It's helped stage protests all over the country against Trump's border policies. While it describes itself as a "nonpartisan grass-roots-driven organization," OFA is the post-Obama White House, working to continue the former president's leftist agenda. OFA is run, in fact, by former campaign advisors and staffers from the Obama White House. The problem is not that Obama is working overtime to defend his flagging legacy but that he is using the wealth and influence of leftist agitators such as Soros and Steyer to destabilize the country.

"OFA," Sperry says, "has formally partnered with one of the angriest resistance groups, Indivisible Project, which has been criticized for using overly aggressive protest tactics against Republicans at town-hall meetings." Indivisible Project was behind the attacks by OFA-trained agitators who stormed Republican districts during the Fourth of July recess in the attempt to shout down "Trump's racist policies," as the Invincible website admits. Obama has helped OFA score between $6 million and $14 million in donations a year, Sperry reports, and is funded in part by the Democracy Alliance, which is the league of leftist power brokers supporting Soros' Open Society Foundations.[16]

OFA, incidentally, is connected to radical groups that have dispatched agitators to protest outside the homes of administration officials, including Homeland Secretary Kirstjen Nielsen, whose privacy was invaded in June 2018 by masked protesters blaring audiotapes of crying immigrant children and chanting, "No justice, no sleep!" throughout the night. These are not the actions of citizens in a democratic republic and not the kind of politics most Americans will appreciate.

Many who had profited from the Obama years were more than ready for that battle to begin. Among the staunch Obama backers was PBS commentator Bill Moyers, former press secretary for Lyndon Johnson and a Baptist seminary graduate, whom I met once when he was invited to speak to a group of evangelical publishers. I knew at the time he was a little left of center, but over the years he has become known for bashing conservatives and Evangelicals. Moyers was so distressed by Clinton's loss that, along with his writer, Michael Winship, he penned a draft inaugural address for the defeated candidate to announce the unveiling of a new "shadow government" to counter and undermine the Trump presidency.

What Moyers was proposing was a radical movement drawn from the legions of angry and humiliated Obama supporters who found themselves suddenly without a country. The aim was to track every plan and proposal of the Trump administration, to raise alarms and dissent, and then to gum up the works and take direct action, as needed, to defeat the Trump agenda at every turn. Every proposal and every executive action would have to be challenged, regardless of the damage done to the country.

Leading the charge would be a core group of political insiders who know how Washington works, along with "mayors, state legislators, public servants, activists and organizers who know the needs of our municipalities, counties, and states across the country." Working behind the scenes, this new government would have its own executive cabinet, secretaries of state, treasury, education, health and human services, and all the rest to deal with the fallout, to provide real leadership, and to relieve the feelings of hopelessness that had overcome the nation since Clinton's defeat.[17]

Hillary never gave that speech, of course. Perhaps she never read it. But in hindsight Moyers' fanciful proposal appears not merely foolish but seditious. Moyers claimed the proposal was in the great tradition still carried on by parties currently out of power in Great Britain. But there is no accommodation in American law or tradition for a "shadow government," and forays carried out by former government officials—such as former secretary of state John Kerry's unauthorized meetings with the leaders of Iran—are not only potentially illegal but extremely dangerous and would likely lead to serious consequences. Nevertheless, Moyers believes he speaks for a large contingent of disoriented refugees from the Obama years who believe their mission is not finished.

A Biblical Parallel?

If Moyers had paid more attention in his Baptist Sunday school class as a kid, he may have learned the lessons of King Ahab and his wicked queen, Jezebel. Instead of veering left as he has as an adult, he might have understood that in the story of Ahab and Jezebel is a foreshadowing of modern America. This parallel was brought to light by Jonathan Cahn in his eye-opening book *The Paradigm*. Cahn, a Messianic rabbi and *New York Times* best-selling author whose books I've had the privilege of publishing, saw a similarity between the Clintons and Ahab and Jezebel, as well as between Barack Obama and Joram (Ahab and Jezebel's son), much like the parallels between ancient Israel and the events of 9/11 Cahn wrote about in *The Harbinger*.

The Paradigm is worth reading for anyone wanting to see how God's hand has been over not only ancient Israel but also modern America. The parallels are astounding. Ahab was in power twenty-two years. He had a power-hungry wife, Jezebel, who brought to Israel the worship of Baal, which included sacrificing babies, a practice not unlike today's abortion. Bill Clinton was also in power twenty-two years from the time he was governor of Arkansas to when his presidential term ended. His power-hungry wife, Hillary, remained in political power as a senator, secretary of state, and unsuccessful presidential candidate. This is similar to Jezebel, who remained in power after the end of Ahab's reign until an unruly, unpredictable outsider named Jehu appeared on the scene, overthrew the worship of Baal, and returned Israel to worship of the one true God. Do you see any parallels to Donald Trump?

In between the reigns of Ahab and Jehu, Israel was ruled by King Joram, who was in power for twelve years, just as Obama was. Joram continued the worship of Baal. And when he met Jehu in battle, Joram said, "Is it peace, Jehu?" Jehu answered, "What peace, so long as the harlotries of your mother Jezebel and her sorceries are so many?" (2 Kings 9:22). Jehu then drew a bow and killed Joram, and he later had Jezebel killed. Back then a person's reign ended when he or she died. Today we have democratic elections or term limits that end someone's reign. But is it possible that somehow Trump will end Obama's influence in the culture and political process? Only time will tell, but as a student of the Bible, I find the parallels here fascinating. While it seems speculation (including Moyers') is rampant, rarely do we look to the Bible to see what's happening.

Meanwhile Obama is still a major influence, and many don't believe his influence is over. In the meantime Obama turned his attention back to community organizing and political activism, where he got his start. In his widely publicized sit-down interview with Britain's Prince Harry for the BBC, Obama said, "I'm really obsessed now with training the next generation of leaders to be able to make their mark on the world. One way I've described it is that I think when you're in politics directly, then you're a player on the field, and there's some element of that you'll never be able to duplicate—the excitement and the thrill and sometimes the agony that goes along with being on the field. And now I'm making that transition to some degree as a coach. And that has its own demands and its own responsibilities and its own impact."[18]

The former president had hinted more than once that if there were enough popular support to mount a challenge to the Twenty-Second Amendment, which limits the president to two terms, he would be willing to run for a third term. He even went as far as telling CNN analyst David Axelrod in December 2016 that he could have beaten Trump if he had been able to run for a third term.[19] The public never took him up on the offer, but as Jason Zengerle pointed out, all he really lacked was the right moment and the right opportunity for a comeback. According to a January 2018 report at Politico.com, Obama has been prepping for a more significant role. He has spoken at political rallies, recorded a robocall, and made a few endorsements. He's made no secret of his long-term plans to be an activist, to help mobilize the next generation of Democratic leaders, and to continue to speak out about his core beliefs. He's even inked a multiyear deal with Netflix to produce films, series, and other projects that "train the next generation of leaders here in the United States and around the world."[20] At some point, the Politico report states, "He'll activate his 15,000-member campaign alumni association for causes and candidates he supports—including the 40 who are running for office themselves. He's already strategizing behind the scenes."[21] There are signs he has been shifting to a higher gear, just waiting for the right moment to reenter the fray.

A Growing Rift

For Donald Trump, the fray began in December 2016 when it was revealed that intelligence officials reported to Congress that they had evidence indicating Russian operatives tried to interfere in the US presidential election, supposedly to help the Trump campaign. Shortly before Obama's term expired, he asked for a report on the situation and called for sanctions against Russian intelligence organizations and several individuals. As part of the Obama administration's response, the State Department expelled thirty-five Russian diplomats and closed two of its US intelligence facilities.

At the time, I believed the sudden announcement of a suspected conspiracy with the inauguration just days away was a bit odd. Something wasn't quite right about the report or the timing of the revelations. Furthermore, insulting the Russians in that manner on the basis of mere conjecture was not a very diplomatic approach. To me and many other Americans, the whole situation sounded fishy, and Donald Trump was justifiably suspicious. So the president-elect asked for an intelligence briefing to confirm what he was being told. Just over two weeks before taking the oath of office Trump was informed the briefing, scheduled for Tuesday, January 3, would be delayed until Friday, January 6, at which point Trump tweeted that he was disappointed the intelligence agencies were so unprepared.

> The "Intelligence" briefing on so-called "Russian hacking" was delayed until Friday, perhaps more time needed to build a case. Very strange![22]

When Senate minority leader Chuck Schumer was shown a copy of Trump's tweet during an appearance on Rachel Maddow's television program, he remarked that Trump was taking a big risk with his criticism. "Let me tell you," he said, "you take on the intelligence community, they have six ways from Sunday at getting back at you. So, even for a practical, supposedly hard-nosed businessman, he's being really dumb to do this." During the discussion that followed, Schumer said, "From what I am told, they are very upset with how he has treated them and talked about them."[23]

Subsequently a CIA official disputed Trump's claim that there had been a delay in delivering the briefing and said a meeting had been arranged for the president-elect with several high-level intelligence officials in New York. Trump received a partial briefing on Tuesday, as planned, but the full briefing was not delivered until Friday, January 6. As reported by the *Washington Post*, the officers taking part in that meeting included Director of National Intelligence James Clapper, CIA Director John Brennan, FBI Director James Comey, and National Security Agency (NSA) Director Adm. Mike Rogers. But before he would have access to the comprehensive review, Trump was told, the document would have to be reviewed by Obama.[24]

The team that would be briefing the president-elect was a noteworthy cast of characters, renowned for their lack of investigatory restraint. All but one (Admiral Rogers) had been caught up in revelations related to the Clinton email scandal. A report from the Office of Inspector General indicated that FBI Deputy Director Andrew McCabe had lied to federal investigators concerning his handling of the Clinton email investigation.[25] Members of the intelligence community leaped to McCabe's defense, but he would be fired by Atty. Gen. Jeff Sessions on March 16, 2018, at the recommendation of the inspector general and the FBI's Office of Professional Responsibility.

But McCabe was not alone. FBI Director James Comey may have lied to Congress when he testified he had not written a report on the email scandal before interviewing Hillary Clinton. Former director of National Intelligence James Clapper and former CIA director John Brennan both lied to Congress. Brennan lied about the CIA spying on Senate Intelligence Committee staff, and Clapper lied about the NSA collecting data on millions of Americans. All three fought the allegations, and in 2015 the internal CIA Accountability Board recommended no accountability for wrongdoing by Brennan.

Brennan had avoided prosecution and apparently believed lying to Congress by CIA personnel was an excusable offense, which may explain his unprovoked verbal attack on President Trump when McCabe was fired two days before his anticipated retirement. There was no disputing the fact that McCabe had lied to Congress and would likely face prosecution, but Brennan lashed out at the president on Twitter, saying:

> When the full extent of your venality, moral turpitude, and political corruption becomes known, you will take your rightful place as a disgraced demagogue in the dustbin of history. You may scapegoat Andy McCabe, but you will not destroy America…America will triumph over you.[26]

Again, the former CIA director was quick to defend a member of the inner circle who had repeatedly broken the law. But there was more to the story. Ohio Republican Jim Jordan, a member of the House Judiciary Committee, told Fox News host Laura Ingraham, "He didn't lie just once; he lied four times." The congressman said, "He lied to James Comey, he lied to the Office of Professional Responsibility, and he lied twice under oath to the inspector general."[27]

Brennan's tirade caused a brief stir, but even the editorial board of the *New York Times* perceived the folly of his intemperate remarks. In an unsigned editorial, published two days after Brennan's tweet, they wrote:

> Declarations like these may be important to make and gratifying to read, but they really shouldn't be coming from those whose integrity depends on them remaining outside the political fray, even in these insane times. For starters, they make it easier for Mr. Trump and his defenders to argue, as they already do, that crucial witnesses in the investigation by the special counsel, Robert Mueller, into the Trump campaign's possible ties to Russia are biased against the president.[28]

There it was. The objectivity of three high-ranking officials associated with the probe into Russian collusion with the Trump campaign was becoming a matter of concern. Schumer had warned the president about the damage the intelligence community could inflict on anyone who dared to question their tactics. Clearly, Trump's suspicion about the objectivity of the partisan heads of the intelligence agencies was warranted, and this became even more apparent after Trump's handpicked appointee, Atty. Gen. Jeff Sessions, recused himself from having any part in the Russian influence investigation.

Sessions' recusal was suspicious, but he said he voluntarily recused himself because of Rule 28 CFR 45.2, which states that DOJ personnel may not participate in a criminal investigation or prosecution if they have a personal or political relationship with any person or organization that may be the subject of the investigation.[29] Since he had been an advisor to the Trump campaign, he turned the investigation over to his deputy, Rod Rosenstein, who then appointed the special counsel for the investigation.

A Trail of Devastation

It was clear to anyone familiar with the close-knit network inside the agencies that this was a huge conflict of interest and a violation of the same rule Sessions had cited for his recusal. The team of lawyers and investigators assembled by Mueller is made up of mostly Democrats and includes many Clinton contributors. One of the DOJ attorneys had represented the Clinton Foundation, and another attended Hillary Clinton's election-night event in New York.

Rosenstein was the official who recommended that President Trump remove James Comey from his post as FBI director for poorly handling the investigation of Hillary Clinton, yet most of the outrage after Comey's firing fell on the president. Rosenstein made it appear he had the president's back but then appointed his close friend Robert Mueller as special counsel to investigate the president and others associated with the Trump campaign.

Look at how none of the agency heads were interested in pursuing Clinton for her misuse of secret government documents, for her unauthorized email server that had been compromised by Russian and Chinese hackers, or for deleting more than thirty thousand emails—one of the most blatantly obvious scandals in American history. But going after the sitting president based on a salacious document paid for by the Clinton campaign and an undisclosed group of big-money backers was another matter. Should anyone be concerned?

Congressman Louie Gohmert, former chief justice of the Twelfth Circuit Court of Appeals, made it clear he is concerned. In April 2018 he published a detailed forty-eight-page report titled, "Robert Mueller: Unmasked," which lays out Mueller's "long and sordid history of illicitly targeting innocent people." In the report Gohmert says the special counsel "lacks the judgment and credibility to lead the prosecution of anyone." He adds that anyone who examines Mueller's record at the FBI will be confronted by a long-established pattern of indicting innocent people and forcing them into bankruptcy by running up their legal fees.[30]

One of Mueller's favorite tricks, he says, is to go after the family of his targets, threatening prosecution and forcing targeted individuals to plead guilty to protect family members. This is possibly how the FBI was able to force a confession from former national security advisor lieutenant general Michael Flynn for lying to the FBI. Flynn had broken no laws, but by going after Flynn's son, Mueller got his man and basked in the praises of the liberal media.

In 2003 then Deputy Atty. Gen. James Comey convinced Atty. Gen. John Ashcroft, whom I have interviewed several times as governor of Missouri and US senator from Missouri, to recuse himself from the investigation into the source of leaks that revealed the identity of CIA agent Valerie Plame. Comey named former US Attorney Patrick Fitzgerald, the godfather of one of Comey's children, as special counsel. Mueller, Comey, and Fitzgerald knew very early in the investigation that Deputy Secretary of State Richard Armitage was the person who leaked Plame's identity, but they weren't interested in Armitage. They wanted either Vice President Dick Cheney or Bush advisor Karl Rove.

In the end they settled for Cheney's chief of staff, Lewis "Scooter" Libby. They offered Libby a chance to flip on his boss, but when he refused, he was charged, tried, and convicted in 2007 for perjury and obstruction of justice. It was one more example of the lengths the partisan defenders of law and order would go to, to destroy an innocent man. Eight years after Libby's conviction Judith Miller, the *New York Times* reporter whose testimony was instrumental in Libby's conviction, recanted her story. George W. Bush had commuted Libby's sentence, and on April 13, 2018, President Trump pardoned Libby, saying, "I don't know Mr. Libby, but for years I have heard that he has been treated unfairly. Hopefully, this full pardon will help rectify a very sad portion of his life."[31]

The same kind of irresponsible prosecution was used against Alaska senator Ted Stevens. The senator, who had represented his state faithfully since 1968, was indicted by the Justice Department in 2008 on spurious charges related to payment for a rural cabin. "One would think before the U.S. government would seek to destroy a sitting U.S. Senator," says Gohmert, "there would be no question whatsoever of his guilt. One would be completely wrong in thinking so when the FBI Director is Robert Mueller."[32]

During congressional debate over the Obama administration's controversial Obamacare bill, Stevens, the longest-serving senator in US history, let it be known that he would be voting against the bill. His one vote could be the difference in whether the bill passed. But the FBI indictment, based on fraudulent testimony, made sure Stevens' vote would never be counted.

Much later, an independent investigation found that the prosecution of Senator Stevens was "permeated by the systemic concealment of significant exculpatory evidence, which would have independently corroborated Senator Stevens' defense and his testimony, and seriously damaged the testimony and credibility" of the FBI's cooperating witness.[33] It was shown that, rather than cheating on payments for his cabin, Stevens had actually overpaid by more than 20 percent.

"Someone should have gone to jail for this illegality within the nation's top law enforcement agency," writes Gohmert. "Instead, Senator Stevens lost his seat, and surprise, surprise, Mueller's FBI helped another elected Republican bite the dust."[34] Senator Stevens was exonerated and returned to civilian life, but tragically he died in a plane crash in August 2010.

Gohmert's report offers a long and disturbing account of the malfeasance and manipulation of the justice system by Mueller, Comey, and their teams of investigators. The destruction of Pennsylvania congressman Curt Weldon is another such example. During the aftermath of the 9/11 terrorist attacks, Representative Weldon dared to point out that the FBI had ignored evidence from the Able Danger investigation, which warned that an al Qaeda cell that included Mohammed Atta had been identified. Under Mueller's leadership, the FBI chose to ignore the evidence that could have prevented that national tragedy.

But here again, Chuck Schumer's warning to the president comes into play. On the morning of October 16, 2006, television news cameras captured the FBI raid on the home of Weldon's daughter, allegedly to see if Weldon improperly helped his daughter win consulting contracts. It was a spectacle manipulated for maximum impact. "The early morning raid by Mueller's FBI with all the media outside, obviously alerted by the FBI, had achieved its goal of colluding to abuse the federal justice system to silence Curt Weldon by ending his political career. Mueller's FBI worked it like a charm."[35]

These and other revelations provide a devastating portrait of the special counsel's abuse of his authority over many years and raise important questions about the motives, tactics, and objectives of the individuals and groups pushing so hard for the Russian collusion investigation. "People say those kinds of things just don't happen in America," Gohmert writes. "They certainly seemed to when Mueller was in charge of the FBI, and they certainly seem to while he is Special Counsel, as well."[36]

The Coming Train Wreck

Columnist and historian Victor Davis Hanson has written extensively on the political theater surrounding the never-ending Russian collusion investigation and predicted in April 2018 that the nation was about to witness a train wreck. Coming from one direction, he said, is Robert Mueller's investigation, in search of any conceivable thing to damage or destroy Donald Trump's presidency. From the other direction comes a series of congressional investigations, Department of Justice referrals, and inspector general reports focused on improper or illegal FBI and DOJ behavior during the 2016 election. Both of these high-powered engines are racing forward at full speed, headed for a dramatic collision.

"Why are the two now about to collide?" Hanson asks. "By charging former National Security Adviser Michael Flynn for lying to the FBI, Mueller emphasized that even the appearance of false testimony is felonious behavior. If that is so, then the DOJ will likely have to charge former Deputy FBI Director Andrew McCabe with perjury or related offenses."[37] According to Hanson:

> Former FBI Director James Comey may also have lied to Congress when he testified that he had not written his report on the Hillary Clinton email scandal before interviewing Clinton. Former Director of National Intelligence James Clapper and former CIA Director John Brennan lied under oath to Congress on matters related to surveillance. Clinton aides Cheryl Mills and Huma Abedin likely lied when they told FBI investigators they had no idea their then-boss, Hillary Clinton, was using an illegal private email server for official correspondence. Both had communicated with Clinton about it.[38]

On at least four occasions, writes Hanson, FBI and Justice Department officials misled the people, saying the Russian dossier compiled by British spy Christopher Steele was the source of information used in applications to the Foreign Intelligence Surveillance Court. The Special Counsel is still looking into the possibility of collusion with Russia. But if the FBI's objective is to uncover and prosecute collusion, the Justice Department will have to look more carefully at the Clinton campaign, which paid Christopher Steele to dig up as much dirt as he could find on the Trump campaign in order to produce evidence of interference by the Russians.

If and when that collision comes, first responders will have a lot of emergency cleanup to do. As this book heads to press, former Trump campaign manager Paul Manafort has been convicted of eight counts of financial fraud. A jury failed to reach a verdict on ten other counts, and the judge declared a mistrial on those charges. But as columnist Jed Babbin wrote in the *American Spectator*, while Manafort was still a "cooperating witness" in Mueller's investigation, he was surprised by a predawn raid on his home on Mueller's orders: "a harsh tactic," Babbin says, "normally reserved for serial killers, drug traffickers, and mafia dons who might destroy evidence."[39]

Manafort's lawyers insisted the charges related to bank fraud and other matters should be dropped because they were outside the authority granted to Mueller to investigate evidence of collusion. Mueller managed to indict and convict Lieutenant General Flynn for lying to federal agents despite the fact that, as the House Permanent Select Committee on Intelligence revealed, former FBI director Comey testified that FBI agents who interrogated Flynn saw no evidence that Flynn was lying. After that two other minor Trump campaign officials, Rick Gates and George Papadopoulos, pleaded guilty to lying to investigators, and several more charges were filed.

Three convictions, all on process crimes, and none of them had anything to do with the Russian affair. But to show that he hadn't forgotten why he was hired, Mueller indicted three Russian companies and thirteen Russian citizens, demanding they appear for questioning. This was obviously a publicity stunt. DOJ lawyers knew the Russian government would never serve indictments from a US court on its citizens, but Mueller and company were caught off guard when one of the Russian companies, Concord Management and Consulting, chose to appear in court to respond to the charges. When they got the news, DOJ attorneys requested a delay so they could build a case, but US District Court Judge Dabney Friedrich said no and scheduled a hearing for the following Wednesday. In a hearing on Paul Manafort's case US District Court Judge T. S. Ellis III berated the government attorneys, saying something a lot of Americans had been thinking for some time.

Judge Ellis said the DOJ lawyers' characterization of the case was false and amounted to: "We said what this investigation was about but we are not bound by it and we were lying." He added, "You don't really care about Mr. Manafort. You really care about what information Mr. Manafort can give you to lead you to Mr. Trump and an impeachment, or whatever."[40] The DOJ team was surprised but not dissuaded by the rebuff.

While these setbacks may not have derailed the investigation, they did raise questions about the strength of Mueller's case. Given the growing concern and scrutiny of Mueller's work, as Politico points out, "even small hitches are welcome news for a White House looking for evidence that the Russia probe has gone too far."[41] Before

Manafort's conviction two federal judges questioned Mueller's authority to bring charges on matters unrelated to the presidential election, including the allegations against Manafort. In response to the honest and encouraging actions of the federal judges, Trump tweeted:

> The 13 Angry Democrats in charge of the Russian Witch Hunt are starting to find out that there is a Court System in place that actually protects people from injustice.[42]

The number thirteen in the president's tweet refers to the thirteen out of seventeen members of Mueller's team who are registered Democrats.[43]

The Never-Ending Struggle

With charges of collusion, lying, and manipulation from both sides, as well as the FBI's use of Orwellian tactics to force confessions from Trump's campaign officials, it's little wonder many have expressed concern about the existence of a bureaucratic entity working behind the scenes in the nation's capital. According to a March 2018 Monmouth University poll, more than 70 percent of Americans, from both political parties, believe a "deep state" of unelected government officials controls the government.[44]

Although many respondents were not familiar with the term *deep state* at first, when given the definition, "a group of unelected government and military officials who secretly manipulate or direct national policy," a majority said they believe such an institution does exist. In addition, 60 percent said they believe unelected bureaucrats wield too much power when it comes to shaping government policy.[45]

Commenting on the results, Patrick Murray, the director of the independent Monmouth University Polling Institute, said, "We usually expect opinions on the operation of government to shift, depending on which party is in charge. But there's an ominous feeling by Democrats and Republicans alike that a 'Deep State' of unelected operatives are pulling the levers of power."[46] President Trump used the term in a January 2018 tweet accusing the "Deep State" Department of Justice of shielding Hillary Clinton aide Huma Abedin, who used a nonsecure private email account while conducting government business.

> Crooked Hillary Clinton's top aid, Huma Abedin, has been accused of disregarding basic security protocols. She put Classified Passwords into the hands of foreign agents. Remember sailors pictures on submarine?

> Jail! Deep State Justice Dept must finally act? Also on Comey & others.[47]

The Monmouth poll also highlighted fears of government surveillance, with 82 percent of respondents believing the government actively spies on private citizens. "This is a worrisome finding," the poll director said. "The strength of our government relies on public faith in protecting our freedoms, which is not particularly robust. And it's not a Democratic or Republican issue. These concerns span the political spectrum."[48]

When CIA whistle-blower Edward Snowden revealed the existence of a massive surveillance program run by the NSA and other even more clandestine agencies, such as the UK's Government Communications Headquarters, the nation was alerted to the fact that every American is potentially vulnerable to government snooping. Millions then realized there are no safe ways to secure private and confidential information or to prevent home and office computers from being hacked by secretive organizations working under the cover of darkness. Snowden revealed that the NSA was spying on tens of millions of Americans, collecting telephone and internet records. Then we learned that Facebook, Google, Yahoo, Instagram, Twitter, and a raft of social media websites were doing much the same thing and selling the information they gathered.

During a private meeting in his home state of Pennsylvania, Rep. Mike Kelly told a group of supporters and friends he was concerned that the former president had set up shop in DC not merely so his younger daughter, Sasha, could graduate from high school but to manage the operation to discredit and derail President Trump. "President Obama himself said he was going to stay in Washington until his daughter graduated," Kelly said. "I think we ought to pitch in to let him go someplace else because he's only there for one purpose and one purpose only, and that is to run a shadow government that is going to totally upset the new agenda."[49]

When video of that meeting was provided surreptitiously to the media, Kelly's office was besieged with questions. In the official response his staff said the congressman does not think Obama is "personally" running a shadow government. However, they said, "He does believe it would be helpful to the new administration if the former president would personally call for an end to all leaks and obstruction by personnel from his administration who currently serve in the Executive Branch under President Trump." The statement noted that Kelly had delivered the remarks to a private audience of Republicans, and he was "sharing the frustration of everyone in the room over how they believe certain Obama administration holdovers within the federal bureaucracy are attempting to upset President Trump's agenda."[50]

Three years after he entered the race for the presidency, President Trump continues to fill arenas with throngs of loud and enthusiastic supporters (page 226). Here he is shown speaking before thousands at a June 2017 rally in Cedar Rapids, Iowa.

White House photo by Stephanie Chasez

President Trump has appropriated more than $700 billion to rebuild and revitalize the armed forces. He is shown here with Vice President Mike Pence and senior military leaders as he signs the National Defense Authorization Act for fiscal year 2018 (page 232).

White House photo by Shealah Craighead

As a graduate of a military school, President Trump loves the military (page 229). Troops at the Marine Corps Air Facility in Quantico, Virginia, welcomed him warmly as he greeted them before delivering remarks to Marine Helicopter Squadron One in December 2017.

White House Photo by Shealah Craighead

Few can deny that the economy has been thriving on President Trump's watch. Unemployment is at a record low, as his policies have given American business a much-needed boost (page 221).

White House Photo by Shealah Craighead

Since his election President Trump has been aggressive about cutting regulatory red tape, which he said grew from roughly 20,000 pages in 1960 to more than 180,000 today. He has determined to save billions of dollars by getting below the 1960s level (page 13).

White House photo by Shealah Craighead

After his face-to-face meeting with North Korean leader Kim Jong-un on June 12, 2018, Trump said he was hopeful for the prospects of peace but warned that the summit was just the beginning of a long diplomatic process (page 80).

Susan Walsh/Associated Press

After the June summit North Korea agreed to repatriate the remains of American soldiers missing in action during the Korean War (pages 80–81). Remains believed to be those of US service members arrived at Joint Base Pearl Harbor—Hickam in Hawaii in August 2018.

White House photo

My friend Mike Evans said (page 196) Israeli Prime Minister Benjamin Netanyahu, shown here with President Trump at the White House, scored his greatest victory with Trump's election. With a Trump-Netanyahu alliance he believes Israel's finest days are yet to come.

White House photo

In August 2018 Trump reinstated economic sanctions on Iran—one of Israel's greatest threats—which had been lifted as part of a 2015 nuclear deal the president had long criticized as horrible and one-sided (page 231).

Image courtesy of Friends of Zion

Even before his election Trump was being compared to the Persian King Cyrus. That comparison gained further prominence when Israeli Temple organizations issued a "temple coin" with Trump's profile and a rendering of King Cyrus (page 199).

Image courtesy of Friends of Zion

When President Trump announced he would move the US embassy to Jerusalem, my friend Mike Evans presented him with the Friend of Zion award in the Oval Office at a meeting with evangelical leaders (page 197).

Image courtesy of Friends of Zion

When Trump visited Jerusalem before the opening of the new US embassy (shown below), banners were posted throughout the city—including on camels—that said "Trump Is a Friend of Zion," "God Bless Trump," and "Trump Make Israel Great" (page 197).

Image courtesy of Friends of Zion

The banners were put up by Friends of Zion, a group founded by my friend Mike Evans. Evans told me that President Trump's bold decision to recognize Jerusalem as Israel's capital gave the Jewish people "exceptional hope" (page 202).

Charisma, the magazine I founded in 1975, was the only Christian publication to publicly endorse Trump in 2016 (page 53). In fact, I devoted the entire October 2016 issue to what I considered to be the most important election of my lifetime.

White House Photo by Shealah Craighead

With the confirmation of Judge Neil Gorsuch (shown above with his wife) to serve on the Supreme Court, Trump kept his campaign promise to select conservatives to fill vacancies on the high court (page 42).

White House Photo by Shealah Craighead

On the National Day of Prayer in May 2018, faith leaders joined Trump as he signed the National Faith and Opportunity Initiative, which will help ensure faith-based groups gain equal access to government funding and are able to exercise their faith (page 171).

White House Photo by Shealah Craighead

The late Billy Graham was the first religious leader to lie in honor at the U.S. Capitol Rotunda. The president and first lady are shown honoring Graham before his memorial service, at which President Trump spoke (pages 209–210).

REUTERS/Kevin Lamarque

Since Trump's election, Evangelicals have had unprecedented access to the president (page 183) and have often been photographed praying with him, as this group of faith leaders did in September 2017 after Hurricane Harvey.

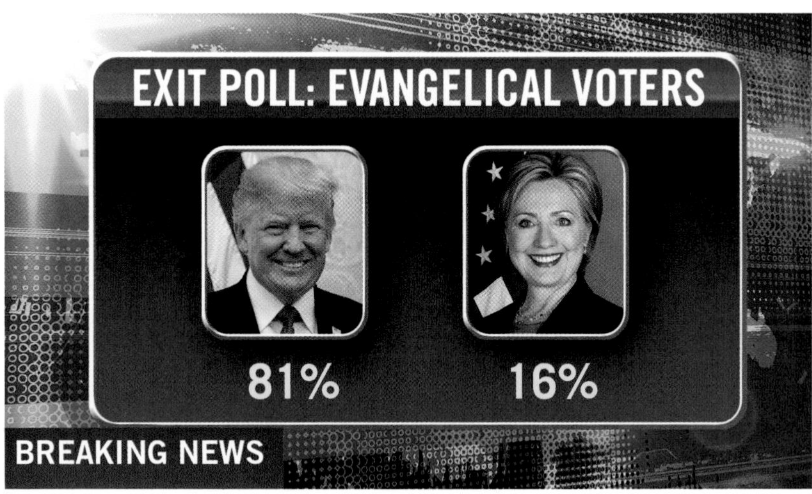

"Fake news" pundits often like to say Evangelicals are divided on Trump, but an overwhelming majority backed him in 2016 (page 38), and I believe a majority of Evangelicals still support the president.

AP Photo/Jose Luis Magana

At the Values Voter Summit in 2015, Trump held up the Bible his mother gave him when he was a child (page 82), which later became one of the two Bibles he placed his hand upon when he was sworn in as president.

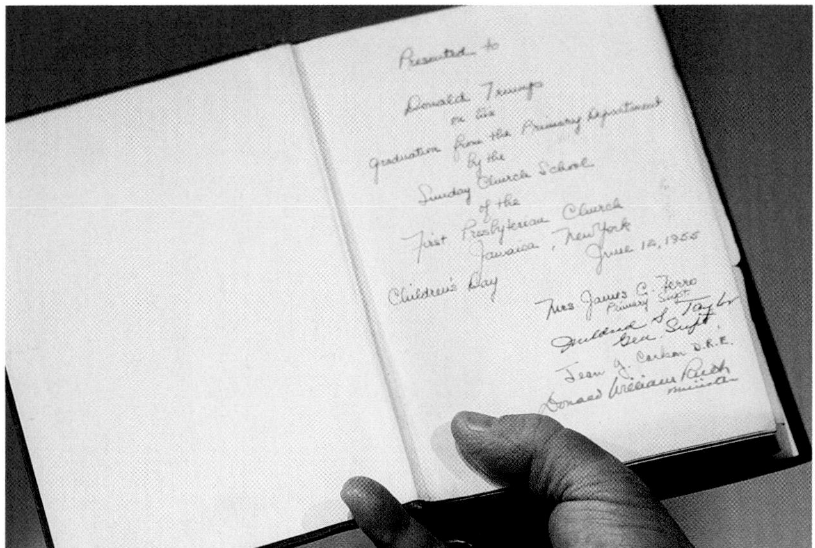

AP Photo/Jose Luis Magana

Trump's childhood Bible, inscribed by his pastor and Sunday school teachers after his graduation from primary Sunday school in 1955, is now on display at the Museum of the Bible in Washington, D.C.

After I met and interviewed Sen. Ted Cruz, I initially endorsed him for president (page 20). But when Donald Trump became the last Republican candidate left standing, I threw my full support behind him, knowing he would be better for the nation than Hillary Clinton.

It was an honor to interview Donald Trump for *Charisma* magazine during the campaign on August 11, 2016. I also had the pleasure of attending his election night party in New York City when Trump was declared the winner (page xiii).

Liberty University

Jerry Falwell Jr., who wrote the foreword to this book, has been a longtime Trump supporter (page 175). Here Trump and his wife, Melania, sit on the front row as Falwell speaks at a private prayer service at St. John's Episcopal Church before the inauguration.

Olivier Douliery/picture-alliance/dpa/AP Images

President Trump spoke to a group of one hundred evangelical leaders in late August 2018 at a White House state dinner to honor the contributions of Evangelicals to American life (page 210).

I posed with Brigitte Gabriel at a conference in California and later interviewed her extensively for this book. A well-known activist on behalf of Israel and the Christian West, Gabriel said she believes Trump is making the world a safer place (pages 189–195).

In addition to secular media interviews, I discussed *God and Donald Trump* on many Christian programs, including *The 700 Club*, where I was honored to be interviewed by my longtime friend Pat Robertson (pages 53–57).

Jim Bakker (shown with his wife, Lori) was the first person to get behind my book *God and Donald Trump* and was the most enthusiastic Trump supporter I met during the campaign.

When I was interviewed on Cornerstone TV in Pittsburgh, I had the opportunity to talk about the supernatural elements of Trump's election, including the many prophecies that had been given that he was going to win in 2016 (page 215–216).

Someone handed the president a copy of *God and Donald Trump* during his trip to the World Economic Forum in Davos, Switzerland, in January 2018 (pages 110–111). I was surprised and understandably pleased when I saw this picture, which was all over social media.

Legitimate Concerns

As noted by the DC publication *The Hill*, Kelly isn't alone in suspecting Obama holdovers of threatening the Trump agenda. The White House press secretary at the time, Sean Spicer, said it's only reasonable to believe that some federal employees may be trying to continue Obama's agenda. "I think that there's no question when you have eight years of one party in office, that there are people who stay in government who are affiliated with and continue to espouse the agenda of the previous administration." During his daily press briefing Spicer said, "I don't think it should come as any surprise that there are people that burrowed into government during eight years of the last administration and may have believed in that agenda and want to continue to seek it."[51]

During a February 2017 CNN interview Kentucky representative Thomas Massie said he believes the deep state controlled by a network of individuals in the permanent bureaucracy is a legitimate threat to the nation. He disagreed with those who believe there's an alliance of former Obama administration officials trying to undermine the Trump administration, but he said the deep state is a legitimate concern. Obama isn't the source of the deep state movement, he said, but he has been integrated into it and used to accomplish its purposes while in office.[52]

When asked about his primary concern, Massie said, "I'm worried it's something deeper than that. I'm concerned that it's an effort on [the part of] those who want a provocation with Russia or other countries to sort of push the president in a direction. So I don't think it's Trump vs. Obama; I think it's really the deep state vs. the president."[53]

In a commentary published one year after President Trump's inauguration, *Newsweek* political writer Sam Schwarz predicted that if Trump and the Republican Party plan on defending their majorities in the House and Senate in the 2018 midterm elections, they're going to have a major factor to contend with: Barack Obama. "The former president enjoyed a busy year since leaving the White House but has largely stayed under the radar," Schwarz wrote. "But he always maintained that he would never leave politics behind." Before his term ended, Obama said he would be politically active, working with candidates seeking to preserve his legacy and accomplishments.[54]

Obama criticized Trump's policies on a number of occasions in 2017, especially regarding issues such as the efforts to repeal Obamacare and deport the Dreamers. He also criticized Trump for his decision to pull out of the Paris Agreement. For most of 2017 the former president's popularity among his core constituency remained high. A September 2017 poll showed that 52 percent of respondents wished Obama was still in office.[55]

If I had heard of the term *deep state* before 2016, I don't remember. But in my few dealings over the years with Washington I began to sense that something was going on behind the scenes because not much changed when the other political party gained control of the White House or Congress. Apparently many Americans feel the same way, if a Monmouth University poll is correct, because more than 80 percent of Americans have a legitimate fear of what the deep state may be doing to undermine and interfere in the way Washington works. If that's the case, Trump and the Republicans may have a lot more to worry about than the former president's appearance on the campaign trail. There is a pattern to all this and a trail that leads to the White House, the Justice Department, the State Department, and halls of Congress. If Victor Davis Hanson is right about the two unstoppable forces approaching from opposite directions, there is a train wreck on the horizon, and God only knows where that could lead.

With all these malevolent forces at home and abroad, President Trump has his work cut out for him. But he is not one to shrink from facing difficult situations. As we will see in the next section, he mounts a strong defense.

PART III

A STRONG DEFENSE

CHAPTER 10

AMERICA AT WAR (WITH ITSELF)

THE ELECTION OF Donald Trump did not create the social and political divide tearing America apart. The forces aligned on the right and the left were already doing that long before Trump or Obama or George W. Bush entered the political arena. But the conflict that has erupted since Trump's victory and Hillary Clinton's defeat has exposed the chasm that divides us more dramatically than any event in the last 150 years.

Americans hardly think any more about the motto that adorns our currency: "E Pluribus Unum." I remember being taught this Latin phrase in school as an example of the dreams of national unity that gave birth to the idea of "From many, one." Today those dreams have all but vanished. The motto once celebrated the birth of a new republic built on mutual interests and our common heritage, along with an almost universal devotion to faith, family, and freedom. But that bond is no longer there. Instead, we're engaged in a bitter feud over core values and beliefs. Who are we, and what do we stand for? Generations of Americans no longer seem to know.

We seldom hear about the culture war that dominated headlines a few years ago. Apparently we're past that point now, and the common culture is in an advanced state of decadence, being ripped apart from the inside out. The national motto, "In God We Trust," which appears not only on our currency but on courthouse walls and monuments of all kinds, has become a source of controversy. We're engaged in a battle over fundamental beliefs and moral convictions, and the result of this decades-long struggle is a dangerous polarization of society between political extremes. There is very little middle ground. In every conceivable way we are a nation divided, which I view not only in political terms but in terms of the spiritual aspect, which I deal with later.

The emphasis on globalism promoted by academic and political elites is a hard-edged repudiation of the common culture. The open-society concept is the enemy of the nation-state. It means tearing down borders and rejecting the laws and customs that have kept America safe and made this nation unique. Rather than celebrating our historic achievements, we're being pushed further and deeper into cultural relativism, social chaos, and the rule of unelected bureaucrats.

The struggle is far from over, of course, and Trump's election has brought a refreshing burst of enthusiasm for conservative principles and ideals. But thanks to the media's unflagging support for the ideology and tactics of the Left, traditional values and the landmarks of Western civilization are taking a beating. The monuments of our collective history are being toppled and hauled away, while defenders of established institutions and traditions are labeled as bigots, racists, homophobes, and worse. Under the tyranny of political correctness, freedom of speech is virtually impossible, religious freedom is threatened, and everyday conversations can be risky and sometimes even lethal.

For centuries men and women from every continent, every race, and every socioeconomic background came to this country to escape classification, but modern liberalism has managed to turn the debate back to race, class, gender, and group identity. As a result, America is becoming fragmented into a collection of warring camps. Dangerous and antisocial behaviors are accepted and even praised by the liberal media. Those who cry loudest about hate and intolerance are often the most hateful and intolerant, using language as a weapon of war and hacking away at the few remaining constructs of social order.

A survey from the American Culture and Faith Institute offers an informative look at the depth of the division. In an interview about the study, George Barna discussed how some Americans are afraid of speaking openly about their love of country or discussing their political views in public.[1] Wearing a ball cap that makes a political statement, such as "Make America Great Again," can start a riot. Bumper stickers have become an open invitation for vandalism. Companies such as Starbucks, Target, Chick-fil-A, and Hobby Lobby are suddenly at the center of controversy because of the social policies and values to which they subscribe. And by allowing football players to express contempt for the nation and the flag—the most visible emblem of our national pride—the National Football League has made itself a punching bag for both the Right and the Left.

The Numbers Speak Volumes

The American Culture and Faith Institute national survey conducted in October and November 2017 discovered two strikingly different definitions of patriotism in America today. There is widespread confusion, it says, about what it means to be patriotic. According to Anne Sorock, executive director of Ear to the Ground Listening Project:

> The findings revealed a fissure in our culture, opportunities to rally around patriotism as a shared value, and also concerns about fluid definitions. They suggest that we are more divided than ever—and neither the left nor the right is content to cede patriotism to the other.[2]

While most Americans believe the country is becoming less patriotic, they tend to believe other people are the problem: they're fine, they say, but their neighbors are unpatriotic, which might explain why only 22 percent of those surveyed said they felt strongly they would be safe wearing a "Make America Great Again" hat.[3] Here's how people responded when asked if patriotism was on the rise in America:

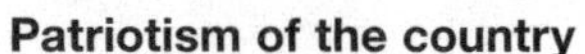

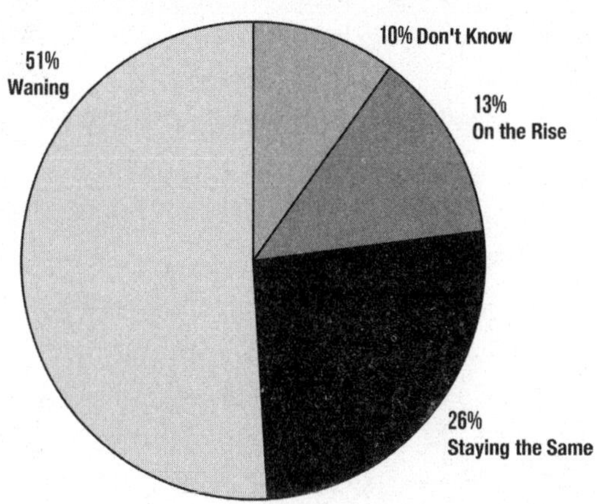

Almost half of the respondents (46 percent) said that it would be completely accurate to describe themselves as "proud to be an American." Here's how that breaks out among conservatives, Republicans, moderates, independents, liberals, and Democrats:

Proud to be an American

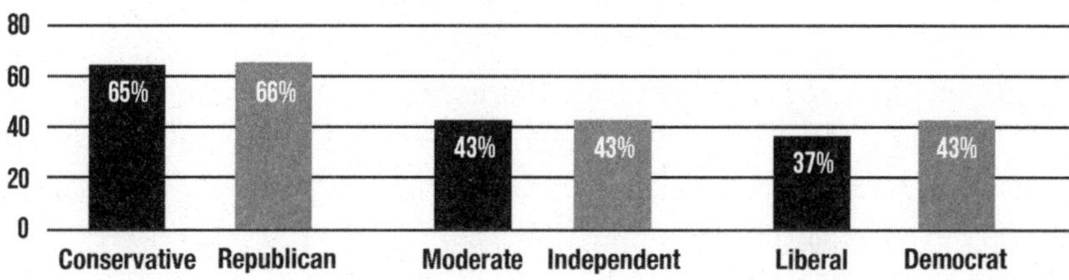

Overall, "freedom of speech" proved to be the most meaningful indicator of the level of patriotism among respondents, with nearly nine out of ten adults (87 percent) saying it was very meaningful to them personally. As you might expect, party and political ideology made a difference in what matters to different groups. According to analysts, "Democrats and independents had similar and significantly lower levels of appreciation for the American flag, the national anthem, the pledge of allegiance, the Bible, and the right to bear arms,"[4] as the following graph illustrates:

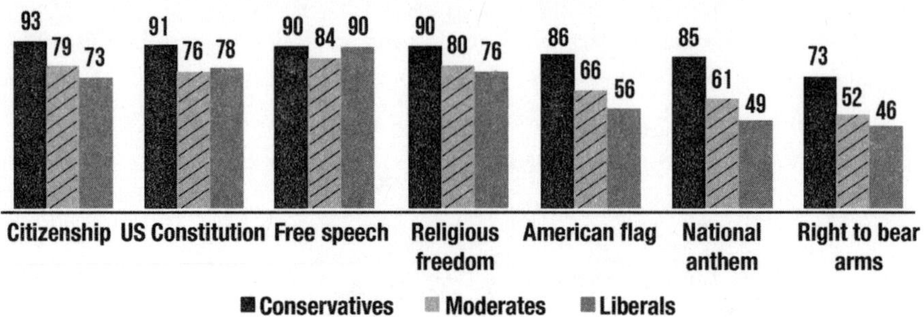

According to the poll, conservatives said the most patriotic organizations and individuals included the National Rifle Association, Chick-fil-A, the Republican Party, Fox News, and Hobby Lobby. The least patriotic organizations to most conservatives are CNN, the *New York Times*, the NFL, Planned Parenthood, Target, and Starbucks. Only between 6 and 9 percent of conservatives considered Colin Kaepernick, Michael Moore, Rachel Maddow, and Al Sharpton to be patriotic.

Liberals, on the other hand, indicated that the most patriotic institutions and people are the Democratic Party, Kaepernick, the US Supreme Court, Planned Parenthood, Moore, the *New York Times*, and the NFL. And, predictably, the least patriotic to liberals are Chick-fil-A, Fox News, and Hobby Lobby.

For poll organizer George Barna, "the NFL 'take a knee' controversy was a cultural flashpoint demanding citizens and leaders to take a stand."[5] The survey showed that conservatives were offended by the NFL, while liberals were excited about the courage of those making a stand. "Trump did the right thing to weigh in," Barna says, "as elected leaders have the responsibility to make sense of the reality unfolding around them."[6]

Ninety-one percent of religious, politically active conservatives turned out to vote in the presidential election in 2016, and 93 percent of that group said they voted for Trump. Most telling, perhaps, is the fact that only 9 percent of religious, politically active conservatives supported Trump in June 2015, but 93 percent of them voted for him in November 2016. Barna says it's also interesting to note that while 58 percent of all Americans voted, a full 91 percent of faith-based voters cast their ballots. Even though many indicated they were still not huge fans of President Trump, they were becoming more comfortable with him on some issues, including his restrictions on abortion and appointment of constitutionalist judges.[7]

I've known Barna for many years. I can't think of a high-profile Christian leader who has written more on worldview than him. He believes a person's worldview is the single most important consideration in evaluating prospects for the nation's future, yet the heated debates over worldviews and basic social and political opinions are pulling the country apart. As a sociologist, Barna concludes that attitudes about God, religion, and the role of faith in our daily lives are the most reliable indicators of America's ability to survive and thrive as a nation.

Liberals and their progressive policies have been waging a cultural and linguistic war in our schools, churches, families, media, and government for decades. Liberals surveyed in Barna's poll said free speech is very important to them, yet there is growing intolerance within the civil debate, and liberals are the most easily offended by points of view that differ from their own. "Cultural marxists have been winning (in our institutions and culture)," says Barna, "but the battle is not over." Barna, who has been conducting national public opinion surveys since the 1970s, feels the cultural debate is hotter than ever today, which is why he founded the American Culture and Faith Institute to focus on what can be done to turn things around.[8]

For more than two decades now, political polarization has been one of the most powerful forces dominating public discourse. According to surveys conducted by the Pew Research Center in June and July 2017, Republicans and Democrats are much more strongly divided on issues like the role of government, environment, race, immigration than on demographic, religious, and educational differences. But what they found most striking, the analysts said, is how little common ground there is on the two opposing sides.

Part of the reason for the shift, they say, is that registered Democrats have moved further and further to the left on key issues, while the views of Republicans and Republican-leaners have moved very little since the mid-1990s. The biggest shifts in the past several years have been Democrats' and Democratic-leaning independents' views regarding race and the role of government, which the analysts feel explains why the views expressed by the general public have taken a more liberal stance. According to their findings:

> In the new study (conducted before violent demonstrations in Charlottesville, Virginia, and recent protests by NFL players), 41% of Americans say racial discrimination is the main reason blacks can't get ahead – up from 18% in 2009 and the highest level dating back to 1994. Virtually all of the change has come among Democrats, with a record 64% saying racial discrimination is the main barrier to blacks getting ahead. Among Republicans and Republican leaners, there has been less change since 2009 (9% then, 14% today). The partisan gap is widening over how much the government should do to help the needy. Half of Americans now say the government should do more to help the needy

> even if it means going deeper into debt, while 43 percent say the government can't afford it. This shift toward more support for the needy is being driven by the 71 percent of Democrats who expressed this view, a dramatic increase since 2011. Only about a quarter (24 percent) of Republicans agree.[9]

The pollsters also found that Democrats are now more likely to favor an active global role for the US, whereas three years ago Republicans and Democrats felt equally skeptical about America playing an active role in world affairs. While 54 percent of Republicans said the US should pay less attention to problems overseas and focus more on problems at home, a majority of Democrats (56 percent) said the country should be globally active, which is up from 38 percent in a similar 2014 survey.[10]

The survey also indicates that acceptance of homosexuality is at record high levels today. Seventy percent of respondents agreed that homosexuality should be accepted. This is the highest percentage in over two decades and the first time that a majority of both Democrats (83 percent) and Republicans (54 percent) favored acceptance of homosexuality.[11]

Wider partisan gap on Trump job rating than for any president in six decades[12]

% approving of president's job during first year

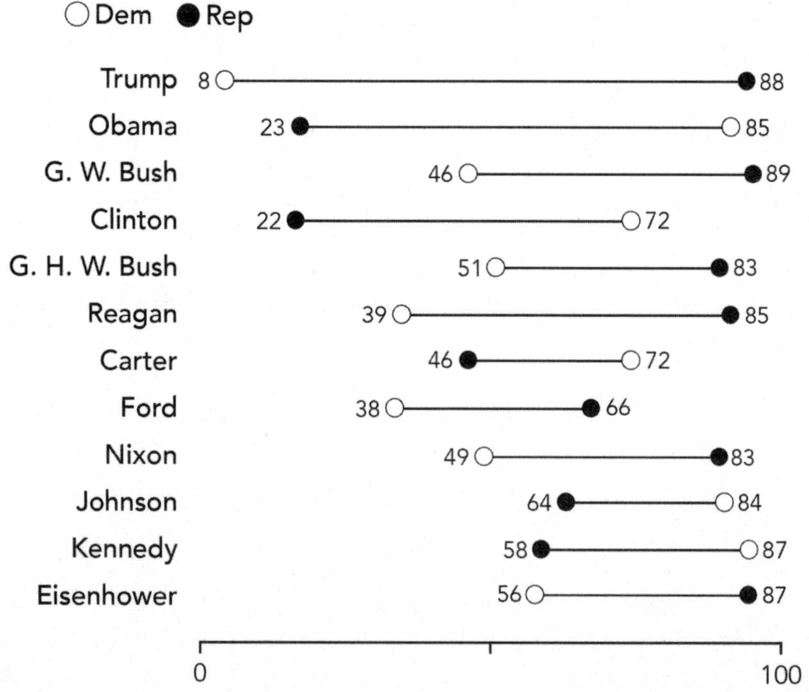

Based on surveys conducted by the Pew center in the first half of 2017, first-year job ratings for President Trump are more polarized than with any president going back to 1953, as the graphic reveals. Generally speaking, we can see a downward trend in job approval ratings for the president from whichever party is not seated in the Oval Office.[13] Even after all the controversy surrounding the Helsinki summit in July 2018 with Vladimir Putin, Trump's approval rating went up according to an NBC News/*Wall Street Journal* poll.[14]

Two Different Worlds

There may be no greater indicator of the disparity between the Left and Right in America today than a comparison of Democratic and Republican attitudes toward traditional values and religious faith. According to a September 2017 NBC News/*Wall Street Journal* poll, the fissures between Republicans and Democrats on cultural issues such as same-sex marriage and religion have grown consistently wider over the past few years. At least 77 percent of Democrats, they said, are "comfortable with social changes" of recent years, while just 30 percent of Republicans felt the same. Forty-two percent of Republicans surveyed support the traditional definition of marriage between one man and one woman, while just 17 percent of Democrats agreed. And in case anyone was wondering, Democrats polled were twice as likely as Republicans to say they never attend church services.[15]

According to the *Wall Street Journal*'s analysis, the divisions in America "reach far beyond Washington into the nation's culture, economy, and social fabric." And, they say, while the high level of polarization began long before Donald Trump's presidency, the 2016 election did more to solidify opinions and attitudes of the two sides than did any other event. These findings help to clarify just how entrenched the cultural differences have become. The findings, they write, "help explain why political divisions are now especially hard to bridge. People who identify with either party increasingly disagree not just on policy; they inhabit separate worlds of differing social and cultural values and even see their economic outlook through a partisan lens."[16]

Addressing similar issues, a *Washington Post* poll in cooperation with the University of Maryland found that nearly three-quarters of Americans believe the United States is as divided today as it was during the Vietnam era—something I vividly remember as a student journalist. Who can forget the violence at the 1968 Democratic convention or the assassination not only of President John Kennedy in 1963 but his brother Robert, who was gunned down five years later as he was running for president? And most tragic of all was the assassination of Martin

Luther King Jr., who since then has become idolized as the one who brought civil rights to millions through his methods of nonviolent protests.

Fully 77 percent of adults age sixty-five and older—that's over three-fourths of the people who were alive and remember the Vietnam War—said the divisions today are as great as they were during the war, with 65 percent of younger adults, age eighteen to twenty-nine, saying the same. The poll also reported that 60 percent believe the political system in the US is dysfunctional, and 36 percent said they're not proud of how democracy works today. This was a surprising increase from the findings of similar polls where people responded that they were not proud of how democracy worked in 1996 (16 percent), 2002 (9 percent), 2004 (10 percent), and 2014 (18 percent).[17]

In other research, pollsters have also noted significant divisions within the political parties and even deeper ones between rural and urban voters. According to a June 2017 report, "The political divide between rural and urban America is more cultural than it is economic, rooted in rural residents' deep misgivings about the nation's rapidly changing demographics, their sense that Christianity is under siege and their perception that the federal government caters most to the needs of people in big cities."[18]

The *Washington Post*-Kaiser Family Foundation survey found that nearly 70 percent of rural residents believe their values are different from those of the people who live in big cities. And approximately 40 percent indicated their values are "very different." Among the poll's urban respondents, half said their values are different from those living in rural or suburban areas, and just under 20 percent of urban respondents said their values are "very different."[19]

There is no question that the United States is engaged in a war of worldviews. The differences between the Right and Left are long-standing and substantial, with little hope of change or compromise. Looking at some of the reasons behind this enormous cultural divide, columnist and author John Hawkins offered a list of seven cultural indicators that the United States is no longer united and that the war of worldviews could become much more than merely a religious or philosophical debate if things continue as they are.

Many conservatives, he writes, are convinced America has gone off the tracks and may be headed for a major split, or possibly even a civil war. Just twenty years ago such a thing would have been unthinkable, even laughable. "Today, the joke isn't so funny," Hawkins says, "because we are a deeply unhealthy society with a dysfunctional government and for all our money, success and storied history, we seem to be on an increasingly dangerous trajectory." Why? For one thing, he says, liberals no longer believe in the Constitution.[20]

Even though they deny it, this is actually what the idea of a "living Constitution" is all about. "You make it up as you go."[21] The Founders intentionally refused to establish the US government as a pure democracy for this reason: because they recognized the instability that would inevitably come from reliance on the whims of public opinion. We're reminded of Benjamin Franklin's response to the woman who asked at the conclusion of the Constitutional Convention in 1787, "Well, Doctor, what have we got—a Republic or a Monarchy?" To that he replied, "A Republic, if you can keep it."[22] What the Founders gave us was a representative republic; however, today many Americans are wondering if we can, in fact, keep it.

A second factor threatening our national unity is what Hawkins refers to as "tribalism," which shows up strikingly in the nation's addiction to social media. Both sides have their preferred outlets and their preferred arguments to use against the other side. Conservatives listen to people such as Rush Limbaugh, Sean Hannity, Ann Coulter, and Donald Trump. Liberals, on the other hand, listen to people such as Elizabeth Warren, Hillary Clinton, Stephen Colbert, and Bill Maher and think anyone who disagrees with them is a racist, bigot, white supremacist, or worse and must be silenced for society to move forward. This makes dialogue difficult. "When every issue is a zero sum war where one tribe must win or lose," Hawkins writes, "a lot of people quite understandably ask, 'What do we gain by staying allied to this other tribe?'"[23]

Other issues pushing us toward dissolution are such things as the size and power of the federal government. As everyone knows, cultural values on the East and West coasts are very different from those in the heartland. But recent laws and social movements have aggressively imposed coastal values on people living in places where those values are not wanted. "When people are unnecessarily forced to live under rules they find abhorrent because the federal government has become an octopus that has inserted its tentacles into every minute crevice of American life," Hawkins writes, "it creates discontent on a wide scale." He adds, "If most Americans wanted to live like people in San Francisco, they'd live in San Francisco."[24]

All this is disturbing, but the issues that have the greatest potential for shredding the fabric of national unity are the ongoing moral decline within our culture and the lack of shared values. We often hear complaints that the American people are losing their manners. It's not just loud and undisciplined children in restaurants but parents and adults of all ages and in all sorts of public places. We also see the breakdown of character and moral discipline in the politicians we elect.

Looking at the "principles, manners and virtue" of Americans today, says Hawkins, we have to wonder how the nation would deal with the kinds of challenges that earlier generations faced, such as the Second World War, the Great Depression, or the Civil War. Few, if any, young people in their twenties could tell you why those events were such challenges in the first place, or why they mattered. The philosopher George Santayana said famously, "Those who cannot remember the past are condemned to repeat it."[25] But in our current condition of cultural, educational, and moral collapse, there's no guarantee the republic the Founders gave us can survive.

The truth is, Americans don't share their admiration for anybody or anything these days. Conservatives and liberals no longer agree on politics, religion, the media, or what qualifies as free speech. We're at the point, as we see so often in today's news, that one man's view of free speech is another man's definition of hate speech. The First Amendment to the US Constitution says, "Congress shall make no law respecting an establishment of religion, or prohibiting the free exercise thereof; or abridging the freedom of speech, or of the press; or the right of the people peaceably to assemble, and to petition the government for a redress of grievances."[26] But all those things have been challenged by the liberal establishment, which is why many are calling for a Constitutional Convention to redefine who we are and what we believe as a nation. This would be a disaster for many of the basic rights we have taken for granted for the last two centuries. Who knows what a new constitution would look like. But for those intent on changing our country to be more godless and socialistic, it would help them achieve their goals.

The Essential Difference

To claim, as many do, that liberals are anti-religious or anti-Christian is one thing, but to show that Democrats believe that churches have a negative impact on society is a couple of steps beyond mere suspicion. But that's precisely what the Pew center's Politics & Policy department discovered when it examined liberal and conservative opinions of the church and other major institutions in the country.

In a July 2017 report Pew found that 36 percent of Democrats believe the impact of the church on society is negative. Just 14 percent of Republicans held that view, but among liberal Democrats 44 percent view churches as a negative influence, while 50 percent of Democrats overall viewed churches as a positive influence.[27]

Wide partisan differences over the impact of major institutions on the country[28]

% who say each has a positive/negative effect on the way things are going in the country

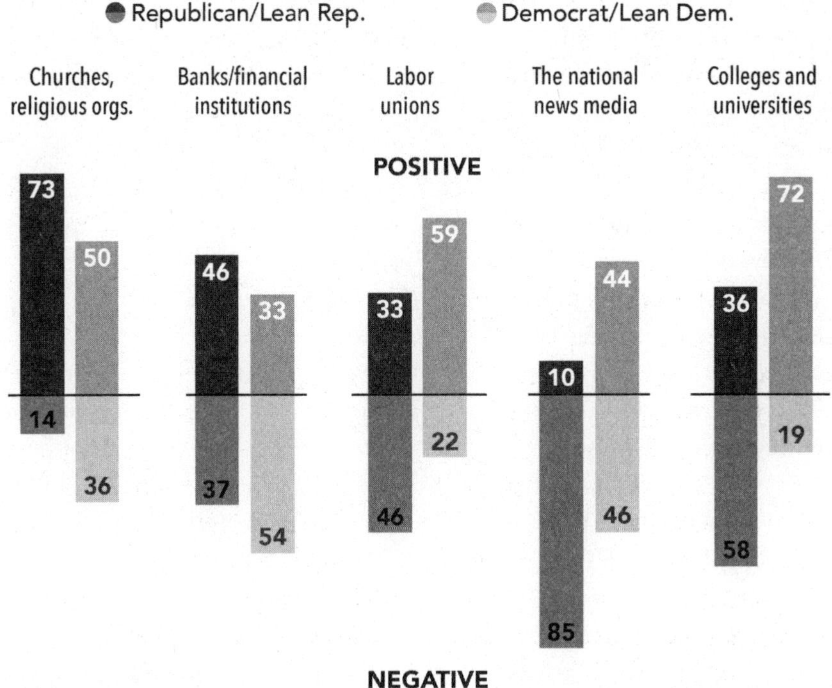

The Pew study revealed that 46 percent of those who don't affiliate with any religion believe churches have a negative impact on society, as do 43 percent of those who seldom or never attend religious services. By way of contrast, the June 2017 survey of 2,504 adults reported that 85 percent of Republicans believe national news media negatively impact society. Only 46 percent of Democrats held that view.[29]

"Among Republicans," the researchers said, "negative views of the news media are shared by large majorities of both conservative Republicans (87%) and moderate and liberal Republicans (80%)."[30] Reacting to the report, Mark Tooley, with the Institute on Religion and Democracy in Washington, DC, said he believes the Democratic party is rapidly on its way to becoming the opposition party to the Christian church in America. "We've [never] really had a political party, as many European nations do, with an opposition to the church," he said, "and hopefully we never will, but the trend seems to be that much of the Democratic Party—a plurality—seems to be heading in that direction."[31]

It would be a great historical irony if the nation were to end up with a two-party system that was essentially a pro-religion political party and an anti-religion political party going head to head in America—a salutary reminder of the English Civil War, with the Protestant Roundheads versus the royalist Cavaliers, which led to the eventual decapitation of the sitting monarch. Hopefully such a fate will never happen here, but "it would be potentially dangerous if one party becomes the almost exclusively pro-religion party and the other party becomes the secular party—which has sometimes occurred in Europe," Tooley said.[32]

"So, a lot of this is just ignorance," Tooley said. He added that "many liberals ideologically are very statist in how they view society, and so for them, the Church and other institutions in civil society may seem peripheral—or unneeded—as the government can do it all on its own." He added that many people hostile to religion fail to fully appreciate the impact religious institutions can have for good in society.[33] But a substantial number of Americans have apparently made up their minds, deciding that the label "No Religion" best describes their belief system.

This is clearly the implication of a widely publicized Pew report from 2012 titled, "'Nones' on the Rise," which showed a steep decline in the number of Americans who identified as Protestant. In the survey of 2,973 adults nationwide Pew asked, "What is your present religion, if any? Are you Protestant, Roman Catholic, Mormon, Orthodox such as Greek or Russian Orthodox, Jewish, Muslim, Buddhist, Hindu, atheist, agnostic, something else, or nothing in particular?" The number who identified as Protestant was 48 percent, down from 53 percent five years earlier. This was in stark contrast to a similar poll from 1960 in which two-thirds of adults identified as Protestant.[34] Catholics showed only a modest 1 percent drop, while Orthodox and Mormons remained steady and the number who indicated "other faith" showed a 2 percent increase. The percentage of those who identified as "religiously unaffiliated" (or "none") increased from 15.3 percent in 2007 to 19.6 percent in 2012.[35]

Whether or not the "none" category has had much traction since the 2012 report, Pew Research Center made an even more remarkable discovery in a 2017 survey looking into the racial component of faith. Pollsters found that "while white Democrats are less likely to be religious than Republicans," Democrats of other ethnicities—generally black or Hispanic—are much closer to Republicans than to liberal Democrats on a whole host of issues, including belief in the God of the Bible.[36] Here's how Pew's analysts illustrated their findings:

In their beliefs about God, nonwhite Democrats more closely resemble Republicans than white Democrats [37]

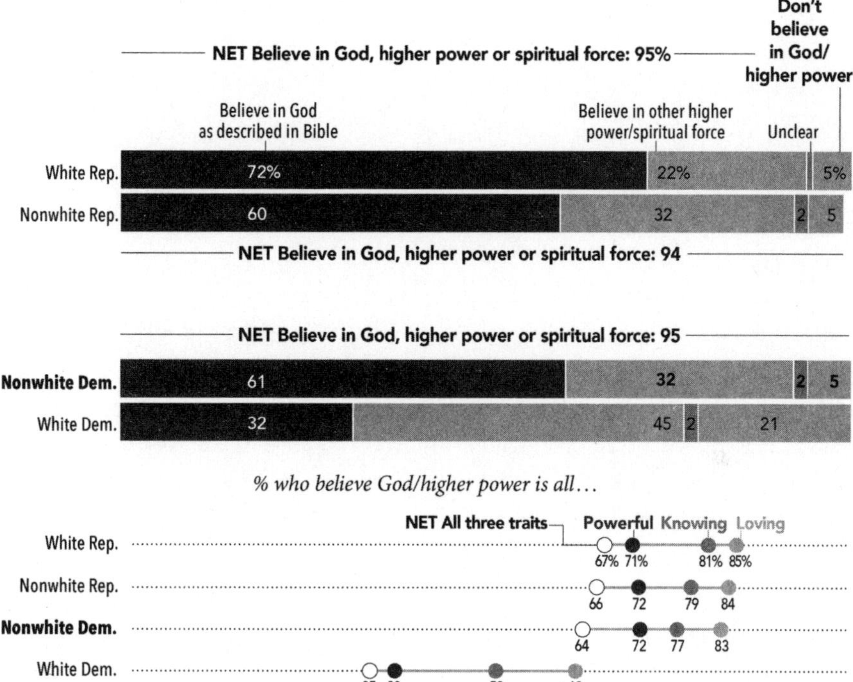

Our nation was founded on Christian principles. Many immigrants (including some of my own family) came for religious freedom. While many would consider America a "post-Christian" society where those who are truly "born again" are no longer a majority of our citizens, that basic belief in God is still strong among Americans. The most recent Pew study of these issues reports that "belief in God as described in the Bible is most pronounced among U.S. Christians. Overall, eight-in-ten self-identified Christians say they believe in the God of the Bible, while one-in-five do not believe in the biblical description of God but do believe in a higher power of some kind. Very few self-identified Christians (just 1%) say they do not believe in any higher power at all."[38]

Pew's 2014 study of religious participation concluded that nonwhite Democrats are as religiously committed as Republicans when it comes to praying and attending church.[39]

On religious attendance, prayer and importance of religion, nonwhite Democrats are more similar to GOP than to white Democrats[40]

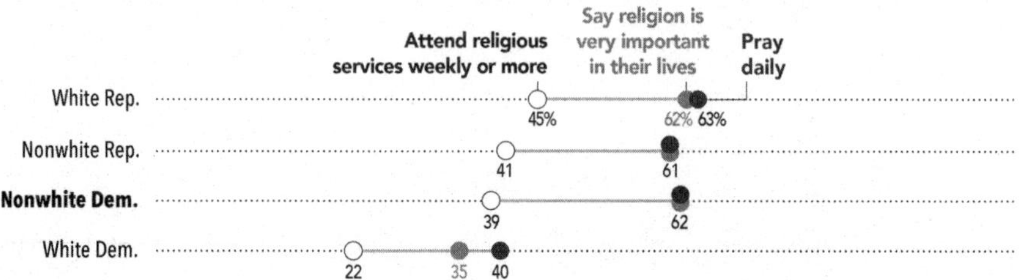

When you narrow the survey results to black Democrats, they are even more religiously committed than Republicans. Nearly half (47 percent) of black Democrats say they attend church at least weekly, and about three-quarters pray daily (74 percent) and say religion is very important in their lives (76 percent). There are some ways that Republicans and nonwhite Democrats do not resemble one another, such as their views on abortion: 58 percent of nonwhite Democrats and 57 percent of black Democrats said abortion should be legal in all or most cases, whereas just 38 percent of Republicans held this view.[41]

When it comes to where they worship, the analysts said, there may not be much overlap. According to the most recent National Congregations Study (2012), while US congregations are growing steadily more racially and ethnically diverse, 86 percent of American congregations "remain overwhelmingly white or black or Hispanic or Asian."[42]

A Seismic Cultural Shift

No single issue so defines the battle taking place within the American culture than the issue of abortion. Since the Supreme Court's 1973 *Roe v. Wade* decision, making abortion legal in all fifty states, data provided by the Centers for Disease Control and Prevention and the pro-abortion Alan Guttmacher Institute indicate that more than sixty million abortions have been performed in this country over the last forty-five years.[43] A survey in 2014 found that approximately 926,000 abortions are performed in this country each year.[44] According to the Guttmacher Institute, 4.6 percent of American women will have an abortion by the time they are twenty years old, 19 percent of women in the United States will have an abortion by age thirty, and nearly one in four (23.7 percent) will have done so by age forty-five.[45]

This is a national tragedy by any reasonable measure, but the issue has become so contentious over the past four decades that it virtually defines the two political parties, with Democrats being overwhelmingly in favor of abortion on demand and

Republicans being overwhelmingly against it. Although groups such as NARAL and Planned Parenthood claim otherwise, abortion is routinely used as contraception of the last resort by women of all ages, both married and single. And despite claims to the contrary, a very small percentage involve the life of the mother, the health of the child, or victims of incest or rape.

Justice Kennedy's resignation announcement in 2018 ignited a flicker of hope in many conservatives for the chance of overturning *Roe v. Wade*. And President Trump's nomination of Brett Kavanaugh is fanning that flame. But despite the sad history of the Supreme Court's disastrous 1973 decision, the most hopeful fact in the abortion debate is the news that a majority of Americans, including Democrats, now have pro-life leanings.[46]

Pro-life leanings of majority of Americans, including Democrats

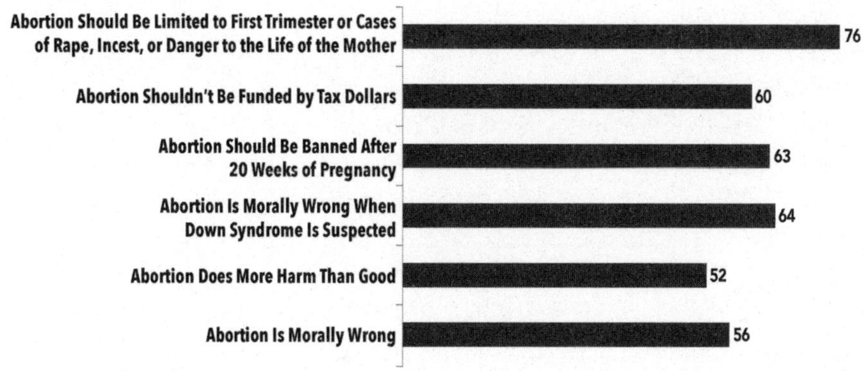

The survey found that strong majorities of Republicans (92 percent), Independents (78 percent), and Democrats (61 percent) feel that abortion should be limited to the first trimester of pregnancy or cases of rape, incest, or danger to the life of the mother. A majority of those who identify as pro-choice (60 percent) also agree with this stance, the poll reported.[47]

These findings were released just in time for the annual March for Life on January 19, 2018. The Washington march is the largest pro-life event in the world and boasted an impressive group of speakers, including Speaker of the House Paul Ryan, several lawmakers and ministry leaders, and President Donald Trump, live by satellite.

"Since his first day in office, President Trump has remained steadfast on his campaign promises to the pro-life cause and has actively worked to protect the unborn," said Jeanne Mancini, who is president of the March for Life. "Over the past year," she said, "the Trump administration has significantly advanced pro-life policy, and it is with great confidence that, under his leadership, we expect to see other pro-life achievements in the years to come."[48] News of this kind is encouraging for the religious and conservative voters who are among Trump's most ardent supporters, but life issues have become a major concern for many in the Democratic Party as well and are apparently attracting voters who have voted for the other side for years.

Issues such as abortion, same-sex marriage, gun control, and illegal immigration are troubling and still hotly debated, but there are signs Trump's conservative agenda is achieving victories in every area of contention. As I mentioned in my introduction, on June 1, 2018, the *New York Times* said it "ran out of words" to describe the incredible successes of the economy under Trump's leadership.[49] Outspoken Democrats such as majority leaders Nancy Pelosi and Chuck Schumer claimed the tax legislation passed in December 2017 would set off a financial Armageddon, but the actual results proved to be just the opposite. In chapter 7, where I discuss the booming economy, I mention the Bureau of Labor Statistics showing employment increased by 223,000 in the May 2018 jobs report, with unemployment dropping to 3.8 percent, the lowest in eighteen years. At the same time, black unemployment was down to 5.9 percent nationally, an all-time record.

Many companies gave bonuses of $1,000 or more, and the mainstream media were compelled to report that millions of Americans would be receiving a tax cut.[50] As Rich Lowry suggested in *Politico Magazine*, the Democrats may have overplayed their hand, pushing a hard-left propaganda message in order to damage Trump, when, in fact, the nation believes Trump's achievements are actually making America great again. "Trump is the racetrack rabbit that keeps Democrats running in a perpetual cycle of outrage," Lowry says. "But a party that's in a perpetual state of hysteria and, on top of that, is operating against the backdrop of an economy with 4.1 [4.0 as of June 2018] percent unemployment, may find it harder than expected to pull off its old tricks."[51]

With Eyes Wide Open

Adding insult to injury, the Democrats' long-term strategy for social change and victory at the polls has turned out to be an utter failure. For at least the past decade they believed they were beneficiaries of a "demographic doomsday clock" that granted them perpetual power. The clock, described in the 2002 book *The Emerging Democratic Majority*, argued that shifting demographic trends, the inflow of immigrants, and the collapse of the white middle class would guarantee a permanent Democratic lock on the White House.[52] After Obama's 2012 reelection, the *Huffington Post* proclaimed, "President Barack Obama did not just win reelection tonight. His victory signaled the irreversible triumph of a new, 21st-century America: multiracial, multi-ethnic, global in outlook and moving beyond centuries of racial, sexual, marital and religious tradition."[53]

The writer celebrated a "New America" and a new multiethnic coalition that included "a good share of the white vote (about 45 percent in Ohio, for example); 70 percent or so of the Latino vote across the country, according to experts; 96 percent of the African-American vote; and large proportions of Asian Americans and Pacific Islanders."[54] No one in the Democratic leadership doubted perennial control of the White House and total dominance of the cultural debate for years to come. Then, out of nowhere, Donald Trump showed up, and everything the Left was counting on flew out of the proverbial window, and the Republican Party suddenly emerged stronger than it had been for more than a century.[55]

Mistaking Obama's eight-year run as a massive realignment, as columnist Sean Trende argued in an article for RealClearPolitics, was a strategic mistake.[56] In fact, Obama virtually destroyed the Democratic Party as an institution. Many of the Democrats' electoral losses in 2016 can be traced directly to the over-the-top "progressive" policies of the Obama administration. "The resulting hunger for change in 2016 was so loud, writes Hayward, that only Hillary Clinton and her campaign team (which includes much of the mainstream media, of course) failed to hear it. Democrats dismissed the 2010 and 2014 midterms as anomalies when they should have seen them as hard evidence that no great realignment had taken place."[57]

Trump's performance with black and Hispanic voters shocked the media as well, although it shouldn't have because what Trump actually says to those constituencies is very different from the caricature image presented by the media. Black voters, who agree strongly with Trump on social and moral issues, have moved slowly but perceptibly to the right. And the Hispanic vote is becoming more Republican with each election cycle. These were important points I made in an entire chapter I devoted to the minority vote in *God and Donald Trump*.

Meanwhile, white voters are tired of the hate-filled attacks from the left. "There is a point," says Hayward, "at which any given group of people will grow weary of being told they're the source of all problems, no matter how much guilt the cultural and educational rackets pump into them."[58]

Pundits on both sides tried to shame evangelical voters who supported Trump in the 2015 primary and 2016 election, but evangelical voters supported the Republican candidate for a very good reason, says Hayward: "Eight years of government-backed progressive proselytization convinced them they needed a strong protector, and they saw one in Trump. Put the evangelicals and Rust Belt working class together, add a few Latinos who want to be fully American, and you've got a big enough monkey wrench to wreck that Democratic Demographic Doomsday Machine for a long time to come."[59]

Regardless of how much the media may try to discredit the president, his achievements are piling up. Even the liberal *New Republic* was surprised how much traction the Democrats have lost among black voters. Just as attention was being focused on how the Democrats could attract white working-class voters, new data showed support for the party slipping among its most reliable voters: the black women voters, who had given Hillary Clinton 94 percent of their support in 2016. But support from this reliable base has dropped significantly since that time. A 2016 Black Women's Roundtable/ESSENCE poll found that 85 percent of black women said the Democratic Party still represents their interests, but by 2017 the number expressing that opinion had fallen to 74 percent.[60]

To make matters worse, several notable defections from the Democratic Party have taken place since the election. Celebrity attorney Alan Dershowitz, though still a liberal, has become a Fox News contributor and vocal Trump supporter. Former Clinton advisor and Microsoft executive Mark Penn weighed in on the Mueller investigation, saying at different times that the Democratic Party had drifted too far to the left and that Mueller's witch hunt needed to end. But perhaps most striking—in light of the role she played in the Benghazi affair and the later charge that she was involved in unmasking targets of FBI investigations—is the news that Susan Rice's son, John David Rice-Cameron, has been elected president of College Republicans at Stanford University and serves as the activism director of the state of California College Republicans.[61]

Fox News once described former UN ambassador Susan Rice as "one of the Obama administration's most unpopular officials among conservatives and Republicans,"[62] a reputation she earned when she attempted to blame the terrorist attack on the American embassy compound in Benghazi, Libya, in 2012 on an offensive YouTube video. Rice was involved in the 2014 deal in which Obama freed five senior Taliban commanders and high-value terrorists in exchange for the US Army deserter Bowe Bergdahl. It has also been reported that she was the person who issued the stand-down order to National Security Council officials developing plans to respond to Russian meddling in the 2016 presidential election.[63] She was consistently one of Obama's most determined defenders.

Surely she must have been shocked when her son decided to go in another direction. To boost membership in the Stanford Republican group, her son helped organize a "Make Stanford Great Again" event on campus. The group hosted Robert Spencer, a controversial expert on radical Islam; pushed for the resignation of a professor with ties to Antifa; pressured the school to reverse a decision to ban American flags on club T-shirts; and hosted the popular Turning Point USA speakers Charlie Kirk and Candace Owens to speak at the event. In fact, it was Owens' lucid discussion of conservative principles that rap sensation Kanye West said he admired and may have led to his later deciding to take the heat and jump on the Trump bandwagon.

When asked what prompted his political conversion, Rice-Cameron said, "This worldview and these principles compel me to promote conservative ideas at Stanford and beyond. I'm driven by a fundamental sense of urgency over the fact that Americans are slowly losing their liberty, and I believe that liberty is being valued less and less. I want to turn the tide, and college campuses are crucial to doing so." When asked how he made the switch, growing up in such a liberal household, he said he changed after listening to other points of view on conservative talk radio. They were words and ideas he had never heard before, and suddenly his eyes were opened.[64]

While it's far too early to declare victory for either side or to assume the battle for the hearts and minds of Americans is over, stories such as these offer a ray of hope. Inscribed on the 1881 Gate at Harvard University, through which Ivy League students and alumni have passed for more than a hundred years, are the words "Ye shall know the truth and the truth shall make you free." The source is not mentioned, but they are the words of Jesus. And even if Harvard no longer recognizes the truth of the inscription, or recognizes the speaker, they offer hope that some will hear the truth, and, as with John David Rice-Cameron, their eyes will be opened, and suddenly they will get it.

The Real War

As a Christian, I don't believe this struggle in America is just Left versus Right or Democrats versus Republicans. I believe it's between light and darkness, between good and evil. There's a spiritual nature to this conflict, which Evangelicals call "spiritual warfare." This isn't just between people. In fact, the Bible says, "We wrestle not against flesh and blood, but against principalities, against powers, against the rulers of the darkness of this world, against spiritual wickedness in high places" (Eph. 6:12, KJV).

On August 19, 2018, my friend John Kilpatrick preached a sermon to his congregation at Church of His Presence in Daphne, Alabama, and told them witchcraft had been unleashed on Donald Trump. He used the reference in 1 Kings 19 when Jezebel unleashed a spirit of witchcraft against the prophet Elijah—the most powerful Old Testament prophet—and left him running for his life and feeling totally discouraged. Someone put a clip of the end of the service, when Kilpatrick called on his congregation to pray for the president. Within a week almost a million people had watched it.

Usually the press and the wider culture seem oblivious to anything the Bible says about such things. But when the sermon went viral, press from around the world began running stories. The *Newsweek* website blared: "Pastor Prays for Trump to Defeat Deep State 'Witchcraft,' Speaks in Tongues."

Newsweek wrote: "Kilpatrick connected America's current scourge of 'witchcraft' that is attacking the president to a biblical struggle in which Trump is in a 'showdown' for power with the shadows of the Deep State. In the video, Kilpatrick can be seen shouting and speaking in tongues as he prays for Trump to defeat the evil 'witchcraft' powers." Then *Newsweek* quoted Kilpatrick saying: "I don't know if you know this, and I don't know if you're going to believe me when I tell you this, but what's happening right now in America is witchcraft is trying to take this country over," prompting an audible response from his audience.[65]

Kilpatrick went on to say:

> I am not being political, but I don't see how President Trump bears up under it. He is as strong as I have ever seen a man be. But here's what the Holy Spirit said to me last night and here's what He said for me to tell you. He said, "Tell the church that so far Trump has been dealing with Ahab. But Jezebel's fixing to step out from the shadows." That's what the Lord said to me....He said, "Pray for him now, because...there's about to be a shift, and the deep state is about to manifest, and it's going to be a showdown like you can't believe." So I'm coming to you as a prophet, as a man of God, and I'm telling you, it's time to pray for the president.[66]

Two days later, August 21, 2018, Paul Manafort was convicted on several counts in a case brought against him by the Mueller investigation. The same day, Trump's former attorney Michael Cohen pleaded guilty to some minor charges. Suddenly the president was in even more hot water than usual. It seemed something had been unleashed. And two days before, it had been predicted by this pastor in Alabama, who is best known in Christian circles as the pastor of the five-year-long revival at Brownsville Assembly of God (also called the Pensacola Outpouring), which drew four million people.

Somehow what Kilpatrick said resonated with Christians all over the country. They perceived something is very wrong, but they couldn't put their finger on it. So when Kilpatrick said it was spiritual warfare and told them to pray, they understood what they were supposed to do.

"Something's been unleashed in our nation," Kilpatrick told me when I interviewed him for a blog I was writing on the subject. "It's like everyone is in a spiritual stupor. It's time for America to turn and repent. This is more than just political differences. Spirits have been unleashed, but if we humble ourselves and pray, God will bring that spirit down."

Time will tell if Christians will heed the call to pray and whether, as Kilpatrick predicted, revival will come to America to heal its wounds or whether Trump will be brought down by these huge unseen forces. But for me and millions of other Christians trying to understand where God is in all this, what Kilpatrick preached explains in spiritual terms the war that seems to be tearing this country apart.

CHAPTER 11

RESOLUTE FAITH AND CONFIDENCE

ONE OF THE first indications Donald Trump was going to be a different sort of president than his predecessors came on January 20, 2017, Inauguration Day. To begin his presidency, the White House invited four evangelical ministers, a Jewish rabbi, and a Catholic archbishop, representing diverse religious and ethnic communities, to offer prayers for the new president and the nation. This would be the largest number of prayers ever offered at an inauguration and an indication the new chief executive understood the importance of faith to the people of this country. The occasion was meant to be an invocation of God's blessing on the nation as well as a statement of the Trump administration's firm commitment to religious liberty.

Throughout the campaign Trump tapped into the emotions of his supporters, giving them hope that America's glory days were not behind us. He energized the base, assuring them of his support, and the crowds at his rallies grew larger with every event. He met with community and religious leaders and listened to their concerns and assured them he heard the message loud and clear. Evangelicals all across the nation told him they were sick and tired of the disrespect they experienced from the secular media. They were concerned about government policies regarding abortion, same-sex marriage, and the right of business owners to determine whom they serve. They wanted a leader who would defend their interests and take a stand for freedom of conscience, and Donald Trump made it clear he was their guy.

After the election many analysts concluded it was the unprecedented and unexpectedly large turnout from the evangelical community that delivered Trump's victory. Eighty-one percent of Evangelicals who voted pulled the lever for Trump, shocking the prognosticators from both political parties. On election eve the *New York Times* compiled tracking polls showing Trump's odds of winning at just 15 percent, 8 percent, 2 percent, and even less than 1 percent.[1] Clinton's supporters were outraged when polling guru Nate Silver dared to suggest before the night was over that Trump had a 29 percent chance of winning the electoral college.[2]

The media and the liberal pollsters never doubted Clinton would be moving to the White House, but they badly misread the voters' mandate for change, and religion turned out to be a big part of it. Clinton was so sure she was going to be the next president. She even bought a $1.16 million house in Chappaqua, New York, to be used by staff and security personnel during her presidential retreats.[3] As it turned out, she wouldn't be needing it, and today the house Clinton bought is a guest cottage.

On January 21, 2017, their first full day in office, President Trump and Vice President Pence attended an interfaith prayer service at Washington's National Cathedral, a tradition dating back to the presidency of George Washington. The event was attended by more than two dozen religious leaders of various faiths. There were no speeches, no political remarks, only prayers and readings. And while most of the guests were from the evangelical community, representatives of the Roman Catholic, Jewish, Orthodox, Mormon, Muslim, Sikh, Buddhist, and Bahá'í traditions were in attendance.

Four months later Trump buoyed the spirits of Evangelicals when he made a strong appeal during the National Day of Prayer for a return to God and a restoration of religious liberty. That event convinced many Evangelicals who were looking for assurance of Trump's commitment that this president would give his support to the issues that were most important to them. They believed his words were more than just rhetoric. In his proclamation for the event, he said:

> We are united in prayer, each according to our own faith and tradition, and we believe that in America, people of all faiths, creeds, and religions must be free to exercise their natural right to worship according to their consciences. We are also reminded and reaffirm that all human beings have the right, not only to pray and worship according to their consciences, but to practice their faith in their homes, schools, charities, and businesses in private and in the public square free from government coercion, discrimination, or persecution.[4]

Religion, he said, is more than an intellectual exercise. It is a practical expression of our beliefs and our commitment to care for those in need and to stand up for those who are suffering for their faith today in many parts of the world. "Even the many prisoners around the world who are persecuted for their faith can pray privately in their cells," he said. "But our Constitution demands more: the freedom to practice one's faith publicly."[5]

This was a striking contrast to the policies of Barack Obama, who issued proclamations but never held a National Day of Prayer observance in the White House. Other past presidents observed in various ways: Bill Clinton invited guests to the White House for prayer during the National Day of Prayer, and Ronald Reagan held observances in the Rose Garden. The first President Bush hosted a "prayer breakfast" in May 1989 in the State Dining Room. I was privileged to attend that event and sat at the same table with the president. There was a lot of talk about prayer during the breakfast, but I found it odd that on the National Day of Prayer there was no actual prayer, other than saying grace before the meal.

In 1952 President Harry Truman established a day of prayer as a national event. Reagan signed a resolution in 1988 to observe the National Day of Prayer on the first Thursday in May each year, and every president since that time has recognized the day with a proclamation. During his eight years in office George W. Bush celebrated the event with a service in the East Room of the White House, but President Obama decided against a White House ceremony and called for a "toned down" National Day of Prayer.[6]

Becky Armstrong, who was the spokesperson for the National Day of Prayer Task Force at that time, said, "It doesn't appear they are going to fulfill our request [to participate]." But she added, "The White House is a small part of what the national day of prayer is all about. Tomorrow there will be dozens of events held in our nation's [capital] and governors from all fifty states have already issued proclamations recognizing the National Day of Prayer." Task Force Chairman Shirley Dobson said she was disappointed by the president's lack of participation and added that "at this time in our country's history, we would hope our President would recognize more fully the importance of prayer."[7]

But Obama didn't reject prayer entirely. Over the coming years he called the nation to prayer during natural disasters, such as Hurricane Sandy, and to pray for the brave men and women taking part in response and recovery efforts. Whether or not Hillary Clinton was interested in commemorating a day of prayer while her husband was president, we do know she helped him to initiate the Ramadan dinner as a White House tradition in 1996. Hillary Clinton hosted 150 Muslim guests at the White House and said she learned about the ritual from her daughter, Chelsea, who had studied Islamic history in school.

President George W. Bush hosted the Ramadan dinner every year during his two terms, including shortly after the 9/11 attacks. He said at the dinner that America's fight was against terrorism, not Islam. The Trump administration did not host the dinner in 2017 but instead sent a personal message: "On behalf of the American people, Melania and I send our warm greetings to Muslims as they celebrate Eid al-Fitr." He said, "During this holiday, we are reminded of the importance of mercy, compassion, and goodwill."[8] In his greeting at the start of Ramadan in May 2018 Trump said, "Our Constitution ensures Muslims can observe Ramadan in accordance with the dictates of conscience and unimpeded by government." He then concluded his remarks with the traditional greeting, "*Ramadan Mubarak*."[9] President Trump hosted a group of Islamic leaders at the White House for an Iftar dinner on June 6, 2018.

Making It Personal

So what does this mean for the evangelical Christians who have been the core of Trump's support? Clearly the president is intent on keeping his promises to safeguard religious liberty and free expression for men and women of all faiths. In the Rose Garden ceremony honoring the National Day of Prayer in May 2018, he announced that he would be signing an executive order establishing a White House Faith and Opportunity Initiative. This would ensure that faith-based communities and related organizations have strong support from the White House and that religious liberty and freedom of conscience are protected throughout all departments of the federal government.

The president spoke at the October 13, 2017, Value Voters Summit in Washington, DC, and assured attendees that religious freedom would be a priority of his administration. This promise came one week after the Justice Department, following the president's instructions, issued a list of twenty principles of religious liberty.[10] Then, in January 2018, the Justice Department raised the profile of religious liberty cases by designating a religious liberty point of contact for all US Attorney's offices.

Major policy changes were announced that same month by the Department of Health and Human Services. It formed a Conscience and Religious Freedom Division, which enabled the agency to focus on effectively enforcing existing laws that protect religious freedom and the rights of conscience.

As I've mentioned in previous chapters, less than four months into his tenure as president Donald Trump made it clear he is a champion for religious liberty, restoring the ideals that have undergirded the nation's freedom and prosperity since its founding. On May 4, 2017, he dealt with two of the most troubling issues for America's houses of worship:

1. Ending enforcement of the so-called Johnson Amendment, which threatened churches and nonprofits with a loss of tax-exempt status if they endorsed any candidate for public office

2. Reinstating the Mexico City Policy, which prevents the funding of the global abortion industry with $9 billion in foreign aid

On April 13, 2017, President Trump overturned the Obama administration's regulation prohibiting states from defunding abortion facilities. In addition, new guidelines stated that tax dollars cannot be used for abortion coverage in Obamacare exchange plans. The Trump administration took action to defend organizations such as the Little Sisters of the Poor, ensuring they won't be forced to comply with the contraceptive mandate of Obamacare, which violates their religious beliefs. The president also ended the Obama-era policy that prevented houses of worship from receiving disaster aid during times of crisis.

President Trump has publicly stood with people of faith and with those who advocate for the sanctity of life, and as I mentioned earlier, he became the first president to address the March for Life rally live via satellite. Mike Pence became the first sitting vice president to address the march in person. Trump's administration has also taken a stand in defense of religious freedom by supporting small-business owners, such as Colorado baker Jack Phillips. Months before the Supreme Court overturned the ruling against Phillips, Trump's DOJ filed a brief on his behalf, agreeing that he should be allowed to operate his business in accordance with his personal convictions and religious beliefs.[11]

One of the best examples of Trump's support of religious freedom is how he made an international incident over the imprisonment of an evangelical American missionary in Turkey. Andrew Brunson, who pastored a small church in the city of Izmir, was arrested in 2016—one of thousands arrested, including journalists, activists, and opponents of President Recep Tayyip Erdogan. He is accused of being a spy with links to the outlawed Kurdistan Workers' Party and to an American-based Muslim imam Fethullah Gülen, whom Turkish authorities blame for the coup attempt. At a State Department conference on religious freedom, attended by Brunson's daughter, Jacqueline Furnari, Mike Pence said Brunson had been accused of "dividing and separating Turkey by simply spreading his Christian faith," according to *Time* magazine.[12]

In July, Vice President Pence tweeted that Turkey should "release Pastor Andrew Brunson NOW or be prepared to face the consequences."[13] The same day President Trump tweeted, "The United States will impose large sanctions on Turkey" for detaining Brunson, whom he called "a great Christian, family man and wonderful human being. He is suffering greatly. This innocent man of faith should be released immediately!"[14] As this book goes to press, Brunson has not been released, but after the sanctions were imposed, Turkey's stock market plunged, losing more than $15 billion (US) in traded value during August 2018, and the Turkish currency, the lira, fell to a record low.

For decades many Americans have feared the intrusion of the federal government into their lives, forcing them to accept policies that contradict long-established tradition and violate our historic religious beliefs. As I mentioned in the introduction of this book, Gov. Mike Huckabee told me he believes Donald Trump represents that part of America that was tired of getting beaten up. One reason so many conservatives turned out for Trump was that they saw him as the kind of guy who fights back.

For the most part President Trump has lived up to his billing. He is a fighter, and he wants to restore the honor and prestige of the United States around the world. Critics claimed he was just a businessman without diplomatic skills. He had no knowledge or experience in foreign affairs and would get us into a third world war. Yet since his first official visits to Europe, China, Japan, and the Middle East, many have hailed him as a hero. His speeches in Riyadh, Saudi Arabia; Warsaw, Poland; Paris; and Davos, Switzerland, were highly acclaimed by most. He was—and is—making what many experts agree is a tremendous difference in international affairs, telling the world that "America is back in business."

On the home front he has rolled back regulations that restrict free trade, energy development, and the use of America's natural resources. As related in other chapters, the president is beginning to drain the swamp in Washington and has taken on the deep state by making dramatic changes to the permanent bureaucracy. None of this has been easy, and the battles are far from over, but Donald Trump has shown that he is a fighter, and he expects to win them all.

Trump's Kingdom Influences

Despite evidence of the president's strong stand for religious and moral values, liberal journalists and media pundits have repeatedly accused Evangelicals of hypocrisy for supporting a person with such a checkered past. Many claimed Trump's endorsement of former Alabama Supreme Court Justice Judge Roy Moore, who was accused of dating teenage girls, was shameless and his evangelical supporters were guilty of moral duplicity.[15]

No one supports everything Trump has said or done—his multiple marriages, the negative things he has said about illegal immigrants, or his Twitter battles with celebrities and political opponents. But the size of his evangelical base, which is large and still growing, is evidence that people of faith have decided his beliefs and motives are good overall. They believe he has their back, and, as pointed out in a previous chapter, evangelical voters took a calculated position based on the political alternatives and their understanding that all people are sinners.

But of course, that is not good enough for those on the left. As an example, Randall Balmer, an Episcopal priest and religion professor at Dartmouth College, recently concluded that the evangelical community has given up on biblical morality. Writing in the liberal English periodical *The Guardian*, Balmer says, "The religious right's wholesale embrace of the Republican party and of Donald J Trump, both as candidate and as president, has necessitated a rewriting of evangelical ethics."[16]

The professor claims evangelicals apparently believe "lying is all right as long as it serves a higher purpose," "vulgarity is a sign of strength," "immigrants are scum," and "white lives matter (much more than others)."[17] Liberals such as Balmer fail to understand that Donald Trump was the only responsible choice for conservatives and people of faith in the 2016 election. They understood only too well what four years of a Clinton presidency would mean. With a culture that is becoming more and more secular, and more hostile to the Christian faith, Evangelicals realized that electing Hillary Clinton would have been infinitely worse than electing Trump, with all his imperfections.

In the culture wars, which the Left has been advancing for the last forty years, Evangelicals were looking for a change agent who would shake up the status quo. They saw Donald Trump as someone who would defend their interests and support their values. That's why they gave Mitt Romney, a Mormon who never reached out to the evangelical community, 79 percent of their votes in 2012. That's roughly the same percentage they gave George W. Bush and John McCain. If Romney had reached out to Evangelicals and supported conservative values as Trump has done, Evangelicals would have supported him just as enthusiastically, and I believe he would have defeated Barack Obama and won the White House. But many Evangelicals stayed home, and Romney lost by 4.98 million votes, or 3.9 percent, which was the evangelical margin.

After struggling through two terms under Obama, who flip-flopped on gay marriage and became an advocate for Planned Parenthood and the abortion industry, millions of Evangelicals and others of goodwill were desperate for a champion. Seventeen Republicans applied for the job, including several with sterling evangelical credentials. Mike Huckabee, a former Baptist pastor, made a strong case, as did former Louisiana governor Bobby Jindal and Sen. Ted Cruz, whom I initially supported. Others such as Sen. Marco Rubio and Dr. Ben Carson spoke openly about their strong Christian faith. They had many dedicated supporters, but none of these candidates caught the voters' imagination.

The question was, Who was strong enough to defeat the Clinton machine? As I documented in my previous book *God and Donald Trump*, most establishment evangelical leaders supported Ted Cruz initially. Trump's support came mainly from Pentecostal and Charismatic Christians in the early stages of the campaign, partly due to the influence of Pastor Paula White Cain and partly because of prophecies that God was raising up a leader like the Persian King Cyrus, a pagan used by God to allow the Jews to return to Jerusalem from the Babylonian captivity.

Trump eventually convinced the broader evangelical community he was for real and earned the greatest evangelical turnout in history. As Dr. Jerry Falwell Jr., president of Liberty University, told me in an interview for *Charisma* magazine, "I said over and over and over: We're not electing a pastor. We're electing a president. When you choose a doctor, you choose the best you can find."[18] Governor Huckabee, who wrote the foreword to *God and Donald Trump*, told me he has tried over and over to explain to reporters that "nobody in the Christian world—certainly not the evangelical world—has any expectation that Donald Trump is one of us." He said he doubted if Trump could find John 3:16 (the most essential Christian text) in a marked New Testament.

In an interview for this book, the former governor told me, "It may be even just his gut instinct. But I do believe that that is what creates this affinity between President Trump and the evangelical community. They see in him someone who sees the world with clarity, and that is not something they have seen in most of their political leaders." The thing that never ceases to amaze, he said, is the president's sincere respect and admiration for the evangelical community. "I do believe part of that is because Evangelicals and Donald Trump see things in binary terms. Good or evil. Right or wrong. Up or down. They don't see anything in...fifty shades of gray. They see it more in terms of very clear choices, and Donald Trump gets very direct with them. He sees things wholly, clearly. He's not a diplomatic, sit-around guy who says, 'Oh, it could be this, but maybe we should consider that!' He's quick with a conclusion."

Dr. Robert Jeffress, the respected pastor of First Baptist Church of Dallas, said that in 2016 the electorate was sick and tired of the status quo. Jeffress told me, "People on both sides of the aisle knew we were in a mess. It took an outsider like Donald Trump to win the election because he demonstrated he has the will and the leadership capability necessary to reverse the downward trajectory of this nation."

Evangelist James Robison, one of the most respected evangelical media personalities in America, did not initially support Trump but ended up being one of his biggest supporters and even a confidant to candidate Trump. He explained Trump this way: "God has only one perfect child: Jesus. All the rest of us are imperfect. The Bible does not whitewash any characters or heroes of the faith. They were all flawed and tragically failed, even as they were seeking to follow God's will. Even the apostle Paul referred to himself as 'chief of sinners.' No one should be surprised when a New York contractor talks like a New York contractor."

Robison says Jesus wants His will to be done "on earth as it is in heaven." It's "not of this world," but it's here now. That's because, he said, kingdom-minded people who are praying know that only *the* Shepherd can lead us to green pastures, but He can lead any leader appropriately. "That's what people have been praying for, never believing that someone like Donald Trump, a businessman from New York, could actually contribute to the positive correction." Robison told me he believes that positive changes are coming because of "kingdom influence" on this president.

As I have tried to explain to secular media, most born-again Evangelicals know God changes lives, including their own, and we understand that no one is perfect. The profane Irish poet and playwright Oscar Wilde said famously, "The only difference between the saint and the sinner is that every saint has a past, and every sinner has a future."[19] I have no doubt he learned that lesson the hard way. But it was essentially this rationale that allowed many Evangelicals to look beyond Donald Trump's indiscretions. Once they made peace with his past, the only question was, Could he stop Hillary Clinton from her inevitable victory? Against all odds, the prophecies that said Trump would win came true. While there was consternation on the left, the religious Right was ecstatic, feeling that "God has given us a reprieve." Jeffress said, "I believe God put Donald Trump in office to give the church more freedom to share the gospel of Jesus Christ."

Answering the Doubters

With Donald Trump keeping so many promises involving issues most Evangelicals believe are important, some would ask, Why does a segment of the evangelical church identify as "Never Trumpers"? Considering that only about 20 percent of Evangelicals did not vote for him in 2016, I would have expected these individuals to come around to support Trump, as I did in 2016, after they began to see what the president has actually accomplished.

To understand this, I interviewed Mark Galli, editor in chief of *Christianity Today* magazine. While *Christianity Today* did not support candidates from either party, one could tell by their editorials that they were not Trump fans. I learned that Galli didn't support him either when both of us were interviewed by the *New York Times* during the week Judge Roy Moore lost his election to the Senate. *Times* writer Laurie Goodstein interviewed me the day of the election and tried to get me to say that Evangelicals were tarnishing their brand. According to Goodstein, supporting someone so imperfect as Trump and his buddy, Roy Moore, we had betrayed our principles.

I've known and admired Galli for many years as he came up through the ranks at *Christianity Today*. Goodstein's lead said he didn't need to wait for the votes to be counted to publish an essay saying: "Whoever wins, there is already one loser: Christian faith." She quoted Galli as writing, "No one will believe a word we say, perhaps for a generation. Christianity's integrity is severely tarnished."

She added, "The sight of white evangelical voters in Alabama giving their overwhelming support to Roy S. Moore...has deeply troubled many conservative Christians, who fear that association with the likes of Mr. Moore is giving their faith a bad name. The angst has grown so deep, Mr. Galli said, that he knows of 'many card-carrying evangelicals' who are ready to disavow the label."[20]

The *New York Times* then quoted Ed Stetzer, executive director of the Billy Graham Center at Wheaton College, a prominent evangelical school in Illinois, as saying "It grieves me. I don't want 'evangelical' to mean people who supported candidates with significant and credible accusations against them. If evangelical means that, it has serious ramifications for the work of Christians and churches."[21]

As a reporter myself, I realized Goodstein had a story line and was looking for some juicy quotes to back it up. I wasn't about to give her the sound bites she wanted, but instead, I tried to explain that with the way the country has been headed the past half century, we needed someone to be disruptive. "I believe God answered our prayers in a way we didn't expect, for a person we didn't even necessarily like," she correctly quoted me as saying, identifying me as the "author of *God and Donald Trump* and founder of Charisma Media."[22]

"Christians believe in redemption and forgiveness, so they're willing to give Donald Trump a chance," I went on to say. Then I added that support by born-again Christians cannot be taken for granted. "If he turns out to be a lecher like Bill Clinton," I said, "or dishonest in some kind of way, in a way that's proven, you'll see the support fade as quickly as it came." That was quoted fairly enough, but in our hour-long interview I tried to explain that Jesus said that "not everyone who says Lord, Lord, will enter into the kingdom of heaven," and there are some people who identify as Christians but don't accept the essential doctrines of the faith. I was simply posing the question whether or not the Never Trumpers and other Trump haters are actually believers at all.[23]

During the interview the writer never mentioned Mark Galli or Ed Stetzer. She interviewed me the day of the election and interviewed both of the others the day after. When the story appeared in print, Goodstein quoted Galli and Stetzer as having deep reservations about Judge Moore and Donald Trump, and quoted Galli as saying that the evangelical brand is "tarnished." She followed that by quoting me: "Mr. Strang said that those who talk about Mr. Trump tarnishing the evangelical brand 'are not really believers—they're not with us, anyway.'"[24]

While I did say that, my words were taken out of context. I had posed the idea hypothetically about unnamed people. Yet my comment created a short-lived Twitter frenzy with people blasting me as saying anyone who didn't agree with me wasn't a believer. Worse than that, it made it look as if I had said Mark Galli and Ed Stetzer, both of whom I respect and consider friends, were nonbelievers. When I read the article online on December 14, 2017, under the headline "Fallout for Evangelicals After a Chaotic Election," I was stunned. I immediately called both men and told them my words were quoted out of context and that I would never have said that Christian leaders are not believers because of political differences. Thankfully both men accepted my explanation, and I learned to be cautious the next time I talk to a reporter for the *New York Times.*

Months later, when I interviewed Mark Galli for this book, I did so to try and understand the Never Trumper mind-set. Galli made it clear he has never been a Never Trumper, per se, even though he did not vote for him and likely would not vote for him in 2020. He mentioned several of Trump's accomplishments—appointing Neil Gorsuch to the Supreme Court, defending religious liberty, bringing North Korea to the negotiating table, and securing the release of three Korean Christians—acknowledging each of those things as important victories for Christians. Moving the US embassy in Israel to Jerusalem was a bold move. He acknowledged that sometimes leaders make bold moves that everyone thinks are wrong but later turn out to be right. "You can't fault Trump for not making bold moves," he said.

He also wanted to set the record straight about a few things from the *New York Times* article. For example, he didn't specifically say the evangelical brand was "tarnished." He told me, "I meant it this way—to people on the left, evangelical support for Trump makes them respect evangelicals less. That's a reality. On the other hand, support for Trump has not tarnished the brand to all the conservatives who voted for Trump."

Where Galli and those who agree with him have a problem is what I now see as a fundamental difference in style. They consider Trump brash, blustering, and a populist. "There are different segments of American life that just do not like populism or the leaders of the populist movement," Galli told me. "They think they are dangerous…just a few steps away from becoming a Hitler or a Stalin." Instead, Galli said he prefers leadership to be understated—to speak softly and carry a big stick.

I asked him if he believed Trump's dalliance with a porn star a dozen years ago diminishes his obvious political successes. He responded, "When he's dealing with

Saudi Arabia or Korea, I [doubt] they're thinking once or twice about whether he had an affair with Stormy Daniels or not." But he went on to say that in the long run, we want our presidents to be good examples of our ideals—people our kids and grandkids can look up to—and he doesn't feel Trump does that. The real conundrum, he said, is how can so many Evangelicals support him when he has had such a checkered past. "For the longest time, Evangelicals have said the character of our leaders is one of the most important aspects of...leadership. And they have now taken a stance and said, 'That's not as important as his policies that are carried out.'...Conservative Evangelicals have taken some time to get respect in the public square. And they want to be seen as legitimate players in the world of culture and politics...along comes Donald Trump, and breaks all of those rules....From the perspective of our international reputation," Galli said emphatically, "Trump is an embarrassment to the country."

While I respect Mark Galli and honor his opinion, we don't agree on a lot of things, including theological doctrines. But we can agree that the most important thing for Christians on both the Left and Right is that there is a higher kingdom. In a way, I understand where Galli and those who share his opinions are coming from. For twenty years I was a registered Democrat, which meant I couldn't vote in the Republican primary when Pat Robertson ran for President in 1988. But when I registered to vote, the 1973 *Roe v. Wade* decision allowing abortion had not yet happened. The biggest issues dividing the nation at the time were the Vietnam War and the civil rights demonstrations in the South. I beat the drum for racial equality then and now, but my political views were in for a major change.

Whom Do You Trust?

Because the Pentecostal movement came out of the black church experience, and because Charismatic churches are among the most integrated in the nation, as a Charismatic Christian, I have always believed I belong at the forefront of the call for racial unity. I have used *Charisma* magazine, which I founded in 1975, as a bully pulpit for four decades, calling for unity in the body of Christ. I held on to my Florida voter registration in the Democratic Party until the party made its hard shift to the left and embraced abortion and gay rights in the party platform. That sent me to the Republican Party, which is now much closer to traditional conservative Christian values than the Democratic Party of today.

Mark Galli helped me understand another important point as well, regarding the attitudes of Evangelicals who are still critical of the president. Because of Trump's rude and offensive comments, especially those they feel denigrate various ethnic groups, these individuals don't believe Trump exemplifies the traits of more refined people; that is, those with higher incomes and better educations (in other words, the "elites"). They feel no affinity for a disruptive personality like Trump's. Instead, they want someone who can "nudge along the status quo," which is not Trump's style.

Pastor Jeffress reminded me that Ronald Reagan once said the term *status quo* is Latin for "the mess we're in."[25] And that may be the crux of the divide between 80 percent, which I call "red Evangelicals," and the 20 percent who tend to be "blue Evangelicals." One has to wonder if "the status quo" will be good enough as the country lurches further to the left, or is a disruptor what we really need to bring a much-needed course correction? Pastor Jeffress said he paid attention to the polls in *Christianity Today* during the campaign to see whom most evangelical leaders were supporting, and only one or two supported Donald Trump. "They missed it," he told me, "and I think a lot of those Christian leaders were miffed that they had so little influence over rank-and-file Evangelicals who didn't listen to them and voted for Trump anyway."

As I have written elsewhere, the secular media only seem interested in Evangelicals if they can find evidence of hypocrisy or bigotry. I've done dozens of radio and television interviews since the publication of *God and Donald Trump*, but the reason CNN and MSNBC wanted to talk to me about Trump had almost nothing to do with my book but how evangelical Christians could defend Donald Trump after the Stormy Daniels scandal erupted.

NPR had similar questions for Stephen Mansfield, an Evangelical who wrote the book *Choosing Donald Trump*, which examined whether Evangelicals and their leaders who vocally supported Trump had done lasting damage to their Christian witness. "Yes," Mansfield said. "I think that they are especially going to lose influence amongst millennials, who are strongly social justice oriented, and the surveys indicate that the vast majority of them are very suspicious of Donald Trump.

"You've got an unusual situation here," he continued, "where the leaders of the religious right are not only having to account to a watching world for why they compromised their religious message to support Donald Trump, but you also are going to have some blowback from the very people that the religious right is trying to reach. The very people these pastors are trying to reach—the young, people of color, etc.—I think they may have lost them and, in some cases, permanently."[26]

While liberals and those who court liberal approval like to throw around charges of hypocrisy regarding Christians and anyone else who doesn't happen to agree with their leftist perspectives, Tucker Carlson, the host of *Tucker Carlson Tonight* on the Fox News Channel, has a different take. As an Episcopalian, Carlson does not identify as an Evangelical, but he understands the Left and its attitudes. Liberals love to accuse Christians of being "holier than thou," he says, but the term is a much better fit for liberal elites and, I would add, for the evangelical Never Trumpers as well.

When New York Atty. Gen. Eric Schneiderman resigned in May 2018 because of multiple accusations of sexual misconduct, Carlson said, "Hypocrisy isn't just a feature of modern liberalism. It's the heart of modern liberalism." Speaking of Schneiderman, he said, "Some of his long-time friends on the left are professing shock. You've heard them. 'We just can't believe it,' they say. 'How can a man so publicly committed to feminism beat women? It just doesn't make sense.' But, of course, it makes perfect sense. Self-righteousness is always a marker for secret creepiness. The people yelling the loudest are usually hiding the most."[27] Carlson added:

> Keep that in mind the next time you hear some Democratic politician lecturing you about your moral inferiority. That's the guy you need to watch carefully. Chances are he's up to something awful behind closed doors.... Ever wonder how people who advocate for abortion can say they stand for children? How a movement that demonizes an entire race can claim to oppose racism? The same way Al Gore can travel by private jet while trying to ban your SUV. Because consistency does not matter to the Left. Only virtue matters. We're good people; therefore, we must rule. You are not; therefore, you must obey. Al Gore doesn't believe he's a hypocrite. Eric Schneiderman probably doesn't think he is either. You can't commit sin if your intentions are pure. And liberals believe their intentions are the purest.[28]

At that point Carlson made an observation that lies at the heart of the conflict between the Left and Right, and between secularists and conservative Christians. He said liberalism is a religion trying to displace Christianity in American culture:

> If that sounds like theology, and not public policy, that's because it is theology. Modern liberalism is...a replacement for the Protestant Christianity that the Left worked so hard to undermine and destroy. Liberals are speaking the language of faith, albeit a faith without God. This is the main reason the Right and Left talk past each other, the reason our public debates are so weird and unsatisfying. One side arrives with facts and stats and arguments. The other brags about its decency. One side is trying to convince; the other side is trying to convert. You can beat a liberal in an argument, but you can never convince him that you won. He cares much more deeply than you do, and therefore knows he's right. By definition. And nothing can convince him otherwise.[29]

It's hard to disagree with his logic. Carlson went on to say, "Somewhere tonight Eric Schneiderman is marinating in his shame. Probably unshaven and alone. His career is over. His reputation is destroyed. He faces years of potential legal action. He is a broken man. He is in agony." Then Carlson concluded, "And yet, on some level, despite all of that, Eric Schneiderman still knows he's a better person than you are."[30]

Pastor Sam Rodriguez, who prayed at Trump's inauguration, believes that things are more politically polarized today than ever. He told me he believes the Democratic Party has moved so far to the left that if Hillary Clinton were to run again, she would be considered by some of the Democratic faithful to be too conservative to get the nomination. Meanwhile, Republicans have moved more to the center, which makes it more broadly appealing to the blue-collar Democrats who voted for Trump.

Pastor Rodriguez is president of the National Hispanic Christian Leadership Conference and has seen this shift up close among Latino voters. Hispanics turned out for Donald Trump at a much higher level than anyone expected, almost 30 percent. For evangelical Hispanics and churchgoing Catholics, the percentage was 66 percent. When he spoke to candidate Trump, he told me, he said that Hispanics are interested in five things: the Supreme Court, religious liberty, educational opportunity, racial unity, and immigration reform, in that order. Hispanics paid close attention to Supreme Court cases involving the Sisters of the Poor, Hobby Lobby, and others, he said, and he believes Obama did more to hurt religious liberty than the previous forty-three presidents combined.

Trusting His Core Beliefs

What do Christian leaders really think about President Trump? I interviewed several who have seen him up close. Jerry Falwell Jr., who was among Trump's earliest supporters and closest allies, told Martha Raddatz on ABC, "One of the reasons I supported him is because he doesn't say what's politically correct; he says what's in his heart, what he believes, and sometimes that gets him in trouble."[31]

Evangelist James Robison agrees. "Here's a man who will not be intimidated or manipulated. He will not be intimidated by any form of political correctness or any manipulative media assault. He just doesn't flinch. The church needs to quit listening to the people who seek to stir controversy and strife—in the media and in the church."

The media have portrayed Trump as arrogant, brash, and a little bit crazy. This was what I expected when I interviewed candidate Trump during the campaign, in August 2016. But that's not what I saw. I found him to be soft-spoken, respectful, and even humble. I've since spoken to other Christian leaders who say the same thing. Behind the scenes he is winsome, and he won them over. However, that was before the election, when politicians will say and do almost anything to get your support. But it turns out that President Trump is very much the same as candidate Trump. And to the leaders of his Faith Leaders Initiative, he is not only the same but maybe even improved since he has been surrounded by wise Christian counsel.

As Falwell told me, "He is personable. He loves people. I think that's one of the true tests of a Christian, whether or not they love people, all people, no matter how important they are. I'm just a son of a preacher who happened to become president of a college, but he still answers his cell phone every two or three weeks when I call him, and he doesn't have to do that. But he is just a people person, and I think he treats the common man the same way he treats billionaires and the same way he treats famous people. And I think that's an indicator of his faith as well."

Jerry Falwell and Robert Jeffress both told me the president is open to people of faith and invites evangelical leaders to the White House and allows them to pray for him in the Oval Office. When Jeffress told Trump that people want to know about his personal faith, the president told him to say that his faith is very important to him and very personal. So Jeffress leaves it at that. When I asked Falwell about Trump's personal faith, he answered me this way: "You know, Jesus said, 'Pray in your closet, and God who sees you in private will reward you openly.' I think that's what Donald Trump does. I think he does speak his mind. I admire that about him. But I do think he is private about his faith, and I think he's not one of these people who is good at explaining his beliefs or doesn't feel comfortable talking about it publicly. And it's just his decision to make."

As to his character, Falwell said, "I've never known him to be anything but 100 percent honest, and he is a man of his word. Whatever he has promised me in the past, he has done." Trump may be reviled by more people than any president since Abraham Lincoln, and the pressure on him is immense. Yet it doesn't seem to bother him. Jeffress said he's been with the president in the Oval Office at times when there were many external distractions, and he was always impressed how calm and collected the president could be under the most adverse circumstances. "I thought I'd have to encourage the president," he told me, "but he was relaxed and jovial, as focused as I've ever seen him. Isn't this the type of person you would want in that seat in the Oval Office?"

Falwell told me every time he calls the president, he says, "What can I do? Is there anything I can do to help you, Mr. President? Please don't give up. Please don't get discouraged. Please don't quit." And he said that President Trump always says,

"Don't worry about me, Jerry. I'm not ever going to back down." Falwell explains, "So I just want to be an encourager to him.... You know, he is the only thing standing between this country and the type of leadership that we had for the last, I don't know how many years, Republican and Democrat, and he's the only one that is for the common man, that puts America first. He's the only one who has the guts to stand up against the attackers and dissenters," he said, "and people who lie about him, and the deep state. We haven't seen that kind of leadership from any president since Ronald Reagan. Maybe since before that. I just think we need to do everything we can as Christians to pray for him."

Speaking of people who lie about the president, while I was wrapping up the final edits of this book, Omarosa Manigault Newman's book, *Unhinged*, released. When she was on the White House staff, the Left and media maligned her, saying she was selling out African Americans—as if blacks should uniformly oppose Trump just because most are Democrats. Yet when she turned on Trump by writing a negative book about him and bashing him in media interviews, she became the darling of the same media, even if the attention was only short-lived.

I met Omarosa at Trump's election party at the New York Hilton in Manhattan. At the beginning of the night, when there still weren't many people in the room, I saw Omarosa surrounded by admirers. I was vaguely familiar with her as some sort of celebrity. Since I had the opportunity, I struck up a conversation with her, never dreaming she'd become controversial or that I'd be writing about it two years later. We talked for quite a while, and I was impressed with how supportive she was of Donald Trump. She shared how Trump had helped her by having her on *The Apprentice*. I quickly learned she had a longtime friendship with the candidate. That night she was excited beyond belief that her friend, for whom she had campaigned so hard, was winning. I got the impression she might even get a job in the White House. So I was shocked when she turned on him after being fired from the White House administration.

As the controversy over her new book, secret recordings, and nasty comments about the president on network television began to come out, I couldn't forget how positive she had been about Donald Trump. Then I saw some of the interviews she did back when she still supported the president. Either she was lying then, or she is lying now. But one thing is certain: people looking for media opportunities can simply criticize Trump and get all the attention they want.

In my conversation with Governor Huckabee, he told me that "Donald Trump is unique in his ability to brush off the harshest criticism and simply to ignore it." He said, "I've never seen anyone like him in this regard. I mean, most people who are as fully under siege as he is would probably be hiding under the desk in the Oval Office and curling up in the fetal position because they would just think, 'I can't even go outside and face the world. I've got all these accusations.' Not even just political ones, the intemperance of heart. It's all this stuff about whether it's Stormy Daniels, or some other woman who fifteen years ago said she had a fling with him.

"Most of those kinds of things would cause a person to just want to say, 'I've gotta run. I can't stay here.' And you know where he ends up? He stares right back in the face of his accusers and challenges them. And I saw it during the campaign. It's one of the reasons why early on I said, 'You know, I think this guy will win.' Everyone else was saying, 'There's no chance. There's no way.' I said, 'Guys, you're getting it wrong.'

"When people would say, 'I can't believe he just said that at the rally,' I would say, 'You don't understand. What he said in that microphone at the podium was what four guys sitting around a booth at the Waffle House leaned close in to each other and said that same morning at breakfast. They were thinking they needed to be careful so no one heard them, but then Trump walks up and says it into the microphone, and they're sitting there saying, "Yeah! Now there's somebody who's talking our language!"' And that's totally beyond the grasp of most of the people who were covering the campaign for the news networks."

According to those who know him best, Donald Trump is a man of resolute faith and confidence. He has been tested over and over, and he has suffered many setbacks and reversals along the way. It would take monumental self-assurance to rise above the slings and arrows that have been aimed at him. But this president has the inner strength to overcome those challenges, and he has the confidence to trust his core beliefs. As Falwell told me, Donald Trump is a man who makes up his own mind on everything. "I think he listens to a lot of people," he said, "but I don't think he lets anyone tell him what to do. I've noticed that about him. He'll take advice from everybody, and he'll listen to everybody, but nobody tells him what to do. Nobody unduly influences him. I've never seen anybody like him. Every other politician I've talked to can be persuaded and can be influenced, but he really can't. He is his own man, and I really respect that."

CHAPTER 12

THE BATTLE FOR JERUSALEM

THE UNREST IN the Middle East and the wars America is fighting in other parts of the world are tied to the one foreign policy issue that may have the greatest long-term significance, which is what to do about Israel and Palestine. Since Israel recaptured the territory Jews call Judea and Samaria but others call the West Bank, there has been a divisive and often violent standoff over whether there should be a one-state or two-state solution. Liberals in Israel and the US tend to opt for the two-state solution. Hard-line conservatives and evangelical Christian Zionists, on the other hand, believe God gave the land to the Jews, and that's the end of the equation.

Even among Evangelicals there is disagreement, however. Some Evangelicals, especially those to the left of center, believe there should be a two-state solution and are often critical of the Israeli government, which they consider to have no religious significance. Many who ascribe to the false doctrine called "replacement theology," frequently associated with reformed theology, believe God bypassed the Jews when He ordained the new covenant to Christian believers, expanding His covenant with Abraham. Therefore, they believe, there is no need to support the Jewish state, and it may even be morally wrong to do so. The doctrine may have made some sense before the establishment of the Jewish state in 1948, but it is clearly incompatible with Scripture and seriously misrepresents the reality of the Middle East today.

One of the thorniest issues in some circles is whether Jerusalem ought to be Israel's capital and whether President Trump was justified in moving America's embassy there. Congress overwhelmingly approved such a move in 1995 in the Jerusalem Embassy Act, which recognized Jerusalem as the capital of Israel and called for Jerusalem to remain an undivided city. Israeli Prime Minister Benjamin Netanyahu and President Trump discussed this in an important meeting a few months into Trump's presidency as part of the president's multination tour of Europe and the Middle East. They discussed not only the Jerusalem Embassy Act, but also Iran and Syria and how to partner to wage war on terrorists in the Middle East.

The purpose of the Jerusalem Embassy Act was to set aside funds for the relocation of the US Embassy from Tel Aviv to Jerusalem by May 31, 1999. Even though the bill became law, Presidents Clinton, Bush, and Obama each signed waivers every six months during their eight-year terms delaying implementation of the law on "national security" grounds. Following suit, Donald Trump also signed waivers, but on December 6, 2017, he announced, "While previous presidents have made this a major campaign promise, they failed to deliver. Today, I am delivering. I've judged this course of action to be in the best interests of the United States of America and the pursuit of peace between Israel and the Palestinians. This is a long-overdue step to advance the peace process and to work towards a lasting agreement."[1]

It would be hard to say who was more ecstatic, the Israelis who had long hoped for America to take this monumental action, or Evangelicals and Christian Zionists for whom this was a top priority. When the president made the announcement, a member of his Faith Leaders Initiative told me, "I believe he did it for us. He knows we believe in him. He knows this is an important issue for us. And I believe that is one of the reasons he did it. I don't believe we lobbied or persuaded him to do it, but I do believe he knew from the very beginning, during the primaries. We had this discussion with them, about core issues. Number one is the sanctity of life. The second is Israel. We knew exactly where he stood on those two issues, and he kept his promise on both of them."

Pastor Frank Amedia of Ohio sees it a little differently. Shortly after Trump was declared the winner of the presidency, in November 2016, Amedia felt led to start a prayer network called POTUS Shield to seek God's favor and guidance for the new leader. He campaigned hard for Trump and even gave him a prophetic word on one occasion. "Trump admits he had no prior understanding of the passionate support for Israel by conservative Christians," Amedia told me. "In fact, he was of the mindset from his experiences in New York that Jews and Christians were deeply divided over Israel."

But something happened as he prepared to speak at an American Israel Public Affairs Committee (AIPAC) event in early 2016, and candidate Trump dared to follow his advisors' counsel to present a five-point plan for Israel that included acknowledging Jerusalem as its capital and relocating the US Embassy there. "Because he has stepped out to bless Israel," Amedia told me, "the force and favor of God were upon him, and through him God's favor was turned up higher, another shade of degrees. Those who bless Israel shall be blessed!"

When the decision was eventually made to move the embassy from Tel Aviv to Jerusalem, President Trump directed the State Department to "begin the process of hiring architects, engineers, and planners so that a new embassy, when completed, will be a magnificent tribute to peace."[2] But when he learned it would take several years and nearly a billion dollars to build the planned embassy, he decided to temporarily move the embassy to the existing US consulate in Jerusalem and to do it for the seventieth anniversary of Israel becoming an independent nation. After that important ceremonial event the architects and engineers would have plenty of time to build a new embassy.

"President Trump has neither a desire to engage in nation-building in the region nor to fight a traditional war. He was adamantly opposed to the Iraq War. The new wars of the twenty-first century are proxy, economic, media, and ideological," Dr. Mike Evans, my longtime friend and the founder and president of the Jerusalem Prayer Team, said in a February 2017 Charisma News article. "Israel is the undisputed proxy champion of the world. Radical Islam has labeled Israel 'The Little Satan.' America has been crowned 'The Big Satan.'"[3] And these two nations are now perceived in some places as the undisputed enemies of Palestinians and those who oppose Israel's autonomy all over the world.

During the embassy dedication, a gala was hosted at the Waldorf Astoria by Mike Evans. Three hundred seventy-five of the most powerful world leaders were there, including Jared and Ivanka Trump Kushner, Sen. Lindsey Graham, Sen. Ted Cruz, former Sen. Joe Lieberman, and Secretary of the Treasury Steven Mnuchin. Speaking at the gala, Evans said that President Donald Trump had kept his promises, unlike earlier presidents who refused to do so. Trump has laid the foundation for a genuine peace process.

When Menachem Begin was prime minister of Israel, he showed Evans a strategic plan he was preparing to present to President Ronald Reagan in the early 1980s. "Israel's conclusion," Evans said, "was that America could not effectively win wars in the Middle East. Wars were fought over such a lengthy period of time. By the time the US reached the region to fight a war, it had reached an end." But that realization revealed a new alignment and a new ally in the world's struggle against terrorism. As Evans writes:

> The reality is that during the Communist era, Israel, a US proxy, had strategically deterred Communists in the Middle East. Now, Israel will become a proxy against radical Islam. There is no information operation in the region that compares to Israeli intelligence. The nation has eyes and ears on the ground in each Arab country. Iran is ground zero

for world terror. Its proxies are destabilizing the entire Middle East. It is in both Trump's and Netanyahu's crosshairs. Israel is incapable of effectively destroying Iran's nuclear reactors alone, which is the reason Netanyahu never moved forward with an operation.[4]

An Insider's Perspective

To get a closer look at the conflict in the Middle East and the battle for Jerusalem, I contacted a woman who was born in the midst of the struggle and survived constant fear and danger before coming to the US to warn Americans about the consequences of doing nothing. She has since become one of the best-known speakers and activists on behalf of Israel and the Christian West. As indicated by her organization's website, Lady Brigitte Gabriel is the founder of ACT for America. She has spoken at the United Nations and met with members of Congress, the British Parliament, the Australian prime minister, senior Pentagon officials, the US Special Operations Command, the FBI, and many others about the threat of radical Islam. She was knighted in Europe in 2016 for her efforts in fighting terrorism and standing up for Western Judeo-Christian values.[5]

When she was just ten years old, radical Islamists fired rockets into her family home, destroying it and seriously injuring her. The family was forced to live for the next several years in an eight-by-ten-foot underground bomb shelter, often surviving on weeds. Gabriel had to crawl through a drainage ditch to get water from a nearby spring while avoiding Islamic snipers. Eventually she fled from Lebanon to Israel but later moved to America and became a citizen of the United States, where she has been recognized as one of the leading terrorism experts in the world.

Gabriel is a regular guest on the Fox News Channel, CNN, MSNBC, and numerous radio programs. She serves on the board of advisors of the Intelligence Summit and is the author of two *New York Times* best sellers, *Because They Hate: A Survivor of Islamic Terror Warns America* and *They Must Be Stopped: Why We Must Defeat Radical Islam and How We Can Do It*. Growing up in a Lebanese Christian family, she lived through unspeakable horrors. Having seen her interviews on television, I admire her courage. I am honored to publish her new book, *Rise: In Defense of Judeo-Christian Values and Freedom*, which released shortly before this book. Recently I interviewed her for the Charisma Podcast Network and learned firsthand what the struggle in that hotly contested region of the world is all about. During our podcast conversation I asked her, "Brigitte, as we witnessed recently in Singapore, Donald Trump is taking bold steps for peace, and his policies are shaking things up. As an expert on the conflict in the Middle East, what do you think the effects of Trump's presidency will be in that part of the world?" Her response and a transcription of the rest of our conversation are as follows:

> GABRIEL: Donald Trump is making the world a safer place and a better place through his strengths. Our enemies know they cannot mess around with this president. He means what he says, and he follows through on his words. If he draws a red line, it means a red line. We see corrupt leaders around the world are already taking notice. This is why North Korea is coming to the negotiating table. This is why we are seeing the Saudis and the Egyptians and the Israelis working together against a common enemy. And this is why we see how he is enforcing the border policies to protect the country. So all in all, he is making the world a safer place.
>
> STRANG: Seismic shifts are happening in the Middle East where Sunni Muslims are allying with Israel against Shiite Muslims in Iran for the first time. What are the prospects for our interest in the region based on these new relationships, and how does that relate to the fight that you have against terrorism?
>
> GABRIEL: I think this is perfect timing because the Saudis and the Israelis started talking to each other, even when President Obama was in office. Except President Obama was more interested in striking up a friendship with the Iranians than supporting and protecting our allies in the Middle East. Today President Trump is capitalizing on the willingness of the Saudis, who basically have a common enemy with the Israelis. It's in their best interest to come together and work together, and this is why the Saudis allow the Israelis to use their air space, because the Saudis know that Iran is building a nuclear weapon, and Iran wants to have [dominance] over the Middle East. So this is why they are willing to come together and work with America and Israel to really facilitate a strong counterbalance to Russia and Iran....
>
> STRANG: What is the significance of moving the US Embassy to Jerusalem? Now several other countries are doing the same, disproving the naysayers who predicted violence in the Middle East. What is your feeling about all of these changes?

GABRIEL: ...The significance of us moving our embassy to Jerusalem is that we are basically showing with our action that we mean business in standing up with our ally. And we are willing to go and fight the world in standing up and imploring Israel's right to exist as a Jewish state with Jerusalem as its capital, and the United States is going to put the embassy there, and a lot of countries are following.

STRANG: With ISIS being decimated in Syria and Iraq, what effect has that had on international terrorism or the future threat of terrorism?

GABRIEL: It has a huge ramification, and it's all for the better. Now, we are not out of the woods with ISIS because even though ISIS lost physical territory, ISIS' caliphate on the internet is still thriving, and they are still recruiting. The fear right now is that almost a third of the Europeans who left the country to go fight with ISIS in Syria have now returned home, including women and children. So the threat is evolving in different ways. We are no longer fighting ISIS with its territory, but we now are fighting ISIS' women who are back in Europe, who look European, who hold European passports, who are there with their children, who have been desensitized to killing.

But in general, these women will not be able to carry out terrorist attacks on massive scales or organize an army the way ISIS leaderships organize. So the threat in general is subsiding....

STRANG: Will Trump's strong stance on securing the borders affect the risk of Islamic terrorism in our country? In other words, what danger has resulted in terrorists coming in illegally across the southern border?

GABRIEL: We have been dealing with Islamic terrorists sneaking through the southern border for over fifteen years now. I talked about that in my book in 2006, titled *Because They Hate*, where I discuss how our government at that time was...identifying some terrorists by name, calling them at that time OTM—"Other Than Mexicans." And what they were referring to was basically Islamic terrorists sneaking through the Mexican border.

Today President Trump is doing the right thing by securing our borders....The risk right now is that Iran has been setting up major Hezbollah centers all over Central America and Latin America. And they are providing cultural centers. They are recruiting and training the people from Central America because they look like Middle Easterners. [They] can blend in, they can learn the language, and then they can sneak through the southern border.

We have already arrested Hezbollah operatives...who have come through the Mexican border, enabled and facilitated by the drug cartel. And so by us securing the border and specifically by building a wall, and going aggressively at building a wall, that will cut down on what type of people are coming through our border, including terrorists. Not just criminals are coming here who are going to take away jobs and benefits, and even are a danger to the safety and security of Americans, but also terrorists. And he is doing the same thing to control the visa immigration, visa migration, all those types of chain migrations, and the result of that would be a more safe and secure America.

STRANG: What would you say is the biggest terrorist threat to America today?

GABRIEL: The radical Left. Without a doubt.... What enables Islamic terrorists is the radical Left who is silencing and sabotaging and acting as shackles around the ankles of those who are trying to keep our community safe, starting with our police officers and our first responders. Right now America is under attack by people from within America who hate America so much that they are willing to give aid and abet our enemies, who share a common goal with them, which is the destruction of America, the way people like you and me see America—as [a] strong, God-loving, God-fearing, patriotic country that was founded on Judeo-Christian principles by great Founding Fathers.... The new Left want to see America brought down in the world, be on the same level as every other country in the world with open borders, open immigration, transgenders in every bathroom, blurring the lines between anything that we have grown up accustomed to as to the America that was founded by our Founding Fathers and this new America today. And so I would say that the radical Left is the greatest threat to America right now.

STRANG: The Palestinian uprising [taking place in Israel today] is smaller than what we hear about in Iraq and Syria, but is terrorism by or inspired by Palestinians a major threat?

GABRIEL: ...What we are seeing right now with terrorism around the world is basically what the Palestinians have perfected and is now being elaborated on by ISIS. So the threat of Palestinian terrorism, who basically initiated car bombings, suicide bombings, killing, lynching, blowing up children, we are now seeing that play worldwide.

We are seeing new resurrection in the Palestinian territories under Hamas, with this venomous hatred against Israelis and the justification of killing...even the youngest among them, even infants, because in the Palestinians' eyes, infants grow to be soldiers. They will always remain a threat as long as they have leaders brainwashing them with hatred toward the state of Israel and Jews in general worldwide.

STRANG: Who is funding most of the violence by extremist groups around the world?

GABRIEL: Iran right now is the major funder of terrorism. Hezbollah has committed attacks on five continents across the globe. After Iran, you are looking at different Islamic states, specifically from the Gulf states, and Saudi Arabia, because of the oil wealth that enables them to support terrorist Islamic organizations. Across the globe, whether it is Al-Shabaab or Al-Nusra, it doesn't matter what country they are. They are being supported by like-minded Islamists who share the same ideology. And what we are seeing also in these certain areas is that Iran has even supported elements of al Qaeda. Iran is even funding Hamas, even though Hamas is a Sunni group. When it comes to them coming together and fighting their enemies, they don't care where the money goes to support Western activities against Israel and the United States because they are the common enemy. So the money pipeline flowing into terrorism worldwide is coming from both directions: the Sunni direction, which is coming out of Saudi Arabia and different countries in the Gulf states, and also from Iran.

STRANG: Is there any evidence of any non-Islamic or non-Muslim groups funding international terrorism?

GABRIEL: Not that I know of, directly. Not directly going for terrorism and the killing of innocent civilians. They might fund the moderate wing or what they perceive as the moderate wing in the West, which is the Muslim Brotherhood movement. Because under Obama, he did not look at the Muslim Brotherhood movement as a terrorist organization or a terrorist group. So look at Muslim Brotherhood operatives within the West, organizations like the Council on American-Islamic Relations or the Islamic Society of North America, or right now you are seeing Linda Sarsour, who is a Palestinian activist and an anti-Semite, now basically is the cochair for the Women's March and leading the women's movement that is very corrupt in the United States, and it's being funded by the likes of the Southern Poverty Law Center, the ACLU, Planned Parenthood, [and] George Soros.

So you've got the Soros foundations funneling money into these radical leftist groups, including Islamic groups that are supposedly operating in a peaceful movement in the West, even though they are basically the stealth arm of the Muslim Brotherhood. They may not be carrying [out] their attacks, but they are carrying on the ideology and enforcing the Muslim Brotherhood project for the world.... And these organizations are receiving funding from the likes of George Soros and leftist organizations.

STRANG: What is the Trump administration going to do to deal with the threat of terrorism?

GABRIEL: The Trump administration is striking and striking hard immediately when they know that...terrorism has been committed. For example, President Trump did not hesitate to strike in Syria, twice already in his first year in office. The first strike was immediately after he became president, basically sending a message that America will not tolerate such barbaric behavior and the killing of innocent people. He has gone aggressively after ISIS, killing ISIS, and this is why ISIS is losing its territory, or practically has lost most of its territory. What President Trump is doing is basically striking immediately where he needs to strike, and he is doing it physically, not with words. We are dealing with an enemy that does not understand words, but they understand and respect strength and actions. And President Trump is acting both in strength with his words as well as with his actions....

STRANG: Is there anything that we ought to know more about concerning diplomatic or military threats in other places, such as North Korea, Europe, or Eastern Europe?

GABRIEL: The wonderful thing about President Trump is that he is putting America first, before other countries like Afghanistan or Iraq. Before, our policy was basically to win hearts and minds. We went into there, and we started building nations. We were borrowing money from China, going terribly into debt. Putting the debt like a shackle around our children's necks in order to basically build schools and highways in Afghanistan for people who loathe us and could [not] care less about what we were building for them.

President Trump is changing all of that. President Trump is of the philosophy of go in, fight the enemy, then pull out, and let them sort it out within themselves. And that is very important because it sends a message to our enemy that you will be destroyed, and we will not rebuild you because we are not wasting our good precious dollars on you while taking it away from our children and going into debt to do so. And countries are taking notice. And this is why President Trump is taking all the right steps in dealing with terrorists, especially Islamic terrorism, and especially in that part of the world, such as the Middle East, Syria, and Iraq. Especially now with the world's eyes on Syria, wondering whether or not America is going to get involved in the war.

As to North Korea, President Trump dealt with such strength with North Korea, and this is what forced North Korea to come to the negotiating table. While the leftist lamestream media was talking about President Trump getting us into a nuclear war, President Trump actually saved the world from a nuclear war and forced the North Koreans to come to the negotiating table by basically letting them know, "You don't want to mess with me because you do not know what I'm going to do to you! You can't even imagine or even know what to expect when I react." And that deterrent—we are getting back now to the same philosophy of strong words to deter our enemies the way we exercised that with the Soviet Union during the Cold War....

President Trump is standing strong. He is standing strong at rebuilding our allies worldwide, whether in Japan, whether in the Middle East, whether in even working relations with China. And what he is about to do with the Iran deal is sending all the right messages in our foreign policy. And having the dream team, or what I call the dream team, Pompeo and Bolton, by his side, now they will be able to get things done.

In Unity of Purpose

It doesn't take a lot of imagination to see that, short of a full-blown miracle, the Middle East will remain a trouble spot and a hotbed of violence and insurrection for years to come. Israel is our strongest ally in the Middle East, and because it is also the smallest nation in the region—8.8 million (6.5 million of them Jews) surrounded by about 400 million Muslims—it depends on America's support and our promise of defense. With the US as a partner and ally, Mike Evans wrote, Israel feels it can withstand the military threats. And not only can Iran's nuclear reactors be neutralized, but the hostile Shiite government can even be pushed into bankruptcy. Such a move would virtually guarantee a regime change and a reduction of tension in the region.

This was the same sort of revolution that took place under the Shah of Iran, he said. "Syria has become a snake-infested swamp filled with the vilest terrorists in the world. Both the Syrian and Iranian matters can be resolved in due course, but it will take the support of one global ally besides the US and Israel. That will be Russia," Evans said, "which explains Donald Trump's refusal to alienate Vladimir Putin."[6]

Evans told me he became Prime Minister Netanyahu's first Christian Zionist friend when they were both in their early thirties. Over the years Evans has raised millions of dollars from his donors for projects benefiting Israel, including his Friends of Zion Museum, and written dozens of books, many of them about Israel. In America. Evans is considered to be one of the most high-profile Christian Zionists, and he believes that not only has Netanyahu scored his greatest victory with the Trump presidency, but so has Trump with Netanyahu, and he believes Israel's finest days are yet to come, thanks to the Netanyahu–Trump alliance. Ultimately the United States will have "a naval base in the Port of Haifa, where US troops can be protected, and special ops can move in and out to decapitate radical Islam."[7] And one more reason the two heads of state are so close: they have two of the same heroes, Winston Churchill and Ronald Reagan.

When Evans was building his pro-Israel coalition in the 1980s, the focus was specifically on prayer. His ministry purchased the home in Haarlem, Netherlands, known as "the Hiding Place," which is where Corrie ten Boom and her family hid Jews before transporting them to safety outside Holland. No Jews were ever captured there, but several members of the ten Boom family died at the hands of the Nazis. Corrie was miraculously released soon after the death of her sister Betsie and was able to tell her story all over the world.

There was a prayer group that met in that home for a full century, from 1844 until 1944, to pray for the Jewish people and the peace of Jerusalem, and Evans' goal was to start it again with the Jerusalem Prayer Team. He also set an audacious goal of one hundred million intercessors praying for the peace of Jerusalem. He claims to have forty-two million intercessors now and says the number will hit one hundred million by 2020, largely through social networks. This has become the base for Evans to pursue his goals. Israel is constantly fighting ideological wars, but since such a tiny nation can't hope to win wars of ideas, it needs friends who can help. So Evans began creating the social networks that led to his building the Friends of Zion Museum in Jerusalem.

Because of my friendship with Mike Evans, I knew about his desire to build the museum long before it became a reality. I admit I was skeptical at first because I knew Evans well enough to know he didn't even like going to museums. I also knew of the great history of Christian Zionism that predates even Jewish Zionism. David Brog, executive director of Christians United for Israel, wrote an amazing book in 2006 that I had the privilege of publishing, called *Standing With Israel*, which documents this. But most Christians—even many Evangelicals who love Israel—don't know this amazing history, nor do most Israeli Jews. So I knew that documenting this special relationship with a museum in Jerusalem was a worthy goal.

When I visited the Friends of Zion Heritage Center, also known as the Friends of Zion Museum, shortly before it officially opened, in 2015, I was awed by its storytelling about Zionism. It was said to be the first "smart museum" in Israel, combining 3D technology, touch screens, and original musical scores and artwork from over 150 Israeli artists, with surround sound in each of its seven exhibitions. Even though I've published books, written, and spoken on Christian Zionism, I learned a few new things and was moved by the genuine love for the Jewish people that comes through at the museum. Today the Friends of Zion Heritage Center is a must-see for the tens of thousands of Christian tourists who visit Jerusalem each year. Interestingly about half of the museum's visitors are Israelis, most of whom don't know how Christians have befriended Jews throughout the years.

When President Trump first visited Jerusalem, he was met by banners put up by Friends of Zion (or FOZ, as it brands itself). Evans said it was a "wonderful opportunity to promote [our] museum and [our] initiative, at the same time, acknowledge a president who is standing for righteousness." So Evans put up banners all over Jerusalem. About half said "Trump is a friend of Zion," and half said "Trump Make Israel Great." And as Evans said, "He certainly has done both."

A few days after Trump announced in December 2017 that he would be moving the US embassy to Jerusalem, Evans presented him with the Friend of Zion award in the Oval Office. He had previously presented the award to President George W.

Bush, Prince Albert II of Monaco, and the former president of Bulgaria, Rosen Plevneliev. He promised to present it to any head of state who moves its embassy to Jerusalem. So far, in addition to President Trump, he has done that for the presidents of Paraguay and Guatemala.

Channel i24 (an English-language station in Jerusalem) sent a reporter to check out the museum. "It's no surprise that all three delegations met here, at the Friends of Zion Museum to learn more about the story of Christian Zionism and why the relationship between the Jewish state and Christians around the world is now more important than ever," TV reporter Mike Wagenheim gushed as he reported favorably on this new Jerusalem tourist attraction. "Many experts say it was US President Donald Trump's evangelical base who ultimately convinced him to move America's Embassy to the Holy City."[8]

The Friends of Zion Museum put banners all over Jerusalem when Donald Trump's visit coincided with Israel's seventieth anniversary celebration in 2017, just a few months into his term. But Trump did not announce what many had hoped he would—that the US would move its embassy there. That announcement would come six months later. "A lot of people were upset about that," Evans told me in an interview for this book, "[but] I believed Donald Trump would keep his word. Actually on the committee I served [on]at the White House…several [committee members] were upset….They said he's not doing it. And I said, 'He's going to do it. He didn't promise he would do it in one year, but he's going to do it.' So I always believed that Donald Trump would do exactly that."

When Vice President Mike Pence visited Jerusalem in January 2018, FOZ put banners all over the city, and they did so again when the US Embassy officially opened in Jerusalem, May 14, 2018. Each time the group was hanging not only banners but also "wraps" on municipal buses driving around the city, and even banners on the backs of camels. "It was pretty funny to see an Arab walking a camel with a sign on it saying 'Trump Make Israel Great,'" Evans said. But that's what happened.

During the festivities, Evans would text me photos and articles from the Israeli press, and I would pass them along and publish some of them on our CharismaNews.com website. The banners were in English (so Trump and Pence could read them), but Evans said many Israelis know enough English to understand what they said. "Now, the interesting thing about the billboards," he told me, "is where…the billboards [were] printed—in Ramallah. All of our billboards were printed by Palestinians….When we have billboards torn, ripped down…usually [by] Jewish leftists that hated Donald Trump…we'd have Palestinian Arabs printing them in Ramallah again and [we] put them back up."

What's the significance of all this? Evans believes that many Israelis still don't know who their friends are. There are around two billion professing Christians in the world, of whom about six hundred million are Bible-believing Christians. "We've had four or five different countries come to us," Evans said, "because of what we're focusing on…creating friends, defending the state of Israel, fighting ideological wars, fighting spirit wars, prayer wars. Even economic wars. Because what we can do through our social network is fantastic. Actually, Facebook was founded on a college campus, but college campuses have become anti-Israel war zones. So we want to take our message back to college campuses utilizing the same tools that the world uses to fight these wars. It's a big project," Evans told me.

The events surrounding the dedication of the new US Embassy were attended by many American Christian Zionists who experienced a sense of euphoria. One who attended was Pastor Jim Garlow of Skyline Church in the San Diego area, who has been to Israel sixteen times. His wife, Rosemary Schindler Garlow, has been there fifty-five times! The Garlows showed up early for the event, and he described a feeling of "almost euphoria" in Jerusalem. "As people began arriving, it was so joyful, almost giddy," he told me. "The delight of the moment was unbelievable. Speaker after speaker referred to Scripture."

One of the most amazing things to Garlow, who is part of the president's Faith Leaders Initiative, is that Trump actually keeps his word on promises he makes. "For someone who isn't really 'one of us,' Trump's policies are so right and correct, especially on saving lives of unborn babies or honoring Israel. He stands on the right side of issue after issue. Plus, he has the unique temperament and personality to take the onslaught of criticism he gets. We're seeing something that can't be explained. He truly is like a Cyrus," Garlow said.

Cyrus was the ancient Persian king who, although he did not believe in the Hebrew God, was used by God according to the prophet Isaiah to enable the Jewish people to return to Jerusalem. In my book *God and Donald Trump* I document how some Christian leaders used this comparison to Trump to explain how God could use someone as imperfect as Trump for His purposes. The comparison was not lost on leaders of the Mikdash Educational Center, a Jewish educational organization that minted a "temple coin" bearing an image of President Trump, alongside an image of King Cyrus, to honor Trump's recognition of Jerusalem as Israel's capital. One thousand copies of the coin, which also mentions the Balfour Declaration, were minted. A second coin in the Cyrus-Trump series has been released as well. The coins can't be used as currency, but you can buy one with a donation.

Jonathan Cahn, whom I mentioned in chapter 9, also sees a connection. He told me, "Trump's proclamation concerning Jerusalem holds striking parallels to the decree of the Persian king Cyrus as recorded in the Bible." He went on to explain that "each proclamation recognizes the right of the Jewish people to the land and Jerusalem as the capital of Israel. The result of Cyrus' decree was the rebuilding of Jerusalem after seventy years. The result of Trump's decree was the inauguration of the American embassy in Jerusalem after seventy years of Israel's existence—*to the exact day.*"

When Pastor John Hagee, the national director of Christians United for Israel, met with President Trump shortly before the embassy's opening, he said the same thing about the president being Cyrus and upped the ante by comparing Trump to Harry Truman, who recognized the state of Israel in 1948 eleven minutes after the new nation was declared into existence and famously said of himself, "I am Cyrus." Hagee told Breitbart News, "I told him that the moment that you do that, I believe that you will step into political immortality, because you are having the courage to do what other presidents did not have the courage to do."[9]

Prime Minister Benjamin Netanyahu was even more specific when he met with President Trump in Washington. "I want to tell you that the Jewish people have a long memory. So we remember the proclamation of the great King Cyrus the Great—Persian King. Twenty-five hundred years ago, he proclaimed that the Jewish exiles in Babylon can come back and rebuild our temple in Jerusalem. We remember, one hundred years ago, Lord Balfour, who issued the Balfour Proclamation that recognized the rights of the Jewish people in our ancestral homeland.

"We remember [seventy] years ago, President Harry S. Truman was the first leader to recognize the Jewish state. And we remember how a few weeks ago, President Donald J. Trump recognized Jerusalem as Israel's capital. Mr. President, this will be remembered by our people throughout the ages. And as you just said, others talked about it. You did it."[10]

Hopeful New Solutions

One of the thorniest issues in the Middle East is whether the Palestinian Authority (PA) should be made a separate state, side by side with Israel. Some on the left still maintain that Israel is occupying the land they captured from what had been part of Jordan in the Six-Day War in 1967. Since then Israel has made peace with Jordan, but many Arabs living in the Gaza Strip as well as what is called the West Bank in the West and Judea and Samaria in Israel demand recognition. Slowly momentum for a two-state solution has gained traction, both among liberals in Israel as well as among American diplomats.

Then a recommendation for a one-state solution has come from an unlikely source: the Messianic Jewish movement in the United States and its lobbying arm in Washington, DC, the Alliance for Israel Advocacy. I've been covering Messianic Jews since the movement emerged from the Jesus movement of the late 1960s–1970s. These are Jews who believe Jesus (Yeshua in Hebrew) was and is the promised Messiah (hence the name Messianic), yet they continue to identify as Jews, often celebrating Jewish feasts and calling their religious leaders rabbi. Charismatics and Evangelicals who love Israel usually embrace Messianic Jews as fellow believers, but the traditional Jewish community typically considers them an anathema, saying the Messianics have converted to Christianity, which they consider non-Jewish and historically hostile to Jews. This has resulted in a perception that Messianic Jews have joined the Jewish community's historic persecutors and thus should be treated as traitors and rejected as fellow Jews.

So when Rabbi Paul Liberman, executive director of the Alliance for Israel Advocacy, and Joel Chernoff, general secretary of the Messianic Jewish Alliance of America, proposed their one-state solution, they were astounded by how well they were received by scores of US Congress members as well as Israeli leaders—including one of Prime Minister Netanyahu's closest allies, Tzachi Hanegbi, who is minister of regional cooperation in Israel. In addition, Liberman has been invited to three meetings at the White House to discuss their bold and viable plan.

As I review and understand this proposal, it is a very simple plan. There would be one Jewish state—Israel—and the nearly one million Arabs who live in the West Bank would be given a financial incentive to voluntarily relocate to neighboring Arab countries, which would also be financially incentivized to receive and assist in resettling them. The one-state solution envisions this happening over a period of ten years. If successful, this plan would change the demographic balance between Jews and Arabs living in Judea and Samaria (the West Bank), thus moving toward the day that Israel could incorporate Judea and Samaria into Israel properly without losing its Jewish majority population and thus Jewish character. Those Arabs remaining in the West Bank would be given full rights of citizenship except the vote.

But would the West Bank Palestinian population be open to or accept this arrangement? Recent independent and authoritative polling done by the Alliance for Israel Advocacy in the West Bank has established that a large majority of the Palestinians living there are so dissatisfied with the horrific quality of life under the PA that they would welcome just such an opportunity.

So how would this be funded? At this time the United States budgets over $600 million annually for the PA (with which the PA funds the families of terrorists) and the United Nations Relief and Works Agency for Palestine Refugees (whose primary function is to resettle Palestinian refugees, which it refuses to do). In essence, this money would be redirected to resettle those Palestinians now desiring a fresh start in neighboring Arab countries, a much more productive and constructive alternative use of those funds. President Donald Trump and his appointee Ambassador to the United Nations Nikki Haley have already threatened to withdraw those funds to the PA when the Palestinians refused to cooperate with the United States' efforts to jump-start Israeli-Palestinian peace talks after he declared Jerusalem the capital of Israel in December 2017. By the way, since 1994 the United States has provided the Palestinians with $5.2 billion through USAID, according to *The Times of Israel*. Trump tweeted in January 2018 that the United States is paying the Palestinians hundreds of millions of dollars a year "for nothing" and complained that, in addition, the United States has received "no appreciation or respect" in return.[11]

So let's do the arithmetic. Over ten years that's $6,000 for each of the 1 million Arabs, yet there are 2.7 million Arabs in the West Bank and Gaza and another 1.4 million Arabs who live in the rest of Israel. Compare that with only 5.9 million Jews who fear they will be outnumbered, with birth rates among Arabs being high and among Jews being fairly low.

Obviously there's work that must be done. And nearby Arab countries would need to accept these immigrants, and the Palestinians would, of course, want to move. But at least it's a step in the right direction. And to me it's prophetically significant that the idea is coming from the Messianic Jewish community. As this book goes to press, the one-state solution in bill form has passed the House Legislative Counsel and is awaiting a congressman to formally propose the bill so that it can be given a name and number, thus becoming a live piece of congressional legislation.

So what does all this mean? According to Mike Evans, the people of Israel now have hope, brought by President Trump's decision to move the American embassy to the holy city of Jerusalem. "The Jewish people felt alone, as they have always felt throughout history, for thousands of years, until Donald Trump courageously stood up and boldly recognized Jerusalem as Israel's capital. It gave them exceptional hope."

Evans said that the Sephardic chief rabbi of Israel, Yitzhak Yosef, articulated what many Israeli Jews believed. Two days before the embassy's opening, the rabbi prayed at a gala hosted by Friends of Zion, in which he called America the "nation of grace" and President Trump the "king of mercy." He then said dramatically that "the recognition of Jerusalem by America can now usher in the Messiah." When I invited Evans to speak at one of our Nights to Honor Israel events in Orlando, Florida, a few years ago, he wowed the crowd with his enthusiastic support of Israel. His message is still inspiring, but nothing could ever be more inspiring to Evangelicals and Charismatic believers than the idea that faithful Jews and believing Christians will be united at last in the celebration of Israel's Messiah.

CHAPTER 13

SHAKING THE CHURCH

WHAT ARE WE to make of all the changes taking place in the world today? We're in the midst of a cultural revolution, and it's no secret that traditional moral values are taking a beating. Looking at the landscape of the past ten to twenty years, and the mounting toll of crimes and crises that fill the daily headlines, it's hard to ignore the feeling that maybe we've gone too far. The culture has drifted way out of bounds and out of control. The hate-filled rhetoric and threats of physical violence coming from the Left reveal just how deeply divided we are as a nation—so divided there seems to be little hope of ever reaching agreement on what's to be done about it.

As I wrote shortly after the publication of my book *God and Donald Trump*, few people outside the four walls of a church pay much attention to what God is doing in the world. To them, "acts of God" are what people call tornadoes and hurricanes. But is it possible God has a plan for this nation? Is it possible He has a plan for His people? In that book I cited several examples of individuals who felt Trump's election was a sign we were being given a second chance.

To put these things in context, perhaps it's worth noting that all is not well in the church today. Not only are there divisions between denominations, but there are intense disagreements over the forms of worship, the music, the structure and order of service, the liturgy, the preparation and role of the clergy, and, not least, over doctrinal integrity. Some churches are more like country clubs where vice is tolerated and old-fashioned evangelism is virtually forbidden. Others, offering bigger, louder, flashier, less-threatening services, have discarded two thousand years of church history to be more "relevant" to the unchurched and otherwise disinterested. Needless to say, such disagreements pose a lethal threat to the community of believers.

Prophetic passages of Scripture, such as the Old Testament Book of Amos and the New Testament Book of 2 Timothy, warn of a falling away in the latter days and a shaking of the church that can lead either to devastation or revival, depending on how the people respond. This nation was founded on Christian principles, and we were led for generations by men and women of exceptional character and moral integrity. But in light of the falling away and the infighting among the faithful, we have to wonder if the church can still make a difference in people's lives. Or is the faith of our fathers so fractured that our moral heritage is becoming irrelevant?

I've made the case that Donald Trump won the evangelical vote by the largest margin in history because Christians believed he alone had the leadership skills and persistence to reverse the death spiral the nation is in. He is not a theologian or even an Evangelical, but whenever he has expressed concern about the moral decline in America, he has been lampooned by the media as a hypocrite and a bigot. Meanwhile, men and women on the left are marching in the streets for abortion on demand and celebrating the right to take the life of an unborn child up to the moment of birth. They're glad same-sex marriage was validated by the Supreme Court and that marijuana is being legalized in state after state. And when it comes to old-fashioned morality, the mantra of the secular culture is simply "anything goes."[1] This too is a sign of biblical judgment.

But most Americans recognize the problems. You don't need to be religious to perceive that something is wrong with the way the country has been going. Two years into his presidency, many on both sides are still shocked that Trump won the election, but they're impressed by what he has managed to accomplish in such a short time—not only with the economy but in the courts, the culture, foreign policy, and the overall sense of well-being. While disappointed Democrats are still raging about the election and doing their best to disrupt his agenda, for many Americans it feels as if we've been given a reprieve.

Keeping the Faith

Considering the magnitude of the shock wave that struck the nation in the 2016 election, millions today feel as if Donald Trump's inauguration was actually a turning point in history. The political world was turned upside down; the agenda of the Left was disrupted, perhaps permanently. Suddenly, rather than a president who defended third-world nations against America and declared on June 28, 2006, that "we are no longer a Christian nation,"[2] we have a president who has promised to restore our national heritage and take a strong stand for religious freedom. People of faith are happy to know he has our backs and that he will be using his bully pulpit and the authority of his office to defend religious liberty. But we are wise enough to know the struggle has only just begun.

Donald Trump's commitment to America's heritage of faith was immediately visible on his Inauguration Day, when the president and First Lady attended a service at St. John's Episcopal Church. Every sitting US president since James Madison has attended a service at St. John's at least once. A crowd of fifty or sixty people gathered at the corner of Sixteenth and I Streets hoping to catch a glimpse of President Trump and Melania as they arrived. The first couple was greeted with shouts of "Trump! Trump! Trump!" as the entourage and a small group of religious leaders and guests made their way into the church. Farther away small groups of millennials and protesters cluttered the streets and security gates to "make a statement," carrying signs that said "Not My President." But inside the sanctuary it was a different story.

The sermon the president heard on that occasion was given by Dr. Robert Jeffress of Dallas' First Baptist Church, who had supported the president throughout the campaign. Jeffress said in part:

> President-elect Trump, you have had your share of critics from the day you announced you were running for president, but you've confounded them at every turn. First, they said you couldn't win the nomination, but you ended up garnering the most votes of any Republican in history. Then they said that was a fluke, but you couldn't win the election. And you handily defeated your opponent. And now your critics say you can't possibly succeed in your agenda.[3]

Drawing on the Old Testament story of Nehemiah, who was called by God to rebuild the broken-down walls of Jerusalem, Jeffress counseled the president to remain strong, like Nehemiah, in the face of resistance and seemingly insurmountable obstacles. At one point Nehemiah's adversaries called out to him, "You need to stop the project and come down from the wall and have a meeting with us." But, Jeffress said, "Nehemiah's response was classic: 'I'm doing a great work...why should I stop the work and come down to you?'"[4]

Then Jeffress continued, "President-elect Trump, you, Vice President-elect Pence, and your team have been called by God and elected by the people to do a great work. It is a work far too important to stop and answer your critics." Drawing to a close, he said:

> Mr. President-elect, I don't believe we have ever had a president with as many natural gifts as you. As you know, the reason I endorsed you within weeks of your announcement that you were running was because I believed that you were the only candidate who possessed the leadership skills necessary to reverse the downward trajectory of our nation. And beginning with Vice President-elect Pence—a great and godly man—you've assembled an unbelievably talented group of advisers around you. But the challenges facing our nation are so great that it will take more than natural ability to meet them. We need God's supernatural power.[5]

Pastor Jeffress went on to say that the same God who empowered Nehemiah nearly twenty-five hundred years ago is available today to all who are willing to humble themselves and ask the Lord for His help. He added, "When President Ronald Reagan addressed the Republican National Convention in my city of Dallas in 1984, he said, 'America needs God more than God needs America. If we ever forget that we are "one nation under God," then we will be a nation gone under.'"[6]

The day after the inauguration, the presidential entourage made the short drive to Washington National Cathedral for a ceremonial interfaith prayer service, which has been a tradition for new presidents ever since the inauguration of George Washington in 1789. Trump did not speak at the service but sat quietly in the front pew, with his children and grandchildren seated behind him, and followed along with the program, closing his eyes in prayer and meditation for lengthy periods of time as each of the religious leaders offered a prayer or a reading.

Some parishioners of the mostly liberal northwest DC congregation had expressed their disapproval of hosting a prayer service for Trump and Pence, but the president nevertheless greeted those in attendance warmly and listened respectfully as more than twenty-five faith leaders from many religious traditions offered prayers and brief readings in honor of the occasion. Among the speakers, my friend Bishop Harry Jackson of Hope Christian Church in Beltsville, Maryland, who serves with the president's Faith Leaders Initiative, prayed that God would grant the new president and his administration "wisdom and grace in the exercise of their duties." And he prayed that President Trump would be able to "serve all people of this nation and promote the dignity and freedom of every person."[7]

A Digital Coup d'État

Throughout the campaign Trump said he was committed to supporting religious liberty and defending the rights of Christians who are being persecuted around the world. During a *Fox & Friends* interview on January 21, 2018, Rev. Franklin Graham was asked for his reaction to the president after his first year in office, to which Graham responded, "He defends the Christian faith more than any president in my lifetime." The son of the late Rev. Billy Graham expressed admiration for President Trump and said, "I'm just grateful to the president. I find him to be an honest person."[8]

Concerning the president's support for issues of faith, Graham said, "I find him to be a person who is concerned about the religious freedoms of Americans, but not just us here in this country. But he's concerned about the religious freedom of people in other countries." He went on to say, "I applaud what he has done this first year, even though he has been attacked since day one. The Left is trying to destroy this man. It's almost like we're in the middle of a digital coup. And that's what it is, it's a digital coup d'état. They are wanting to force him out of office. They want to take control of our government. We need to pray for this man.... If [President Trump] succeeds, we all succeed." He added, "If he fails, we all fail."[9]

A legislative measure brought to the president's attention early in his campaign was the First Amendment Defense Act (FADA), which was written to defend the rights of religious believers to practice their faith without undue restraint. It was sponsored by Sen. Mike Lee, with 37 cosponsors in the Senate, and Rep. Raul Labrador, with 171 cosponsors in the House.

The media and LGBT community reacted with alarm, but when asked if he would support the bill, Trump said, "If I am elected president and Congress passes the FADA, I will sign it to protect the deeply held religious beliefs of Catholics and the beliefs of Americans of all faiths."[10] It remains to be seen whether the FADA legislation will survive in Congress, with partisans on both sides currently lined up to debate the issues. The arguments pro and con are predictable, but regardless of how the legislation fares in the Senate, this is an issue that isn't going away anytime soon. The problem is simply too big to ignore.

But Trump's promise of support couldn't change the minds of his die-hard critics, including many outspoken opponents within the faith community. Ever since he announced his candidacy in 2015, religious leaders of all persuasions had been taking potshots at Trump, calling him everything but a gentleman. The liberal *Huffington Post* published a list of Evangelicals who were "firmly against Trump" at the time, including the president of the Southern Baptist Convention's Ethics & Religious Liberty Commission, Russell Moore; former president Jimmy Carter; former George W. Bush speechwriter Peter Wehner; Sojourners founder Jim Wallis; the celebrated author and evangelical pastor Max Lucado, and a couple of others.[11]

During an interview on the Christian Broadcasting Network (CBN), Moore could hardly disguise his animosity for the president. He said Donald Trump is "changing the moral character of people" and claimed Trump's supporters "had to excuse things that they've never had to excuse before." Too many Christians have been "scared silent," he said, and don't speak up.[12] On another occasion, Moore said that anyone who supports Donald Trump is guilty of serious error. "The religious Right," he added, "turns out to be the people the religious Right warned us about."[13] Not everyone in his denomination agreed with Moore or appreciated his remarks, but the liberal media couldn't get enough of the apparent split among evangelical leaders.

Wehner, a senior fellow at Washington's Ethics and Public Policy Center, excoriated Trump in several columns in the *New York Times*, even comparing him to the German philosopher Friedrich Nietzsche, who influenced Nazi leader Adolf Hitler. Trump's philosophy, Wehner said, prioritizes strength and power over concern for the poor and powerless. He added that his bullying of adversaries and his lack of compassion represent a worldview that is "incompatible with Christianity." And he said that "in rallying around Mr. Trump, evangelicals have walked into the trap."[14]

These were the sorts of attacks that would bring joy to embittered Democratic voters, seeing the faithful turning against their own kind. Wehner criticized Jerry Falwell Jr., the president of Liberty University, who heaped praise on Trump during the campaign and said on one occasion that he believes "Donald Trump is God's man to lead our nation." At the same time, Wehner said, Eric Metaxas, the Christian author of popular biographies of William Wilberforce and Dietrich Bonhoeffer, "rhapsodized about Mr. Trump and argued that Christians 'must' vote for him because he is 'the last best hope of keeping America from sliding into oblivion.'" He also decried Pastor Robert Jeffress for saying that "any Christian who would sit at home and not vote for the Republican nominee" is "motivated by pride rather than principle."[15]

For Max Lucado, the issue of concern was apparently that Trump doesn't sound like a Christian. "I'm a pastor," he said in a blog, a version of which was published in the *Washington Post*. "I don't endorse candidates or place bumper stickers on my car. But I am protective of the Christian faith," he said. "If a public personality calls on Christ one day and calls someone a 'bimbo' the next, is something not awry? And to do so, not once, but repeatedly, unrepentantly and unapologetically? Can we not expect a tone that would set a good example for our children?

"We stand against bullying in schools," Lucado said. "Shouldn't we do the same in presidential politics?" He added, "When it comes to language, Mr. Trump inhabits a league of his own. Some of my friends tell me that his language is a virtue. But I respectfully part company with my Christian colleagues who chalk up his abrasive nature to candor."[16] This was just the kind of feedback the Never Trumpers and the liberal media were dying to hear.

A Different Perspective

During an interview by Scott Ross on CBN's *700 Club* on June 21, 2018, Anne Graham Lotz, Billy Graham's daughter and Franklin Graham's sister, agreed that Trump's choice of words isn't always what she and other Christians would prefer to hear. "I know we have issues with the way he expresses himself," she said. "But his policies have been stunningly supportive of biblical values. Right now he has my applause and my prayers...because I think he's in a very dangerous place, you can feel the enemy trying to tear him to shreds, including his policies that have taken a stand on biblical values."[17]

Speaking about the drift away from the Christian faith in many parts of the nation today, Ross asked, "Have we lost our fear of God?" Lotz responded, "Yes, yes. We have, within the church and outside the church. It's stunning. You know, we live our lives as though He's not holy, as though He's not almighty, as though He's not pure....And fear of God is just that. It's being afraid of God in a healthy sense. So that keeps us from sin, it keeps us right before Him.

"Just like my father," she said. "I was, in a sense as a girl growing up, afraid of my father. I wouldn't have done anything to displease him." Then she said, "I wouldn't have wanted to hurt him or disappoint him or make him cross. And so a fear of God is rooted in love for God. But you don't want to hurt Him. You don't want to displease Him. And then there's a reverence. You know, God is God and we are we. And that's a big difference."[18]

Addressing the apparent lack of faith in the younger generation, Lotz said she felt that part of the problem is that "Christian parents have not passed on the truth that leads to faith to their children. Maybe we left it up to the churches or to the professionals and we didn't do it ourselves," she said. "But something is disconnected because instead of the nation getting better, we've gotten worse. We've gotten farther away from God's Word. And it could be that, in response to what my father did, talking about spiritual warfare, [the devil has] just come in like a flood to try to undo any impact from my father's ministry or other people's ministries or the church. But we know in the end that we'll be triumphant."[19]

I remember watching Billy Graham's funeral on television and the moving eulogies each of his children gave. I especially remember the powerful words Lotz spoke that day, emphasizing that she felt the date her father died was strategic from heaven's point of view. She said, "February 21, 2018 is the day when Jews focused on scripture reading that focuses on the death of Moses. Moses was the great liberator. He brought people, millions of people, out of bondage to slavery, got them to the edge of the Promised Land, and God took him to heaven, and then God brought Joshua to lead them into the Promised Land to take them home."[20]

She went on to explain, "My father also is a great liberator. He brought millions of people out of bondage to sin, and he gets us to the edge of heaven, the edge of the promised land, and then God has called him home." She then challenged those listening: "Could it be that God is going to bring Joshua to lead us into the promised land to lead us to heaven, and do you know what the New Testament name is for Joshua? It's Jesus, and I believe this is a shot across the bow from heaven. And I believe God is saying, 'Wake up, church! Wake up, world! Wake up, Anne! Jesus is coming. Jesus is coming.'"[21]

In the CBN interview Ross followed up on the discussion of Lotz's famous father, asking, "Was he disappointed about the way things have been going in America or in the world?" She said she has seen the impact of her father's preaching all over the world. Lives have been changed, millions came to faith, and many of those people are in ministry today. Their lives are better, she added, "but the impact on our nation, you know, something's missing, isn't it?"[22]

Coming from the world of business and real estate development, Donald Trump was not familiar with the language and customs of the evangelical community when he came to the White House. Although he had been a close friend and supporter of the late Dr. Norman Vincent Peale in New York and attended services at Marble Collegiate Church, he was suddenly being exposed to a different perspective and a different kind of religious experience. But through his friendship with evangelical leaders such as Paula White Cain, James Robison, Robert Jeffress, and a few others, he was gaining a deeper appreciation for the concerns of the millions of evangelical voters who gave him the critical margin of victory.

Very early in his administration the president began assembling an advisory board of faith leaders with whom he could meet from time to time and who would be available by telephone to offer insight on issues of concern to the churches. Then, in mid-July 2017, he invited a group of two dozen evangelical leaders to meet with him in the Oval Office for a few minutes before a daylong listening session with the Office of Public Liaison (OPL). As reported by CBN, the group discussed a wide variety of issues with the OPL, focusing especially on religious liberty, criminal justice reform, and America's support for the nation of Israel.[23]

Among the leaders in attendance were Tony Perkins of the Family Research Council; Paula White Cain of New Destiny Christian Center in Apopka, Florida; former congresswoman Michele Bachmann; Ralph Reed of the Faith and Freedom Coalition; Gary Bauer of American Values; Robert Jeffress of First Baptist Church in Dallas; Jack Graham of Prestonwood Baptist Church in Plano, Texas; Jim Garlow of Skyline Church in La Mesa, California; Rodney Howard-Browne of the River at Tampa Bay Church; Mike Evans, founder of Friends of Zion Museum in Jerusalem; and Richard Land of the Southern Evangelical Seminary in Charlotte.

The meeting had been arranged by a special assistant to the president and included a prayer time, to which, as several members of the group reported, the president was exceptionally receptive. Afterward Perkins told friends and supporters of his organization that the Trump administration was "genuinely interested and responsive to the concerns of the evangelical community." After fourteen years in Washington, he said, "I am more optimistic that we can change the course of this country."[24]

Tony Suarez, executive vice president of the National Hispanic Christian Leadership Conference, said he had been concerned about the lack of action from Washington on immigration reform but said, "I don't blame the White House. I blame Congress." He added that the meeting with Trump was relaxed and unhurried, "like friends getting together."[25] It's true, the president has been a friend to the Christian community. My friend, former congressman Bob McEwen, who serves as executive director of the Council for National Policy, told a group of politically active Christians at a meeting I attended in Washington a year into Trump's first term that if you can't "see God's hand on Donald Trump, you are deaf, dumb, and blind."[26] At this point in his presidency a majority of Christians and like-minded conservatives would likely agree.

A Nation at Risk

One of the reasons I wrote the book *God and Donald Trump* was to take a closer look at the phenomenon that took place in the 2016 election. How was it possible, I wondered, that Donald Trump was able to win such a stunning victory when the media, the polls, and the entire political establishment were against him? As it turns out, it wasn't because the Russians hacked the election, it wasn't because James Comey reopened the Clinton email investigation, and it wasn't because men were telling their wives to vote for Trump, as the Left wanted us to believe. So for me the question became, Was it possible that God, seeing the moral spiral we were in, raised up someone who couldn't care less about political correctness and political protocol but had the temperament and convictions to make America great again?

I made this point when I was interviewed on CNN and MSNBC. They wanted to know how Evangelicals who believe in morality and righteous living could support Donald Trump after the Stormy Daniels scandal emerged. I said most Christians didn't hold him accountable for his past indiscretions—that's God's business—but the question gave me an opening to talk about the bigger issues and to say that Christians are praying for the president and we believe God answered our prayers by giving us a strong and capable leader who, despite his failings, has a clear vision for the future and is standing strong for the policies and standards we believe in.

Praying for an Awakening

Dr. James Dobson has been a popular and highly respected broadcaster for more than forty years, and as an influential Christian psychologist and author, he has helped millions of American families with their questions about the conflict between contemporary culture and issues of faith. During my interview with him for this book, I wanted to hear his thoughts on the seismic shifts brought about by President Trump's election and how the changes taking place may have affected the institution of the family as well as the evangelical community and nation.

STRANG: Thank you, Dr. Dobson, for taking time to share your thoughts on the changes taking place in the country since Donald Trump's election. I know you've had close personal contact with several US presidents as a counselor and friend. So I would be curious to hear about that, and I would especially like to know how you compare President Trump to the other presidents you've known.

DOBSON: Having worked with five United States presidents over the past thirty-eight years, I have had the opportunity to consider the philosophies and priorities of each. The first was Jimmy Carter, who asked me to participate on his White House Conferences on the Families. I then consulted for five years with Ronald Reagan, who began our relationship by asking, "What can my administration do to strengthen the nation's families?" That was followed by infrequent conversations at the White House with [George] Herbert Walker Bush, and his son George W. Bush. Now I am privileged to serve Donald Trump as one of his faith advisors on numerous matters, from mental illness to drug addictions. This personal history has given me a perspective from which to respond to your question today.

I found each of these presidents to be honorable men who were dedicated to the welfare of the nation and its families. I respected them all in their time. However, the five of them were "flawed vessels," as has been every human being who ever lived. For the most part, each president worked tirelessly to serve his country in what turned out to be an impossibly complex task. They had to learn to live with constant criticism from those who wanted to humiliate and demoralize them. As Kermit the Frog said on *Sesame Street*, "It ain't easy being green."

STRANG: How do you rate President Trump on issues of concern to Christian conservatives?

DOBSON: To this point in Donald Trump's first term, I believe he has been more dedicated to the sanctity of human life and the welfare of the family than any of his predecessors. His language is sometimes crude, and his record as a "family man" has been shoddy. However, he appears to understand that "as the family goes, so goes the nation." If you doubt that, ask his grown children. Each of them praises him enthusiastically as a man and as a father.

Since his inauguration in 2017, President Trump fought for and achieved the largest tax cut in the nation's history. He nominated a great Supreme Court justice, Neil Gorsuch, who seems committed to the preservation of life and constitutional protections for religious liberty. Trump has moved the majority of Republican members of Congress to double the child tax credit, which will benefit struggling families everywhere. As we talk, the White House is working on parental leave measures and numerous other legislative efforts to assist families.

Indeed, Trump has fulfilled almost every promise he has made to the pro-family and pro-life communities, including a vigorous effort, now underway, to lessen the opioid epidemic and other illicit drug problems. He is the first president in history to hold events on the National Day of Prayer in the Rose Garden, although George W. Bush celebrated the NDOP with services in the White House every year during his eight years in office. I could write a book outlining the other reasons I am supportive of Donald J. Trump. Although less than perfect, I am grateful to have him as our president, despite the incessant hatred that has been thrown at him to this point.

STRANG: The 2016 national election clearly divided the nation into two warring camps, with conservatives and the liberals becoming increasingly hostile to each other. What do you suggest we, as Christians, do to bring Americans together again?

DOBSON: I don't believe there is a quick solution to the political and social conflict that currently divides us. America hasn't been this agitated internally since slavery tore the nation to shreds in the years leading up to 1860. The five years that followed produced a tragic civil war that resulted in six hundred thousand deaths on battlefields and in disease-ridden prisons on both sides. What could have pitted brother against brother in this way and made them willing to slaughter and maim each other? The passions unleashed during that time were too great to be settled by compromise or negotiation. The chasm between them was just too great to be bridged. The result was a bloodbath that haunts our national memory today.

I'm not suggesting that America is again marching toward another cruel war. I certainly pray not. I do believe, however, that today's contrasting belief systems are powerfully ingrained and breathtakingly dangerous. Some commentators suggest that our leaders should just "walk across the aisle" and restore harmony. That is simplistic and foolish. Though compromise on some issues is possible, the core principles that are tearing us apart are too ingrained to be "talked out."

Take the matter of abortion, for example, and the cultural war that led to it. It has raged for more than forty-six years. Abortion must be outlawed; it cannot be reconciled. We must not forget the brutal murders of sixty million babies, with no end in sight. Can we accept the redefinition of marriage imposed on us by the Supreme Court? Marriage began with a pronouncement by the Creator in the Garden of Eden. He said, as recorded in Genesis 2:24, "For this cause, a man shall leave his father and mother and cleave to his wife, and the two shall be one flesh." After at least five thousand years as the norm, we have abandoned His plan for the family. Have we forgotten that marriage between a man and woman is a metaphor for the relationship between Christ and His church? Can we throw that teaching on the ash heap of history?

STRANG: As you say, these are fundamental issues, and everyone in the country will be affected in some way by how the culture, and Christians in particular, responds to the ongoing threats to religious liberty. So I would like to ask, What's your prescription for people of faith who recognize the risks and want to stand up for their rights as Christians and as citizens of this great country?

DOBSON: Looking forward, are we willing to abandon principles of religious liberty as guaranteed to us by the Constitution? Shall we acquiesce when public schools brazenly indoctrinate our children with libertine sexual enticements and other beliefs that contradict biblical teachings being taught at home? Can we forget the efforts of a former president to "fundamentally change" the God-inspired principles that were handed down to us by our Founding Fathers? And finally, will we turn our backs on our Lord and Savior, Jesus Christ, whose very name generates outrage and hatred from advocates of the Far Left? Remember that He said, "I came not to bring peace, but a sword."

Which of these core values are we willing to sacrifice in a vain search of unity and utopia? I pray there is none. If we Christians feel strongly about things that matter most to us, you can be sure those on the other side are equally impassioned by their own worldview. They are fighting for their beliefs. But we must do the same if future generations are to understand and follow biblical teachings. Thus, adherents to each point of view, Left and Right, are at loggerheads over differing beliefs that aren't likely to be harmonized anytime soon.

STRANG: What then is the solution to the cultural war that's raging all around us?

DOBSON: I submit that, at its base, the conflict we face today is spiritual in nature. Most of the contentious issues that divide us are rooted in Scripture and theology. Those of us on the conservative side aren't dealing with mere differences of opinion. We are trying to live by standards that are eternal and "God breathed." Those principles are not negotiable. We must, however, defend them within the context of love for our fellow human beings. That is a given for followers of Jesus Christ. Our task is to defend our beliefs without insulting or wounding those with whom we disagree.

To summarize my perspective, peace and harmony as a people will only be achieved by another Great Awakening that would sweep the nation in a spirit of repentance and commitment. Will this occur in the light of waning churches and a generation of millennials who seem less interested in matters of faith than their grandparents and forebearers? I don't know. It has happened twice before in earlier times. This should be our prayer for America and the world.

God's Chaos Candidate

Dr. Michael L. Brown, who is one of the most articulate thinkers in the Charismatic world, agrees with Dobson about the good things the president is doing. "Sometimes we look through spiritual eyes that are too pristine, meaning that we have a hard time recognizing how God could use someone with so many flaws.... While we hold standards high for church leaders and things like that, you have to recognize that in life-and-death national crises, God may use people [who are] very unlikely." Then he said Donald Trump is, as others have said, "a divine wrecking ball, or God's chaos candidate, [because] he's one of these guys that really doesn't care about the political gamble."

Half an hour after Trump was declared the winner of the election, Frank Amedia, pastor of Touch Heaven Church in Ohio, felt the Lord telling him to create a protective shield around the new president. As I mentioned briefly in a previous chapter, he called it POTUS Shield, reflecting not only a commitment to pray for the president, but Frank says the acronym stands for the Prophetic Order of the United States. As he explained it, "To be a prophetic, humble, and powerful force of skilled intercessors...to place a shield of prayer, prophecy, unity, and faith around our president, vice president, and to be a spearhead of spiritual force for transformation of our federal court system and our nation. No geographic boundaries, no political boundaries, no limitations other than to be grounded in the Word of God and to give Him glory."

Frank told me he believes the president has what he calls a "breaker anointing" that attracts challenges like a magnet. This gives him the ability to ferret out the source of his enemies and to fearlessly wear them down and withstand their barrages without flinching. It's no secret now that Trump feeds off adversity. He loves taking on a challenge. "It makes him stronger, bolder, more determined," Frank told me, "and acts to prove his causes to himself, from which he grows even more persistent. He has the resolve of a seasoned warrior and the tenacity of a fierce competitor."

I've known Frank since we met at the Western Wall in Jerusalem in 2007. We both attended the Christian celebration of the Feast of Tabernacles, which the Jews call Sukkot. The last day is Simchat Torah and is a celebration of the end of one year of reading the Torah and starting over at Genesis 1 again. There were at least ten thousand at the Western Wall that day—mostly Orthodox Jews. It was amazing to see them dancing, carrying the Torah scrolls above their heads. In that massive crowd Frank and I had mutual friends who introduced us, and over the years, we've stayed in touch due to our mutual love for Israel.

When the media, the polls, and everyone else was saying Donald Trump could never win the presidency, Frank told me he knew Trump would win. He not only prophesied this but was very involved in the campaign. As I reported in my previous book *God and Donald Trump*, Frank had access to Trump's advisors and persuaded Corey Lewandowski to hand a written prophecy to candidate Trump as he was boarding his plane to return to Mar-a-Lago from Ohio. The prophecy said basically, "If you will humble yourself before Me (meaning the Lord), you will be the next president of the United States." We can only speculate, but I believe Trump read the prophecy and humbled himself as well as he knew how. And since that time the president has been a defender of traditional values and an advocate for the freedom of men and women around the world to worship according to their own beliefs and traditions.

Defending the Church

The president made it clear even before he entered the presidential sweepstakes that he would use the power and influence of the United States to defend the interests of men and women in the faith community. Since that time he has taken an interest in the plight of Christians suffering from persecution around the world. According to David Curry, the president and CEO of Open Doors USA, which works on behalf of persecuted Christians, religious liberty will be one of the most critical issues facing the Trump administration over the next several years. It is, he said, "the central issue that they're going to have to deal with, whether you're looking at it through the lens of immigration, whether you're looking at it through the lens of terrorism."[27]

As Open Doors and like-minded relief agencies have pointed out, Islamic extremism is now the greatest threat to Christians in other nations. Curry said that "2016 was the worst year of persecution of Christians on record, with a shocking 215 million Christians experiencing high levels of persecution for their faith." Governments such as North Korea, Somalia, Afghanistan, Pakistan, and Sudan are actively engaged in the repression and persecution of believers. He added that "nearly one in every twelve Christians in the world today lives in an area or in a culture in which Christianity is illegal, forbidden or punished. And yet today the world is largely silent on the shocking wave of religious intolerance."[28]

Evidence that the president has taken the challenge seriously was the appointment of former US senator and former Kansas governor Sam Brownback on July 26, 2017, as ambassador-at-large for International Religious Freedom. While Democrats criticized Brownback's traditional Christian values, especially as it relates to the LGBT community, Evangelicals cheered his record on religious freedom. It would take a tie-breaking vote from Vice President Pence, who serves as president of the Senate, to secure the confirmation, but the appointment received high praise in the faith community.

"Confirmation of Sam Brownback as the Ambassador-at-Large sends a message to the world," said Oklahoma senator James Lankford, "that religious freedom is a priority of the United States government."[29] And it signaled that the president would be an advocate for religious freedom around the world. Many in the faith community had been hoping to see more evidence of support for religious freedom from the

State Department. A few days before Brownback was confirmed, the White House issued a statement from the president saying, "Faith breathes life and hope into our world. We must diligently guard, preserve, and cherish this unalienable right."[30]

In January 2018 the Trump administration placed Pakistan on its Special Watch List because of its severe violations of religious freedom. In doing so, the administration took a stand for religious freedom around the world. It also designated ten more "countries of particular concern." Then, in May 2018, the State Department Office of International Religious Freedom released the annual report for 2017. Secretary of State Mike Pompeo, who had been confirmed to his post just a month earlier, called a press conference to announce release of the new report. Subsequently Ambassador Brownback provided a special briefing on the report, which covered two hundred countries and territories.

"This report is a testament to the United States' historic role in preserving and advocating for religious freedom around the world," said Secretary Pompeo.[31] The International Religious Freedom Act, which became law in 1998, guaranteed that religious freedom would be an issue of concern in US foreign policy. In his remarks Secretary Pompeo assured those in attendance that President Trump and Vice President Pence will stand "with those who yearn for religious liberty." After announcing that the State Department would hold the first ever "Ministerial to Advance Religious Freedom" and that it would be about "action," not just a discussion group, the Secretary said:

> Religious freedom is indeed a universal human right that I will fight for, one that our team at the department will continue to fight for, and one that I know President Trump will continue to fight for. The United States will not stand by as spectators. We will get in the ring and stand in solidarity with every individual who seeks to enjoy their most fundamental of human rights.[32]

As the administration was preparing for its first ever global summit on religious liberty in July 2018, Pew Research Center reported that 28 percent of all countries in 2016 had "high" or "very high" levels of government restrictions on religion, up from 25 percent the prior year. Among all nations, "China had the highest levels of government restrictions on religion, while India had the highest levels of social hostilities involving religion. Both countries had the highest levels of restrictions in these respective categories, not only among the 25 most populous countries but also in the world at large."[33]

As a group, Middle Eastern and Northern African governments were the worst violators of religious liberty on a regional level, Pew found, followed by the Asia-Pacific region, Europe, Sub-Saharan Africa, and the Americas.[34] In his remarks at the release of the State Department's 2017 International Religious Freedom Report, Secretary Pompeo called religious freedom "a right belonging to every individual on the globe," and he added that "religious freedom was vital to America's beginning. Defending it is critical to our future."[35]

President Trump and Vice President Pence have made a priority of maintaining an open dialogue with America's churches and church leaders, and the vice president reaffirmed that commitment in his remarks to the more than eleven thousand members of the Southern Baptist Convention who attended the annual meeting in Dallas on June 13, 2018. He spoke first about the progress the administration has made, protecting life, preserving religious liberty, helping the persecuted church, and standing with Israel. But those gains, he said, cannot be sustained without engaged churchgoing Americans.

During his remarks he said, "I believe that your voice, your compassion, your values, and your ministries are more needed than ever before.... But you should also know that we recognize that the most important work in America doesn't happen in the White House or anywhere in Washington, DC, for that matter." Then he said:

> We know the most meaningful work, the most transformative work happens where you live, where your ministries impact: in the hearts and minds of the American people. The truth is, no podium that President Trump and I will ever stand behind will be of greater consequence than the pulpits you stand behind every Sunday morning. No policy we enact will ever be more meaningful than the ministries you lead. And no action we take will ever be more powerful than your prayers.[36]

For a president whose administration began with a monumental shock wave and whose words and deeds continue to set off aftershocks around the globe, it may come as a shock of even greater magnitude that his administration has become such a strong defender of religious liberty. But for people of faith, it's really no surprise. One of the most famous events in Bible history is a story about the risks and rewards of standing for religious freedom—it's the story of Queen Esther, who risked her life to approach the throne of King Ahasuerus to explain that General Haman was lying to the king in order to destroy the Hebrew slaves living in Persia.

When Esther's cousin asked her to approach the king with the truth, he made one of the most striking declarations in biblical literature, saying, "If you remain silent at this time, relief and deliverance will arise for the Jews from another place and you and your father's house will perish. And who knows whether you have not attained royalty for such a time as this?" After hearing the challenge, Esther said, "I will go in to the king, which is not according to the law; and if I perish, I perish" (Esther 4:14–16, NASB). Providentially the king listened to Esther, her people were spared, and Haman became the victim of his own conspiracy.

The story of Queen Esther is a moving tribute to the power of loyalty and selfless courage that has been celebrated by Jewish families for countless generations. But as Gen. Jerry Boykin told me in a previous chapter, "I am absolutely convinced that he was raised up for such a time as this." The analogy is a good one because the consequences of failure in both cases are so great.

As I bring this chapter to a close, I can offer no better statement of what I believe the Trump aftershock is really all about. Who knows whether Donald Trump has been lifted up to help this nation avert or at least delay impending disaster. He is not a perfect man, and we are not perfect people, but for many in the household of faith, President Trump has been chosen for such a time as this. The only question now is, How will America respond?

CONCLUSION

A SEISMIC SHAKE-UP

THE BIGGEST AFTERSHOCK from the 2016 presidential election may be that the American people have wised up under Donald Trump's tutelage. Most Americans no longer trust the "fake news" mainstream media or their so-called "experts." We're all skeptics now. We get our news from multiple and alternative sources, such as the internet, talk radio, and Fox News. We don't need liberal pundits to interpret the facts for us any longer. With good information from objective sources, we can do that for ourselves now.

It's no secret that the mainstream media don't report the news anymore. Good news about our thriving economy or the fact that Trump's policies are giving American business a much-needed boost is apparently too much to expect. Instead, the news is all about Trump's perceived failings, twenty-four hours a day, while ignoring the news people really need to know. Consequently ratings for CNN, MSNBC, and other liberal news outlets are in the tank. On the other hand, the ratings are soaring for the only channel offering a fair and balanced picture of what's actually happening. Hosts on the Fox News Channel are sharp and well informed, and they invite contrary opinions. Audiences have flocked to the one honest network, which is a sign that the public is a lot more discerning these days and the complacency of the American people is gone forever.

For many years the late CBS News anchor Walter Cronkite ended his daily broadcasts by saying, "And that's the way it is." But even then the news broadcasted by the big three networks wasn't actually the way it was. There was a lot of mischief in America's newsrooms, and Cronkite was as much a part of it as anyone. The mainstream news outlets are constantly complaining about Trump's tweets and his over-the-top tirades against the press. Labeling reports from CNN and other cable networks as "fake news" drives them crazy, but as several polls have shown, the president's criticism of the media is actually scoring major points with the voters. Conservatives in the heartland have been convinced for years that they can't get a fair shake from the liberal press, making it harder to elect conservative candidates and almost impossible for their beliefs to be reported fairly.

As I related earlier, a 2017 Quinnipiac poll found that 80 percent of Republican voters said they trust President Trump more than they trust the media. A similar survey of American voters by the British publication *The Economist* reported that voters trust Trump more than the *New York Times*, the *Washington Post*, or CNN by a 70 percent margin. Fewer than 15 percent sided with the media. Perhaps the most surprising discovery is that when respondents were asked if they would be willing to support "a presidential candidate who has done immoral acts in his or her private life," Democratic voters were less forgiving than Republicans. Fully 48 percent of Republicans said they would be willing to back a candidate with moral failings in the past, while only 19 percent of those in the party of Bill and Hillary Clinton said they would support such a person. Politics has a lot to do with it, but while Democratic voters were focused on vilifying the president, conservative and Christian voters were much more forgiving because they understand that all people are sinners.

For the most part, President Trump has lived up to his billing. He is a fighter, and he wants to restore the honor and prestige of the United States around the world. His critics claim he's just a self-serving businessman with no knowledge of politics, the economy, or diplomacy. He has so little knowledge of foreign affairs, they said, he'll end up getting us into World War III. But when he made his first diplomatic visits to Israel, Europe, China, the Middle East, and later the summit in Singapore, most cheered him as a hero. He spoke in Saudi Arabia, Paris, and Warsaw, and made headlines at the World Economic Forum in Switzerland, where he spelled out his pro-business agenda to the home turf of the international elites. The media did their best to downplay his success on the world stage, but it was obvious the president was doing an amazing job.

Back in Washington he rolled back taxes, ordered the termination of thousands of redundant and restrictive regulations, expanded free trade with our partners around the world, and pulled America out of the Paris Agreement, which penalized American industry and funded environmental extremists. Slowly but surely, he is beginning to drain the swamp by reorganizing the permanent bureaucracy in Washington and giving the deep state a run for the money. It hasn't been easy, and it's far from over, but Donald Trump is a fighter, and who would be willing to bet against him?

No one supports everything he has said or done. The media have portrayed Trump as arrogant, brash, and vulgar, and that was probably the kind of person I expected to encounter when I interviewed candidate Trump during the 2016 campaign. But that's not what I found. He was soft-spoken, respectful, and a true gentleman, and I've talked with others since that time who've said much the same thing.

After he won the presidency, he proved to be exactly the same person I saw on the campaign trail, only perhaps a little more focused on the day-to-day business of leading a great nation.

Seismic Cultural Changes

My objective in writing this book has been to document the seismic shifts that have taken place since the earthquake that brought Donald Trump to the White House and launched Hillary Clinton on her never-ending apology tour. This book has been written with the understanding that things can change. We may not get everything we wanted, and it may take longer than we'd like to fulfill all of Trump's policies and plans. But some things will never go back to the way they were. Years from now Neil Gorsuch will still be on the Supreme Court, taxes will still be lower, Supreme Court rulings defending the rights of bakers and florists will still be in place, and thousands of suffocating government regulations will be off the books forever.

While I have tried to document how the president has spurred the economy, boosted the military, and delivered a truly remarkable brand of muscular diplomacy, there's no guarantee this will continue. A quote attributed to Yogi Berra had it about right: "It's tough to make predictions, especially about the future." There are forces at play that can make some of the president's accomplishments appear less successful—that is certainly the goal of his political opponents. This happened to the second Bush presidency when constant attacks from the liberal media drove the president's poll numbers down to less than 30 percent. That might not have happened if the president had bothered to defend himself against the media's slander. But nothing that happens in the months and years ahead can lessen the seismic impact of all the good things that have already been accomplished since Donald Trump took up residence in the people's house.

Even if President Trump turned out to be a pseudoconservative or a closet globalist, as many Never Trumpers seem to think, that wouldn't undo the advances he has made in religious liberty or the support his administration has given to persecuted Christians around the world. These and other items on the list of Trump's accomplishments during his first five hundred days in office, which are included in the appendix to this book, reveal just how dramatic the changes have been. Even if the War on Terror fails to rack up win after win, as it has done so far, or if our southern borders remain porous to infiltration by illegals, that cannot diminish the seismic shift brought about by ISIS losing 90 percent of its caliphate. The tolerance for Islamic extremism and anti-American protests orchestrated and funded by Obama through his Organizing for Action campaign may be disruptive for a time, but such tactics cannot endure for long. The people will tolerate only so much of that behavior from the former president.

In foreign policy things may not always go Trump's way, and his string of diplomatic successes could conceivably come to an end, but that will not move the American embassy out of Jerusalem or spur North Korea to revert to the suicidal mission it has been pursuing for the last seventy years. If Republicans were to lose both the House and the Senate, it would no doubt mean setbacks from the conservative agenda, but even that will not vindicate the deep state and the corrupt FBI, Justice Department, and CIA officials who were helping Hillary Clinton and laying traps for Donald Trump during the pivotal 2016 election.

Had Clinton been elected, the world would never have known about the text messages between FBI agents Peter Strzok and Lisa Page saying they would make sure Trump was never elected and if he were, they had an insurance policy. What we know now is that the FBI agent involved in the investigation into Clinton's email scandal took steps to bury the matter and then launched a probe into Donald Trump and a fabricated story about Russian collusion in the election. Strzok texted his partner in crime that he couldn't think of a single person in America who should vote for Trump, and he was going to use his influence and authority to make sure Clinton won. That sort of corruption may be normal behavior in a third-world banana republic but not in the United States of America. And now that these and other facts have been exposed to the light of day, the people want answers. Justice cannot be denied, and the deep state genie, once exposed, cannot be put back in the bottle.

Democrats keep talking about a big "blue wave," when they think the public will come over to their side. But that hasn't happened. While this could change with any election, I believe it's because so many Americans have concluded Republicans sounded more like people with common sense, while Democratic candidates looked and sounded radical, scary, and lawless. Fundamentally American politics is about law and order, favoring rules over chaos and lawlessness. George Soros has spent billions to activate violent anarchist groups such as Antifa and Black Lives Matter and attack conservatives in all sorts of venues, including their homes and places of business, but the people see what's going on, and a majority say they've had enough of the Left's agenda.

Restoring Cultural Institutions

The damage done by the liberal agenda over the last forty years can no longer be denied. In education America's colleges and universities have been contaminated by leftist elites for generations. Rather than learning about our great history, traditions, and values, students are being indoctrinated by radical professors and taught to shame anyone who doesn't kowtow to their leftist ideology. Public school students are barely learning history, language skills, or anything that will actually help them succeed in life. They're being taught lurid details of human sexuality and being indoctrinated with leftist propaganda. The miseducation of the younger generation has been going on for years, but the word is out, and changes are coming.

Trump is pushing back, and the confirmation of Betsy DeVos as secretary of education was an important first step. Although she is being attacked and threatened every day by defenders of the liberal agenda, neither she nor the president is backing down. They are making dramatic improvements to the system to restore the integrity of America's classrooms. The new policies are guaranteed to drive the Left crazy, but parents and others who care about the well-being of future generations of Americans realize we've been cheated and America's children have been intellectually and morally abused. There is nothing of greater long-term consequence than the education of our children, and here too change is on the way.

In the justice system President Trump has appointed a long list of conservative judges to the federal courts. By July 2018 at least forty-three federal judges, including one associate justice of the Supreme Court of the United States, had been confirmed by the Senate. In addition, twenty-two judges were confirmed for the US Court of Appeals, and twenty for the US District Courts had been confirmed by the Senate. By midyear there were eighty-eight appointments still awaiting confirmation, and appointments were being announced at a record pace.

In addition to the confirmation of Justice Gorsuch, President Trump has nominated Brett Kavanaugh to replace the retiring Justice Kennedy and will likely have at least one more opportunity to nominate conservative jurists to the Supreme Court before leaving office. These men and women will have an opportunity to restore the foundations of our legal system for generations to come. And nothing will have a greater impact of the legacy of the president. The importance of the federal courts cannot be overestimated. While the Supreme Court only rules on between eighty and one hundred cases each year, the federal courts will handle as many as four hundred thousand cases, which means that judgments handed down at this level can have immense and long-lasting importance.

These are just a few of the changes taking place since Trump's inauguration—victories for conservatives and stunning aftershocks for those who have been working for decades to transform this country into a socialist utopia. But the list of seismic changes goes on and on. As we've seen in the debates taking place in Europe today, the citizens of those countries are emulating America's example of commonsense solutions to complex problems. In the UK, Brexit is a symbol of the growing desire for freedom, autonomy, and the people's desire to control their own destiny without bowing to the edicts of an Orwellian superstate.

Ronald Reagan said that men and women everywhere long for freedom, but it must be fought for, protected, and handed on to the next generation, or it will be lost. Today in China, Japan, and North Korea, people are watching what's happening here, and they want what we have. They've discovered that Donald Trump means what he says. He wants to create a level playing field for all Americans, and he has shown that he will use our great military power if necessary. Under the Obama administration other nations played us for fools, and the American president actually bowed before tyrants and dictators. But under the Trump administration the game has changed. Our allies and adversaries will have to rethink their policies concerning America.

For the past several years the police have been getting a bad rap from the media and from many on the left. Obama never stood up for the police. He often took the side of criminals and troublemakers and inspired hatred for the men and women in blue who put their lives on the line for our safety. The Obama administration routinely accused police officers of racism and cruelty. Even minor incidents were manipulated to provide opportunities for leftists, anarchists, and violent protesters to attack the police. But Donald Trump is having none of that. He goes to police ceremonies, lauds our men and women in uniform, honors them, and helps whenever they need a hand. It's much the same with the military. He has appropriated more than $700 billion to rebuild and revitalize the armed forces. As a graduate of a military school, he loves the military. And for the most part our soldiers, sailors, and airmen are proud to serve this president. At graduation ceremonies at the US Naval Academy in May 2018, Trump stayed for more than ninety minutes following his commencement address to shake hands and speak with the newly commissioned naval officers, and they reciprocated his appreciation and admiration.

Leading From the Front

From the time he entered the race for the presidency, in May 2015, Trump has been shaking up the world of politics. His rallies, which have continued ever since that time, are often filled to capacity with throngs of loud and enthusiastic supporters—sometimes twenty-five thousand or more—and he goes to places most Republican politicians have never visited. Blue-collar workers love him, and he relates to them. He worked on the job site with his brothers as a young man. He admires these workers, he understands how they feel, and they love him in return. Many of them, including union workers, have left the Democratic Party because they believe in Trump's message.

While Democrats have turned left and ignored the interests of American workers, paying more attention to the demands of illegal aliens than to the success and security of our own citizens, Trump and his supporters are making it clear they want to "make America great again." And they're gaining friends and supporters around the world, not by kowtowing to foreign interests but by putting "America First." The voters in Pennsylvania, Wisconsin, Ohio, Michigan, and Iowa could see where this president was going, and that's why they went for him in 2016. They're happy now with the new factories, the new business growth, and the low unemployment numbers. These people plan to stick with Trump. There will be no more "leading from behind." America will be leading from the front from now on—the only way to lead. And, not surprisingly, other nations are following.

Very few leaders have shown such strength of character in the face of adversity—Winston Churchill being one of only a few in the last century. But considering the world we might have entered if Hillary Clinton had won the election, we are fortunate indeed to have a leader with such a strong sense of purpose at this critical moment in history. He takes orders from no one but seeks input from all, even his enemies. Money can't buy him; he has plenty of that. Politics eludes him, and he seldom follows the party line. His signature is not for sale. Like Gen. George Patton in many ways, he believes in his destiny and his duty, and he wants to do the most direct and sensible thing.

The deep state is an enormous adversary community within the permanent bureaucracy and would love to do him in. This includes a large number of Democrats but also several members of his own party, yet they're not able to shake him. President Trump has more accomplishments at this point in his presidency than any other president in history. Globalist puppet master George Soros lamented in a June 2018 interview in the *Washington Post* that the rise of Donald Trump and the anti-establishment movement has been a major disruption to his open-borders agenda. "Everything that could go wrong has gone wrong," he said. He admitted he didn't expect Trump to win in November and added, "Apparently, I was living in my own bubble."[1] I hope he will stay in his bubble indefinitely.

Like many people I've spoken to since the 2016 election, I believe Donald Trump feels he is following his destiny. He has been given a divine mandate, and he doesn't care what anyone thinks or says about the way he's doing his job. He wants to do what he believes is right, and he truly wants to make America great again. Much to everyone's surprise, he has kept his campaign promises on issue after issue. Even his most ardent supporters have been stunned by how many of the goals listed at the start of his campaign have already been accomplished. A glance at the list of five hundred accomplishments in the appendix is eye-opening, and on issues where we're still waiting for results, such as immigration and the border wall, he is pushing Congress to deliver the goods. In almost every way, he is shaking things up, but it has been encouraging to see that, despite everything his adversaries and the mainstream media have thrown at him, this president is still standing. He is an achiever, a man of resolute faith, and a man of his word. We're fortunate indeed to have such a leader.

"God's love redeems the world," President Donald Trump declared in his greeting at Passover and Easter in 2018. He also shared:

> My fellow Americans…during the sacred holiday of Passover, Jewish families around the world give thanks to God for liberating the Jewish people from bondage in Egypt and delivering them to the promised land of Israel. For Christians, we remember the suffering and death of God's only Son and His glorious resurrection on the third day. On Easter Sunday we proclaim with joy, "Christ has risen!"
>
> Both of these sacred celebrations remind us that God's love redeems the world. Almost three thousand years ago, the prophet Isaiah wrote, "Darkness covers the Earth, but the Lord rises upon you and His glory appears over you. For the Lord will be your everlasting light."
>
> In America, we look to the light of God to guide our steps, we trust in the power of the Almighty for wisdom and strength, and we praise our Heavenly Father for the blessings of freedom and the gift of eternal life.[2]

If our nation can begin to truly trust in God and let His light guide our steps, then that's the greatest aftershock of all.

APPENDIX

PRESIDENT DONALD J. TRUMP'S 500 DAYS OF AMERICAN GREATNESS

Our families will thrive. Our people will prosper. And our nation will forever be safe and strong and proud and mighty and free.

—President Donald J. Trump

500 DAYS: In his first 500 days in office, President Donald J. Trump has achieved results domestically and internationally for the American people.[1]

- Since taking office, President Trump has strengthened American leadership, security, prosperity, and accountability.
- After 500 days, the results are clear: the American economy is stronger, American workers are experiencing more opportunities, confidence is soaring, and business is booming.
- President Trump has re-asserted American leadership on the world stage, secured vital investments in our military, and stood up against threats to our national security.
- President Trump has put the American people first and made government more accountable.

AMERICA'S ECONOMY IS STRONGER: The American economy is stronger today and American workers are better off thanks to President Trump's pro-growth agenda.

- Nearly 3 million jobs have been created since President Trump took office.
    - ▷ 304,000 manufacturing jobs have been created since President Trump took office, and manufacturing employment stands at its highest level since December 2008.

    - ▷ 337,000 construction jobs have been created since President Trump took office, and construction employment stands at its highest level since June 2008.

- Under President Trump, the unemployment rate has dropped to 3.8, the lowest rate since April 2000, and job openings have reached 6.6 million, the highest level recorded.
    - ▷ 67 percent of Americans believe now is a good time to find a quality job, according to Gallup.
    - ▷ Only under President Trump have more than 50 percent of Americans believed it is a good time to find a quality job since Gallup began asking the question 17 years ago.
- President Trump prioritized job training and workforce development to empower workers to seize more opportunities, signing an Executive Order to expand apprenticeship opportunities.
- President Trump has restored confidence in the American economy, with confidence among both consumers and businesses reaching historic highs.
    - ▷ Consumer confidence in current conditions has reached a 17-year high, according to the Conference Board.
    - ▷ Optimism among manufacturers has hit record highs under President Trump, according to the National Association of Manufacturers.
    - ▷ Small business optimism has sustained record-high levels under President Trump, according to the National Federation of Independent Business.
- President Trump signed the historic Tax Cuts and Jobs Act into law, cutting taxes for American families and making American business more competitive.
    - ▷ American families received $3.2 trillion in gross tax cuts and saw the child tax credit double.
    - ▷ The top corporate tax rate was lowered from 35 percent to 21 percent so American businesses could be more competitive.
- President Trump has rolled back unnecessary job-killing regulations beyond expectations.

- ▷ In 2017, President Trump far exceeded his promise to eliminate regulations at a two-to-one ratio, issuing 22 deregulatory actions for every new regulatory action.
- ▷ The Administration rolled back rules and regulations harming farmers and energy producers, such as the Waters of the United States Rule and the Clean Power Plan.
- ▷ Regional and community banks and credit unions got relief after President Trump signed legislation reducing harmful requirements imposed by the Dodd-Frank Act.

- Since taking office, President Trump has advanced free, fair, and reciprocal trade deals that protect American workers, ending decades of destructive trade policies.
    - ▷ Days after taking office, the President withdrew the United States from the Trans-Pacific Partnership negotiations and agreement.
    - ▷ President Trump's Administration is working to defend American intellectual property from China's unfair practices through a range of actions.
    - ▷ The President improved the KORUS trade agreement with the Republic of Korea, which will allow more US automobile exports to South Korea with lower tariffs and increase US pharmaceutical access to South Korea.
    - ▷ American agriculture has gained access to new markets under President Trump.

AMERICA IS WINNING ON THE WORLD STAGE: President Trump has re-asserted American leadership on the world stage and is achieving results for the American people.

- President Trump followed through on his promise to move the US Embassy in Israel to Jerusalem.
- President Trump ordered an end to United States participation in the horrible Iran deal and immediately began the process of re-imposing sanctions that had been lifted or waived.
    - ▷ The President has taken action to confront aggression by Iran and its proxies.

- ▷ The Department of the Treasury has issued a range of sanctions targeting Iranian activities and entities, including the Islamic Revolutionary Guard Corps-Qods Force.

- Under President Trump, the United States has led an unprecedented global campaign to achieve the peaceful denuclearization of the Korean peninsula.
- President Trump's leadership has contributed to the return of 17 Americans held overseas.
  - ▷ In May 2018 alone, Venezuela released one American and North Korea released three Americans who came home to the United States.
- The President has secured historic increases in defense funding in order to rebuild our Nation's military with the resources they need, after years of harmful sequester.
  - ▷ President Trump signed legislation to provide $700 billion in defense spending for fiscal year (FY) 2018 and $716 billion for FY 2019.
- The United States has worked with international allies to decimate ISIS.
- President Trump ordered strikes against Syria in response to the regime's use of chemical weapons in April 2017 and April 2018.
- The Trump Administration has imposed a range of sanctions on the Maduro dictatorship in Venezuela, including sanctions targeting Maduro and other senior government officials.

AMERICA'S COMMUNITIES ARE SAFER AND MORE SECURE: President Trump has worked to secure our borders, enforce our immigration laws, and protect the safety and security of American communities.

- Despite limited resources and obstruction from Congress, President Trump has worked to take control of our border and enforce our immigration laws.
  - ▷ President Trump has called on Congress to provide the resources needed to secure our borders and close loopholes that prevent immigration laws from being fully enforced.
- President Trump authorized the deployment of the National Guard to help secure our borders.

- President Trump's Administration has carried out immigration enforcement efforts based on the rule of law.
  - ▷ From the start of President Trump's Administration to the end of FY 2017, US Immigration and Customs Enforcement (ICE) Enforcement and Removal Operations (ERO) made 110,568 arrests of illegal aliens.
  - ▷ Arrests made in this timeframe represented a 42 percent increase from the same timeframe in FY 2016.
  - ▷ Of the 110,568 arrests made, 92 percent had a criminal conviction, pending criminal charge, were an ICE fugitive, or had a reinstated final order of removal.
- President Trump has made clear that his Administration will continue to combat the threat of MS-13 in order to protect communities from the horrendous violence the gang has spread.
  - ▷ In 2017, the Department of Justice worked with partners in Central America to file criminal charges against more than 4,000 members of MS-13.
- The Trump Administration has cracked down on the import and distribution of illegal drugs in order to stop them from reaching our communities and causing even more devastation.
  - ▷ As of April 2018, US Border Patrol has seized 284 pounds of fentanyl in FY 2018, already surpassing the total of 181 pounds seized in FY 2017.
- The President has launched a nationwide effort to fight the opioid crisis, which has devastated communities across America.
  - ▷ The President's Opioid Initiative seeks to reduce drug demand, cut off the flow of illicit drugs, and save lives by expanding treatment opportunities.
- President Trump signed an omnibus spending bill, which provides nearly $4 billion to address the opioid epidemic.
  - ▷ The bill included $1 billion for grants focused on the hardest-hit States and Tribes and provided funding for a public-private research partnership on pain and addiction.

AMERICA'S GOVERNMENT IS MORE ACCOUNTABLE: Since taking office, President Trump has worked to ensure government is more accountable to the American people.

- President Trump has confirmed the most circuit court judges of any President in their first year, and secured Justice Neil Gorsuch's confirmation to the United States Supreme Court.
- President Trump has signed legislation to bring more accountability to the Department of Veterans Affairs and provide our veterans with more choice in the care they receive.
    - ▷ President Trump signed the Department of Veterans Affairs Accountability and Whistleblower Protection Act of 2017, improving processes for addressing misconduct.
    - ▷ President Trump signed the VA Choice and Quality Employment Act into law, authorizing $2.1 billion in additional funds for the Veterans Choice Program.
- President Trump successfully eliminated the penalty for Obamacare's burdensome individual mandate.
- The President's Administration is seeking to provide more affordable health coverage and broader access to affordable alternatives to Obamacare plans.
- President Trump has released a blueprint to lower drug prices for Americans.
- President Trump has ensured that the religious liberties and conscience of Americans are protected and respected by the Federal government.
    - ▷ President Trump signed an Executive Order to protect the free speech and religious liberties of groups such as the Little Sisters of the Poor.
    - ▷ The Department of Justice issued guidance to all executive agencies on protecting religious liberty in federal programs.

ACKNOWLEDGMENTS

A BOOK SUCH AS this covering such a broad spectrum of ideas and issues cannot be produced without a great publishing team. Fortunately I didn't have to look for a publisher. As the owner of Charisma House and the FrontLine book imprint, I've been able to bring together a great team, and over the years we've published more than three thousand titles, including fourteen *New York Times* best sellers, such as Jonathan Cahn's groundbreaking book *The Harbinger.*

Now that I've taken up book writing late in my career, it has been interesting to work with the team as an author and not just the boss. I would love to mention everyone in the publishing group, but it would be a very long list. I do, however, want to express my gratitude and appreciation to those who've worked closest with me on this project, including Marcos Perez, our publisher, and Debbie Marrie, vice president of product development, who polished the manuscript with the help of Kimberly Overcast. They're terrific, and they lead a remarkably talented group.

In my four decades in the publishing business I've hired many editors, writers, and freelancers. I know most of the best in the industry, and none is better than Dr. Jim Nelson Black. He has worked with many well-known authors and has written several books of his own. I have gotten to know Jim as we've worked together on several major books over the years, and I asked him to collaborate with me on *God and Donald Trump.* He did such a great job I tapped him again to help with this sequel. Much of the research you've read in these pages is his, and his editing skills are greatly appreciated. Thank you, Jim.

The backbone of the publishing process is the typesetting, cover design, and printing quality, which is the responsibility of Frank Hefeli and his team, including Justin Evans, our design director, who captured the "seismic" theme on the cover and also tied it in to his excellent cover design for *God and Donald Trump.* Lucy Diaz Kurz, vice president of marketing; our sales director, Ken Peckett; and our sales representative to the mass market, Ned Clements, are truly top of the line. They helped *God and Donald Trump* exceed expectations and become a national best seller. Now they're doing it again.

Thanks is also due to Deb Hamilton of Hamilton Strategies and Jenny Henneberry of GuestBooker.com, who arranged the interviews on Fox News, CNN, MSNBC, and many Christian media outlets, along with reviews of *God and Donald Trump* in unlikely places such as Politico.com. I also want to say thank you to my new administrative assistant, Chris Schimbeno, who helped keep things moving while I was away working on the manuscript. And of course, I want to acknowledge Joy Strang, my wife of forty-six years, who was supportive in many ways during this process. In her role as CFO and COO of our company, she provided excellent leadership while I was otherwise occupied, as did Ken Hartman, our controller; and Dr. Steve Greene, executive vice president of the Charisma Media Group.

I also want to express my heartfelt thanks and praise to our Lord not only for His leading in this writing project but for allowing a lowly newspaper reporter to be able to grow and in some small way to touch the world through media. This book is one more example of His mercy and grace.

ABOUT THE AUTHOR

Stephen E. Strang is CEO of Charisma Media in Lake Mary, Florida, and the founder of *Charisma* magazine, the leading Pentecostal-Charismatic magazine in the world. The success of *Charisma* has spawned other magazines and led to book and Bible publishing in both English and Spanish. He has traveled the world and, among many other things, has interviewed four US presidents, including President Donald Trump. He has also been invited to speak at the United Nations.

He has received many awards from both religious and secular organizations, including the prestigious William Randolph Hearst Award. He was named by *Time* magazine in 2005 as one of the twenty-five most influential Evangelicals in America. Lee University conferred on him an honorary degree in 1995. He was nominated as Entrepreneur of the Year and received awards from the State of Florida for creating jobs in the publishing industry.

Now he adds best-selling author to his resume, thanks to the success of his first major book, *God and Donald Trump*, which also opened doors for him to appear several times on Fox News, CNN, and MSNBC, as well as several major Christian media outlets.

Raised in a Christian home, he is the son and grandson of Assemblies of God ministers. He remembers accepting Christ at age five at home and received the baptism in the Holy Spirit at age twelve at a youth camp. He was deeply affected by the Jesus movement and the burgeoning Charismatic movement while a journalism student at the University of Florida, where he founded and led a Charismatic student group on campus. This foreshadowed the founding of *Charisma* magazine a couple of years later while he worked several years as a newspaper reporter for the *Orlando Sentinel*.

For forty-six years he has been married to the love of his life, Joy Strang. In 1981 they cofounded the company now known as Charisma Media. They live in Longwood, Florida, and are the proud parents of Cameron and Chandler and grandparents of Cohen.

ENDNOTES

Introduction—Shaken to the Core

1. Neil Irwin, "We Ran Out of Words to Describe How Good the Jobs Numbers Are," *New York Times*, June 1, 2018, https://www.nytimes.com/2018/06/01/upshot/we-ran-out-of-words-to-describe-how-good-the-jobs-numbers-are.html.
2. "List of Tax Reform Good News," Americans for Tax Reform, July 2, 2018, https://www.atr.org/sites/default/files/assets/National%20List%20of%20Tax%20Reform%20Good%20News.pdf.
3. Michael Goodwin, "The Left Needs to Face Reality: Trump Is Winning," *New York Post*, June 30, 2018, https://nypost.com/2018/06/30/the-left-needs-to-face-reality-trump-is-winning/.

Chapter 1—Capital Psychosis

1. Erik Wemple, "Study: 91 Percent of Recent Network Trump Coverage Has Been Negative," *Washington Post*, September 12, 2017, https://www.washingtonpost.com/blogs/erik-wemple/wp/2017/09/12/study-91-percent-of-recent-network-trump-coverage-has-been-negative/?utm_term=.454b12f1e818.
2. Rich Noyes and Mike Ciandella, "Study: The Liberal Media's Summer of Pummeling Trump," *NewsBusters* (blog), September 12, 2017, https://www.newsbusters.org/blogs/nb/rich-noyes/2017/09/12/liberal-medias-summer-pummeling-trump.
3. Brent Bozell and Tim Graham, "Bozell & Graham Column: Trump vs. Our Perpetually Panicked Press," *NewsBusters* (blog), March 6, 2018, https://www.newsbusters.org/blogs/nb/tim-graham/2018/03/06/bozell-graham-column-trump-vs-our-perpetually-panicked-press.
4. Bozell and Graham, "Bozell & Graham Column: Trump vs. Our Perpetually Panicked Press."
5. Julia Glum, "The Moment Liberals Knew Trump Won: 24 Horrified Quotes, Pictures and Tweets That Capture Election 2016," *Newsweek*, November 8, 2017, http://www.newsweek.com/trump-election-anniversary-liberal-reactions-clinton-loss-704777.
6. *The Rachel Maddow Show*, NBC Universal, August 15, 2016, http://www.msnbc.com/transcripts/rachel-maddow-show/2016-08-15.
7. *CNN Live Event/Special*, "Election Night in America: Clinton Carries California; Hidden Trump Voters," Cable News Network, November 8, 2016, http://transcripts.cnn.com/TRANSCRIPTS/1611/08/se.08.html.

8. Keith Olbermann, *The Closer*, "The Terrorists Have Won," The Scene, November 9, 2016, https://thescene.com/watch/gq/the-closer-with-keith-olbermann-the-terrorists-have-won?mbid=email_cne_thescene_hotsheet.
9. Andrew Sullivan, "The Republic Repeals Itself," New York Media LLC, November 9, 2016, http://nymag.com/daily/intelligencer/2016/11/andrew-sullivan-president-trump-and-the-end-of-the-republic.html.
10. Jeff Jarvis (@jeffjarvis), "I'll say it: This is the victory of the uneducated and uninformed. Now more than ever that looks impossible to fix. They now rule," Twitter, November 8, 2016, 10:51 p.m., https://twitter.com/jeffjarvis/status/796243909890506752.
11. Michael Moore, "Morning After To-Do List," Facebook, November 9, 2016, 10:13 a.m., https://www.facebook.com/mmflint/posts/10153913074756857.
12. Ana Navarro (@ananavarro), "All pollsters should be tarred and feather. Every single one of them. Next time someone shows me a poll, I'm using it to wrap dead fish," Twitter, November 9, 2016, 7:13 a.m., https://twitter.com/ananavarro/status/796370050383024128.
13. Joy Behar, *The View*, November 9, 2016, viewed at https://www.dailywire.com/news/10662/lol-joy-behar-meltdown-over-trump-too-good-amanda-prestigiacomo.
14. Gary Abernathy, "Why Would We Abandon Trump? He's Doing What He Said He Would Do.," *Washington Post*, December 8, 2017, https://www.washingtonpost.com/opinions/why-would-we-abandon-trump-hes-doing-what-he-said-he-would-do/2017/12/08/2aae3682-db95-11e7-a841-2066faf731ef_story.html?utm_term=.274224dbfa52.
15. Abernathy, "Why Would We Abandon Trump? He's Doing What He Said He Would Do."
16. Abernathy, "Why Would We Abandon Trump? He's Doing What He Said He Would Do."
17. Katty Kay, "Why Trump's Supporters Will Never Abandon Him," BBC, August 23, 2017, https://www.bbc.com/news/world-us-canada-41028733.
18. Kay, "Why Trump's Supporters Will Never Abandon Him."
19. Kay, "Why Trump's Supporters Will Never Abandon Him."
20. "Most Republicans Trust the President More Than They Trust the Media," *The Economist*, August 3, 2017, https://www.economist.com/news/united-states/21725822-there-also-broad-support-shutting-down-outlets-perceived-biased-most-republicans.
21. Kathy Frankovic, "Moral Judgments Often Split Along Party Lines," YouGov PLC, March 19, 2018, https://today.yougov.com/topics/philosophy/articles-reports/2018/03/19/moral-judgments-often-split-along-party-lines.
22. Michael Medved, "Why Democrats Are Suddenly Unforgiving Moralists," MichaelMedved.com and Salem National, March 22, 2018, http://www.

michaelmedved.com/column/why-democrats-are-suddenly-unforgiving-moralists/.

23. Frankovic, "Moral Judgments Often Split Along Party Lines."
24. Michael Medved, "For Dems, Hunting Is Worse Than Abortion," MichaelMedved.com and Salem National, March 22, 2018, http://www.michaelmedved.com/column/for-dems-hunting-is-worse-than-abortion/.
25. Jonathan Wilson-Hartgrove, "Why Evangelicals Support President Trump, Despite His Immorality," *Time*, February 16, 2018, http://time.com/5161349/president-trump-white-evangelical-support-slaveholders/.
26. Michael Gerson, "The Last Temptation," *The Atlantic*, April 2018, https://www.theatlantic.com/magazine/archive/2018/04/the-last-temptation/554066/.
27. "Hostility to Religion: The Growing Threat to Religious Liberty in the United States," Family Research Council, July 2014, https://downloads.frc.org/EF/EF14G25.pdf.
28. Masterpiece Cakeshop, Ltd., et al. v. Colorado Civil Rights Commission et al., 16–111 U.S. (2017), https://www.supremecourt.gov/opinions/17pdf/16-111_j4el.pdf.
29. Hugh Hewitt, "Why Christians Will Stick With Trump," *Washington Post*, October 5, 2017, https://www.washingtonpost.com/opinions/why-christians-will-stick-with-trump/2017/10/05/7d7d2bb6-a922-11e7-850e-2bdd1236be5d_story.html?utm_term=.8f935c878477.
30. Hewitt, "Why Christians Will Stick With Trump."
31. James Strock, "This SOTU, Trump Can Move to Drain the Swamp for Good," *The Hill*, January 30, 2018, http://thehill.com/opinion/white-house/369187-this-sotu-trump-can-move-to-drain-the-swamp-for-good.
32. Brink Lindsey and Steven M. Teles, "Trump Made the Swamp Worse. Here's How to Drain It," *New York Times*, October 26, 2017, https://www.nytimes.com/2017/10/26/opinion/trump-made-the-swamp-worse-heres-how-to-drain-it.html.
33. "President Donald J. Trump Is Delivering on Deregulation," White House, December 14, 2017, https://www.whitehouse.gov/briefings-statements/president-donald-j-trump-delivering-deregulation/.
34. Thomas Binion, "The Incredible Trump Agenda: What Most Americans Don't Know About the War the President Has Waged," Fox News Network LLC, March 2, 2018, http://www.foxnews.com/opinion/2018/03/02/incredible-trump-agenda-what-most-americans-dont-know-about-war-president-has-waged.html.
35. Joseph P. Williams, "The Battle for the Judiciary," *U.S. News & World Report*, August 2, 2017, https://www.usnews.com/news/the-report/articles/2017-08-02/democrats-take-aim-at-trumps-judicial-appointments.

36. Allan Smith, "Trump Is Quietly Moving at a Furious Pace to Secure 'The Single Most Important Legacy' of His Administration," *Business Insider*, July 27, 2017, http://www.businessinsider.com/trump-judges-attorneys-nominations-2017-7.
37. Donald J. Trump (@realDonaldTrump), "Hundreds of good people, including very important Ambassadors and Judges, are being blocked and/or slow walked by the Democrats in the Senate...," Twitter, March 14, 2018, 6:02 a.m., https://twitter.com/realdonaldtrump/status/973907142649397251?lang=en.
38. John Kruzel, "Why Trump Appointments Have Lagged Behind Other Presidents," Poynter Institute, March 16, 2018, http://www.politifact.com/truth-o-meter/statements/2018/mar/16/donald-trump/why-trump-appointments-have-lagged-behind-other-pr/.
39. "Press Briefing by Press Secretary Sarah Sanders," White House, March 7, 2018, https://www.whitehouse.gov/briefings-statements/press-briefing-press-secretary-sarah-sanders-030718/.
40. Saunders, "Trump, Democrats Create Logjam in Diplomat Confirmations," *American Spectator*, April 1, 2018, https://spectator.org/trump-democrats-create-logjam-in-confirmation-of-diplomats/.
41. Saunders, "Trump, Democrats Create Logjam in Diplomat Confirmations."
42. Debra J. Saunders, "Trump Against the World," *American Spectator*, December 3, 2017, https://spectator.org/trump-against-the-world/.
43. Saunders, "Trump Against the World."
44. Saunders, "Trump Against the World."
45. Kristen Soltis Anderson, "The Democratic Base Wants Congress to Oppose Trump. That May Not Sell With Independents," *Washington Examiner*, March 28, 2018, https://www.washingtonexaminer.com/opinion/the-democratic-base-wants-congress-to-oppose-trump-that-may-not-sell-with-independents?_amp=true.
46. Sam Schwarz, "Support for Donald Trump's Impeachment Is Higher Than His Re-election Chances," *Newsweek*, December 20, 2017, http://www.newsweek.com/donald-trump-impeachment-reelection-2020-753546.
47. "NBC News/Wall Street Journal Survey—Study #17409," Dow Jones & Company Inc., October 2017, https://www.wsj.com/public/resources/documents/17409NBCWSJOctober2017Poll.pdf.
48. Anderson, "The Democratic Base Wants Congress to Oppose Trump."

Chapter 2—The Tipping Point

1. Laura Reston, "Americans Love an Underdog—Just Not Lincoln Chafee, Jim Webb, or Martin O'Malley," *New Republic*, October 14, 2015, https://newrepublic.com/article/123116/americans-love-underdog-just-not-chafee-webb-or-omalley.
2. Clyde Wayne Crews Jr., "Obama's Legacy: Here's a Raft of Executive Actions Trump May Target," *Forbes*, January 16, 2017, https://www.forbes.com/sites/

waynecrews/2017/01/16/obamas-legacy-heres-a-raft-of-executive-actions-trump-may-target/#54dfc45c2dce.

3. Crews Jr., "Obama's Legacy."
4. Kenneth P. Vogel, "George Soros Rises Again," Politico LLC, July 27, 2016, https://www.politico.com/story/2016/07/george-soros-democratic-convention-226267.
5. "George Soros: Media Mogul," Media Research Center, accessed July 20, 2018, https://www.mrc.org/special-reports/george-soros-media-mogul.
6. Sebastian Mallaby, "'Go for the Jugular,'" *The Atlantic*, June 4, 2010, https://www.theatlantic.com/business/archive/2010/06/go-for-the-jugular/57696/.
7. David Horowitz and Richard Poe, *The Shadow Party* (Nashville: Nelson Current, 2006), xi.
8. Malcolm Gladwell, *The Tipping Point: How Little Things Can Make a Big Difference* (Boston: Back Bay Books, 2000), 295.
9. Richard G. Lee, *The Coming Revolution* (Nashville: Thomas Nelson, 2012), introduction, https://books.google.com/books?id=q39hk2x6uloC&q.
10. "Remarks by President Trump to the World Economic Forum," White House, January 26, 2018, https://www.whitehouse.gov/briefings-statements/remarks-president-trump-world-economic-forum/.
11. Keith Bradsher, "Trump, in Davos Speech, Sticks to Script as He Declares America Open for Business," *New York Times*, January 26, 2018, https://www.nytimes.com/2018/01/26/business/davos-world-economic-forum-trump.html.
12. John Lloyd, "Commentary: Global Takeaways From Trump's Davos Speech," Reuters, January 26, 2018, https://www.reuters.com/article/us-lloyd-davos-commentary/commentary-global-takeaways-from-trumps-davos-speech-idUSKBN1FF2C8.
13. "Remarks by President Trump to the World Economic Forum," White House.
14. Bradsher, "Trump, in Davos Speech, Sticks to Script as He Declares America Open for Business."
15. Claire Zillman, "Wilbur Ross Tells Davos: U.S. Is Done 'Being a Patsy' on Trade," *Fortune*, January 24, 2018, http://fortune.com/2018/01/24/davos-2018-trump-wilbur-ross-trade-war-tariff/.
16. "Remarks by President Trump to the World Economic Forum," White House.
17. Bradsher, "Trump, in Davos Speech, Sticks to Script as He Declares America Open for Business."
18. "Stocks Rise as Trump Declares America 'Open for Business,'" CBS Money Watch, January 26, 2018, https://www.cbsnews.com/news/stock-futures-rise-as-trump-declares-america-open-for-business/.
19. Eamon Quinn, "Stocks Hit New Highs on 'Palatable' Trump Speech at Davos," *Irish Examiner*, January 27, 2018, https://www.irishexaminer.com/breakingnews/business/stocks-hit-new-highs-on-palatable-trump-speech-at-davos-825059.html.

20. "Remarks by President Trump to the World Economic Forum," White House.
21. Andrew Ross Sorkin, "What Happens to the Markets if Donald Trump Wins?," *New York Times*, October 31, 2016, https://www.nytimes.com/2016/11/01/business/dealbook/what-happens-to-the-markets-if-donald-trump-wins.html.
22. Paul Krugman, "What Happened on Election Day," *New York Times*, accessed July 23, 2018, https://www.nytimes.com/interactive/projects/cp/opinion/election-night-2016/paul-krugman-the-economic-fallout.
23. George Soros, "Remarks Delivered at the World Economic Forum," January 25, 2018, https://www.georgesoros.com/2018/01/25/remarks-delivered-at-the-world-economic-forum/.
24. Soros, "Remarks Delivered at the World Economic Forum."
25. Ryan Saavedra, "Soros Threatens: Trump 'Will Disappear in 2020 or Even Sooner,'" Daily Wire, January 25, 2018, https://www.dailywire.com/news/26347/soros-snaps-trump-will-disappear-2020-or-even-ryan-saavedra.
26. Soros, "Remarks Delivered at the World Economic Forum."
27. Eric Lichtblau, "George Soros Pledges $10 Million to Fight Hate Crimes," *New York Times*, November 22, 2016, https://www.nytimes.com/2016/11/22/us/politics/george-soros-hate-crimes.html.
28. Thomas E. Mann, "Admit It, Political Scientists: Politics Really Is More Broken Than Ever," *The Atlantic*, May 26, 2014, https://www.theatlantic.com/politics/archive/2014/05/dysfunction/371544/.
29. Dennis Prager, "Will the Second Civil War Turn Violent?" Dennis Prager.com, May 2, 2017, http://www.dennisprager.com/will-the-second-civil-war-turn-violent/.
30. "Political Polarization in the American Public," Pew Research Center, June 12, 2014, http://assets.pewresearch.org/wp-content/uploads/sites/5/2014/06/6-12-2014-Political-Polarization-Release.pdf.
31. Russell Blair, "The Politics of Anger: Rhetoric, Intolerance Seen as Rising in U.S.," *Hartford Courant*, June 18, 2017, http://www.courant.com/politics/hc-baseball-shooting-political-anger-20170615-story.html.
32. Blair, "The Politics of Anger."
33. Charles Hurt, "This Trap Was Set Well Before Trump Won," *Washington Times*, March 18, 2018, https://www.washingtontimes.com/news/2018/mar/18/trap-was-set-well-trump-won/.
34. Hurt, "This Trap Was Set Well Before Trump Won."
35. James Strock, "This SOTU, Trump Can Move to Drain the Swamp for Good," *The Hill*, January 30, 2018, http://thehill.com/opinion/white-house/369187-this-sotu-trump-can-move-to-drain-the-swamp-for-good.
36. Strock, "This SOTU, Trump Can Move to Drain the Swamp for Good."
37. "Judicial Watch: State Department Records Show Obama Administration Helped Fund George Soros' Left-Wing Political Activities in Albania," Judicial Watch Inc.,

April 4, 2018, https://www.judicialwatch.org/press-room/press-releases/judicial-watch-doj-records-show-obama-administration-helped-fund-george-soros-left-wing-political-activities-albania/.

38. "Judicial Watch: State Department Records Show Obama Administration Helped Fund George Soros' Left-Wing Political Activities in Albania," Judicial Watch Inc.
39. Alexi McCammond, "Democrats Don't Want Tom Steyer's Impeachment Guide," Axios, April 3, 2018, https://www.axios.com/tom-steyer-impeachment-guide-campaign-2018-election-1d8f9649-08a5-45d8-a1c0-93fcb89d73d7.html.
40. Adelle Nazarian, "Tom Steyer's 'Need to Impeach' Trump Drive Reveals Division Among Democrats," Breitbart.com, April 7, 2018, http://www.breitbart.com/california/2018/04/07/tom-steyers-need-to-impeach-trump-drive-reveals-division-among-democrats/.
41. Susan Davis and Scott Detrow, "A Year Later, the Shock of Trump's Win Hasn't Totally Worn Off in Either Party," NPR Morning Edition, November 9, 2017, https://www.npr.org/2017/11/09/562307566/a-year-later-the-shock-of-trumps-win-hasn-t-totally-worn-off-in-either-party.

Chapter 3—Trump's Fast-Start Agenda

1. Dana Milbank, "Trump Supporters Are Talking About Civil War: Could a Loss Provide the Spark?," *Washington Post*, October 18, 2016, https://www.washingtonpost.com/opinions/trump-supporters-are-talking-about-civil-war-could-a-loss-provide-the-spark/2016/10/18/f5ce081a-9573-11e6-bb29-bf2701dbe0a3_story.html?.
2. Chris Cillizza (@CillizzaCNN), "I think this is who she sort of is -- at least in the context of a debate. Hyper aggressive," Twitter, February 4, 2016, 6:57 p.m., https://twitter.com/TheFix/status/695441165974269952.
3. Olga Khazan, "Would You Really Like Hillary More if She Sounded Different?," *The Atlantic*, August 1, 2016, https://www.theatlantic.com/science/archive/2016/08/hillarys-voice/493565/.
4. Elspeth Reeve, "Why Do So Many People Hate the Sound of Hillary Clinton's Voice?," *The New Republic*, May 1, 2015, https://newrepublic.com/article/121643/why-do-so-many-people-hate-sound-hillary-clintons-voice.
5. Emily Crockett, "This Awful Morning Joe Clip Shows How Not to Talk About Hillary Clinton," Vox Media Inc., updated February 3, 2016, https://www.vox.com/2016/2/3/10909354/morning-joe-hillary-clinton-shouts-bob-woodward.
6. Francis Wilkinson, "Hillary Clinton's 85 Slogans Explain 2016 Campaign," *Denver Post*, October 20, 2016, https://www.denverpost.com/2016/10/20/hillary-clintons-85-slogans-explain-2016-campaign/.
7. "Memorandum for the Heads of Executive Departments and Agencies," White House, January 20, 2017, https://www.whitehouse.gov/presidential-actions/memorandum-heads-executive-departments-agencies/.

8. Victor Davis Hanson, "Hanson: How Trump Is Succeeding by Not Playing by the Rules," *Mercury News*, updated April 6, 2018, https://www.mercurynews.com/2018/04/05/hanson-how-trump-is-succeeding-by-not-playing-by-the-rules/.
9. Hanson, "Hanson: How Trump Is Succeeding by Not Playing by the Rules."
10. "Alexander the Great," History.com, https://www.history.com/topics/ancient-history/alexander-the-great.
11. Victor Davis Hanson, "Trump Is Cutting Old Gordian Knots," *National Review*, April 5, 2018, https://www.nationalreview.com/2018/04/trump-cuts-gordian-knots-with-unconventional-methods/.
12. Donald J. Trump (@realDonaldTrump), "North Korean Leader Kim Jong Un just stated that the "Nuclear Button is on his desk at all times," Twitter, January 2, 2018, 4:49 p.m., https://twitter.com/realDonaldTrump/status/948355557022420992; Donald J. Trump (@realDonaldTrump), "The Chinese Envoy, who just returned from North Korea, seems to have had no impact on Little Rocket Man," Twitter, November 30, 2017, 4:25 a.m., https://twitter.com/realDonaldTrump/status/936209447747190784.
13. Matthew Kazin, "Trump Tariffs Could Dent Economic Growth; President Should Meet With China's Xi, Kevin Brady Says," Fox Business, July 15, 2018, https://www.foxbusiness.com/economy/trump-tariffs-could-dent-economic-growth-president-should-meet-with-chinas-xi-kevin-brady-says.
14. Paul Szoldra and Associated Press, "Here's Who Is Paying the Agreed-Upon Share to NATO—and Who Isn't," *Business Insider*, February 16, 2017, http://www.businessinsider.com/nato-share-breakdown-country-2017-2.
15. "Remarks by President Trump at NATO Unveiling of the Article 5 and Berlin Wall Memorials—Brussels, Belgium," White House, May 25, 2017, https://www.whitehouse.gov/briefings-statements/remarks-president-trump-nato-unveiling-article-5-berlin-wall-memorials-brussels-belgium/.
16. Donald J. Trump (@realDonaldTrump), "Many NATO countries have agreed to step up payments considerably, as they should," Twitter, May 27, 2017, 3:03 a.m., https://twitter.com/realdonaldtrump/status/868407229380268033?lang=en.
17. Hannity Staff, "IT'S OVER: Trump 'TERMINATES' NAFTA, Unveils New 'US-Mexico Trade Agreement,'" Sean Hannity and Hannity.com, August 27, 2018, https://www.hannity.com/media-room/its-over-trump-terminates-nafta-unveils-new-us-mexico-trade-agreement/.
18. Tessa Berenson, "Donald Trump Offers Conservatives a Deal on Supreme Court," *Time*, March 21, 2016, http://time.com/4266700/donald-trump-supreme-court-nominations/.
19. Debra J. Saunders, "Trump, Democrats Create Logjam in Diplomat Confirmations," *American Spectator*, April 1, 2018, https://spectator.org/trump-democrats-create-logjam-in-confirmation-of-diplomats/.

20. "Remarks by President Trump to March for Life Participants and Pro-Life Leaders," White House, January 19, 2018, https://www.whitehouse.gov/briefings-statements/remarks-president-trump-march-life-participants-pro-life-leaders/.
21. Kimberlee Shaffir, "The 'Mexico City Policy': Why Does It Matter?," CBS Interactive Inc., January 27, 2017, https://www.cbsnews.com/news/the-mexico-city-policy-why-does-it-matter-donald-trump-abortion/.
22. "Remarks by President Trump to March for Life Participants and Pro-Life Leaders," White House.
23. "Remarks by President Trump to March for Life Participants and Pro-Life Leaders," White House.
24. "Remarks by President Trump in Cabinet Meeting," White House, October 16, 2017, https://www.whitehouse.gov/briefings-statements/remarks-president-trump-cabinet-meeting-4/.
25. "The Index of Consumer Sentiment," University of Michigan, accessed July 6, 2018, http://www.sca.isr.umich.edu/files/tbmics.pdf.
26. Rex Tillerson, "Raqqa's Liberation From ISIS," US Department of State, October 20, 2017, https://translations.state.gov/2017/10/20/raqqas-liberation-from-isis/.
27. JMattera, "Trump on the Somali Pirates: 'I Would Wipe Them Off the Face of the Earth,'" Human Events, March 18, 2011, http://humanevents.com/2011/03/18/trump-on-the-somali-pirates-i-would-wipe-them-off-the-face-of-the-earth/.
28. Jenna Johnson and Jose A. DelReal, "Trump Vows to 'Utterly Destroy ISIS,'" *Washington Post*, September 24, 2016, https://www.washingtonpost.com/politics/trump-vows-to-utterly-destroy-isis--but-he-wont-say-how/2016/09/24/911c6a74-7ffc-11e6-8d0c-fb6c00c90481_story.html?.
29. Richard Baris, "Trump's First Year Accomplishments Compiled in Shockingly Long List," Rasmussen Reports LLC, December 29, 2017, http://www.rasmussenreports.com/public_content/political_commentary/commentary_by_richard_baris/trump_s_first_year_accomplishments_compiled_in_shockingly_long_list.
30. "Enhancing Public Safety in the Interior of the United States," Executive Order 13768, *Federal Register*, January 25, 2017, https://www.federalregister.gov/documents/2017/01/30/2017-02102/enhancing-public-safety-in-the-interior-of-the-united-states.
31. Mason Weaver, "Why Trump's Signing of Omnibus Bill Was Sheer Genius," WorldNetDaily.com, March 29, 2018, http://www.wnd.com/2018/03/why-trumps-signing-of-omnibus-bill-was-sheer-genius/.
32. Weaver, "Why Trump's Signing of Omnibus Bill Was Sheer Genius."
33. Donald J. Trump (@realDonaldTrump), "Because of the $700 & $716 Billion Dollars gotten to rebuild our Military, many jobs are created and our Military is again rich," Twitter, March 25, 2018, 3:33 a.m., https://twitter.com/realdonaldtrump/status/977855968364171264?lang=en.
34. Weaver, "Why Trump's Signing of Omnibus Bill Was Sheer Genius."

35. Richard Feloni, "Here Are the 12 Business Leaders Trump Hosted for His First Big White House Meeting," *Business Insider*, January 23, 2017, http://www.businessinsider.com/business-leaders-trump-white-house-meeting-2017-1.
36. Rachel Cao, "Dow Chemical CEO on Trump: This Is the Most Pro-Business Administration Since the Founding Fathers," CNBC, February 23, 2017, https://www.cnbc.com/2017/02/23/dow-chemical-ceo-on-trump-this-is-the-most-pro-business-administration-since-the-founding-fathers.html.
37. "2018 Second Quarter Manufacturers' Outlook Survey," National Association of Manufacturers, accessed July 7, 2018, http://www.nam.org/outlook/.
38. Baris, "Trump's First Year Accomplishments Compiled in Shockingly Long List."
39. Toby Harnden, "Barack Obama: Nasa Must Try to Make Muslims 'Feel Good,'" *Telegraph*, July 6, 2010, https://www.telegraph.co.uk/news/science/space/7875584/Barack-Obama-Nasa-must-try-to-make-Muslims-feel-good.html.
40. "NASA Acting Administrator Statement on the NASA Authorization Act of 2017," NASA, March 21, 2017, https://www.nasa.gov/press-release/nasa-acting-administrator-statement-on-the-nasa-authorization-act-of-2017.

Chapter 4—In the Lion's Den

1. Tim Hains, "Trump on McCain: 'He Is a War Hero Because He Was Captured... I Like People Who Weren't Captured,'" RealClearHoldings LLC, July 19, 2015, https://www.realclearpolitics.com/video/2015/07/19/trump_on_mccain_he_is_a_war_hero_because_he_was_captured_i_like_people_who_werent_captured.html.
2. Hollie McKay, "Trump, Mattis Turn Military Loose on ISIS, Leaving Terror Caliphate in Tatters," Fox News, December 8, 2017, http://www.foxnews.com/world/2017/12/08/trump-mattis-turn-military-loose-on-isis-leaving-terror-caliphate-in-tatters.html.
3. New Day, "Pentagon to Pay for Wall; Citizenship Question on Census; NFL Expands Helmet Rule; Evangelicals Still Support Trump.," Cable News Network, March 28, 2018, http://transcripts.cnn.com/TRANSCRIPTS/1803/28/nday.02.html.
4. Shimon Cohen, "Half-Shekel Coin Bears Profile of Trump," Arutz Sheva, February 21, 2018, http://www.israelnationalnews.com/News/News.aspx/242249.
5. "Trump Tweets Regarding Immigration; U.S. and South Korea Kick Off War Games; White Evangelicals Split Over Trump's Personal Life," Cable News Network, April 1, 2018, http://transcripts.cnn.com/TRANSCRIPTS/1804/01/cnr.01.html.
6. "MSNBC Live With Craig Melvin," NBC Universal, March 30, 2018, archived at https://archive.org/details/MSNBCW_20180330_170000_MSNBC_Live_With_Craig_Melvin/start/2760/end/2820.

7. "Bill of Rights," National Archives, accessed July 8, 2018, https://www.archives.gov/founding-docs/bill-of-rights-transcript.
8. *New Day*, "Pentagon to Pay for Wall; Citizenship Question on Census; NFL Expands Helmet Rule; Evangelicals Still Support Trump," Cable News Network, March 28, 2018, http://transcripts.cnn.com/TRANSCRIPTS/1803/28/nday.02.html.
9. Marc A. Thiessen, "Why Conservative Christians Stick With Trump," *Washington Post*, March 23, 2018, https://www.washingtonpost.com/opinions/why-conservative-christians-stick-with-trump/2018/03/23/2766309a-2def-11e8-8688-e053ba58f1e4_story.html?utm_term=.6f60173b6d1a.

Chapter 5—Trump's Bully Pulpit

1. "NBC: Donald Trump Interviewed by Tom Brokaw on *The Today Show*—August 21, 1980," Factbase, accessed July 9, 2018, https://factba.se/transcript/donald-trump-interview-today-show-august-21-1980.
2. Conor Friedersdorf, "When Donald Trump Became a Celebrity," *The Atlantic*, January 6, 2016, https://www.theatlantic.com/politics/archive/2016/01/the-decade-when-donald-trump-became-a-celebrity/422838/.
3. James Traub, "Trumpologies," *New York Times Magazine*, September 12, 2004, https://www.nytimes.com/2004/09/12/magazine/trumpologies.html.
4. Traub, "Trumpologies."
5. Traub, "Trumpologies."
6. Traub, "Trumpologies."
7. Mayhill Fowler, "Obama: No Surprise That Hard-Pressed Pennsylvanians Turn Bitter," HuffPost, updated May 25, 2011, https://www.huffingtonpost.com/mayhill-fowler/obama-no-surprise-that-ha_b_96188.html.
8. Michael C. Haverluck, "Trump's 50% Approval Trumps Obama's 45%," One News Now, February 23, 2018, https://www.onenewsnow.com/politics-govt/2018/02/23/trumps-50-approval-trumps-obamas-45.
9. Time staff, "Here's Donald Trump's Presidential Announcement Speech," *Time*, June 16, 2015, http://time.com/3923128/donald-trump-announcement-speech/.
10. Jose A. DelReal, "Donald Trump Announces Presidential Bid," *Washington Post*, June 16, 2015, https://www.washingtonpost.com/news/post-politics/wp/2015/06/16/donald-trump-to-announce-his-presidential-plans-today/?utm_term=.98adce22b890.
11. Politico wrote: "In fact, birtherism, as it's been called, reportedly began with innuendo by serial Illinois political candidate Andy Martin, who painted Obama as a closet Muslim in 2004." Kyle Cheney, "No, Clinton Didn't Start the Birther Thing; This Guy Did," Politico, September 16, 2016, https://www.politico.com/story/2016/09/birther-movement-founder-trump-clinton-228304.

12. Kori Schulman, "'The President's Speech' at the White House Correspondents' Dinner," White House, May 1, 2011, https://obamawhitehouse.archives.gov/blog/2011/05/01/president-s-speech-white-house-correspondents-dinner.
13. Donald J. Trump (@realDonaldTrump), "An 'extremely credible source' has called my office and told me that @BarackObama's birth certificate is a fraud," Twitter, August 6, 2012, 1:23 p.m., https://twitter.com/realDonaldTrump/status/232572505238433794.
14. Donald J. Trump (@realDonaldTrump), "I am starting to think that there is something seriously wrong with President Obama's mental health," Twitter, October 16, 2014, 1:23 a.m., https://twitter.com/realDonaldTrump/status/522664117438775296.
15. James Lewis "What Does Donald Trump Really Believe?," *American Thinker*, February 28, 2016, http://www.americanthinker.com/articles/2016/02/what_does_donald_trump_really_believe.html.
16. Donald J. Trump (@realDonaldTrump), "I use Social Media not because I like to, but because it is the only way to fight a VERY dishonest and unfair 'press,' now often referred to as Fake News Media," Twitter, December 30, 2017, 2:36 p.m., https://twitter.com/realdonaldtrump/status/947235015343202304?lang=en.
17. Mathew Ingram, "Love and Hate: The Media's Co-Dependent Relationship With Donald Trump," *Fortune*, March 1, 2016, http://fortune.com/2016/03/01/media-love-hate-trump/.
18. Ingram, "Love and Hate."
19. "President Trump Job Approval," RealClearHoldings LLC, accessed July 9, 2018, https://www.realclearpolitics.com/epolls/other/president_trump_job_approval-6179.html.
20. Douglas Ernst, "Jim Acosta Says Voters Too Stupid to Grasp Trump 'Act': 'Their Elevator Might Not Hit All Floors,'" *Washington Times*, April 24, 2018, https://www.washingtontimes.com/news/2018/apr/24/jim-acosta-says-voters-too-stupid-to-grasp-trump-a/.
21. John Nolte, "Nolte—Media Fail: Trump's Approval Rating Average Hits Year-Long High," Breitbart, May 1, 2018, http://www.breitbart.com/big-government/2018/05/01/media-fail-trumps-approval-rating-average-hits-year-long-high/.
22. Kimberly Fitch, "Both Sides of the Aisle Agree: The Media Is a Problem," Gallup, January 29, 2018, http://news.gallup.com/opinion/gallup/226472/sides-aisle-agree-media-problem.aspx?.
23. Art Swift, "Democrats' Confidence in Mass Media Rises Sharply From 2016," Gallup, September 21, 2017, https://news.gallup.com/poll/219824/democrats-confidence-mass-media-rises-sharply-2016.aspx.
24. Nolte, "Nolte—Media Fail."
25. Nolte, "Nolte—Media Fail."

26. Alexandra Topping, "'Sweden, Who Would Believe This?': Trump Cites Non-Existent Terror Attack," *The Guardian*, February 19, 2017, https://www.theguardian.com/us-news/2017/feb/19/sweden-trump-cites-non-existent-terror-attack.
27. Cheryl Chumley, "Trump Clarifies 'Sweden' Comment, as Press Goes Bonkers," WND.com, February 20, 2017, http://www.wnd.com/2017/02/trump-clarifies-sweden-comment-as-press-goes-bonkers/.
28. Jon Miller, "The 9 Most Absurd Lies the Media Told About Trump in 2017," CRTV.com, December 27, 2017, https://www.crtv.com/video/9-most-absurd-lies-the-media-told-about-trump-in-2017--white-house-brief.
29. Miller, "The 9 Most Absurd Lies the Media Told About Trump in 2017."
30. *The Lead With Jake Tapper*, "Trump Transition Sought Secret Communications With Russia?; North Korea Test-Fires 3rd Missile in Three Weeks," Cable News Network, May 29, 2017, http://transcripts.cnn.com/TRANSCRIPTS/1705/29/cg.01.html; Donald J. Trump (@realDonaldTrump), "It is my opinion that many of the leaks coming out of the White House are fabricated lies made up by the #FakeNews media," Twitter, May 28, 2017, 5:33 a.m., https://twitter.com/realdonaldtrump/status/868807327130025984?lang=en; Donald J. Trump (@realDonaldTrump), "The Fake News Media works hard at disparaging & demeaning my use of social media because they don't want America to hear the real story!," Twitter, May 28, 2017, 5:20 p.m., https://twitter.com/realdonaldtrump/status/868985285207629825?lang=en.
31. Donald J. Trump (@realDonaldTrump), "Sorry folks, but if I would have relied on the Fake News of CNN, NBC, ABC, CBS, washpost or nytimes, I would have had ZERO chance winning WH," Twitter, June 6, 2017, 5:15 a.m., https://twitter.com/realdonaldtrump/status/872064426568036353?lang=en.
32. Donald J. Trump (@realDonaldTrump), "The FAKE MSM is working so hard trying to get me not to use Social Media," Twitter, June 6, 2017, 4:58 a.m., https://twitter.com/realdonaldtrump/status/872059997429022722?lang=en.
33. Donald J. Trump (@realDonaldTrump), "The Fake News Media hates when I use what has turned out to be my very powerful Social Media—over 100 million people!," Twitter, June 16, 2017, 5:23 a.m., https://twitter.com/realdonaldtrump/status/875690204564258816?lang=en.
34. Combined total followers of these accounts as of July 26, 2018: Donald J. Trump (@realDonaldTrump), Twitter, https://twitter.com/realDonaldTrump; President Trump (@POTUS), Twitter, https://twitter.com/potus; Donald J. Trump (@DonaldTrump), Facebook, https://www.facebook.com/DonaldTrump/; President Donald J. Trump (@POTUS), https://www.facebook.com/POTUS/.
35. Mark Joyella, "Sean Hannity Unrivaled as Fox News Posts 66th Consecutive Quarter at No. 1," July 3, 2018, https://www.forbes.com/sites/markjoyella/2018/07/03/sean-hannity-unrivaled-as-fox-news-posts-66th-consecutive-quarter-at-number-

one/#a933e2d536d2; "The Most-Followed Twitter Accounts on Earth," CBS Interactive Inc., accessed July 26, 2018, rankedhttps://www.cbsnews.com/pictures/the-biggest-twitter-accounts-on-earth/14/; "List of Most-Followed Twitter Accounts," Wikipedia, https://en.wikipedia.org/wiki/List_of_most-followed_Twitter_accounts.

36. Donald J. Trump (@realDonaldTrump), "The Fake News is going crazy making up false stories and using only unnamed sources (who don't exist)," Twitter, April 30, 2018, 3:49 p.m., https://twitter.com/realdonaldtrump/status/991087278515769345?lang=en.
37. Donald J. Trump (@realDonaldTrump), "The White House is running very smoothly despite phony Witch Hunts etc.," Twitter, April 30, 2018, 4:02 p.m., https://twitter.com/realdonaldtrump/status/991090373417152515?lang=en.
38. Emily Stewart, "Wonder What Michelle Wolf Said to Make Everyone So Mad? Read It Here," Vox, April 30, 2018, https://www.vox.com/policy-and-politics/2018/4/30/17301436/michelle-wolf-speech-transcript-white-house-correspondents-dinner-sarah-huckabee-sanders.
39. Andrea Mitchell (@mitchellreports), "Apology is owed to @PressSec and others grossly insulted [by] Michelle Wolf at White House Correspondents Assoc dinner which started with uplifting heartfelt speech by @margarettalev," Twitter, April 29, 2018, 8:03 a.m., https://twitter.com/mitchellreports/status/990607447160164352?lang=en.
40. Reince Priebus (@Reince), "An R/X rated spectacle that started poorly and ended up in the bottom of the canyon," Twitter, April 28, 2018, 8:22 p.m., https://twitter.com/reince/status/990431023992320000?lang=en.
41. Gov. Mike Huckabee (@GovMikeHuckabee), "Those who think that the tasteless classless bullying at the WHCD was an example of the 1st Amendment should never condemn bullying, bigoted comments, racist bile or hate speech," Twitter, April 29, 2018, 7:59 a.m., https://twitter.com/govmikehuckabee/status/990606414287724550?lang=en.
42. Donald J. Trump (@realDonaldTrump), "The White House Correspondents' Dinner was a failure last year, but this year was an embarrassment to everyone associated with it," Twitter, April 29, 2018, 7:38 p.m., https://twitter.com/realdonaldtrump/status/990782291667488768?lang=en.
43. Donald J. Trump (@realDonaldTrump), "The White House Correspondents' Dinner is DEAD as we know it," Twitter, April 30, 2018, 5:10 a.m., https://twitter.com/realdonaldtrump/status/990926480329859073?lang=en.
44. Kate Samuelson, "Michelle Wolf's Routine Was 'Not in the Spirit' of Our Mission, Says WHCA President," *Time*, April 30, 2018, http://time.com/5259517/whca-president-michelle-wolf-routine-not-in-spirit-of-mission/.
45. Liz Peek, "Michelle Wolf Assault Was Perfectly in Tune With How Liberal Media Views the Trump White House," Fox News, April 30, 2018, http://www.foxnews.

com/opinion/2018/04/30/liz-peek-michelle-wolf-assault-was-perfectly-in-tune-with-how-liberal-media-views-trump-white-house.html.

46. Nic Newman and Richard Fletcher, "Audience Perspectives on Low Trust in the Media," Reuters Institute (University of Oxford), accessed July 25, 2018, https://reutersinstitute.politics.ox.ac.uk/our-research/bias-bullshit-and-lies-audience-perspectives-low-trust-media.
47. Rob Wile, "When It Comes to News, America Is in a State of 'Pure Polarization,' Physicist Says," *Miami Herald*, updated April 4, 2018, http://www.miamiherald.com/news/business/article207841309.html.
48. Wile, "When It Comes to News, America Is in a State of 'Pure Polarization,' Physicist Says."
49. Lyman Abbott, cited in *The Outlook*, February 27, 1909; quoted in the *New York Times*, March 6, 1909.
50. Victor Davis Hanson, "Trump Syndromes," *National Review*, March 6, 2018, https://www.nationalreview.com/2018/03/president-donald-trump-creates-hysterical-hatred-and-fervent-support/.
51. Hanson, "Trump Syndromes."
52. "Trump Administration Embraces Heritage Foundation Policy Recommendations," Heritage Foundation, January 23, 2018, https://www.heritage.org/impact/trump-administration-embraces-heritage-foundation-policy-recommendations.
53. Hanson, "Trump Syndromes."
54. "How New Yorkers See the World: View of the World From 9th Avenue," Brilliant Maps, June 7, 2015, https://brilliantmaps.com/new-yorkers-world/.
55. Salena Zito, "The Media Assault on Trump Could Win Him a Second Term," *New York Post*, April 29, 2017, https://nypost.com/2017/04/29/the-media-assault-on-trump-could-win-him-a-second-term/.
56. Zito, "The Media Assault on Trump Could Win Him a Second Term."
57. Aaron Blake, "Trump Voters Don't Have Buyer's Remorse. But Some Hillary Clinton Voters Do," *Washington Post*, April 23, 2017, https://www.washingtonpost.com/news/the-fix/wp/2017/04/23/trump-voters-dont-have-buyers-remorse-but-some-hillary-clinton-voters-do/?utm_term=.3bb4836a60ae; "President Trump Is Least Popular President at 100-Day Mark," *Washington Post*, April 27, 2017, https://www.washingtonpost.com/page/2010-2019/WashingtonPost/2017/04/23/National-Politics/Polling/release_466.xml?tid=a_inl.
58. "President Trump Is Least Popular President at 100-Day Mark," *Washington Post*.
59. Zito, "The Media Assault on Trump Could Win Him a Second Term."
60. Salena Zito, "Anti-Trump Hysteria Has Only Hardened His Voters' Support," *New York Post*, April 14, 2018, https://nypost.com/2018/04/14/anti-trump-hysteria-has-only-hardened-his-voters-support/.

61. Darrell Delamaide, "Media Courts Backlash With Constant Assault on Trump," MarketWatch, June 30, 2017, https://www.marketwatch.com/story/media-courts-backlash-with-constant-assault-on-trump-2017-06-30.
62. Glenn Greenwald, "CNN Journalists Resign: Latest Example of Media Recklessness on the Russia Threat," The Intercept, June 27 2017, https://theintercept.com/2017/06/27/cnn-journalists-resign-latest-example-of-media-recklessness-on-the-russia-threat/.
63. Delamaide, "Media Courts Backlash With Constant Assault on Trump."
64. Delamaide, "Media Courts Backlash With Constant Assault on Trump."

Chapter 6—Muscular Diplomacy

1. Stephen Loiaconi, "Trump: 'I've Been Preparing All My Life' for North Korea Summit," Sinclair Broadcast Group, June 8, 2018, https://wjla.com/news/nation-world/trump-ive-been-preparing-all-my-life-for-north-korea-summit.
2. NBC News, "Flashback: Donald Trump Says He'd 'Negotiate Like Crazy' With North Korea | NBC News," YouTube, August 9, 2017, https://www.youtube.com/watch?v=sQUaQo2j42Y.
3. "Press Conference by President Trump," White House, June 12, 2018, https://www.whitehouse.gov/briefings-statements/press-conference-president-trump/.
4. "Press Conference by President Trump," White House.
5. "READ: Full Text of Trump-Kim Signed Statement," Cable News Network, June 12, 2018, https://www.cnn.com/2018/06/12/politics/read-full-text-of-trump-kim-signed-statement/index.html; "Press Conference by President Trump," White House.
6. Mark Landler, "Trump and Kim See New Chapter for Nations After Summit," *New York Times*, June 11, 2018, https://www.nytimes.com/2018/06/11/world/asia/trump-kim-summitmeeting.html.
7. Micah Meadowcroft, "War, Mission, & Memory: Dr. Somerville's Childhood in South Korea," *Hillsdale Forum*, March 31, 2016, https://hillsdaleforum.com/2016/03/31/war-mission-memory-dr-somervilles-childhood-in-south-korea/.
8. "Trump 'Bold' Talk on North Korean Christians," Religion News Service, June 12, 2018, https://religionnews.com/2018/06/12/press-release-trump-bold-talk-on-north-korean-christians/.
9. "Message to South Koreans on Reunification," NorthKoreanChristians.com, accessed July 24, 2018, http://www.northkoreanchristians.com/unification-korea.html.
10. These interesting parallels were brought to my attention by Kathie Walters of Macon, Georgia, a longtime friend who ministers around the world and has spent many years researching revivals.

11. Ben Archibald, "Donald Trump's Scots Aunt Is Dead Ringer for US President," *Scottish Sun*, October 20, 2017, https://www.thescottishsun.co.uk/news/1729757/donald-trumps-aunt-hairdo-president-scot/; "Desperate Prayers by Trump's Great Aunts in 'Sanctuary' Cottage Said to Spark Hebrides Revival in Scotland," World Tribune, October 18, 2017, http://www.worldtribune.com/desperate-prayers-by-trumps-aunts-in-sanctuary-cottage-said-to-spark-hebrides-revival-in-scotland/.
12. Chang May Choon, "Trump-Kim Summit: South Korea's Moon Jae in Hopes for Bold Decisions and Miraculous Result," *Straits Times*, June 11, 2018, https://www.straitstimes.com/asia/east-asia/singapore-summit-south-koreas-moon-hopes-for-bold-decisions-and-miraculous-result.
13. "History of North Korea," Liberty in North Korea, accessed July 26, 2018, https://www.libertyinnorthkorea.org/learn-north-korea-history/.
14. Carey Lodge, "Christians 'Hung On a Cross Over Fire,' Steamrollered and Crushed to Death in North Korea," *Christian Today*, September 23, 2016, https://www.christiantoday.com/article/christians-hung-on-a-cross-over-fire-steamrollered-and-crushed-to-death-in-north-korea/96190.htm.
15. Russell Goldman, "How Trump's Predecessors Dealt With the North Korean Threat," *New York Times*, August 17, 2017, https://www.nytimes.com/2017/08/17/world/asia/trump-north-korea-threat.html.
16. Goldman, "How Trump's Predecessors Dealt With the North Korean Threat."
17. Peter Baker and Choe Sang-Hun, "Trump Threatens 'Fire and Fury' Against North Korea if It Endangers U.S.," *New York Times*, August 8, 2017, https://www.nytimes.com/2017/08/08/world/asia/north-korea-un-sanctions-nuclear-missile-united-nations.html.
18. "Trump Sometimes 'Felt Foolish' Using Harsh Rhetoric Against North Korea," *The Hill*, June 12, 2018, http://thehill.com/homenews/administration/391783-trump-i-felt-foolish-using-harsh-rhetoric-against-north-korea-in-the.
19. "Press Conference by President Trump," White House.
20. *CNN Newsroom*, "Trump Speaks on Meeting With Kim Jong-un, IG Report, Immigration," Cable News Network, June 15, 2018, http://transcripts.cnn.com/TRANSCRIPTS/1806/15/cnr.01.html.
21. "North Korea Relief," Samaritan's Purse, accessed July 10, 2018, https://www.samaritanspurse.org/donation-items/north-korea-relief/.
22. Samaritan's Purse, "Mission of Mercy: Samaritan's Purse Airlifts Emergency Aid to Victims of Devastating Floods in North Korea," ReliefWeb, August 31, 2007, https://reliefweb.int/report/democratic-peoples-republic-korea/mission-mercy-samaritans-purse-airlifts-emergency-aid.
23. Franklin Graham, "Thank you, Mr. President, Mike Pompeo, and all of the administration's advisors for being willing to work for peace," Facebook, June 13, 2018, 7:08 a.m., https://www.facebook.com/FranklinGraham/posts/1961344047255100.

24. Jessilyn Justice, "Trump Confronted Kim Jong Un About Atrocities Against Christians," CharismaNews.com, June 12, 2018, https://www.charismanews.com/politics/71603-trump-confronted-kim-jong-un-about-atrocities-against-christians.
25. Justice, "Trump Confronted Kim Jong Un About Atrocities Against Christians."
26. Jessilyn Justice, "North Korea Crushed Christians Under Steamroller, Hung Them on Crosses Above Fire, New Report Says," CharismaNews.com, September 28, 2016, https://premium.charismanews.com/article/60218.
27. Open Doors, "World Watch List 2018," Open Doors USA, accessed July 10, 2018, https://www.opendoorsusa.org/wp-content/uploads/2017/05/WWL2018-Booklet-11518.pdf.
28. Justice, "Trump Confronted Kim Jong Un About Atrocities Against Christians."
29. Justice, "Trump Confronted Kim Jong Un About Atrocities Against Christians."
30. "Press Conference by President Trump," White House.
31. Judson Berger, "Trump to 'Hannity': Kim Jong Un to Start Denuclearization 'Virtually Immediately,'" FOX News Network LLC, June 12, 2018, http://www.foxnews.com/politics/2018/06/12/trump-to-hannity-kim-jong-un-to-start-denuclearization-virtually-immediately.html.
32. J. Lee Grady, "10 Bizarre Facts About North Korea." *Charisma*, June 13, 2018, https://www.charismamag.com/blogs/fire-in-my-bones/37295-10-bizarre-facts-about-north-korea.
33. Grady, "10 Bizarre Facts About North Korea."
34. Lucas Tomlinson, "ISIS Has Lost 98 Percent of Its Territory—Mostly Since Trump Took Office, Officials Say," Fox News, December 26, 2017, http://www.foxnews.com/politics/2017/12/26/isis-has-lost-98-percent-its-territory-mostly-since-trump-took-office-officials-say.html.

Chapter 7—Trump's Booming Economy

1. Peter Roff, "Good News Doesn't Always Travel Fast," *U.S. News & World Report*, January 16, 2018, https://www.usnews.com/opinion/thomas-jefferson-street/articles/2018-01-16/the-economy-is-booming-under-trump-but-mainstream-media-wont-tell-you-that.
2. Thomas Cooley and Peter Rupert, "U.S. Economic Snapshot," Rupert-Cooley Economic Snapshot, June 1, 2018, https://www.econsnapshot.com/2018/06/.
3. Neil Irwin, "We Ran Out of Words to Describe How Good the Jobs Numbers Are," *New York Times*, June 1, 2018, https://www.nytimes.com/2018/06/01/upshot/we-ran-out-of-words-to-describe-how-good-the-jobs-numbers-are.html.
4. Donald J. Trump (@realDonaldTrump), "In many ways this is the greatest economy in the HISTORY of America and the best time EVER to look for a job!," Twitter, June 4, 2018, 1:42 p.m., https://twitter.com/realdonaldtrump/status/1003738744061603843?lang=en.

5. Bloomberg, "Trump Says 'This Is the Greatest Economy in the HISTORY of America,'" *Fortune*, June 7, 2018, http://fortune.com/2018/06/07/trump-eisenhower-greatest-economy-history-america/.
6. Wayne Allyn Root, "The Trump Miracle," Townhall.com, June 5, 2018, https://townhall.com/columnists/wayneallynroot/2018/06/05/the-trump-miracle-n2487181.
7. Roff, "Good News Doesn't Always Travel Fast."
8. Roff, "Good News Doesn't Always Travel Fast."
9. Roff, "Good News Doesn't Always Travel Fast"; Patrice Lee Onwuka, "Black Americans' Record Employment, Tax Cuts and More," Independent Women's Forum, January 9, 2018, http://iwf.org/news/2805497/Black-America-Winning-With-Record-Employment,-Tax-Cuts-and-More.
10. Roff, "Good News Doesn't Always Travel Fast."
11. Roff, "Good News Doesn't Always Travel Fast."
12. Bob Bryan, "Nancy Pelosi Says Companies' Bonuses to Workers Because of the Tax Bill Are 'Crumbs,'" *Business Insider*, January 11, 2018, http://www.businessinsider.com/nancy-pelosi-tax-bill-bonuses-crumbs-2018-1.
13. Naomi Jagoda, "Trump Compares Pelosi's 'Crumbs' Comments to Clinton's 'Deplorables' Remark," *The Hill*, February 1, 2018, http://thehill.com/policy/finance/371847-trump-compares-pelosis-crumbs-comments-to-clintons-deplorables-remark.
14. Andy Puzder, "What Trump-Haters Don't Get About the Incredible Power of American Capitalism," Fox News, April 23, 2018, http://www.foxnews.com/opinion/2018/04/23/andy-puzder-what-trump-haters-dont-get-about-incredible-power-american-capitalism.html.
15. Puzder, "What Trump-Haters Don't Get About the Incredible Power of American Capitalism."
16. Puzder, "What Trump-Haters Don't Get About the Incredible Power of American Capitalism."
17. Puzder, "What Trump-Haters Don't Get About the Incredible Power of American Capitalism."
18. Puzder, "What Trump-Haters Don't Get About the Incredible Power of American Capitalism."
19. Andy Puzder, "If Democrats Decide to Pivot From Trump and Run on an Economic Message, They're Doomed," Fox News, May 25, 2018, http://www.foxnews.com/opinion/2018/05/25/andy-puzder-if-democrats-decide-to-pivot-from-trump-and-run-on-economic-message-re-doomed.html.
20. Puzder, "If Democrats Decide to Pivot From Trump and Run on an Economic Message, They're Doomed."
21. Matthew Boyle, "Donald Trump Jr.: Trump Economy Most Helping 'Forgotten Men' in 'Forgotten Land Everywhere Between New York City and Malibu,'" Breitbart.

com, June 4, 2018, http://www.breitbart.com/big-government/2018/06/04/exclusive-trump-jr-trump-economy-helping-forgotten-men-forgotten-land-everywhere-new-york-city-malibu.

22. Boyle, "Donald Trump Jr."
23. Boyle, "Donald Trump Jr."
24. Boyle, "Donald Trump Jr."
25. Gregg Re, "GDP Report Shows Booming 4.1 Percent Growth, as Trump Touts 'Amazing' Numbers," Fox News, July 27, 2018, http://www.foxnews.com/politics/2018/07/27/gdp-report-shows-booming-4-1-percent-growth-as-trump-touts-terrific-numbers.html.
26. Kimberly Amadeo, "US Economic Outlook for 2018 and Beyond," TheBalance.com, updated July 11, 2018, https://www.thebalance.com/us-economic-outlook-3305669.
27. "National Debt," US Department of the Treasury, accessed July 30 2018, https://www.treasury.gov/resource-center/faqs/Markets/Pages/national-debt.aspx.
28. "National Debt," US Department of the Treasury.
29. "National Debt," US Department of the Treasury.
30. Brennan Weiss, "Here's What a Top Intel Chief Says Is the Biggest Internal Threat to US National Security," *Business Insider*, February 13, 2018, http://www.businessinsider.com/dan-coats-biggest-threat-national-security-national-debt-2018-2.
31. Andy Biggs, "'The Single, Biggest Threat to National Security,'" *Washington Times*, May 8, 2018, https://www.washingtontimes.com/news/2018/may/8/the-single-biggest-threat-to-national-security-is-/.
32. Moody's: US' Economic Strength and Integral Role in Global Capital Markets Counterbalance Deteriorating Fiscal Position," Moody's Investors Services, February 9, 2018, https://www.moodys.com/research/Moodys-US-economic-strength-and-integral-role-in-global-capital--PR_379378.
33. Secretary of Defense James N. Mattis, "Remarks by Secretary Mattis on the National Defense Strategy," US Department of Defense, January 19, 2018, https://www.defense.gov/News/Transcripts/Transcript-View/Article/1420042/remarks-by-secretary-mattis-on-the-national-defense-strategy/; Andy Biggs, "The Threat to National Security That Hardly Anyone Is Watching," June 11, 2018, https://www.dailysignal.com/2018/06/11/the-threat-to-national-security-that-hardly-anyone-is-watching/; Biggs, "'The Single, Biggest Threat to National Security.'"
34. Biggs, "'The Single, Biggest Threat to National Security.'"
35. Kimberly Amadeo, "U.S. Debt by President: By Dollar and Percent," TheBalance.com, April 13, 2018, https://www.thebalance.com/us-debt-by-president-by-dollar-and-percent-3306296.
36. Amadeo, "U.S. Debt by President."
37. Amadeo, "U.S. Debt by President."

38. Garland S. Tucker III, "Looming Debt Crisis Isn't Just a Fiscal Crisis—It's a Crisis of Morality," *Investor's Business Daily*, April 13, 2018, https://www.investors.com/politics/commentary/looming-debt-crisis-isnt-just-a-fiscal-crisis-its-a-crisis-of-morality/.
39. Tucker, "Looming Debt Crisis Isn't Just a Fiscal Crisis."
40. Tucker, "Looming Debt Crisis Isn't Just a Fiscal Crisis"; Sir Alexander Tytler wrote: "A democracy…can only exist until the people discover they can vote themselves largesse out of the public treasury. From that moment on, the majority always votes for the candidate promising the most benefits from the public treasury, with the result that democracy always collapses over loose fiscal policy ("Alexander Fraser Tytler Quotes," Goodreads Inc., accessed July 30, 2018, https://www.goodreads.com/author/quotes/5451872.Alexander_Fraser_Tytler).
41. Tucker, "Looming Debt Crisis Isn't Just a Fiscal Crisis."
42. Jesse Hathaway, "Congress Still Ignoring Country's Dangerously Growing Debt," *Investor's Business Daily*, May 14, 2018, https://www.investors.com/politics/commentary/congress-still-ignoring-countrys-dangerously-growing-debt/.
43. Conor Sen, "Trump's Economic Gamble Might Just Work," *Chicago Tribune*, February 28, 2018, http://www.chicagotribune.com/news/opinion/commentary/ct-perspec-economy-trump-deficits-growth-productivity-0301-20180228-story.html.
44. Sen, "Trump's Economic Gamble Might Just Work."
45. Saleha Mohsin, "Mnuchin Urges Markets to Shrug Off Tax Cuts, Debt Worries," Bloomberg, updated February 23, 2018, https://www.bloomberg.com/news/articles/2018-02-23/mnuchin-says-trump-policies-will-raise-wages-without-inflation.
46. Sen, "Trump's Economic Gamble Might Just Work."
47. Sen, "Trump's Economic Gamble Might Just Work."

Chapter 8—Billionaire Radicals

1. Charles Riley, "What Happens at Davos?," CNN Money, January 20, 2018, http://money.cnn.com/2018/01/19/news/economy/davos-what-is-wef/index.html.
2. "Transcript of Donald Trump Interview With the Wall Street Journal," *Wall Street Journal*, updated January 14, 2018, https://www.wsj.com/articles/transcript-of-donald-trump-interview-with-the-wall-street-journal-1515715481.
3. Riley, "What Happens at Davos?"
4. "Remarks by President Trump to the World Economic Forum," White House.
5. "Remarks by President Trump to the World Economic Forum," White House.
6. Peter S. Goodman and Keith Bradsher, "Trump Arrived in Davos as a Party Wrecker. He Leaves Praised as a Pragmatist," *New York Times*, January 26, 2018, https://www.nytimes.com/2018/01/26/business/trump-davos-speech-response.html.

7. Ian Schwartz, "Trump: I Didn't Realize How 'Vicious,' 'Fake' Press Could Be Until I Became a Politician," RealClearPolitics, January 26, 2018, https://www.realclearpolitics.com/video/2018/01/26/trump_in_davos_it_wasnt_until_i_became_a_politician_that_i_realized_how_vicious_fake_the_press_can_be.html.
8. Victor Davis Hanson, "Is Trump an Island?," *National Review*, December 19, 2017, https://www.nationalreview.com/2017/12/trump-accomplishments-speak-themselves-despite-media-attacks/.
9. "Soros Clones: 5 Liberal Mega-Donors Nearly as Dangerous as George Soros," Media Research Center, accessed July 12, 2018, https://www.mrc.org/special-reports/soros-clones-5-liberal-mega-donors-nearly-dangerous-george-soros; "George Soros: Media Mogul," Media Research Center, accessed July 12, 2018, https://www.mrc.org/special-reports/george-soros-media-mogul.
10. "About ONO," Organization of News Ombudsmen, accessed July 12, 2018, https://www.newsombudsmen.org/about-ono/.
11. "George Soros: Media Mogul," Media Research Center.
12. "Soros Clones: 5 Liberal Mega-Donors Nearly as Dangerous as George Soros," Media Research Center, accessed July 31, 2018, https://www.mrc.org/special-reports/soros-clones-5-liberal-mega-donors-nearly-dangerous-george-soros.
13. Neil Maghami, "True Believers: George Soros and the Religious Left's War on President Trump," Capital Research Center, June 7, 2017, https://capitalresearch.org/article/true-believers-george-soros-and-the-religious-lefts-war-on-president-trump/.
14. Jim VandeHei and Chris Cillizza, "A New Alliance of Democrats Spreads Funding: But Some in Party Bristle at Secrecy and Liberal Tilt," *Washington Post*, July 17, 2006, http://www.washingtonpost.com/wp-dyn/content/article/2006/07/16/AR2006071600882_pf.html.
15. VandeHei and Cillizza, "A New Alliance of Democrats Spreads Funding."
16. Maghami, "True Believers."
17. Dan Gainor, "Soros Spends Over $48 Million Funding Media Organizations" [Part 2 of 4], Media Research Center, August 26, 2014, https://www.mrc.org/commentary/soros-spends-over-48-million-funding-media-organizations.
18. Asra Q. Nomani, "Billionaire George Soros Has Ties to More Than 50 'Partners' of the Women's March on Washington," Women in the World Media LLC, January 20, 2017, https://womenintheworld.com/2017/01/20/billionaire-george-soros-has-ties-to-more-than-50-partners-of-the-womens-march-on-washington/.
19. VandeHei and Cillizza, "A New Alliance of Democrats Spreads Funding."
20. Bloomberg Billionaires Index, July 31, 2018, https://www.bloomberg.com/billionaires/.
21. Andy Kroll, "Meet the Megadonor Behind the LGBTQ Rights Movement," *Rolling Stone*, June 23, 2017, https://www.rollingstone.com/politics/politics-features/meet-the-megadonor-behind-the-lgbtq-rights-movement-193996/.

22. Kroll, "Meet the Megadonor Behind the LGBTQ Rights Movement."
23. "AB-2943 Unlawful Business Practices: Sexual Orientation Change Efforts," California Legislature 2017–2018 Regular Session, published May 30, 2018, https://leginfo.legislature.ca.gov/faces/billTextClient.xhtml?bill_id=201720180AB2943.
24. Discpad, "George Soros' Lost 1998 60 Minutes Interview (CC)," YouTube, November 24, 2016, https://www.youtube.com/watch?v=rd39zUvreOU.
25. "Making of the Puppet Master," *Glenn Beck*, November 12, 2010, http://www.foxnews.com/story/2010/11/12/glenn-beck-making-puppet-master.html.
26. Prashanth Perumal, "The Incredible Life of Billionaire Investing Legend George Soros," *Business Insider*, January 24, 2017, http://www.businessinsider.com/george-soros-billionaire-investor-profile-2017-1.
27. "About Us," Open Society Foundations, accessed July 31, 2018, https://www.opensocietyfoundations.org/about.
28. Richard Poe, "George Soros' Coup," Newsmax.com, vol. 6, no. 5 (May 2004).
29. "Organizations Funded by George Soros and His Open Society Foundations," DiscoverTheNetworks.org, accessed July 31, 2018, http://www.discoverthenetworks.org/individualProfile.asp?indid=977.
30. Rebecca Hagelin, "Soros vs. America," Townhall.com, February 16, 2018, https://townhall.com/columnists/rebeccahagelin/2018/02/16/draft-n2449953.
31. Jay Richards, "Soros Funding of Sojourners Is Only the Tip of the Iceberg," *National Review*, August 25, 2010, https://www.nationalreview.com/corner/soros-funding-sojourners-only-tip-iceberg-jay-richards/.
32. Robert A. Sirico, "Soros' Catholic Useful Idiots: Faith-Based Groups Stray When Accepting Progressive Cash," *Washington Times*, August 30, 2016, https://www.washingtontimes.com/news/2016/aug/30/george-soros-catholic-useful-idiots/.
33. "Mission Statement," Faith in Public Life, accessed July 31, 2018, https://www.faithinpubliclife.org/mission-statement.
34. Maghami, "True Believers."
35. "1500 Interfaith Clergy Call on Republican Lawmakers to Reject Trump's Presidential 'Cabinet of Bigotry,'" Faith in Public Life, November 23, 2016, https://www.faithinpubliclife.org/clergyrejectcabinetofbigotry.
36. John Gehring, "Prophetic Prayer & Moral Resistance," Commonweal, February 1, 2017, https://www.commonwealmagazine.org/prophetic-prayer-moral-resistance.
37. "4,000 Faith Leaders Oppose Trump's Forthcoming Executive Action Targeting Refugees From Muslim-Majority Countries," Faith in Public Life, February 23, 2017, https://www.faithinpubliclife.org/4000-faith-leaders-oppose-muslim-ba.
38. "Faith Leaders Denounce Trump's New Executive Order Targeting Muslim Refugees, Call for Immediate Repeal," Faith in Public Life, March 6, 2017, https://www.faithinpubliclife.org/ohio-clergy-denounce-new-muslim-ban.
39. Maghami, "True Believers.

40. "Be Not Afraid?," Faith in Public Life, June 2013, https://docs.wixstatic.com/ugd/03e723_528c111e09fd4fef8f6102ba47316187.pdf.
41. Matthew Vadum, "Left-Wing Radicalism in the Church: The Catholic Campaign for Human Development," Capital Research Center, September 1, 2009, https://capitalresearch.org/article/left-wing-radicalism-in-the-church-the-catholic-campaign-for-human-development-2/.
42. Maghami, "True Believers."
43. "About PICO," PICO National Network, accessed July 13, 2018, archived at https://web.archive.org/web/20170515134943/piconetwork.org/about.
44. "Father John Baumann, SJ, Discusses PICO and Community Organizing for Passionate Leaders in Social Entrepreneurship Speaker Series," Holy Names University, October 31, 2014, https://www.hnu.edu/about/news/father-john-baumann-sj-discusses-pico-and-community-organizing-passionate-leaders-social.
45. David Hogberg, "The Gamaliel Foundation: Alinsky-Inspired Group Uses Stealth Tactics to Manipulate Church Congregations," *Foundation Watch*, July 2010, https://capitalresearch.org/article/the-gamaliel-foundation-alinsky-inspired-group-uses-stealth-tactics-to-manipulate-church-congregations/.
46. "Full Transcript: *Face the Nation* on March 11, 2018," CBS Interactive Inc., March 11, 2018, https://www.cbsnews.com/news/full-transcript-face-the-nation-on-march-11-2018-2/.
47. Todd Starnes, "WaPost Columnist Calls Pro-Trump Evangelicals 'Slimy, Political Operatives,'" March 12, 2018, https://www.toddstarnes.com/show/wapost-columnist-calls-pro-trump-evangelicals-slimy-political-operatives/.
48. Starnes, "WaPost Columnist Calls Pro-Trump Evangelicals 'Slimy, Political Operatives.'"
49. David Horowitz and Richard Poe, *The Shadow Party* (Nashville: Nelson Current, 2006), 243.
50. Horowitz and Poe, *The Shadow Party*.
51. "WikiLeaks Reveals How Billionaire 'Progressives' Run the Democratic Party," *Investor's Business Daily*, November 2, 2016, https://www.investors.com/politics/editorials/wikileaks-reveals-the-billionaire-progressives-that-run-the-democratic-party/.
52. "Remarks by President Trump to the World Economic Forum," White House.
53. "Remarks by President Trump to the World Economic Forum," White House.
54. "Remarks by President Trump to the World Economic Forum," White House.
55. Kenneth P. Vogel, "George Soros Rises Again," Politico, July 27, 2016, https://www.politico.com/story/2016/07/george-soros-democratic-convention-226267.

Chapter 9—Obama's Third Term

1. Dan Alexander, "How Barack Obama Has Made $20 Million Since Arriving in Washington," *Forbes*, January 20, 2017, https://www.forbes.com/sites/

danalexander/2017/01/20/how-barack-obama-has-made-20-million-since-arriving-in-washington/#1006876e5bf0.

2. Alexander, "How Barack Obama Has Made $20 Million Since Arriving in Washington"; "Hillary Clinton: 'We Came Out of the White House Dead Broke,'" RealClearHoldings LLC, June 9, 2014, https://www.realclearpolitics.com/video/2014/06/09/hillary_clinton_we_came_out_of_the_white_house_dead_broke.html.
3. Peter Schweizer, *Throw Them All Out* (New York: Houghton Mifflin, 2011), xvi.
4. Schweizer, *Throw Them All Out*, 76–77.
5. Schweizer, 77.
6. Schweizer, 80.
7. "Memorandum for the President, From Carol Browner, Ron Klain, Larry Summers, Subject: Renewable Energy Loan Guarantees and Grants," Briefing Memo, White House, October 25, 2010, 1–8, https://archive.org/stream/gov.gpo.fdsys.CHRG-112hhrg76267/CHRG-112hhrg76267_djvu.txt. Cited in Schweizer, *Throw Them All Out*, 83.
8. "DOE Loan Programs," United States Government Accountability Office, April 2015, https://www.gao.gov/assets/670/669847.pdf.
9. "Solar Energy," United States Government Accountability Office, August 2012, https://www.gao.gov/assets/650/647732.pdf.
10. David Williams, "Solar Energy Delivers Too Little Bang for Billions Invested," *Forbes*, February 25, 2015, https://www.forbes.com/sites/realspin/2015/02/25/solar-energy-delivers-too-little-bang-for-billions-invested/#6da216ad49f3.
11. Jason Zengerle, "Barack Obama Is Preparing for His Third Term," *GQ*, January 17, 2017, https://www.gq.com/story/barack-obama-preparing-for-third-term.
12. Zengerle, "Barack Obama Is Preparing for His Third Term."
13. Zengerle, "Barack Obama Is Preparing for His Third Term."
14. Zengerle, "Barack Obama Is Preparing for His Third Term."
15. Paul Sperry, "The Myth of Obama's 'Disappearance,'" *New York Post*, June 30, 2018, https://nypost.com/2018/06/30/obamas-disappearance-is-a-myth/.
16. Sperry, "The Myth of Obama's 'Disappearance.'"
17. Bill Moyers and Michael Winship, "Hillary Clinton's Inaugural Address," Moyers & Co., December 6, 2016, https://billmoyers.com/story/hillary-clintons-inaugural-address/.
18. Conor Friedersdorf, "Barack Obama Reflects on Leaving the Presidency" (from a BBC podcast recorded by Prince Harry of Wales), *The Atlantic*, December 27, 2017, https://www.theatlantic.com/politics/archive/2017/12/barack-obama-reflects-on-leaving-the-presidency/549236/.
19. Michael Kranish, "President Obama Says He Could Have Beaten Trump—Trump Says 'NO WAY!,'" *Washington Post*, December 26, 2016, https://www.washingtonpost.com/news/post-politics/wp/2016/12/26/president-

obama-says-he-would-have-beaten-trump-if-i-had-run-again/?utm_term=.3a715025b787.

20. Warner Todd Huston, "Obama: My Netflix Projects Will Help 'Train the Next Generation of Leaders' and Heal Our Political Divide," Breitbart, May 24, 2018, https://www.breitbart.com/big-hollywood/2018/05/24/obama-wants-netflix-projects-to-ease-americas-political-divide/.
21. Edward-Isaac Dovere, "Inside Obama's Midterm Campaign Plans," Politico, January 18, 2018, https://www.politico.com/story/2018/01/18/obama-midterm-campaign-plans-trump-345491.
22. Donald J. Trump (@realDonaldTrump). "The 'Intelligence' briefing on so-called 'Russian hacking' was delayed until Friday, perhaps more time needed to build a case," Twitter, January 3, 2017, 5:14 p.m., https://twitter.com/realdonaldtrump/status/816452807024840704?lang=en.
23. *The Rachel Maddow Show*, NBC Universal, January 3, 2017, http://www.msnbc.com/transcripts/rachel-maddow-show/2017-01-03.
24. John Wagner and Greg Miller, "Trump Alleges Delay in His Briefing on 'So-Called' Russian Hacking; U.S. Official Says There Wasn't One," *Washington Post*, January 4, 2017, https://www.washingtonpost.com/news/post-politics/wp/2017/01/03/trump-says-a-delay-in-his-briefing-on-so-called-russian-hacking-is-very-strange/?.
25. "A Report of Investigation of Certain Allegations Relating to Former FBI Deputy Director Andrew McCabe," Office of the Inspector General, February 2018, https://static01.nyt.com/files/2018/us/politics/20180413a-doj-oig-mccabe-report.pdf.
26. John O. Brennan (@JohnBrennan), "When the full extent of your venality, moral turpitude, and political corruption becomes known, you will take your rightful place as a disgraced demagogue in the dustbin of history," Twitter, March 17, 2018, 5:00 a.m., https://twitter.com/johnbrennan/status/974978856997224448?lang=en.
27. Tim Hains, "Reps. Jim Jordan and Mark Meadows: McCabe Lied Four Times, DOJ Needs to 'Come Clean,'" RealClearHoldings LLC, March 30, 2018, https://www.realclearpolitics.com/video/2018/03/30/reps_jim_jordan_and_mark_meadows_mccabe_lied_four_times_doj_needs_to_come_clean.html.
28. "The Wrong People Are Criticizing Donald Trump," *New York Times*, March 19, 2018, https://www.nytimes.com/2018/03/19/opinion/trump-mccabe-republicans.html.
29. Eliza Relman, "Jeff Sessions Explains Why He Recused Himself From Trump Campaign-Related Investigations," *Business Insider*, June 13, 2017, https://www.businessinsider.com/jeff-sessions-on-recusing-himself-trump-investigation-russia-2017-6.
30. Louie Gohmert, "Robert Mueller: Unmasked," accessed August 2, 2018, https://1zwchz1jbsr61f1c4mgf0abl-wpengine.netdna-ssl.com/wp-content/uploads/2018/04/Gohmert_Mueller_UNMASKED.pdf.

31. Peter Baker, "Trump Pardons Scooter Libby in a Case That Mirrors His Own," *New York Times*, April 13, 2108, https://www.nytimes.com/2018/04/13/us/politics/trump-pardon-scooter-libby.html.
32. Gohmert, "Robert Mueller: Unmasked," 19.
33. Rollcall Staff, "Recalling the Injustice Done to Sen. Ted Stevens," CQ Roll Call, October 28, 2014, https://www.rollcall.com/news/recalling_the_injustice_done_to_sen_ted_stevens_commentary-237407-1.html.
34. Gohmert, "Robert Mueller: Unmasked," 20.
35. Gohmert, "Robert Mueller: Unmasked," 10.
36. Gohmert, "Robert Mueller: Unmasked," 11.
37. Victor Davis Hanson, "The Double Standards of the Mueller Investigation," *Investor's Business Daily*, April 30, 2018, https://www.investors.com/politics/columnists/the-double-standards-of-the-mueller-investigation/.
38. Hanson, "The Double Standards of the Mueller Investigation."
39. Jed Babbin, "Time to Shut Mueller Down," *American Spectator*, May 7, 2018, https://spectator.org/time-to-shut-mueller-down/.
40. Babbin, "Time to Shut Mueller Down."
41. Darren Samuelsohn and Josh Gerstein, "Mueller's Courtroom Bruises Cheer Trump Team," Politico, May 7, 2018, https://www.politico.com/story/2018/05/07/trump-mueller-russia-probe-judges-573221.
42. Donald J. Trump (@realDonaldTrump), "The 13 Angry Democrats in charge of the Russian Witch Hunt are starting to find out that there is a Court System in place that actually protects people from injustice," Twitter, May 7, 2018, 4:39 a.m., https://twitter.com/realdonaldtrump/status/993455375755173892.
43. Samuelsohn and Gerstein, "Mueller's Courtroom Bruises Cheer Trump Team."
44. "Public Troubled by 'Deep State,'" Monmouth University, March 19, 2018, https://www.monmouth.edu/polling-institute/documents/monmouthpoll_us_031918.pdf/.
45. "Public Troubled by 'Deep State,'" Monmouth University.
46. "Public Troubled by 'Deep State,'" Monmouth University.
47. Donald J. Trump (@realDonaldTrump), "Crooked Hillary Clinton's top aid, Huma Abedin, has been accused of disregarding basic security protocols," Twitter, January 2, 2018, 4:48 a.m., https://twitter.com/realdonaldtrump/status/948174033882927104?lang=en.
48. "Public Troubled by 'Deep State,'" Monmouth University.
49. Max Greenwood, "GOP Rep: Obama Running 'Shadow Government' to Undermine Trump," *The Hill*, March 10, 2017, http://thehill.com/blogs/blog-briefing-room/news/323457-gop-rep-obama-running-a-shadow-government-to-undermine-trump.
50. Greenwood, "GOP Rep: Obama Running 'Shadow Government' to Undermine Trump."

51. Greenwood, "GOP Rep: Obama Running 'Shadow Government' to Undermine Trump."
52. WCPO staff, "Kentucky Congressman Claims 'Deep State' Undermining President Trump," WCPO, updated February 17, 2017, https://www.wcpo.com/news/state/state-kentucky/kentucky-congressman-claims-deep-state-undermining-president-trump.
53. WCPO staff, "Kentucky Congressman Claims 'Deep State' Undermining President Trump."
54. Sam Schwarz, "Obama Is Returning to Politics in 2018, and Trump Should Be Worried," *Newsweek*, January 17, 2018, http://www.newsweek.com/barack-obama-trump-returning-politics-783421.
55. "2018 Shaping Up Big for Democrats," Public Policy Polling, September 28, 2017, https://www.publicpolicypolling.com/wp-content/uploads/2017/10/PPP_Release_National_92817-1.pdf.

Chapter 10—America at War (With Itself)

1. Ginni Thomas, "Poll Shows Nation Divided Between America First and Blame America First [Video]," The Daily Caller, December 17, 2017, http://dailycaller.com/2017/12/16/poll-shows-nation-divided-between-america-first-and-blame-america-first-video/.
2. "A Tale of Two Patriotisms," Ear to the Ground, accessed August 2, 2018, https://www.eartotheground.us/a-tale-of-two-patriotisms.
3. "American Views on Patriotism," American Culture and Faith Institute, October–November 2017, https://www.culturefaith.com/wp-content/uploads/2017/12/Patriotism-Summary.pdf.
4. "American Views on Patriotism," American Culture and Faith Institute.
5. Thomas, "Poll Shows Nation Divided Between America First and Blame America First."
6. Thomas, "Poll Shows Nation Divided Between America First and Blame America First."
7. Thomas, "Poll Shows Nation Divided Between America First and Blame America First."
8. Thomas, "Poll Shows Nation Divided Between America First and Blame America First."
9. Carroll Doherty, "Key Takeaways on Americans' Growing Partisan Divide Over Political Values," Pew Research Center, October 5, 2017, http://www.pewresearch.org/fact-tank/2017/10/05/takeaways-on-americans-growing-partisan-divide-over-political-values/.
10. Doherty, "Key Takeaways on Americans' Growing Partisan Divide Over Political Values."

11. Doherty, "Key Takeaways on Americans' Growing Partisan Divide Over Political Values."
12. Doherty, "Key Takeaways on Americans' Growing Partisan Divide Over Political Values."
13. Doherty, "Key Takeaways on Americans' Growing Partisan Divide Over Political Values."
14. Michael C. Bender, "Donald Trump's Approval Rating Inches Higher, Buoyed by Republican Support," *Wall Street Journal*, July 22, 2018, https://www.wsj.com/articles/donald-trumps-approval-rating-inches-higher-buoyed-by-republican-support-1532293201.
15. Julia Manchester, "Poll: Americans Deeply Divided on Cultural and Economic Issues," *The Hill*, September 6, 2017, http://thehill.com/blogs/blog-briefing-room/news/349378-poll-americans-deeply-divided-on-cultural-and-economic-issues.
16. Janet Hook, "Political Divisions in U.S. Are Widening, Long-Lasting, Poll Shows," *Wall Street Journal*, September 6, 2017, https://www.wsj.com/articles/political-divisions-in-u-s-are-widening-long-lasting-poll-shows-1504670461.
17. John Wagner and Scott Clement, "'It's Just Messed Up': Most Think Political Divisions as Bad as Vietnam Era, New Poll Shows," *Washington Post*, October 28, 2017, https://www.washingtonpost.com/graphics/2017/national/democracy-poll/.
18. Jose A. DelReal and Scott Clement, "Rural Divide," *Washington Post*, June 17, 2017, https://www.washingtonpost.com/graphics/2017/national/rural-america/.
19. DelReal and Clement, "Rural Divide."
20. John Hawkins, "7 Forces Driving America Toward Civil War," Townhall.com, April 21, 2018, https://townhall.com/columnists/johnhawkins/2018/04/21/draft-n2473193.
21. Hawkins, "7 Forces Driving America Toward Civil War."
22. Benjamin Franklin, as quoted in *Respectfully Quoted: A Dictionary of Quotations*, accessed August 2, 2018, https://www.bartleby.com/73/1593.html.
23. Hawkins, "7 Forces Driving America Toward Civil War."
24. Hawkins, "7 Forces Driving America Toward Civil War."
25. George Santayana, *The Life of Reason* (Massachusetts: Massachusetts Institute of Technology, 2011), 172.
26. "Bill of Rights," National Archives.
27. "Sharp Partisan Divisions in Views of National Institutions," Pew Research Center, July 10, 2017, http://www.people-press.org/2017/07/10/sharp-partisan-divisions-in-views-of-national-institutions/.
28. "Sharp Partisan Divisions in Views of National Institutions," Pew Research Center.
29. "Sharp Partisan Divisions in Views of National Institutions," Pew Research Center.
30. "Sharp Partisan Divisions in Views of National Institutions," Pew Research Center.

31. Bill Bumpas, "Poll: GOP vs. Dems Is Really Religion vs. Anti-Religion," American Family News Network, July 14, 2017, https://www.onenewsnow.com/church/2017/07/14/poll-gop-vs-dems-is-really-religion-vs-anti-religion.
32. Bumpas, "Poll: GOP vs. Dems Is Really Religion vs. Anti-Religion."
33. Bumpas, "Poll: GOP vs. Dems Is Really Religion vs. Anti-Religion."
34. S. Michael Craven, "The Latest Pew Survey: Christianity Losing, Secularism Winning," *Christian Post*, October 15, 2012, https://www.christianpost.com/news/the-latest-pew-survey-christianity-losing-secularism-winning-83325/.
35. "'Nones' on the Rise," Pew Research Center, October 9, 2012, http://assets.pewresearch.org/wp-content/uploads/sites/11/2012/10/NonesOnTheRise-full.pdf.
36. Jeff Diamant and Gregory A. Smith, "Religiously, Nonwhite Democrats Are More Similar to Republicans Than to White Democrats," Pew Research Center, May 23, 2018, http://www.pewresearch.org/fact-tank/2018/05/23/religiously-nonwhite-democrats-are-more-similar-to-republicans-than-to-white-democrats/.
37. Diamant and Smith, "Religiously, Nonwhite Democrats Are More Similar to Republicans Than to White Democrats."
38. "When Americans Say They Believe in God, What Do They Mean?," Pew Research Center, April 25, 2018, http://www.pewforum.org/2018/04/25/when-americans-say-they-believe-in-god-what-do-they-mean/.
39. Diamant and Smith, "Religiously, Nonwhite Democrats Are More Similar to Republicans Than to White Democrats."
40. Diamant and Smith, "Religiously, Nonwhite Democrats Are More Similar to Republicans Than to White Democrats."
41. Diamant and Smith, "Religiously, Nonwhite Democrats Are More Similar to Republicans Than to White Democrats."
42. Diamant and Smith, "Religiously, Nonwhite Democrats Are More Similar to Republicans Than to White Democrats."
43. "The State of Abortion in the United States," National Right to Life Committee Inc., January 2018, https://www.nrlc.org/uploads/communications/stateofabortion2018.pdf.
44. "The State of Abortion in the United States," National Right to Life Committee Inc.
45. "Abortion Is a Common Experience for U.S. Women, Despite Dramatic Declines in Rates," Guttmacher Institute, October 19, 2017, https://www.guttmacher.org/news-release/2017/abortion-common-experience-us-women-despite-dramatic-declines-rates.
46. "Americans' Opinions on Abortion," Knights of Columbus, January 2018, https://www.kofc.org/un/en/resources/communications/abortion-limits-favored.pdf.
47. "Americans' Opinions on Abortion," Knights of Columbus; Jennifer Harper, "New Poll Reveals Pro-Life Leanings Among Majority of Americans, Including

Democrats," *Washington Times*, January 18, 2018, https://www.washingtontimes.com/news/2018/jan/18/new-poll-reveals-pro-life-leanings-among-majority-/.

48. Harper, "New Poll Reveals Pro-Life Leanings Among Majority of Americans, Including Democrats."
49. Irwin, "We Ran Out of Words to Describe How Good the Jobs Numbers Are."
50. "List of Tax Reform Good News," Americans for Tax Reform, accessed August 2, 2018, https://www.atr.org/sites/default/files/assets/National%20List%20of%20Tax%20Reform%20Good%20News.pdf.
51. Rich Lowry, "Have Democrats Overplayed Their Trump Hand?," *Politico Magazine*, February 14, 2018, https://www.politico.com/magazine/story/2018/02/14/democrats-trump-presidency-216999. Statistic updated.
52. Josh Hayward, "Democrats Lose the Future by Trusting Their Demographic Doomsday Clock," Breitbart.com, November 23, 2016, http://www.breitbart.com/big-government/2016/11/23/democratic-demographic-doomsday-clock/.
53. Howard Fineman, "Barack Obama Reelection Signals Rise of New America," *Huffington Post*, updated November 7, 2012, https://www.huffingtonpost.com/2012/11/06/barack-obama-reelection_n_2085819.html.
54. Fineman, "Barack Obama Reelection Signals Rise of New America."
55. Hayward, "Democrats Lose the Future by Trusting Their Demographic Doomsday Clock."
56. Sean Trende, "The God That Failed," RealClearHoldings LLC, November 16, 2016, https://www.realclearpolitics.com/articles/2016/11/16/the_god_that_failed_132363.html.
57. Hayward, "Democrats Lose the Future by Trusting Their Demographic Doomsday Clock."
58. Hayward, "Democrats Lose the Future by Trusting Their Demographic Doomsday Clock."
59. Hayward, "Democrats Lose the Future by Trusting Their Demographic Doomsday Clock."
60. Graham Vyse, "Democrats Are Losing Their Most Loyal Voters: Black Women," *New Republic*, October 2017, https://newrepublic.com/minutes/144925/democrats-losing-loyal-voters-black-women.
61. "Surprise! Susan Rice's Son Now Leads Republicans," WND.com, May 31, 2017, http://www.wnd.com/2018/05/surprise-susan-rices-son-now-leads-republicans/.
62. Caleb Parke, "Susan Rice's Son Is Outspoken Pro-Trump GOP Leader at Stanford," Fox News Network LLC, May 31, 2018, http://www.foxnews.com/us/2018/05/31/susan-rices-son-is-outspoken-pro-trump-gop-leader-at-stanford.html.
63. Saagar Enjeti, "Report: Susan Rice Told NSC Officials to 'Stand Down' in Response to Russian Meddling Attempts," The Daily Caller, March 9, 2018, http://

dailycaller.com/2018/03/09/report-susan-rice-obama-stand-down-russian-election-meddling/.

64. Parke, "Susan Rice's Son Is Outspoken Pro-Trump GOP Leader at Stanford."
65. Benjamin Fearnow, "Pastor Prays for Trump to Defeat Deep State 'Witchcraft,' Speaks in Tongues," *Newsweek*, August 23, 2018, https://www.newsweek.com/alabama-pastor-john-kilpatrick-witchcraft-trump-jezebel-speaking-tongues-1087386.
66. Pray Alabama, "Pray Against Witchcraft Coming Against President Trump," Facebook, August 20, 2018, 2:27 p.m., https://www.facebook.com/116678935084921/videos/241848136380412/.

Chapter 11—Resolute Faith and Confidence

1. Josh Katz, "Who Will Be President?," *New York Times*, updated November 8, 2016, https://www.nytimes.com/interactive/2016/upshot/presidential-polls-forecast.html.
2. Victor Davis Hanson, "Hillary's 'Sure' Victory Explains Most Everything," *National Review*, January 30, 2018, https://www.nationalreview.com/2018/01/expected-clinton-victory-explains-federal-employee-wrongdoing/.
3. Pardes Seleh, "Hillary Was So Sure She Would Win the Presidency That She Bought a $1.16 Million Home for White House Staff," IJR.com, September 10, 2017, https://ijr.com/the-declaration/2017/09/970572-hillary-sure-win-presidency-bought-1-16-million-home-white-house-staff/.
4. "President Donald J. Trump Proclaims May 4, 2017, as a National Day of Prayer," White House, May 4, 2017, https://www.whitehouse.gov/presidential-actions/president-donald-j-trump-proclaims-may-4-2017-national-day-prayer/.
5. "President Donald J. Trump Proclaims May 4, 2017, as a National Day of Prayer," White House.
6. Kristi Keck, "Obama Tones Down National Day of Prayer Observance," CNN, May 6, 2009. http://www.cnn.com/2009/POLITICS/05/06/obama.prayer/.
7. Keck, "Obama Tones Down National Day of Prayer Observance."
8. "Statement From President Donald J. Trump on Eid al-Fitr," White House, June 24, 2017, https://www.whitehouse.gov/briefings-statements/statement-president-donald-j-trump-eid-al-fitr/.
9. "Presidential Message on Ramadan," White House, May 15, 2018, https://www.whitehouse.gov/briefings-statements/presidential-message-ramadan/.
10. "Federal Law Protections for Religious Liberty," Office of the Attorney General, October 6, 2017, https://www.justice.gov/opa/press-release/file/1001891/download.
11. Robert Barnes, "Trump Administration Sides With Colorado Baker Who Refused to Make Wedding Cake for Gay Couple," *Denver Post*, September 7, 2017, https://

www.denverpost.com/2017/09/07/trump-sides-with-colorado-baker-who-refused-to-make-gay-wedding-cake/.

12. Ciara Nugent, "Who is Andrew Brunson, the Evangelical Pastor at the Center of Trump's Threat Against Turkey?," *Time*, July 27, 2018, http://time.com/5351025/andrew-brunson-trump-turkey-sanctions/.
13. Mike Pence (@VP), "To President Erdogan and the Turkish government, I have a message, on behalf of the President of the United States of America," Twitter, July 26, 2018, 7:49 a.m., https://twitter.com/vp/status/1022494110735851521?lang=en.
14. Donald J. Trump (@realDonaldTrump), "The United States will impose large sanctions on Turkey for their long time detainment of Pastor Andrew Brunson, a great Christian, family man and wonderful human being," Twitter, July 26, 2018, 8:22 a.m., https://twitter.com/realdonaldtrump/status/1022502465147682817?lang=en.
15. Laurie Goodstein, "Has Support for Moore Stained Evangelicals? Some Are Worried," *New York Times*, December 14, 2017, https://www.nytimes.com/2017/12/14/us/alabama-evangelical-christians-moore.html.
16. Randall Balmer, "Under Trump, America's Religious Right Is Rewriting Its Code of Ethics," *The Guardian*, February 18, 2018, https://www.theguardian.com/commentisfree/2018/feb/18/donald-trump-evangelicals-code-of-ethics.
17. Balmer, "Under Trump, America's Religious Right Is Rewriting Its Code of Ethics."
18. Stephen Strang, "Investing in Liberty," *Charisma*, July 2018, 26.
19. Oscar Wilde, *A Woman of No Importance* (London: Theatreprint, 1992).
20. Goodstein, "Has Support for Moore Stained Evangelicals?"
21. Goodstein, "Has Support for Moore Stained Evangelicals?"
22. Goodstein, "Has Support for Moore Stained Evangelicals?"
23. Goodstein, "Has Support for Moore Stained Evangelicals?"
24. Goodstein, "Has Support for Moore Stained Evangelicals?"
25. Ronald Reagan, "Address Before a Joint Session of the Tennessee State Legislature in Nashville," The American Presidency Project, March 15, 1982, http://www.presidency.ucsb.edu/ws/?pid=42270.
26. Jessica Taylor, "After 'Choosing Donald Trump,' Is the Evangelical Church in Crisis?," NPR, October 29, 2017, https://www.npr.org/2017/10/29/560097406/after-choosing-donald-trump-is-the-evangelical-church-in-crisis.
27. Ian Schwartz, "Tucker Carlson: Modern Liberalism Is a Religious Movement," RealClearHoldings LLC, May 10, 2018, https://www.realclearpolitics.com/video/2018/05/10/tucker_carlson_modern_liberalism_is_a_religious_movement.html?spotim_referrer=social_rail.
28. Schwartz, "Tucker Carlson: Modern Liberalism Is a Religious Movement."
29. Schwartz, "Tucker Carlson: Modern Liberalism Is a Religious Movement."
30. Schwartz, "Tucker Carlson: Modern Liberalism Is a Religious Movement."

31. "Jerry Falwell Jr. on President Trump: He 'Doesn't Say What's Politically Correct,'" ABC News, YouTube, August 20, 2017, https://www.youtube.com/watch?v=_2QqAZydbTE.

Chapter 12—The Battle for Jerusalem

1. "Statement by President Trump on Jerusalem," White House, December 6, 2017, https://www.whitehouse.gov/briefings-statements/statement-president-trump-jerusalem/.
2. "Statement by President Trump on Jerusalem," White House.
3. Michael D. Evans, "Dr. Mike Evans: Trump and Netanyahu Have a Lot to Discuss," Charisma News, February 10, 2017, https://www.charismanews.com/politics/opinion/62923-dr-mike-evans-trump-and-netanyahu-have-a-lot-to-discuss.
4. Evans, "Dr. Mike Evans: Trump and Netanyahu Have a Lot to Discuss."
5. "About Our Founder," ACT for America, accessed August 3, 2018, http://www.actforamerica.org/aboutbrigitte.
6. Evans, "Dr. Mike Evans: Trump and Netanyahu Have a Lot to Discuss."
7. Evans, "Dr. Mike Evans: Trump and Netanyahu Have a Lot to Discuss."
8. i24NEWS, "Christian Zionism and the Jerusalem Embassy Move," YouTube, May 25, 2018, https://www.youtube.com/watch?v=IT_REC7ntCA.
9. Joel B. Pollak, "Exclusive: Hagee Says Trump, Like Truman, Earned 'Political Immortality' by Moving Embassy to Jerusalem," Breitbart, May 11, 2018, https://www.breitbart.com/big-government/2018/05/11/john-hagee-trump-jerusalem-embassy/.
10. "Remarks by President Trump and Prime Minister Netanyahu of Israel Before Bilateral Meeting," White House, March 5, 2018, https://www.whitehouse.gov/briefings-statements/remarks-president-trump-prime-minister-netanyahu-israel-bilateral-meeting-2/.
11. Dov Lieber, "How Much Aid Does the US Give Palestinians, and What's It For?," *Times of Israel*, January 3, 2018, https://www.timesofisrael.com/how-much-aid-does-the-us-give-palestinians-and-whats-it-for/.

Chapter 13—Shaking the Church

1. Steve Strang, "What Is God Saying One Year After the Inauguration?," CharismaNews.com, January 19, 2018, https://www.charismanews.com/politics/elections/69204-what-is-god-saying-one-year-after-the-inauguration.
2. BarackObamadotcom, "10 Questions: Religion in America," YouTube, December 17, 2007, https://www.youtube.com/watch?v=35sGJrWKcmY&feature=related.
3. Time staff, "Read the Sermon Donald Trump Heard Before Becoming President," *Time*, January 20, 2017, http://time.com/4641208/donald-trump-robert-jeffress-st-john-episcopal-inauguration/.
4. Time staff, "Read the Sermon Donald Trump Heard Before Becoming President."
5. Time staff, "Read the Sermon Donald Trump Heard Before Becoming President."

6. Time staff, "Read the Sermon Donald Trump Heard Before Becoming President."
7. "The National Prayer Service for the Fifty-Eighth Presidential Inaugural," Washington National Cathedral, January 21, 2017, https://cathedral.org/wp-content/uploads/2017/01/Inaugural-Prayer-Service-2017.pdf.
8. "Rev. Graham: Trump 'Defending Christian Faith' More Than Any Recent President," FOX News Network LLC, January 21, 2018, http://insider.foxnews.com/2018/01/21/franklin-graham-donald-trump-defending-christianity-more-any-recent-president.
9. "Rev. Graham: Trump 'Defending Christian Faith' More Than Any Recent President," FOX News Network LLC.
10. Tim Chapman, "Trump Should Move Forward on Religious Liberty Order," *The Hill*, February 16, 2017, http://thehill.com/blogs/pundits-blog/religion/319867-trump-should-move-forward-on-religious-liberty-order.
11. Carol Kuruvilla, "Why These Evangelical Leaders Are Firmly Against Trump," *Huffington Post*, July 22, 2016, https://www.huffingtonpost.com/entry/why-these-evangelical-leaders-are-firmly-against-trump_us_578d0d14e4b0fa896c3f6fc2.
12. Kuruvilla, "Why These Evangelical Leaders Are Firmly Against Trump."
13. Brandon Showalter, "Russell Moore: Religious Right Has Become the People They Warned Against," *Christian Post*, October 25, 2016, https://www.christianpost.com/news/russell-moore-religious-right-become-people-they-warned-against-first-things-erasmus-171094/.
14. Peter Wehner, "The Theology of Donald Trump," *New York Times*, July 5, 2016, https://www.nytimes.com/2016/07/05/opinion/campaign-stops/the-theology-of-donald-trump.html?mtrref=www.google.com&gwh=CE54134672E08077A38160293FDD2181&gwt=pay&assetType=opinion.
15. Wehner, "The Theology of Donald Trump."
16. Max Lucado, "Trump Doesn't Pass the Decency Test," *Washington Post*, February 26, 2016, https://www.washingtonpost.com/posteverything/wp/2016/02/26/max-lucado-trump-doesnt-pass-the-decency-test/?; Max Lucado, "Decency for President," February 24, 2016, https://maxlucado.com/decency-for-president/.
17. "Anne Graham Lotz: Her Book, America, and Remembering Billy Graham: Part 2," CBN.com, accessed August 3, 2018, http://www1.cbn.com/anne-graham-lotz-her-book-america-and-remembering-billy-graham-part-2.
18. "Anne Graham Lotz: Her Book, America, and Remembering Billy Graham: Part 2," CBN.com.
19. "Anne Graham Lotz: Her Book, America, and Remembering Billy Graham: Part 2," CBN.com.
20. "Honoring the Life of Billy Graham," Billy Graham Evangelistic Association, March 2, 2018, https://memorial.billygraham.org/funeral-service-transcript/.
21. "Honoring the Life of Billy Graham," Billy Graham Evangelistic Association.

22. "Anne Graham Lotz: Her Book, America, and Remembering Billy Graham: Part 2," CBN.com.
23. Heather Sells, "Faith Leaders Pray for Trump in Oval Office, Enjoy 'Open Door' at White House," CBN News, July 12, 2017, http://www1.cbn.com/cbnnews/us/2017/july/faith-leaders-enjoy-open-door-at-white-house.
24. Sells, "Faith Leaders Pray for Trump in Oval Office, Enjoy 'Open Door' at White House."
25. Sells, "Faith Leaders Pray for Trump in Oval Office, Enjoy 'Open Door' at White House."
26. "Authors Discuss President Trump," CSPAN, December 17, 2017, archived at https://archive.org/details/CSPAN2_20171217_231500_Authors_Discuss_President_Trump.
27. Lauren Markoe, "Trump Must Aid Persecuted Christians or His Presidency Will Fail, Says Open Doors," Religion News Service, January 11, 2017, https://religionnews.com/2017/01/11/trump-must-aid-persecuted-christians-or-his-presidency-will-fail-says-open-doors/.
28. Markoe, "Trump Must Aid Persecuted Christians or His Presidency Will Fail, Says Open Doors."
29. Kate Shellnutt, "Sam Brownback Finally Confirmed as America's Religious Freedom Ambassador," *Christianity Today*, January 24, 2018, https://www.christianitytoday.com/news/2018/january/sam-brownback-is-ambassador-international-religious-freedom.html.
30. "President Donald J. Trump Proclaims January 16, 2018, as Religious Freedom Day," White House, January 16, 2018, https://www.whitehouse.gov/presidential-actions/president-donald-j-trump-proclaims-january-16-2018-religious-freedom-day/.
31. "Release of the 2017 Annual Report on International Religious Freedom," US Department of State, May 29, 2018, https://www.state.gov/secretary/remarks/2018/05/282789.htm.
32. "Release of the 2017 Annual Report on International Religious Freedom," US Department of State.
33. Katayoun Kishi, "Key Findings on the Global Rise in Religious Restrictions," Pew Research Center, June 21, 2018, http://www.pewresearch.org/fact-tank/2018/06/21/key-findings-on-the-global-rise-in-religious-restrictions/.
34. "Global Uptick in Government Restrictions on Religion in 2016," Pew Research Center, June 21, 2018, http://www.pewforum.org/2018/06/21/global-uptick-in-government-restrictions-on-religion-in-2016/.
35. "Release of the 2017 Annual Report on International Religious Freedom," US Department of State.
36. "Remarks by Vice President Pence at the Southern Baptist Convention Annual Meeting," White House, June 13, 2018, https://www.whitehouse.gov/briefings-

statements/remarks-vice-president-pence-southern-baptist-convention-annual-meeting/.

Conclusion—A Seismic Shake-up

1. Michael Kranish, "'I Must Be Doing Something Right': Billionaire George Soros Faces Renewed Attacks With Defiance," *Washington Post*, June 9, 2018, https://www.washingtonpost.com/politics/i-must-be-doing-something-right-billionaire-george-soros-faces-renewed-attacks-with-defiance/2018/06/09/3ba0e2b0-6825-11e8-9e38-24e693b38637_story.html?noredirect=on&utm_term=.424d6fcb2b0a.
2. Craig Bannister, "Trump: 'God's Love Redeems the World,'" CNSNews.com, April 2, 2018, https://www.cnsnews.com/blog/craig-bannister/trump-gods-love-redeems-world.

Appendix—President Donald J. Trump's 500 Days of American Greatness

1. "President Donald J. Trump's 500 Days of American Greatness," White House, June 4, 2018, https://www.whitehouse.gov/briefings-statements/president-donald-j-trumps-500-days-american-greatness/.

INDEX

C

G

H

O

P

Q

R

S

T

STAY IN TOUCH WITH STEPHEN E. STRANG

- Follow him on Twitter @sstrang.
- Like him on Facebook @stephenestrang.
- Subscribe to the *Strang Report* twice-weekly newsletter at signup.strangreport.com/.
- Listen to the *Strang Report* podcast at strangreport.cpnshows .com/.
- Subscribe to *Charisma* magazine or other Charisma Media publications. Call 1-800-749-6500 during office hours EST or order online at Shop.CharismaMag.com.

If you enjoyed *Trump Aftershock*, tell your friends, post about it on social media, and leave a review at Amazon.com.

Charisma Media
600 Rinehart Road
Lake Mary, Florida 32746
www.charismahouse.com

FREE Bonus CONTENT!

To further increase your understanding of Trump's accomplishments since taking office, access this additional resource:

Why We Are Winning: Hundreds of Ways Trump Has Made America Great Again

TrumpAftershock.com/gift

15986